OXFORD STUDIES IN ANALYTIC THEOLOGY

Analytic Theology utilizes the tools and methods of contemporary analytic philosophy for the purposes of constructive Christian theology, paying attention to the Christian tradition and development of doctrine. This innovative series of studies showcases high-quality, cutting-edge research in this area, in monographs and symposia.

OXFORD STUDIES IN ANALYTIC THEOLOGY

Series Editors
Michael C. Rea   Oliver D. Crisp

Analytic Theology and the Academic Study of Religion

WILLIAM WOOD

OXFORD
UNIVERSITY PRESS

OXFORD
UNIVERSITY PRESS

Great Clarendon Street, Oxford, OX2 6DP,
United Kingdom

Oxford University Press is a department of the University of Oxford.
It furthers the University's objective of excellence in research, scholarship,
and education by publishing worldwide. Oxford is a registered trade mark of
Oxford University Press in the UK and in certain other countries

Published in the United States of America by Oxford University Press
198 Madison Avenue, New York, NY 10016, United States of America

British Library Cataloguing in Publication Data
Data available

Library of Congress Control Number: 2020942864

ISBN 978-0-19-877987-2

DOI: 10.1093/oso/ 9780198779872.001.0001

Preface

This book is an exercise in bridge-building. I want to explain analytic theology to other theologians and to scholars of religion, and to explain those other fields to analytic theologians, many of whom remain far more steeped in philosophy than in theology, let alone in the academic study of religion. I am convinced that all sides would benefit if analytic theology were given a seat at the interdisciplinary table where—ideally—theologians, continental philosophers of religion, and scholars of religion sometimes gather. Analytic theology can flourish in the secular academy and, moreover, flourish as theology, rather than as philosophy of religion aimed at solving specifically Christian puzzles.

I have been writing about analytic theology for the better part of a decade, and I have already said some of what I want to say in the best way that I am capable of saying it. So at various points throughout the book, I have drawn freely from the following published articles, though none is reproduced in full: "Modeling Mystery," *Scientia et Fides* 4 (2016): 39–59; "Traditions, Trajectories, and Tools in Analytic Theology," *Journal of Analytic Theology* 4 (2016): 254–66; "Analytic Theology as a Way of Life," *Journal of Analytic Theology* 2 (2014): 43–60; "Philosophical Theology in the Religious Studies Academy: Some Questions for Analytic Theologians," *Journal of the American Academy of Religion* 81 (2013): 592–600; "On Behalf of Traditional Philosophy of Religion. Roundtable on Kevin Schilbrack, *Philosophy and the Study of Religions*," *Journal of the American Academy of Religion* 83 (2015): 236–60; "On the New Analytic Theology, or: The Road Less Travelled," *Journal of the American Academy of Religion* 77 (2009): 941–60.

I am very grateful for the personal and intellectual friendship of Chuck Mathewes. He helped me think about how to bring analytic theology into dialogue with the wider field of religious studies, and he also pushed me to understand the project as one of mutual translation between disciplines. For three years, I have been a Senior Fellow in the University of Virginia's "Religion and Its Publics" project, co-directed by Chuck Mathews and Paul Dafydd Jones. I have learned so much from the other Fellows, and they will all recognize how much of the book grows directly out of our discussions together. So special thanks to Chuck (again) and Paul, and to Elizabeth Bucar, Shaun Casey, Slavica Jakelic, Thomas A. Lewis, Vincent Lloyd, Tyler Roberts, Ted A. Smith, and Darlene Fozard Weaver. I would also like to thank the postdocs and graduate students involved in the "Religion and Its Publics" project, from whom I have also learned much: Creighton Coleman, Lucila Crena, Brady Daniels, Mae Speight, and Shelly Tilton. Evan Sandsmark deserves special thanks for reading, editing, and commenting on nearly the whole book. Any remaining faults are his, not mine. (Just kidding.)

Several friends commented at length on various draft chapters. I'd especially like to thank Brian Leftow, Vincent Lloyd, Timothy Pawl, Darren Sarisky, Donovan Schaefer, and Kevin Schilbrack. Many thanks as well to Ed Brooks, Simon Cuff, Sam Filby, Jason Lepojärvi, Ben Page, and Ed Watson.

I have discussed this project with many other colleagues over the years, both informally and in formal seminars or lectures. I cannot begin to remember everyone who has helped me, and so this list is surely incomplete, but thanks to Andrew K. M. Adam, Margaret Adam, Nicholas Adams, Ata Anzali, James M. Arcadi, Max Baker-Hytch, Katie Bastide, Tim Baylor, E. A. Bazzano, Matthew Benton, Brian Black, Joseph Blankholm, Annie Blazer, Deborah Casewell, Sarah Coakley, Aaron Cotnoir, Joseph Cregan, James Crocker, Oliver Crisp, Dafydd Daniel, Sarah Dees, Daniel De Haan, Samuel Dickinson, Trent Dougherty, Alexandria Eikelboom, Peter Gent, Paul Gleason, Amber Leigh Griffioen, Peter Groves, Brendan Harris, Mark Harris, Eric Hoenes, Hud Hudson, Gavin Hyman, Chris Insole, Lorraine Juliano Keller, Emily S. Kempson, Karen Kilby, Hannah Kim, Cameron Kirk-Giannini, Kate Kirkpatrick, Joanna Lawson, Joanna Leidenhag, Joseph Lenow, Todd LeVasseur, Vicki Lorrimar, Read Marlatte, Beatrice Marovich, Luke Martin, T. J. Mawson, Bryan McCarthy, Tom McCall, Christa L. McKirland, Karin Meyers, Andrew Moore, Teresa Morgan, R. T. Mullins, Hindy Najman, Madhavi Nevader, Heather Ohaneson, Simon Oliver, Jotham Parsons, Faith Glavey Pawl, John Perry, Martin Pickup, Gregory Platten, Oliver Pooley, Joel Rasmussen, Michael Rea, Nathan Rein, John Ritzema, Gonzalo Rodriguez-Pereyra, Jonathan C. Rutledge, John Saladino, Kurtis Schaeffer, Lydia Schumacher, Alec Siantonas, Wes Skolits, Emily Smith, Martin Smith, Gregory Stacey, Sally Stamper, Charlie Stang, Richard Swinburne, Amy Taylor, Kevin Timpe, Alan Torrance, Andrew Torrance, Audrey Truschke, J. T. Turner, Olli-Pekka Vainio, Aku Visala, Graham Ward, Emma Wasserman, Jordan Wessling, Christopher Willard-Kyle, Scott Williams, Judith Wolfe, Peter Woodford, Christopher Woznicki, Mark Wynn, Sameer Yadav, Jamie Yeo, Johannes Zachhuber, and Simeon Zahl.

The early stages of my research were funded by a grant from the John Templeton Foundation, and I am grateful for their support. I would especially like to thank Alexander Arnold and Michael J. Murray for their personal encouragement.

Finally, I am grateful to Gillian Hamnett. She read many drafts of many chapters, including some of the very early, very crappy drafts, which—believe me—was a real labor of love. In more ways than one, I wrote this book for her.

Contents

PART I
INTRODUCTION

Across three short chapters, Part I introduces the book as a whole and briefly outlines the argument in Parts II–IV. I aim to hold together three very different audiences: analytic theologians and philosophers of religion, other academic theologians, and scholars of religion. I want to build bridges across the various intellectual gaps that currently divide them. Yet the more I insist that analytic theology obviously counts as legitimate academic work because it draws on the norms of inquiry that govern academic philosophy, the more I risk alienating theologians who rightly insist that theology should not be assimilated to philosophy. But the more successfully I show that analytic theology really counts as a legitimate form of Christian theology, the more easily I allow it to fall under existing critiques of theology. Holding all three audiences together will therefore be quite challenging, but not, I hope, impossible.

1

The Value and Distinctiveness
of Analytic Theology

Several years ago, at an American Academy of Religion job interview, I was asked about the difference between philosophical theology and philosophy of religion.[1] The question was tricky. Answering it well would require me to say something about "theology," on the one hand, versus "religion," on the other. Additional disciplinary traps loomed. In context, my interviewer clearly meant to use the label "philosophical theology" to refer to *analytic* philosophy of religion—which he regarded as a kind of theology. Not without reason: despite its name, analytic "philosophy of religion" doesn't focus much on religion per se, but on a fairly narrow range of questions posed by Western, usually Christian monotheism. And while the theology that is produced in divinity schools may be quite philosophical, it is not often influenced by analytic philosophy. In departments of religion, philosophy of religion is usually not analytic either, and is often called "philosophy of religions," in the plural, further marking the distance from its analytic cousin.

I cannot say that I answered my interviewer's question well, but it hardly mattered. Under a barrage of follow-up queries, it emerged that my answer had missed his real point entirely. I was not being asked a substantive question about different kinds of academic work. I was being asked an ideological question. I was being asked to declare my colors and choose sides: *Philosophical theology or philosophy of religion? Analytic or continental?* "All of the above" was not an acceptable answer.

Amid this fraught disciplinary context, I seek to carve out a place for the emerging field of "analytic theology." As a provisional definition, by "analytic theology" I mean theology—typically constructive, systematic, Christian theology—that uses the tools and methods of analytic philosophy.[2] By way of ostension, the label "analytic theology" refers to the kind of work commended by the prominent collection *Analytic Theology: New Essays in the Philosophy of Theology*, edited by Michael Rea of the University of Notre Dame and Oliver Crisp, now of the

---

[1] Chapters 1–3 collectively do the work of a more traditional Introduction. Each chapter can be read alone, but only together do they introduce the book as a whole.
[2] This definition presupposes that we know what analytic philosophy is. I return to this question in Chapter 4.

Analytic Theology and the Academic Study of Religion. William Wood, Oxford University Press (2021). © William Wood.
DOI: 10.1093/oso/9780198779872.003.0001

University of St Andrews.[3] In addition, there is now a thriving online open-access *Journal of Analytic Theology*, as well as the Oxford University Press series of which this book is a part, *Oxford Studies in Analytic Theology*.[4] For now at least, there can be no question that analytic theology is growing rapidly.

But there is a Templeton-sized elephant in the room. The growth of analytic theology has been fueled by a seemingly bottomless well of funding from the John Templeton Foundation and other Templeton Trusts. No one could reasonably doubt this fact; the question is what to make of it. Economic pressures are forcing the humanities to adopt grant-based funding models better suited to the harder sciences, and I worry that real humanistic inquiry will not survive our emerging culture of "grant capture." But this is where we are, and what really matters is whether analytic theology is valuable, not whether it has been heavily supported by Templeton funding. Because I am convinced that analytic theology is valuable, I am glad that the Templeton Foundation has supported it. As I noted in the Preface, my own work on the early stages of this book was supported by a small Templeton grant. I can report with absolute confidence that no one from Templeton ever tried to influence the work itself. In fact, they have been remarkably restrained, since from their point of view, I basically took their money and then turned in a very different book, several years later than I promised.

I aim to hold together three very different audiences: analytic theologians and philosophers of religion, other academic theologians, and scholars of religion. I want to build bridges across the various intellectual gaps that currently divide them. There has been very little engagement across these gaps, in part because few scholars have the conceptual skills to cross them adroitly. With these audiences in mind, I defend analytic theology along two very different fronts. On the one hand, many contemporary theologians are skeptical of analytic theology. Indeed, they do not regard it as theology at all, but rather as an especially pernicious—perhaps even idolatrous—form of philosophy. I find this disdain quite interesting. After all, by any measure, the contemporary theological scene is remarkably pluralistic, and although theologians do disagree, often sharply, about theological method, for the most part those disagreements take place within a framework of healthy respect for methodological diversity. Yet the same theologians who are prepared to countenance a bewildering array of conceptual tools drawn from deconstruction, hermeneutics, phenomenology, process thought—the list is endless—then go on to treat analytic theology with a suspicion that

---

[3] Oliver D. Crisp and Michael C. Rea, eds., *Analytic Theology: New Essays in the Philosophy of Theology* (New York: Oxford University Press, 2009).

[4] https://journals.tdl.org/jat/index.php/jat/index; https://global.oup.com/academic/content/series/o/oxford-studies-in-analytic-theology-osat.

borders on hostility. Against this line of criticism, I defend an account of analytic theology that is robustly theological.

On the other hand, prominent theorists of religion assert that, in principle, theology cannot ever be a genuine academic discipline with a legitimate place in the contemporary academy. Some deny that theology exemplifies the free, open-ended pursuit of knowledge that characterizes academic research. Others insist, on broadly postmodern grounds, that theology serves oppressive and harmful regimes of power. I argue that analytic theology presents a counterexample to these criticisms, and that it therefore shows one way that theology can flourish in the contemporary university. In fact, much of what I say also applies to non-analytic forms of theology, and nearly all of it applies to non-Christian analytic theology, but my own focus is squarely on analytic Christian theology. (I will usually drop the qualifier "Christian," however.)

Defending analytic theology along both fronts will be tricky. The more I insist that analytic theology obviously counts as legitimate academic work because it draws on the norms of inquiry that govern academic philosophy, the more I risk alienating theologians who rightly insist that theology should not be assimilated to philosophy. On the other hand, the more successfully I show that analytic theology really counts as a legitimate form of Christian theology, the more easily I allow it to fall under existing critiques of theology.

My defense of analytic theology is not one-sided. Analytic theologians also have much to learn from other theologians and scholars of religion. For example, I agree that analytic theologians should take divine transcendence and the apophatic tradition more seriously than they have. Analytic theologians would also benefit from a sustained dialogue with the traditions of genealogy and critique that are at the heart of the contemporary study of religion. Analytic theologians tend to ignore the myriad ways in which patterns of physical and social power shape our most fundamental concepts, rational norms, and taken-for-granted assumptions. No doubt they would also benefit from more exposure to the religious and philosophical thought of non-Christian and non-Western traditions.

Before continuing, I would like to head off two predictable ways of misunderstanding my argument. First, I do not claim that Christian theology must conform to the intellectual standards of the secular university in order to be viable. That is not at all my view. As far as I am concerned, Christian theology requires no "secular" justification at all. Theology is the queen of the sciences, and if the university now has no place for theology, that reflects badly on the university, not badly on theology. My own claim is rather different: it is *good* that some forms of theology conform to the intellectual standards of the secular university. Analytic theology is one such form. This claim, though narrow in scope, still requires further justification—indeed, even many Christians would not assent to it. The second way to misunderstand my argument would be to read it as yet another suggestion that there is something wrong with studying religions (including

Christianity) in purely naturalistic, scientific, or social scientific ways. That isn't my view either. I am not engaged in a protective strategy designed to insulate theology from critique. If anything, as I make clear in Chapter 12, I think scholars of religion should feel free to critique theology much more deeply than they currently do.

From Analytic Philosophy of Religion to Analytic Theology

The descriptor "analytic theology" is becoming steadily more prominent, as is the kind of inquiry it names. Despite this growing prominence, however, one might wonder whether analytic theology is anything new or special, or whether it is just ordinary philosophical theology—or even analytic philosophy of religion—with a new name. This question is made more pressing by the fact that so far at least, the roster of self-identified analytic theologians is largely coextensive with the roster of analytic philosophers of religion. Accordingly, many theologians worry that "analytic theology" is little more than a brand name, a convenient label adopted by a small group of conservative analytic philosophers of religion as they try to mount a hostile takeover of the theological academy.

For their part, scholars of religion can only be amused by this development, steeped as they are in the highly contentious internal debates that characterize the academic study of religion. By their lights, should they think about it at all, analytic theology presents a rare spectacle: otherwise-respected philosophers who demand that their work also be recognized as theology. To many scholars of religion, "theology" is a label to be shunned, not reclaimed—it often functions as a slur. Theorists of religion are prone to describing theology not as a form of inquiry but as a form of data: theology and theologians are what proper theorists of religion theorize *about*. Religion is not the study of religion, by definition. The task of this book is to argue that analytic theology is a genuine form of theology, yet a form of theology that confounds the sterile critiques typically offered by exclusivist scholars of religion. (I use the label "exclusivist" to name those scholars of religion who hold that theology is not a legitimate academic discipline, and who therefore would deny it any place in a broader field of religious studies.[5])

But in order to understand analytic theology, we must first disambiguate it from other related forms of philosophical and theological inquiry. And in good analytic fashion, the best way to do that is by drawing some distinctions, beginning with

---

[5] Not all scholars of religion are exclusivists in this sense. See the discussion in Chapter 3. I admit that I also like the resonance between this use of "exclusivist" and the position that is called "exclusivism" in philosophical discussions about religious diversity. See https://www.iep.utm.edu/reli-div/, accessed July 4, 2020.

philosophy of religion. On my understanding, the specific task of philosophy of religion—or, at least, analytic philosophy of religion—is to use the tools of philosophy to investigate arguments for and against the existence of God, as well as to investigate the properties or attributes that the major monotheistic traditions would ascribe to God: omnipotence, omniscience, omnibenevolence, and so forth. Philosophy of religion, in short, concerns what might be called (non-pejoratively, at least here) "bare theism."

Analytic philosophy of religion has flourished since the 1970s. Although theists remain a minority in most philosophy departments, it is certainly true that analytic philosophy of religion has become a natural entry point for Christian theists who want their Christian commitments to shape their academic work. Indeed, following the landmark work of Alvin Plantinga, William Alston, and others:

> it became apparent to the philosophical profession that realist theists were not outmatched by naturalists in terms of the most valued standards of analytic philosophy: conceptual precision, rigor of argumentation, technical erudition, and an in-depth defense of an original worldview...In philosophy it became, almost overnight, 'academically respectable' to argue for theism, making philosophy a favored field of entry for the most intelligent and talented theists entering academia today.[6]

Unsurprisingly, Christian philosophers have sometimes turned their attention toward the philosophical problems posed by specifically Christian doctrines. This sort of work has come to be called "philosophical theology." The line between philosophy of religion and philosophical theology has always been fuzzy. Philosophical theology, as I understand it, uses the tools of philosophy to investigate the theological claims made by a specific religious tradition. Thus, Christian philosophical theology investigates the meaning, coherence, and truth of specifically Christian doctrines like the Trinity, the incarnation, and the atonement.[7]

---

[6] So says atheist and naturalist Quentin Smith in "The Metaphilosophy of Naturalism," in *Philo* 4 (2001): 196.

[7] Important collections of philosophical theology that might now be labeled "analytic theology" include Ronald J. Feenstra and Cornelius Plantinga, Jr., *Trinity, Incarnation, and Atonement: Philosophical and Theological Essays* (Notre Dame, IN: University of Notre Dame Press, 1989), Michael Rea, ed., *Oxford Readings in Philosophical Theology*. Volume 1: Trinity, Incarnation, Atonement; Volume 2: Providence, Scripture, and Resurrection (New York: Oxford University Press, 2009), Oliver Crisp, ed., *A Reader in Contemporary Philosophical Theology* (New York: Continuum, 2009), Anna Marmodoro and Jonathan Hill, eds., *The Metaphysics of the Incarnation* (New York: Oxford University Press, 2011).

What about "analytic theology?" At the moment there is no sharp distinction between "analytic theology" and "analytic philosophical theology." To some degree, I hope to change that, by pushing analytic theology to be even more theological. So although this book is primarily a defense of analytic theology, it is also an intervention in some internal debates among analytic theologians about how they should understand their own emerging field. For now, the label "analytic theology" functions as a quick and easy way of letting you know what you are getting when you wade into this particular kind of inquiry: you get certain presuppositions and assumptions and not others, a certain kind of writing, appeals to some intellectual influences and interlocutors but not others, a certain set of intellectual villains, and so forth. In my view, the label "analytic theology" is better as a shorthand description for this kind of inquiry than the more venerable "philosophical theology." It is better because it is more specific. There are many different kinds of intellectual work that can justifiably be called philosophical theology—Kant uses the term, Schleiermacher uses the term, and there are many contemporary forms of philosophical theology that have nothing to do with analytic philosophy. The label "analytic theology" describes those that do.

In my experience, arguments between analytic theologians and their critics quickly break down in the face of persistent mutual misunderstanding. Critics of analytic theology tend to assume that it is a form of a priori philosophical reasoning that is utterly divorced from the touchstones of Christian scripture and tradition. Frequently, those same critics also have an outdated understanding of analytic philosophy and do not recognize how far analytic philosophy has evolved from its origins in logical positivism and conceptual analysis. From the other direction, analytic philosophers and theologians often do not recognize how opaque their assumptions and methods can be to scholars outside the analytic guild. Too often, they equate the analytic style of arguing with rationality itself, rather than seeing it as a narrow and specialized method that has limitations as well as virtues.

My first task after the three-chapter introduction, then, is to try to make analytic philosophy and analytic theology more intelligible to critics. I begin in Chapter 4, with a brief discussion of contemporary analytic philosophy, understood as a distinctive style of writing and thinking. I conclude Chapter 4 with a question that few analytic thinkers consider themselves: Are there limitations, as well as virtues, to the analytic quest for clarity? However analytic philosophers might answer this question, analytic theologians, steeped in the Christian narrative of the Fall, should agree that there are such limitations. Chapter 5 is an extended attempt to address the still-open question "What is Analytic Theology?" Drawing on several contemporary examples, I argue that analytic theology is best understood as a form of faith seeking understanding and a form of constructive theology. I then point out that analytic theology is evolving in some unexpected—and unexpectedly self-critical—ways.

Interlude: On the "Narrowness" of Analytic Philosophy of Religion

Scholars from other disciplines are sometimes surprised at just how Western and Christian analytic philosophy of religion can seem. Indeed, analytic philosophy of religion could probably be renamed "the philosophy of theism" or even "Christian philosophy" without affecting much of the underlying work at all. This point is sometimes presented as a sort of "gotcha," but most analytic philosophers of religion would happily admit that they have no *philosophical* stake in defending the current name of their subspecialty. Similarly, most of them have no philosophical interest in "religion" as such. As it turns out, the label "philosophy of religion" is another holdover from the vexed history of modern European thought on "religion."[8] Early modern and Enlightenment thinkers equated "religion" with a denatured, putatively universal, but still implicitly Protestant Christian monotheism. For example, even though Immanuel Kant calls his treatise *Religion within the Limits of Reason Alone*, it is really about *Protestant Christianity* within the limits of reason alone.[9] The same implicit assumption—that something counts as a "religion" to the degree that it approximates Protestant Christianity—has continued to shape the development of Western philosophical reflection on religions. The end result is that much analytic philosophy of religion is implicitly the philosophy of Christianity despite explicitly bearing the moniker "philosophy of religion."

By and large, analytic philosophers of religion have been content with this state of affairs. Their non-analytic colleagues find it constricting. They want the field to expand its horizons, become more pluralistic in its methods, and focus more on the heterogeneous phenomena of religion, rather than on Christianity or bare monotheism.[10] Depending on how the argument is construed, I have some sympathy for both sides.[11] Happily, however, for the purposes of this book, I can

---

[8] Merold Westphal, "The Emergence of Modern Philosophy of Religion," in Philip L. Quinn and Charles Taliaferro, eds., *Blackwell Companion to Philosophy of Religion*, (Malden, MA: Blackwell, 1997), 111–20. For a recent history of "religion" in Western thought, see Brent Nongbri, *Before Religion: A History of a Modern Concept* (New Haven, CT: Yale University Press, 2015).

[9] Immanuel Kant, *Religion within the Limits of Mere Reason and Other Writings*, trans. and ed. Allen Wood and George di Giovanni (New York: Cambridge University Press, 2018).

[10] See, for example, Kevin Schilbrack, *Philosophy and the Study of Religions: A Manifesto* (Malden, MA: Wiley-Blackwell, 2014); Thomas A. Lewis, *Why Philosophy Matters to the Study of Religion and Vice Versa* (New York: Oxford University Press, 2015); J. Aaron Simmons, "Living in the Existential Margins: Reflections on the Relationship between Philosophy and Theology," *Open Theology* 5 (2019): 147–57; J. L. Schellenberg, "Is Plantinga-Style Christian Philosophy Really Philosophy?" in J. Aaron Simmons, ed., *Christian Philosophy: Conceptions, Continuations, and Challenges* (New York: Oxford University Press, 2018), 229–43.

[11] So long as the critique is aimed at the field, rather than at individual philosophers and their work, I am sympathetic. It would indeed be good if the field were more pluralistic. But it is perfectly legitimate for any individual philosopher to follow her own intellectual interests, even if that means she focuses on narrowly theistic or Christian topics. All scholars study what interests them, and ignore things they find less interesting. How could it be otherwise? See William Wood, "On Behalf of

sidestep the issue altogether. This book is explicitly framed as a defense of analytic Christian theology. Whatever we might think about the current state of philosophy of religion, analytic Christian theology cannot become less analytic or less Christian without becoming something else altogether. (Of course, analytic theology so defined can still learn from non-analytic and non-Christian interlocutors.) One way to understand the charge that analytic philosophy of religion is too narrow is like this: analytic philosophy of religion *has always been* analytic theology. In that case, my defense of analytic theology would also extend to analytic philosophy of religion. So be it—but I do not need to make (or reject) that case myself. Still, anyone who does affirm this criticism of analytic philosophy of religion should at least be happy that analytic philosophers of religion are starting to own up to the theological character of their work.[12]

The Value and Distinctiveness of Analytic Theology

Analytic philosophers of religion like to tell a tidy—perhaps too tidy—story to explain their recent turn to theology. In this story, heroic analytic philosophers have leapt in to fill the intellectual vacuum left by neglectful contemporary theologians. Contemporary theologians, so the story runs, no longer even try to elucidate the meaning, coherence, and truth of key Christian doctrines. Lo! Analytic theology to the rescue! Analytic philosophers can now do the intellectual heavy lifting that theologians are unwilling or unable to do themselves.[13] Without question, this view reflects a certain disciplinary chauvinism. In fact, a great deal of theology over the past quarter-century has used philosophy to deepen our grasp of the central doctrines of the Christian faith—it just hasn't used analytic philosophy. Analytic theologians should, therefore, resist the temptation to construe the debate between analytic theology and other forms of academic theology like this: on the one side, there is analytic theology standing together with orthodoxy, tradition, and truth; whereas on the other side, there is mainstream academic theology, stuck in the mire with postmodern heterodoxy, revision, and relativism. Of course, this is not an accurate picture of either side.

At the same time, however, analytic philosophical theology really has focused on fundamental questions about the meaning, logical coherence, and truth of

---

Traditional Philosophy of Religion." Roundtable on Kevin Schilbrack, *Philosophy and the Study of Religions. Journal of the American Academy of Religion* 83 (2015): 236–60.

[12] Simmons, "Living in the Existential Margins," 149. J. L. Schellenberg, "Is Plantinga-Style Christian Philosophy Really Philosophy?," 240–43.

[13] Alvin Plantinga, "Christian Philosophy at the End of the Twentieth Century," in James F. Sennett, ed., *The Analytic Theist: An Alvin Plantinga Reader* (Grand Rapids, MI: Eerdmans, 1998), 340–41; Oliver Crisp, in Crisp and Rea, eds., *Analytic Theology*, 39.

Christian doctrines in a way that other forms of academic theology have not. Analytic theology's focus on these questions constitutes its most valuable and distinctive contribution to academic theology. And analytic philosophical tools and methods really are very helpful for addressing such questions. For instance, many Christian doctrines involve claims about modality—about what sorts of actions or states of affairs are possible, necessary, or impossible. Analytic philosophers have developed very sophisticated, technically rigorous ways of framing arguments about necessity, possibility, and impossibility. Consider the doctrine of the incarnation. We might wonder how it is possible for a single agent to be both fully human and fully divine. Or, more specifically, we might wonder whether a "kenotic" Christology is the best way to understand the incarnation. (Kenotic Christologies argue that God the Son, the divine Logos, the second person of the Trinity, "emptied himself" of his divinity and voluntarily renounced some of the divine attributes when he became a human man.[14]) Whether kenotic Christologies are possibly true is a viable research question, one that analytic theology is well positioned to investigate. If kenotic Christologies are not so much as possibly true, then they cannot really help us understand the doctrine of the incarnation.

Many people, including many "ordinary" Christians, really do have questions about the meaning, logical coherence, and truth of Christian doctrines. One does not have to be a Christian to agree that these are important questions and that thinking carefully about them is valuable intellectual work. So it is good that there is a mode of inquiry that explicitly foregrounds such questions. This is one reason why analytic theology is especially well suited for the secular university. Analytic theology draws on the same norms of inquiry and argument found in philosophy and other secular academic disciplines and uses them to address difficult questions about Christian doctrine. Analytic theology can, therefore, teach students—and, frankly, other scholars as well—that tricky theological questions are actually amenable to respectful, rational investigation. In the contemporary climate, that in itself is a valuable contribution.

Analytic theology has other distinctive things to offer theologians and scholars of religion. As Kevin Schilbrack has helpfully reminded us, religious communities make metaphysical claims, claims about the nature of reality as such.[15] At the same time, scholars of religion—and, for that matter, most academic theologians—are often quite skeptical about metaphysical claims. From an analytic point of view, this hostility to metaphysics is very strange, more reminiscent of the long-gone, bad old days of logical positivism than of the best contemporary philosophy. Analytic theologians, by virtue of their philosophical training, can

---

[14] The scriptural grounding for kenotic Christology is Philippians 2:6–7: "though [Christ] was in the form of God, he did not count equality with God a thing to be grasped, but emptied himself, taking the form of a servant." For a classic analytic example, see Peter Forrest, "The Incarnation: A Philosophical Case for Kenosis," *Religious Studies* 26 (2000): 127–40.

[15] Schilbrack, *Philosophy and the Study of Religions*, 149–74.

help other theologians and scholars of religion make sense of the metaphysical claims that inevitably arise when we study religious adherence.

Furthermore, analytic theology is typically metaphysically realist, as opposed to anti-realist, and methodologically constructive, as opposed to historical-exegetical. Both options are the norm in analytic philosophy, but far less common among other humanistic disciplines. With respect to realism, analytic theologians talk rather easily about the realm of the transcendent—about God rather than about religion, where religion can be understood as a human construction. Moreover, that talk treats its objects of inquiry as things that are really out there, independent of human minds, even when those objects are "things" like God, God's property of being omniscient, Christ's divine nature, and so forth. All of this will seem wanton to many practitioners of religious studies (including theologians), who are more likely to be committed to some form of "interpretation universalism."[16] According to interpretation universalism, our cognitive engagement with the world is always already an interpretation of the world, and all such interpretations are mediated by cultural-linguistic conceptual schemes that vary across time and across populations. It follows, supposedly, that we never engage with the world as it is in itself—for what would that even be?—but rather with the world as an interpretation that is jointly constructed for us and by us. I am much more sympathetic to metaphysical realism than to interpretation universalism, but for now it suffices to say that both sides would benefit from a more sustained engagement with the alternative point of view. This is another reason to welcome analytic theology into the religious studies academy. At the moment, interpretation universalism is nearly unchallenged among scholars of religion, and metaphysical realism is nearly unchallenged among analytic theologians. This situation is not ideal for either side.

With respect to constructive thought, analytic theologians usually try to offer their own accounts of the meaning or truth of some Christian doctrine or claim, rather than just interpreting or exegeting other historical accounts. That is, analytic arguments feature direct assertions of one's own views about reality, often in propositional form, and direct contradictions of alternative views. That style of argument often seems arrogant and confrontational to outsiders, even though analytic insiders regard it as the norm. In my view, contemporary academic theologians are far too suspicious of constructive thought. There is a sense in which one has to "earn" the right to be constructive, and that only major scholars, at the height of their careers, have really earned that right.[17] But this assumption

---

[16] The phrase "interpretation universalism" comes from Nicholas Wolterstorff, "Between the Pincers of Increased Diversity and Supposed Irrationality," in William J. Wainwright, ed., *God, Philosophy and Academic Culture: A Discussion between Scholars in the AAR and the APA* (Atlanta, GA: Scholars Press, 1996), 18.

[17] This claim is not an exceptionless generalization, but I believe that it holds widely. A few quick examples from major contemporary systematicians: Graham Ward's first book is a study of Derrida

forecloses far too many avenues for interesting and fruitful work. Analytic theology can, therefore, help theologians remember the value of constructive theology.[18]

Finally—brace yourself—analytic theology is fun. Not for everyone, and maybe not for most people, but for some of us, analytic modes of inquiry yield real intellectual pleasure. Of course, the fact that some of us find analytic theology fun does not automatically mean that it is valuable. But its fun-ness does contribute to its value. We scholars do not talk enough about intellectual pleasure (and I say more in Chapter 14), but academic inquiry, and especially humanistic inquiry, should be pleasurable. Even scholars who do not enjoy analytic modes of inquiry themselves should accept that some of us do enjoy it. That recognition alone ought to lead them to view analytic theology with less suspicion. Analytic theology is a mode of inquiry that focuses on important aspects of important topics—paradigmatically, the meaning, coherence, and truth of Christian doctrines—and for some people, it is also really fun. Frankly, that is as strong an argument as anyone could want for why analytic theology is valuable.

and Barth: *Barth, Derrida and the Language of Theology* (New York: Cambridge University Press, 1995). His constructive turn came later. David Tracy's first book is a study of Bernard Lonergan: *The Achievement of Bernard Lonergan* (New York: Herder and Herder, 1970), and only later did he turn to constructive topics. Katherine Sonderegger also began her career as a Barth scholar, before turning to constructive topics: *That Jesus Christ was Born a Jew: Karl Barth's Doctrine of Israel* (University Park, PA: Pennsylvania State University Press, 1992). Nor is this a criticism: the same point holds for my own first book, on Pascal: *Blaise Pascal on Duplicity Sin and the Fall* (New York: Oxford University Press, 2013).

[18] I develop this point more in Chapter 2, and still more in Chapter 5.

2

Three Theological Objections

History, Mystery, Practice

Other than general skepticism about analytic philosophy, theological objections to analytic theology cluster around three major objections. I call them the objection from history, the objection from mystery, and the objection from practice.[1] I respond to these objections at greater length in later chapters. But I would like to say a preliminary word about all three objections. My initial response to the objections from history and mystery is the same: when properly understood, these are not *global* objections—that is, in-principle objections that apply to anything that counts as analytic theology. Rather, they are *local* objections, objections that at most apply to specific analytic thinkers, not analytic theology as such. In a way this conclusion should be unsurprising. There are better and worse analytic theologians, just as there are better and worse theologians of all kinds. My response to the objection from practice is different. I think there is a sense in which analytic theology can be understood as a spiritual practice. I develop that argument at length in Chapter 10.

The Objection from History

Many academic theologians regard theology primarily as a historical discipline, and they regard analytic theology as perniciously ahistorical. No one can deny that the development of Christian orthodoxy seems messy and historically contingent. More radically still, perhaps all Christian truth claims are unavoidably historically contingent even in their very formulations. Can we really know now what it meant in the fourth century to claim that the Son is *homoousios* with the Father? And if we cannot, or if it meant something radically different from what we mean today with our Creedal statements that the Father and Son are "of one Being," or "consubstantial," then how can we be sure that ancient Christians and modern Christians are even making the same claims? This question is especially pertinent for analytic theologians, since they tend to formulate Christian doctrines as abstract, timelessly true propositions. Further challenges arise. Premodern ways

---

[1] I take it that the main objection to analytic theology from scholars of religion is simply that it is *theology*. I address this objection throughout the book, but especially in Chapters 3 and 11.

Analytic Theology and the Academic Study of Religion. William Wood, Oxford University Press (2021). © William Wood.
DOI: 10.1093/oso/9780198779872.003.0002

of reading and thinking are often very different from analytic ways of reading and thinking, and premodern argument typically looks very different from analytic argument.[2] All too often, analytic theology pays little attention to such complexities. So the objection is that analytic theology does not take history or historical contingency seriously enough. Sometimes, this objection takes an even more direct form: analytic theologians are simply ignorant of the history of doctrine, and of historical sources more generally.

The objection from history makes a very important point. Or rather, it makes several important points that are often conflated. Consider first the suggestion that analytic theologians are ignorant of the history of doctrine, or unable to handle historical sources skillfully. I agree that some analytic theologians and philosophers of religion do not take historical sources seriously enough. I also agree that analytic theologians sometimes misunderstand premodern ways of reading and thinking. But in such cases, the fault lies with the individual thinkers who make these mistakes, not with the analytic method itself. After all, when we turn from analytic theology to analytic philosophy, it is immediately apparent that there are many excellent analytically trained historians of philosophy—think of John Cottingham on René Descartes, or Allen Wood on Immanuel Kant, for example.[3] So it is certainly possible for analytic thinkers to treat historical sources with contextual nuance and sensitivity. The fault lies with those who do not, not with the analytic method itself.

Now consider a different version of the objection. Call it the objection from historical contingency or the genealogical objection. Here the suggestion is that analytic theologians ignore the messy history of Christianity, along with the myriad ways that non-rational forces have shaped Christian doctrines. Suppose Constantine had backed Arius, for instance, or suppose Cyril of Alexandria were less politically astute. Christian doctrine might well be very different. Yet no one would argue that every claim formulated under the influence of historically contingent circumstances is in principle unwarranted or false. Such a suggestion would rule out any truth claim whatsoever, not least those of the natural sciences. So someone making the genealogical objection would have to argue that there is something about specifically religious—maybe even specifically Christian—claims such that the sheer fact that they have a messy history somehow vitiates them, with the result that they are not plausible or true. But note that this is not

---

[2] The scholars who emphasize this point tend also to push the objection that analytic theology and philosophy of religion are guilty of ontotheology and idolatry. See the discussion in Part III. For a discussion of the ways that patristic debates differ from modern debates, one that is applicable to, but not aimed specifically at, analytic thought, see Lewis Ayres, *Nicaea and Its Legacy* (New York: Oxford University Press, 2004), esp. 384–435. At least some analytic theologians would concede the point with respect to patristic thought, but not with respect to premodern thought more generally, because they see strong affinities between analytic theology and scholastic theology.

[3] As in, e.g., Allen W. Wood, *Kant's Rational Theology* (Ithaca, NY: Cornell University Press, 2009); John Cottingham, *Cartesian Reflections* (New York: Oxford University Press, 2008).

itself a historical claim, and it cannot be adjudicated by further appeals to historical evidence. Rather, it is a disguised philosophical or theological claim that can only be adjudicated by arguments about, for example, the nature of revelation, or the nature of God. After all, who is to say that the Holy Spirit cannot work through Constantine, or through skillful Church politicians? So far from being an objection to analytic theology, this version of the objection from history becomes simply more fodder for argument, more grist for the analytic mill. As an objection to analytic theology *as such*, this objection does not hold much promise. Indeed, I would even say the opposite: analytic theology can help us uncover hidden philosophical assumptions that sometimes lurk behind historical claims. This in itself is a valuable contribution to theology and the study of religion.

Another version of the objection from history holds more promise as a global objection to analytic theology as such. Even so, it does not finally succeed. The objection from history could be understood as an objection to the kind of abstract thinking that is typical in analytic theology. The "objection from abstraction" runs like this: analytic theologians do not focus on the concrete, historical revelation of God in Christ; instead, they theorize about their own constructed abstractions, which are far more tractable. So instead of deepening our understanding of the living God of the Christian faith, analytic theologians do little more than solve their own self-constructed problems, by appealing to their own self-constructed abstract models:

> This is a familiar tale: the analytic philosopher of religion does not deal with the God of any tradition or encounter, but with a conceptual construct, a simulacrum or "the God of the philosophers"...The philosopher conceptually constructs a being which is labeled "God" and then proceeds to prove or disprove the existence of this being. In other words, the philosopher begins with the *possibility* that this conceptual construct *actually* pertains to reality. This is part of a more general tendency in modern philosophy—both continental and analytic—to prioritize the possible over the actual.[4]

This objection has some purchase. There is indeed a very real and literal sense in which analytic theology is avowedly ahistorical: analytic thinkers typically do try to construct abstract conceptual models, and articulate timelessly true propositions and definitions.[5] Yet even though it has real purchase, at bottom, this version of the objection from history misunderstands the character of most contemporary analytic theology and is therefore best regarded as yet another local

---

[4] Simon Oliver, "Analytic Theology," *International Journal for Systematic Theology* 12 (2010): 467–68.
[5] As did the great medieval theologians, so at a minimum, anyone who faults analytic theology on this score should also fault Anselm, Aquinas, Bonaventure, and the like. In fact, I'm quite confident that this style of abstract reasoning is universal across the Christian tradition, but we certainly see it among the scholastics and proto-scholastics.

objection, properly aimed at specific analytic thinkers, rather than a global objection aimed at analytic theology per se.

The objection seems to assume that analytic theology is an entirely a priori project. That is, it assumes that analytic theology must begin with abstract, a priori reflection about God, the kind of reflection we can do from the proverbial philosopher's armchair, when it should instead begin with concrete attention to scripture or tradition. But the assumption that analytic theology is entirely a priori is false. It might describe some instances of analytic philosophy of religion—perhaps it describes Richard Swinburne's work in the 1970s, though I have my doubts even there. But as an objection to contemporary analytic theology, it seriously misses the mark.[6] Most contemporary analytic theology does begin with scripture and tradition rather than with armchair a priori theorizing, and is therefore best understood as an example of faith seeking understanding, rather than a priori natural theology. The best way to redeem this claim is by considering some concrete examples of analytic theology. Accordingly, I defer further argument until Chapter 5, where I look at the work of Timothy Pawl and William Hasker. But as a placeholder, consider these statements by Hasker:

> Supposing that the events concerning Jesus do constitute some sort of divine revelation, that revelation is available to us only if we have some reasonably reliable information as to what those events actually were. The events, however, are accessible to us only through the writings of the New Testament...But if we are not willing to be Trinitarian skeptics, I submit that we will do well to take seriously the consensus of the universal Church, rather than going off in a fundamentally different direction on our own. In the light of these reflections, I propose that the best place to begin in our investigation of the doctrine of the Trinity is with the Church Fathers of the late fourth century.[7]

Even from these remarks, it should be clear that Hasker is not beginning his study "from the armchair," as an a priori exercise. Rather, he begins from a position of faith seeking understanding, with attention to scripture and tradition, and in dialogue with the "universal Church." In this respect, he is entirely typical of recent analytic theology.

---

[6] There is simply an enormous difference in the scholarly aim, target audience, and philosophical methodology of a work like Richard Swinburne's *The Coherence of Theism* (New York: Oxford University Press, 1977) and the work of contemporary, self-avowed analytic theologians like those discussed in Chapter 5. This is not to denigrate Swinburne—far from it. *The Coherence of Theism* was written in a very hostile academic climate, well before the contemporary resurgence of philosophy of religion had taken root, in the waning days of ordinary language philosophy, when nearly all respectable philosophers still assumed that religious assertions were meaningless, emotive, or otherwise non-referential. We should bear that context in mind when assessing whether Swinburne's style of reasoning now seems unfashionably a priori.

[7] William Hasker, *Metaphysics and the Tri-Personal God* (OUP 2013), 7, 9.

I now want to switch from a more defensive mode of argument to a more positive mode. One reason why analytic theology seems ahistorical to other theologians is because it is so constructive. Constructive theologians try to offer their own accounts of the meaning or truth of some doctrine or claim of the Christian tradition, rather than merely interpreting existing historical accounts. Constructive argument is common in philosophy but less common in other humanistic disciplines.

Analytic theology foregrounds explicit truth claims about God, Christ, salvation, or whatever is under discussion. A work of constructive analytic theology is finally *about* reality itself (including the divine reality) rather than about other texts or other thinkers. It is important not to draw this distinction too sharply. No one can think in an intellectual vacuum. The analytic theologian will, of course, engage with other texts and thinkers, but she will usually engage with them by assessing whether the arguments of those texts or thinkers are cogent or true. The ultimate aim is always to make true statements about God, or whatever aspect of reality is under discussion. Crucially, this means that analytic thinkers sometimes engage with historical sources in an ahistorical way—for example, by using modern modal metaphysics to try to understand the Christological claims of the Council of Chalcedon. This would be an illegitimate move if the goal were to understand Chalcedon on its own terms, or to give an account of what the fifth-century church thought about Christ. But if the goal is to develop a true or possibly true Christology, then it is perfectly legitimate to draw on contemporary philosophical tools that the fifth-century church fathers lacked.

The Objection from Mystery

According to another set of objections, analytic theology falters because it is not well suited for grappling with the mystery and paradox that lie at the heart of the Christian faith. I take the objection from mystery quite seriously, and I devote the bulk of Part III to defending analytic theology from various related worries about idolatry, ontotheology, univocity, and so-called "theistic personalism." So here I will be brief. Like the objection from history, the objection from mystery resolves into several more specific objections that are best understood as local, not global.

One way to understand the objection from mystery is as a claim that analytic theology is a form of intellectual hubris—smug complacency run amok. I call this the "objection from misplaced certainty." We might ask: Is it not the case that many analytic theologians believe that they have grasped the truth completely, once and for all, that they know God as he is, that they have dispelled all mysteries, and is this not a form of hubris? Certainly it is possible for an individual analytic theologian to think this way, but I doubt that many of them do. (Thus Brian Leftow: "I give many perfect-being arguments in what follows. As I give them, I have a nagging fear that I am just making stuff up. This is not due to uncertainty about God's being perfect. Rather, our ideas of what it is to be perfect are inconsistent and flawed, and there is no guarantee that they match up with what God's perfection really is."[8]) In any case—once again—there is nothing about the analytic method of inquiry that entails complacent certainty or being closed off to the possibility of future correction. And surely we would not want to say that anyone who asserts a truth claim is thereby guilty of hubris. To assert a claim at all is to assert it as true, and implicitly to assert that its contradiction is not true; but this can't always be hubris or inquiry would be impossible. So even though one does hear this kind of objection fairly regularly, I doubt that the real worry here is that analytic theologians are too confident that they are right and other people are wrong.

I think the real worry is something else, a related objection, and one that is much harder to dismiss: that analytic theology is inevitably guilty of "conceptual idolatry" or "ontotheology." This is a difficult objection to assess, not least because it is not entirely clear what conceptual idolatry and ontotheology even are or what it would mean to be guilty of them. The most salient version of the charge goes something like this: if the goal of analytic theology is to use the tools of human reason to come to know God better, then surely that kind of inquiry presupposes that God can be known, which in turn presupposes that our concepts can "grasp" God, which means that God is an object in the world, fundamentally like us, just bigger and more powerful. A related form of the objection would argue: if the goal of analytic theology is to give philosophical explanations of Christian doctrines, then analytic theology constitutively presupposes that doctrines are like scientific theories, fit to be reductively analyzed, rather than mysteries, or proper objects of faith.

As I say, these are difficult objections to answer, and I address them at length in later chapters. But I do want to note at the outset that no analytic theologian or philosopher of religion would agree that God is "a thing in the world," and every major analytic theologian affirms a strong distinction between God, who creates out of nothing, and creatures, who are entirely dependent on God at every moment of their existence. Of course, it may turn out that some analytic theologians fail to maintain the distinction between creator and creature despite their best intentions. But showing that this is the case would require detailed exegetical and conceptual work. It cannot simply be assumed.

Next, critics of analytic philosophical theology sometimes argue that analytic thinkers treat the Christian tradition instrumentally, as little more than a novel source of conceptual puzzles to be solved. This instrumental focus can also be a way of denying mystery and paradox. According to Thomas Weinandy, "Because God, who can never be fully comprehended, lies at the heart of all theological

---

[8] Brian Leftow, *God and Necessity* (New York: Oxford University Press, 2012), 11–12.

enquiry, theology by its nature is not a problem solving enterprise, but rather a mystery discerning enterprise."[9] This worry is also a version of the objection from mystery.

Yet the Christian tradition has never equated mystery or paradox with bare logical contradiction. Even on the most venerable and orthodox accounts, the mystery of the Trinity is not the "mystery" of how a logical contradiction can be true. So, for example, an abstract analytic model of the Trinity that tries to reconcile God's three-in-oneness actually removes a significant barrier to discerning the real mystery of the Trinity. We are better able to appreciate the mystery of the Trinity in all its depth when we appreciate that the doctrine of the Trinity is not a flat-footed falsehood like "1+1+1 = 1." Analytic models do not aim to "replace" the triune God, or dispel the mystery of the Trinity. Quite the contrary. Analytic theology can contribute to the "mystery discerning" task of theology by pursing its distinctively analytic task of elucidating the meaning, coherence, and truth of Christian doctrine.[10]

The Objection from Practice

The final objection may be called the objection from practice. Many theologians would say that all genuine theology is in the first instance practical: aimed not at achieving better explanatory theories about God, but at fostering greater love for God and neighbor. Genuine theology, in short, is a spiritual *praxis*, one deeply woven together with a Christian life of prayer, virtue, and participation in the sacraments.[11] Analytic theology seemingly exhibits none of this. The worry, then, is that analytic theology is spiritually sterile and therefore not really a form of genuine theology at all.

Michael Rea raises this worry himself in his introduction to the *Analytic Theology* volume. He agrees that analytic theology is not a spiritual practice, yet denies that this fact constitutes a genuine objection. On his view, all theology is a second-order *theoretical* discipline, and therefore not a source of spiritual nourishment. For spiritual nourishment, we should look to scripture, not theology,

---

[9] Thomas Weinandy, *Does God Suffer?* (Notre Dame, IN: University of Notre Dame Press, 2000), 32.

[10] See William Wood, "Modeling Mystery," *Scientia et Fides* 4 (2016): 1–21.

[11] One finds this vision expressed from many different quarters: from classic liberation theology (Gustavo Gutiérrez, *A Theology of Liberation* [New York: Orbis, 1973]) to contemporary postmodern theology (Kevin J. Vanhoozer, ed., *The Cambridge Companion to Postmodern Theology* [New York: Cambridge University Press, 2003], 24–25, 43). See also Sarah Coakley: "systematic theology without contemplative and ascetic practice comes with the danger of rendering itself void; for theology in its proper sense is always implicitly *in via* as practitional" (*God, Sexuality, and the Self* [New York: Cambridge University Press, 2013], 45).

and certainly not to academic theology.[12] Rea's response makes sense. It seems unlikely that all genuine theology is practical; nor has this view been the consensus of the Christian tradition. Theoretical tasks like "clarifying, systematizing, and model-building" have always featured in theological discourse. But even though his response makes sense, I believe that Rea cedes too much ground to opponents of analytic theology. For there is a sense in which analytic theology can foster wisdom, moral improvement, and love for God, and so may be understood as a spiritual practice. Or so I shall argue in Chapter 10.

To set the scene here I will only ask: When we talk about theology as praxis, are we talking about a direct, first-order praxis, like *lectio divina*, worship, or prayer? Or are we talking about a practice that indirectly contributes to the spiritual life and thereby serves the Christian Church in some more remote way? If we mean the former, then much of what we would generally regard as good theology falls short. Whatever we think of major modern theologians like Karl Barth or Hans Urs von Balthasar, their central works are exercises in academic systematic theology. They are not devotional manuals in disguise. But if we mean the latter, then this is actually a very difficult charge to make stick. Who but God himself is in a position to say what is indirectly spiritually valuable to someone somewhere? (Believe it or not, I have met people who sincerely claim that they feel closer to God as a result of reading Richard Swinburne.) It is a mistake, and furthermore a presumptuous mistake, to assume that analytic philosophical theology cannot *in principle* be spiritually nourishing. Suppose that God causes your heart to swell with gratitude as you come to believe that the Brower-Rea model of the Trinity at last preserves that mysterious doctrine from incoherence. Who am I to insist that such a possibility is absurd? God's love rains down on logicians too, after all.

Conclusion

So the objections from history and mystery may have some purchase on individual analytic theologians, but they are not a reason to dismiss analytic theology as such. And contrary to our expectations, there may be a way to treat analytic theology as a spiritual practice. At this point, someone might fairly say that I have made things too easy for myself. Even if it is true that the kinds of worries that I have been discussing are local and not global, if it should turn out that they are sufficiently widespread, then that would indeed show that *something* is awry with the current state of analytic theology. Fair enough. But the charge that these errors are widespread among analytic theologians is an empirical claim. Establishing its truth would require considerable exegetical and argumentative work. The burden

---

[12] Michael Rea, in Crisp and Rea, eds., *Analytic Theology*, 18–19.

of doing that difficult work falls not on me but on the person who wants to make the charge. He or she would have to read a great deal of contemporary analytic theology—including its best recent exemplars—and argue that each of them makes the same characteristic errors, and then argue that we have some further reason to think that those errors generalize to analytic theology as such. I am not aware of anyone who has even attempted to do the difficult work required to establish this kind of claim.

Looking ahead, I respond further to the objection from history in Chapter 5, where I consider some contemporary examples of analytic theology and argue that they are rightly understood as examples of constructive theology. I respond to the objections from mystery and practice in Part III. I first try to show other theologians that analytic theology is properly Christian and properly theological. I begin, in Chapter 6, by arguing that the Christian doctrine of creation furnishes the theological warrant for analytic theology. The doctrine of creation establishes the value of theological inquiry as such, and also establishes the value of analytic philosophy, understood minimally as a systematic extension of our God-given faculties of rational reflection. On this account, analytic theology can be a valuable tool to help us distinguish theological truth from theological error. Across Chapters 7–9, I offer a connected argument that analytic theology is not especially vulnerable to charges of idolatry, ontotheology, univocity, or so-called "theistic personalism." These charges represent some of the most common theological objections to analytic theology, and so it is important to address them carefully. Yet in a way, they are all versions of the same worry: that analytic theologians do not take divine transcendence seriously enough, and effectively turn God into an exalted creature. I argue that once we have a better understanding of the charges themselves, and the distinctively analytic ways of thinking about God, we can see that analytic theologians are able to preserve a sufficiently sharp distinction between God and creatures. Chapter 10 concludes the theological defense of analytic theology with an argument that analytic theology is far from spiritually sterile, and can even be understood as a spiritual practice.

3

Analytic Theology in the Religious Studies Academy

By training and inclination, I am first and foremost a Christian theologian, but this book is more than just a theological defense of analytic theology. I also aim to find a place for analytic theology within the broader religious studies academy. It must be said that I face an uphill battle. The religious studies academy is famously fractious. Methodological disagreement, vituperation, and overheated rhetoric abound. Even so, scholars from every camp are likely to regard analytic theology with a jaundiced eye. The first problem, of course, is that analytic theology is *theology*. Whether theology has a place in the modern, secular university is a vexed question, and the stakes involved in answering it are high. By now the traditional battle lines between theology and the study of religion are well known, even shopworn. To exclusivist scholars of religion, theology is not a real academic discipline at all, and at best offers only spiritual or moral instruction. As mentioned in Chapter 1, I use the label "exclusivist" to describe scholars of religion who hold this pejorative view about theology.[1] Many individual scholars of religion are not exclusivists in this sense, either because they agree that theology is a legitimate academic discipline or because they do not think about theology at all. Theologians often assume that every individual scholar of religion is obsessed with theology. In fact, many individual scholars of religion are completely indifferent to theology, and for legitimate reasons, but it is still fair to say that the academic study of religion *as a field* has avowedly defined itself in opposition to theology.

According to exclusivist scholars of religion, theology trades on authority rather than free and open inquiry, and posits spooky unverifiable entities that, by definition, cannot be investigated by normal, empirical methods.[2] The rhetoric here runs hot. For example, Russell T. McCutcheon has built a career around judging what counts as proper scholarly work in the field. In his capacity as intellectual gatekeeper, he explicitly denies that academic theologians count as

---

[1] There is considerable overlap between the scholarly views that I call "exclusivist" and the views of those Tyler Roberts calls "locativists." Tyler Roberts, *Encountering Religion: Responsibility and Criticism after Secularism* (New York: Columbia University Press, 2013).

[2] For a useful way into the literature here, see Linell Cady and Delwin Brown, eds., *Religious Studies, Theology, and the University: Conflicting Maps, Changing Terrain* (New York: SUNY Press, 2002), especially p. 26, n. 2.

Analytic Theology and the Academic Study of Religion. William Wood, Oxford University Press (2021). © William Wood.
DOI: 10.1093/oso/9780198779872.003.0003

colleagues or dialogue partners.[3] According to McCutcheon, scholars of religion should be "critics" of the traditions they study, but theologians can only be "caretakers" of those traditions. The roles of scholarly critic (outsider) and non-scholarly caretaker (insider) are mutually exclusive.[4] His teacher, Donald Wiebe, goes even further: Wiebe likens theology to an infectious disease.[5]

Bruce Lincoln, in his well-known "Theses on Method," offers one of the most prominent accounts of the distinction between scholarly discourse and religious discourse. Lincoln's account, therefore, also marks the distinction between the study of religion and theology. On the side of the study of religion we have fallibility, historical and empirical inquiry, and the possibility of critique; on the side of theology we have authoritarianism, pseudo-infallibility, and cheerleading.

> History of Religions, in the sharpest possible contrast [to religion itself], is that discourse which speaks of things temporal and terrestrial in a human and fallible voice, while staking its claim to authority on rigorous critical practice. [It is] thus a discourse that resists and reverses the orientation of [the religious] discourse with which it concerns itself. To practice history of religions in a fashion consistent with the discipline's claim of title is to insist on discussing the temporal, contextual, situated, interested, human, and material dimensions of those discourses, practices, and institutions that characteristically represent themselves as eternal, transcendent, spiritual, and divine...[6]

> Although critical inquiry has become commonplace in other disciplines, it still offends many students of religion, who denounce it as "reductionism." This charge is meant to silence critique. The failure to treat religion "as religion"—that is, the refusal to ratify its claim of transcendent nature and sacrosanct status—may be regarded as heresy and sacrilege by those who construct themselves as religious, but it is the starting point for those who construct themselves as historians.[7]

> When one permits those whom one studies to define the terms in which they will be understood, suspends one's interest in the temporal and contingent, or fails to distinguish between "truths", "truth-claims", and "regimes of truth", one

---

[3] Russell T. McCutcheon, *The Discipline of Religion: Structure, Meaning, Rhetoric* (New York: Routledge, 2003), 146–47.

[4] Russell T. McCutcheon, *Critics Not Caretakers: Redescribing the Public Study of Religion* (New York: SUNY Press, 2001), 103; "A Direct Question Deserves a Direct Answer: A Response to Atalia Omer's "Can a Critic Be a Caretaker too?" *Journal of the American Academy of Religion* 80 (2012): 1079.

[5] Theology "cannot complement the academic study of religion but can only 'infect' it." Donald Wiebe, *Politics of Religious Studies* (New York: Palgrave, 1999), 155.

[6] Theses 3 and 4. Lincoln's "Theses on Method" have been widely reprinted, but they were originally published as Bruce Lincoln, "Theses on Method," *Method and Theory in the Study of Religion* 8 (1996): 225–27.

[7] Lincoln, "Theses on Method," Thesis 12.

has ceased to function as historian or scholar. In that moment, a variety of roles are available: some perfectly respectable (amanuensis, collector, friend and advocate), and some less appealing (cheerleader, voyeur, retailer of import goods). None, however, should be confused with scholarship.[8]

According to Lincoln, scholars of religion can only investigate "the temporal, contextual, situated, interested, human, and material dimensions" of religious traditions. To be sure, scholars can *critique* the metaphysical ("transcendent"—i.e., theological) claims made by religious adherents, but "critique" cannot really mean "evaluate" or "assess," since the outcome of the critique is predetermined. Scholarly critique cannot end in commendation, by definition: those who commend religious claims cease practicing scholarship altogether, according to Lincoln. Accordingly, the scholar qua scholar must insist that religions characteristically *mis*represent themselves as "eternal, transcendent, spiritual, and divine."

Even scholars of religion who do not seem especially hostile to theology implicitly deny its academic credentials. For example, Gregory D. Alles begins his textbook, *Religious Studies: A Global View*, with a simple distinction: "The aim of the study of religions is knowledge about religions. The aim of theology is to formulate religious truth." So far so good. But as he continues, it becomes clear that Alles regards "religious truth" as something that falls outside the scope of typical academic inquiry, because it is "non-epistemic" and so cannot constitute knowledge.

It is true that at times people who are by profession theologians also formulate and transmit knowledge. When they do so, they are engaged in the study of religions. But in the world in which we now live, the most interesting religious claims, those that would seem to be most central to the theological enterprise— to take traditional examples, claims about God and forgiveness or rebirth and release—do not count as knowledge in a strict sense, even if religious people sometimes make equivocal use of the verb "to know." Furthermore, in the world in which we now live it seems like a poor use of time and energy to try to make such claims count as knowledge.

While theology—more broadly, serious religious reflection—has its place, that place is not the study of religions. For example, the study of religions does not aspire to make "progress in discovering the truths of religion"...That is partly because at least for the foreseeable future there seems to be no progress to be made. [9]

[8]   Lincoln, "Theses on Method," Thesis 13.
[9]   Gregory D. Alles, ed., *Religious Studies: A Global View* (New York: Routledge, 2008), 5–6. The point that religious claims are "non-epistemic" comes on page 6, after the cited block quotation.

Alles's distinction between theology and the study of religions turns on the claim that only scholars of religion can "transmit knowledge." He assumes that theological claims do not count as knowledge, and asserts that when religious adherents use the verb "to know," they use it equivocally. Later he notes that people are "entitled to disregard religious claims…in a manner in which they are not entitled to disregard, for example, the existence of the ground on which they walk or, more abstractly, Newton's equations defining motion."[10] He therefore seems to think that truth-directed inquiry cannot feature persistent disagreement or lack of progress. This view seems to depend on the further assumption that truth-directed inquiry must look like inquiry in the empirical sciences. In the empirical sciences, persistent disagreement is irrational once it is clear which way the evidence points. Theology cannot look like that, and so it is not a genuine form of truth-directed inquiry. QED.

Alles obviously wants to distinguish theology from the study of religion in a charitable, non-tendentious way. He denies that "religious claims are somehow inherently flawed," agrees that theology "has an extremely important place within religious communities," and identifies himself as a "religious insider in at least one tradition." But he also insists that while theology has its place, "that place is not the study of religions."[11] Given his further assertion that theology is "non-epistemic," it seems to follow that theology has no place in the contemporary university at all. Even though theology can be valuable in its own domain, that domain is not the properly academic domain of knowledge, evidence, and truth-directed argument. It is entirely legitimate to distinguish—even sharply distinguish—theology from the study of religion, by pointing out that they are two different forms of academic inquiry, with different aims, and that we should not confuse the one with the other. It is another thing altogether to say that only the study of religion, and not theology, really counts as a legitimate form of academic inquiry. For all his charitable words toward theology, Alles seems to take this second route, and he is by no means alone among scholars of religion.

But consider this: in any modern university, often right down the hall from the department of religion, we find another academic discipline, philosophy, with sterling intellectual credentials and its own methodological norms, norms that do seem to legitimate exactly the practice that our own opponents of theology will not countenance—namely, the practice of making and assessing truth claims about God. For exclusivist theorists of religion, this fact is awkward.

Take the career of the late Syracuse philosopher William P. Alston. Most of his work is straightforwardly philosophical, with no reference at all to religious belief. Alston also wrote *Perceiving God*, which defended the rationality of religious

---

[10] Alles, ed., *Religious Studies: A Global View*, 7.
[11] Alles, ed., *Religious Studies: A Global View*, 6–7.

belief.[12] Yet even though *Perceiving God* argues that it is rational to believe claims like "God is appearing to me now," it is universally regarded as a work of philosophy (and a very fine one, too) rather than theology. It would be laughable to assert that *Perceiving God* is not really philosophy, more laughable still to assert that it is not even a legitimate academic work. Now consider that Alston also wrote articles that are even more directly about God. For example, in "Two Cheers for Mystery!" he argues that God is mysterious in some ways, but not in all ways.[13] Should we call this philosophy or theology? Suppose "Two Cheers" is theology and suppose we agree that theology is not legitimate academic work. What, then, is the difference between *Perceiving God* (philosophy) and "Two Cheers" (theology) such that one is clearly academic work and the other is not? Or is "Two Cheers" legitimate academic work in the philosophy department that somehow magically becomes illegitimate "edifying discourse" two doors down the hall in the department of religion? How would one ever defend *that* result?

Here analytic theology re-enters the picture. Contemporary analytic philosophy shows that theology need not confine itself to historicist or empiricist methods in order to count as a genuine form of academic inquiry. The methods of analytic epistemology and metaphysics—which flourish in every philosophy department—are also appropriate tools with which to investigate questions about the divine. Analytic theology draws on these same methods. There is, therefore, no reason to regard analytic theology as methodologically illegitimate unless one is prepared also to regard wide swaths of contemporary philosophy as similarly illegitimate. I take this conclusion to be a *reductio* of all efforts to exclude analytic theology from the academy on methodological grounds.

"Well, so what?" comes the reply. No doubt some scholars of religion are so suspicious of analytic philosophy that they would happily commend that whole field to the flames as well. Obviously a full explanation and defense of analytic philosophy would require a book of its own. But in the next chapter, I do try to allay this suspicion, at least partially, and I also say a bit more in Chapter 11. For now I would only ask suspicious scholars of religion to extend to analytic metaphysics and epistemology the same charity they want other scholars to extend toward their own preferred methods of inquiry. Certainly, no one is obliged to abandon their own preferred methods and practice analytic inquiry instead. But at the same time, no wants to see their own preferred methods simply dismissed out of hand as illegitimate, especially by opponents who have no real expertise in those methods.[14] So I encourage suspicious scholars of religion at least to bear in

---

[12] William P. Alston, *Perceiving God* (Ithaca, NY: Cornell University Press, 1991).

[13] William P. Alston, "Two Cheers for Mystery!" in Andrew Dole and Andrew Chignell, eds., *God and the Ethics of Belief: New Essays in Philosophy of Religion* (Cambridge: Cambridge University Press, 2005), 99–116.

[14] Analytic philosophers are sometimes guilty of the same thing. That is, some analytic ideologues do dismiss alternative methods of inquiry out of hand and in ignorance. That's bad. They shouldn't do that. But it also isn't a reason to return the favor.

mind that analytic metaphysics and epistemology are well-established academic subfields, which should give them considerable prima facie plausibility.

Analytic Theology in Dialogue

Although this book is primarily a defense of analytic theology, I also want to make a positive case to theologians and scholars of religion that analytic theology can be a valuable dialogue partner. The case is considerably easier with respect to academic theologians. For all their differences, analytic and non-analytic theologians both inhabit the Christian thought world. With respect to scholars of religion, I have a much trickier case to make. I agree that theology (analytic or not) is a different form of inquiry than the study of religions, but as a field, the religious studies academy functions best when it explicitly welcomes a variety of approaches, including theology. To make this case, I draw on my own background in analytic theology to intervene in three debates that continue to preoccupy the field of religious studies as a whole.

The first debate concerns naturalism and reductionism. Scholars of religion typically distinguish "methodological" naturalism from "metaphysical" or "ontological" naturalism, and claim to practice the former but not the latter.[15] While individual scholars of religion can—and often should—practice methodological naturalism, it turns out that one cannot justify such a requirement as a global norm that applies to the field of religious studies as a whole. Attempts to justify methodological naturalism as a global norm inevitably presuppose controversial metaphysical claims, and thereby collapse into ontological naturalism—a position that I call "ontological naturalism on the cheap." It follows that any naturalism-based barriers to admitting analytic theology into the field of religious studies are not global, intellectual barriers. They are at most local, prudential barriers that apply to individual scholars, depending on their specific scholarly aims.

The second debate concerns the role of "critique" in the academic study of religion. The term "critique" has a technical meaning in contemporary academic contexts. It does not just mean criticism, or even negative evaluation. Rather, critique is a "thought style" by which we "expose hidden truths and draw out unflattering and counterintuitive meanings that others fail to see."[16] Bruce Lincoln's "Theses on Method" (discussed earlier in this chapter) give a good sense of what critique looks like in the academic study of religion. I agree that critique can be valuable, but in the contemporary religious studies academy it has become

---

[15] See Chapter 12. Briefly, methodological naturalism asserts that we may only appeal to natural things or causes in our theories and explanations. Metaphysical or ontological naturalism asserts that there are no non-natural things or causes.

[16] Rita Felski, *The Limits of Critique* (Chicago: University of Chicago Press, 2015), 2.

ubiquitous, to the point where it threatens to crowd out other, equally legitimate methods of inquiry. Exclusivist theorists of religion have recently turned to critique in their continuing effort to exclude theology from the academy. Yet for a variety of reasons, critique is not well suited for this role. Analytic theologians clearly see the limitations of critique precisely because the thought style of critique differs so sharply from that of analytic theology. I argue that we must supplement critique's epistemology of power with a more analytic epistemology of truth, one that treats religious adherents as rational agents, guided by their beliefs about what is the case.

This engagement with critique sets the stage for the third debate, which concerns the role of normative inquiry in the academic study of religion. Critique is inherently normative, and once it becomes apparent that the study of religion not only welcomes but even depends on normative inquiry in the form of critique, it becomes much harder to bar other forms of normative inquiry, including theology. I first discuss the vexed role of normativity in the study of religion, and consider some recent defenses of normative inquiry. I then argue that analytic theology shows one way to understand post-critical inquiry in the study of religions, a model I call "rigorous appreciation." Rigorous appreciation prizes attachment and engagement rather than suspicion and subversion. It is a form of critical inquiry in the broader sense, even though it is not a form of critique in the specialized sense. I conclude with a modest proposal on behalf of comparative analytic theology.

Conclusion

With this book, I hope to articulate an attractive vision of analytic theology, provoke a more fruitful interdisciplinary conversation, and help scholars across the religious studies academy understand one another better. My aims are modest, and minimally polemical. I agree that theology and the study of religion are very different forms of inquiry. I do not claim that analytic theology is the only way to study theology, still less the only way to study religion. Nor do I claim that all departments of religion or faculties of theology must include analytic theology, as if those that do not are somehow deficient. But analytic theology is a legitimate form of theology and a legitimate form of academic inquiry, and it can be a valuable conversation partner within the wider religious studies academy. That claim, though modest, still has real weight and still requires defense.

PART II
FOUNDATIONS

Chapters 4 and 5 try to get clear about what analytic philosophy and analytic theology really are. I begin with a brief discussion of contemporary analytic philosophy, understood as a distinctive style of writing and thinking. I conclude Chapter 4 with a question that few analytic thinkers ever consider: In addition to its virtues, are there limitations to the analytic quest for clarity? However analytic philosophers might answer this question, analytic theologians, steeped in the Christian narrative of the Fall, should agree that there are such limitations. Chapter 5 is an extended attempt to address the still-open question "What is Analytic Theology?" Drawing on several contemporary examples, I argue that analytic theology is best understood as both a form of faith seeking understanding and a form of constructive theology. I then point out that analytic theology is evolving in some unexpected—and unexpectedly self-critical—ways.

4

Why Do They Write That Way?

Analytic Philosophy and its Discontents

A deep gulf of misunderstanding separates analytic philosophers from scholars in other humanistic disciplines. The same gulf also separates analytic theologians from the rest of the religious studies academy. Explaining and addressing this gulf is one of the major tasks of this book as a whole. There is no doubt that the gulf is a joint construction, and that analytic and non-analytic thinkers have collectively created it and allowed it to persist. Analytic philosophers sometimes lack hermeneutical charity. But at the same time, other humanists often misunderstand what analytic philosophy really is. I want to persuade non-analytic colleagues of the value of analytic theology, and so I must allay some of these misunderstandings. Yet I also want analytic theologians and philosophers to recognize that the analytic style of writing and thinking comes with its own limitations. Like all forms of inquiry, analytic theology has "characteristic deformations," typical excesses, and common ways of going wrong.[1] Many of its characteristic deformations are inherited from analytic philosophy. Analytic theologians can accept this criticism without conceding the value of analytic philosophy or analytic theology.

Contemporary Analytic Philosophy

All too often, even well-meaning scholars are simply unable to appreciate the intellectual virtues that prevail in traditions of inquiry very different from their own. By way of example, I once had a conversation about the problem of evil with a friend who is a conventionally trained theologian. She had just read some analytic theodicies, and she found them by turns both impenetrable and repulsive. As we talked, however, it became clear that she did not really understand what they were trying to accomplish. She assumed that any properly philosophical response to the problem of evil would be, if not pastoral, then at least practical or existential: it should raise and address questions about what evil and suffering mean for

---

[1] I discuss the term "characteristic deformations" further below. The term is inspired by Lauren Winner's account of "characteristic damage" in *The Dangers of Christian Practice* (New Haven, CT: Yale University Press, 2018).

Analytic Theology and the Academic Study of Religion. William Wood, Oxford University Press (2021). © William Wood.
DOI: 10.1093/oso/9780198779872.003.0004

the human condition. I explained that most analytic theodicies and defenses address a very different set of questions, mainly about whether the amount of evil we observe in the world renders the existence of God either logically impossible or evidentially improbable. She was surprised to learn that these questions were regarded as important.

I found our exchange quite revealing. The questions that preoccupied analytic philosophers on the problem of evil were not "live" questions for her at all. Of course, I do not mean that it had literally never occurred to her that evil and suffering pose difficult challenges to Christian belief. But the analytic approach to these challenges was utterly alien. She was not used to thinking about God in terms of logical possibilities or evidential probabilities. The analytic philosophers she read did not raise the questions most important to her, and the questions they did raise seemed irrelevant to her concerns. The analytic "problem of evil" was so far from her own thought-world that when she encountered it, she was not able to recognize it as a problem, and so she was not really sure what the philosophers she had read were even attempting to do.

I have also had many similar exchanges from the other direction. When colleagues trained in analytic philosophy read contemporary academic theology, they often find it baffling. I recall a case when a good friend cornered me at a philosophy conference and—struggling to keep his facial expression neutral and nonjudgmental—asked me oh-so-casually: "Bill, do theologians ever *make arguments*?" It was a sincere question, and he was not attacking me or my discipline. He had recently read some contemporary theology, but had not seen anything that he could recognize as argument in it, and so he concluded that, for some reason, contemporary academic theologians do not make arguments at all. He was not at home in the thought-world of contemporary academic theology, and so he could not appreciate what theological argument looks like. (I assured him that theologians do indeed make arguments.)

The Analytic Style: Propositions, Precision, Transparency

As a first step toward identifying the causes of this gulf of misunderstanding, I would point to the unique rhetorical style of analytic philosophy. Michael Rea offers a useful outline of the analytic style of philosophizing in his introduction to the original *Analytic Theology* volume. According to Rea, paradigmatic instances of the analytic style conform to the following prescriptions:

(1) Write as if philosophical positions and conclusions can be adequately formulated in sentences that can be formalized and logically manipulated; (2) Prioritize precision, clarity, and logical coherence; (3) Avoid substantive (non-decorative) use of metaphor and other tropes whose semantic content

outstrips their propositional content; (4) Work as much as possible with well-understood primitive concepts, and concepts that can be analyzed in terms of those; (5) Treat conceptual analysis (insofar as it is possible) as a source of evidence.[2]

There is plenty to quibble with here, but the exact details of the list need not concern us too much. The fact is that we can all recognize paradigmatic instances of analytic philosophy when we see them, precisely because of this rhetorical style. This style is one of analytic philosophy's signal contributions, but it is not an unmixed blessing. It is fair to say that theologians and scholars of religion often find analytic philosophy to be quite off-putting precisely because of this formalized, extremely precise style. More importantly, they tend to think that the analytic style just couldn't possibly be the right mode of discourse for doing theology or even valuable philosophy.

Analytic writing expresses analytic thinking: when one has been trained as an analytic philosopher, one learns to address some problems and ignore others, and one learns to write about the problems one addresses in certain ways and not others. Too many analytic philosophers do not recognize that they write and think as they do as a result of disciplinary socialization. Consider the common refrain that analytic philosophy uniquely exhibits rhetorical virtues like precision, parsimonious expression, logical coherence, rigor, and—above all—clarity.[3] This refrain is not false, but it does display a certain naive triumphalism. Somehow I doubt that continental philosophers or theologians cheerfully prize writing that is vague, wordy, incoherent, rigor-free, and unclear. Moreover, what counts as clear, parsimonious, and rigorous writing will vary according to the community for which one writes. Analytic philosophy may be clear to readers trained in the analytic tradition, but it is not clear to every intelligent reader. Nor is it surprising that analytic philosophers often find contemporary theology unclear. Note, too, that someone with continental commitments might reasonably call analytic writing "thin" instead of "clear," and might reasonably call densely allusive continental writing "rich" instead of "obscure." Rhetorical virtues do not transcend disciplinary socialization. Analytic philosophy is not the unmediated language of thought.

Transparency and Truth Claims

The practice that is most central to analytic philosophy—and therefore to analytic theology—is the practice of making and assessing explicit propositional truth claims. Of course, this is not to insist that only analytic philosophers make truth

---

[2] Michael Rea, in Crisp and Rea, eds., *Analytic Theology*, 5–6; see also 17–26.
[3] See, e.g., Crisp and Rea, eds., *Analytic Theology*, 5–6, 35, 55, 83, 280.

claims, still less that no one else cares about truth. But analytic philosophy foregrounds the practice of making and assessing explicit propositional truth claims in a way that goes beyond what we usually find in other humanistic disciplines. This has two important consequences. First, because philosophers treat this practice as central, they naturally try to formulate their propositional claims as precisely as possible. Thus one hallmark of much analytic philosophy is not just precision, but a kind of hyperprecision, which—in all honesty—can be annoying to those who are unused to it. Second, because analytic philosophers focus so closely on truth claims, they also privilege argumentative transparency. This is my own, less tendentious rendering of the common analytic claim to be especially "clear." The paradigmatic form of analytic argumentation is a series of explicit propositional claims, laid out as stepwise arguments, ideally presented in linear, if not deductive, form. Once one understands how to read analytic philosophy, which does take some getting used to, it is usually fairly easy to grasp the claims an author wants to make and the exact reasons he or she offers in support of those claims. One is then in a position to assess whether the author's reasons really do support his or her claims, and to assess whether the claims themselves are true. Doing this is what it is to be an analytic philosopher.

These methodological assumptions explain, at least in part, why analytic philosophy takes the form that it does. Because analytic philosophers trade in precise, propositional truth claims, and because they try to argue as transparently as they can, analytic persuasion takes place at the micro level, at the level of the specific, individual claim. By contrast, much of the persuasive reasoning in other forms of theology and philosophy—and maybe in other humanities as well—takes place not at this micro level, but at the relatively macro level of, for example, "offering a rival reading of a central text" or even at the still broader level of offering a "rival worldview." The crucial point is that even though that reading or worldview will, of course, be supported by smaller claims, one often does not argue or engage with non-analytic work primarily at the level of those small claims. When one reads Heidegger for instance, one rarely finds him making explicit arguments against the specific claims of intellectual opponents that he cites by name, as one finds in analytic philosophy. Instead, one finds him offering a new reading of Aristotle, Kant, or Hegel, for example, or even rethinking the whole tradition of Western philosophy from the bottom up. I take it that we are meant to embrace or reject his work as a whole depending on whether we find it productive for our own thought. If we respond by saying, "Well, but the problem is that Aristotle didn't quite say that, you see," then there is a genuine sense in which we are missing the point of what Heidegger is trying to do.

This difference helps to explain the common reaction that occurs when analytic philosophers read non-analytic work, and vice versa. To the stereotypical analytic philosopher, continental thought seems to feature ungrounded assertion after ungrounded assertion with virtually no argument at all. But the persuasive force does not always function at the level of the individual claim, but at the level of the whole piece or even the whole system, which stands or falls according to whether it helps us make sense of ourselves and the world. From the other direction, to someone untrained in analytic philosophy, a typical piece of analytic writing can seem trivial, sterile, and irrelevant because it is so closely and narrowly argued.

Contemporary Analytic Philosophy: Beyond Classical Analysis

These differences in rhetorical style go a long way toward explaining the gulf of misunderstanding that obtains between analytic and non-analytic thinkers. But it is also true that theologians and scholars of religion tend to have an outdated conception of analytic philosophy, because they do not recognize the extent to which it has evolved since the 1970s. Scholars unacquainted with contemporary analytic philosophy are apt to associate it with conceptual analysis, or perhaps even with logical positivism—narrow methods that have historically proven very unfriendly to the rest of the humanities. Theologians in particular may also assume that analytic philosophers rely on an Enlightenment-style foundationalist epistemology that seems especially unfriendly to religious belief. Although these assumptions about analytic philosophy remain widely held, they are actually quite out of date.

It turns out (somewhat amusingly, I admit) that most analytic philosophers now repudiate the method of analysis, at least if by "analysis" we mean the specific kind of conceptual investigation that reigned from (roughly) the 1930s until the 1970s.[4] On that understanding, analytic philosophy is chiefly a method of linguistic analysis in which philosophers either analyze complex concepts into their constituent parts (e.g., from *bachelor* to *unmarried male*) or carefully attend to ordinary language to determine what makes words and sentences meaningful. Of course, some self-identified analytic philosophers continue to analyze concepts and linguistic structures, but many more do not. Outside of philosophy faculties, few scholars recognize the extent of this shift away from classical analysis.

Consider this description of analytic philosophy provided by Harriet Harris and Christopher Insole in their introduction to a volume aimed at assessing the

---

[4] Opponents sometimes construe this point as a blow that strikes squarely at the heart of analytic philosophy, but it really isn't. The suggestion that this situation should embarrass analytic philosophers rests on false assumptions about the nature of analytic philosophy. Analytic philosophy cannot be identified with the project of giving necessary and sufficient conditions for the extensions of terms or concepts, and so it is not embarrassing that philosophers cannot give necessary and sufficient conditions for "analytic philosophy."

impact of analytic philosophy on the philosophy of religion. According to Harris and Insole, analytic philosophy "most distinctively" exhibits:

> the dissection of sentence structures and investigation of language as the best means of investigating concepts. The focus on language and meaning comes from a conviction that the best way of understanding ourselves and the world is to look at what we think, and the best way of getting at what we think is to analyze what we say.... Analytic philosophers vary from one another and disagree, for example, over the extent to which the philosophical task is to state definitions. But it is a sufficient generalization for now to say that they proceed by isolating beliefs for individual consideration, breaking arguments down step by step, and taking apart sentences word by word, and that they do this in order to spare us from confusion and specious argument.[5]

This is a fine description of the classical method of analysis. Yet it is not an accurate description of the way that contemporary analytic philosophers now understand their own work.[6] It remains true—as Harris and Insole write—that analytic philosophy often proceeds by "isolating beliefs [or propositions] for individual consideration," and by "breaking arguments down step by step." And it even remains true that they often attend carefully to linguistic structures. What has changed in more recent decades, however, is *why* analytic philosophers attend carefully to language, and how they understand their own philosophical task when they do.

Timothy Williamson now holds the chair at Oxford once held by A. J. Ayer. According to Williamson, analytic philosophy no longer confines itself to how we must talk about a subject matter, rather than the subject matter itself.[7] Whereas

---

[5] Harriet Harris and Christopher Insole, eds., *Faith and Philosophical Analysis: The Impact of Analytical Philosophy on the Philosophy of Religion* (Burlington, VT: Ashgate, 2005), 1–2.

[6] In fairness to Harriet and Insole, this account of analytic philosophy did indeed have considerable influence on philosophy of religion for many years. It is also worth emphasizing that Harriet and Insole here echo Michael Dummett's well-known attempt to define analytic philosophy by appealing to distinctively "analytic" views about thought and language. According to Dummett, "What distinguishes analytical philosophy, in its diverse manifestations, from other schools is the belief, first, that a philosophical account of thought can be attained through a philosophical account of language, and, secondly, that a comprehensive account can only be so attained." See Michael Dummett, *Origins of Analytical Philosophy* (London: Duckworth, 1993), 4. Dummett's claim certainly describes the views of an earlier generation of philosophers who identified with the analytic tradition, and it has some purchase as a general description of one phase of that tradition. But, as many commentators have noted, as a characterization of analytic philosophy per se, Dummett's claim is more aspirational than descriptive; he defends it because he wants it to be true, not because it actually is true. See Hans-Johann Glock, *What Is Analytic Philosophy?* (New York: Cambridge University Press, 2008), 130; and Neil Levy "Analytic and Continental Philosophy: Explaining the Differences," *Metaphilosophy* 34 (2003): 289–90.

[7] Timothy Williamson, "How Did We Get Here from There? The Transformation of Analytic Philosophy," *Belgrade Philosophical Annual* 27 (2014): 7–37. Nicholas Wolterstorff offers another useful corrective to those who continue to identify analytic philosophy with linguistic analysis—or worse,

an earlier generation of analytic philosophers regarded linguistic structures and concepts as the *objects* of their inquiry, today most philosophers would say that they study the general features of reality—things in the world, not words or concepts. Our language and our concepts—"what we say" and "what we think" about a subject matter—now have the secondary status of *evidence* to which a philosopher appeals to support her theories about the world.[8] They are no longer the primary objects of inquiry in their own right. As Michael Rea puts it, analytic philosophers now strive to develop "true explanatory theories…in areas of inquiry (metaphysics, morals, and the like) that fall outside the scope of the natural sciences."[9]

The Surprising Return of Metaphysics

In other words, metaphysics—good old-fashioned pre-Kantian metaphysics—has returned to analytic philosophy with a vengeance:

> recent decades have seen the growth and flourishing of boldly speculative metaphysics within the analytic tradition. Far from being inhibited by logical positivist or ordinary language scruples, such analytic metaphysics might be described by those unsympathetic to it as *pre-critical*, ranging far outside the domain of our experience, closer in spirit to Leibniz than to Kant.[10]

Closer in spirit to Leibniz than to Kant, but perhaps even closer in spirit to Aristotle. Not only is contemporary analytic philosophy rife with unashamedly metaphysical speculation, but it often appears to presuppose a form of premodern essentialism. Many analytic metaphysicians would cheerfully agree that a given existing thing has "essential" properties that determine what kind of thing it

with logical positivism. In his chapter "How Philosophical Theology Became Possible within the Analytical Tradition of Philosophy," found in Crisp and Rea, *Analytic Theology*, he writes:

> the theme of limits on the thinkable and the assertable has lost virtually all interest for philosophers in the analytic tradition. Of course, analytic philosophers do still on occasion charge people with failing to think a genuine thought or make a genuine judgment. But the tacit assumption has come to be that such claims will always have to be defended on an individual, ad hoc basis; deep skepticism reigns among analytic philosophers concerning all grand proposals for demarcating the thinkable from the unthinkable, the assertable from the non-assertable. (Wolterstorff in Crisp and Rea, eds., *Analytic Theology*, 2009: 157)

For an additional short piece on recent developments in analytic philosophy, see Dean Zimmerman, "Three Introductory Questions: Is Analytic Philosophical Theology an Oxymoron, Is Substance Dualism Incoherent, What's in This Book Anyway" in Peter van Inwagen and Dean Zimmerman, eds., *Persons Human and Divine* (New York: Oxford University Press, 2007), 1–13.

[8] Williamson, "How Did We Get Here from There?" 16.
[9] Michael Rea, in Crisp and Rea, eds., *Analytic Theology*, 4.
[10] Williamson, "How Did We Get Here from There?" 7.

most fundamentally is, as well as other "accidental" properties that determine its other attributes.[11] Philosophers can theorize about the (really existing) properties of things, including their (really existing) essential properties, and thereby get at fundamental truths about those things. This kind of essentialism is no longer regarded as a discredited blind alley but as "intuitive and commonsensical and...defensible—not spooky and weird."[12]

There is an interesting story to be told about how a philosophical tradition that was once constitutively hostile to metaphysics has evolved into a tradition that embraces extravagant metaphysical speculation of a sort that would make Aquinas blush. That story should be told, but I cannot tell it here. In briefest outline, the return of metaphysics was driven by technical developments in modal logic (the logic of necessity and possibility). Prior to these developments, nearly all philosophers, from David Hume in the eighteenth century to W. V. O. Quine in the twentieth, assumed that the only coherent notion of necessity was narrowly logical or semantic necessity: only statements or propositions could be necessary, and only then because necessity was equated with analyticity. (For example, "All bachelors are unmarried males" is necessarily true, because it is analytically true—true by virtue of the meanings of the terms used in the statement.) Beginning in the 1950s, Ruth Barcan Marcus, Saul Kripke, and other logicians developed mathematically rigorous, intuitively plausible accounts of necessity and possibility on which objects and properties can also be called necessary or possible. In the wake of these developments, metaphysical realism and Aristotelian essentialism no longer seem untenable. For instance, we might say that my specific biological origins constitute one of my essential properties. There is no "possible world,"—no way the world could have gone—such that I myself exist but am the product of a different sperm and egg. By contrast, consider another of my properties: *currently living in England*. I would still be myself (narrowly construed as "the same numerically identical human being") even if I lacked that property. It is an accidental property.

One could tell a parallel story about developments in epistemology, and especially the epistemology of religious belief. Just as there was a time when conceptual analysis reigned supreme among analytic philosophers, and metaphysics was thoroughly discredited, so there was a time when a narrow foundationalism was the default epistemology among analytic philosophers, with the result that religious beliefs were treated as almost paradigmatically unjustifiable.[13] That time is

---

[11] Here I caution that this view is not just identical to the "essentialism" that is often deprecated in other humanistic disciplines. One can hold the view that things have essential properties while also denying that, e.g., race, gender, or (for that matter) religion are essential properties.

[12] Stephen P. Schwartz, *A Brief History of Analytic Philosophy: From Russell to Rawls* (Chichester: Wiley-Blackwell, 2012), 210.

[13] Classical foundationalism, associated with Enlightenment figures like Descartes and Locke, assumes that all rationally held beliefs, including theistic beliefs, must be either indubitable, incorrigible, or evident to the senses, or else deducible from other beliefs that are so justified. For a classic

also past. Although epistemology remains one of the most important analytic subspecialties, no single epistemological theory dominates, and many widely held theories are quite friendly to religious belief. As a result, charges of irrationality against theistic beliefs must be made "on an individual *ad hoc* basis" rather than "by appealing to some general epistemological theory" like the demand that all beliefs must be grounded in apodictically certain evidence.[14]

These developments in epistemology also explain the otherwise puzzling fact that analytic philosophy of religion has flourished even though few philosophers take themselves to have knockdown arguments for the existence of God. Since it can be rational to believe in God even when one cannot show that God exists, "the dominant attitude has been that nothing of any great epistemological importance hangs on whether or not one can give arguments for God's existence."[15] Opponents of analytic philosophy of religion continue to assume, wrongly, that it is committed to Lockean or Cartesian epistemological projects. In this respect at least, analytic philosophy of religion is authentically post-Enlightenment, if not quite postmodern.

Contra Clarity?

I hope that the previous section has helped scholars who are not well acquainted with contemporary analytic philosophy to understand the current state of the field. If I were to leave matters here, however, then I would only be telling part of the story. Ignorance is not the only reason why someone might be skeptical of analytic philosophy: someone might understand the analytic style all too well and yet still reject it. Some critical theorists and continental philosophers have a much deeper critique, one that is well worth bringing to light. Their critique goes beyond ordinary disciplinary disagreements about what counts as "clear" prose, and manifests as a fundamental suspicion of "clarity" itself. On some accounts of language and politics, clear prose and ordinary language are politically conservative, even regressive. On these accounts, clear prose cannot ever be a vehicle for radical thought, and so truly critical thinkers must avoid plain speech and ordinary language. This suggestion will seem like sheer perversity to analytic thinkers, but it is a principled view, with deep roots in the continental tradition.

work of philosophy of religion that relies on such assumptions, see Antony Flew, "The Presumption of Atheism," *Canadian Journal of Philosophy* 2 (1972), 29–46.

[14] Nicholas Wolterstorff, "How Philosophical Theology Became Possible within the Analytical Tradition of Philosophy," 160–61.
[15] Wolterstorff, "How Philosophical Theology Became Possible within the Analytical Tradition of Philosophy," 163.

To a certain extent, these roots grew in the soil furnished by the dense German philosophical prose of the eighteenth and nineteenth centuries—Immanuel Kant, and, above all, G. W. F. Hegel. Similarly, in the twentieth century, Heidegger's investigation of Being initially seemed to require a new technical language, and when he had exhausted that language, he turned to poetry as the best vehicle for expressing the fundamental mystery of Being.[16] As for the specific link between radical politics and difficult prose, Theodor Adorno's 1951 *Minima Moralia* is a classic source of skepticism about plain speech. According to Adorno, the demand for clarity is tantamount to a demand for conventional, staid, superficial thinking. So-called intellectuals who valorize clarity only reinforce the cultural and political status quo, since what counts as clear speech is always determined by socially dominant and politically regressive groups with power. Clear speech inevitably expresses conventional wisdom and the logic of the marketplace:

> A writer will find that the more precisely, conscientiously, appropriately he expresses himself, the more obscure the literary result…The logic of the day, which makes so much of its clarity, has naively adopted this perverted notion of everyday speech…Only what [people] do not need first to understand, they consider understandable; only the word coined by commerce, and really alien ated, touches them as familiar…[Intellectuals] who would escape it must recognize the advocates of communicability as traitors to what they communicate.[17]

A decade later, Herbert Marcuse makes a similar argument, this time explicitly aimed at analytic philosophy:

> Analytic philosophy often spreads the atmosphere of denunciation and investigation by committee. The intellectual is called on the carpet. What do you mean when you say…? Don't you conceal something? You talk a language which is suspect. You don't talk like the rest of us, like the man in the street, but rather like a foreigner who does not belong here. We have to cut you down to size, expose your tricks, purge you. We shall teach you to say what you have in mind, to "come clear," to "put your cards on the table."[18]

Marcuse gives the imaginary target of this analytic attack a ready retort: if he could say what he wanted to say with ordinary language "he would probably have done so in the first place." Here, once again, clear speech is incapable of expressing truly novel insights.

---

[16] Jeffrey Powell, ed., *Heidegger and Language* (Bloomington, IN: Indiana University Press, 2013).

[17] Theodor Adorno, *Minima Moralia*, trans. E. F. N. Jephcott (New York: Verso, 2005 [1951]), fragment 64, "Method and Style," 101.

[18] Herbert Marcuse, *The One-Dimensional Man: Studies in the Ideology of Advanced Industrial Society* (New York: Routledge, 1991 [1964]), 196–97.

These views still have intellectual currency. The contemporary philosopher Judith Butler explicitly cites Adorno when she argues that "to speak in ways that are already accepted as intelligible is precisely to speak in ways that do not make people think critically, that accept the status quo, and that do not make use of the resource of language to rethink the world radically."[19] Elsewhere, Butler develops a similar point by citing the Marcuse passage above.[20] In the field of literary theory, Rita Felski argues that contemporary critics are often mistrustful of a clear, simple, and direct prose style, because they regard these qualities as inherently ideological. She cites the feminist theorist and filmmaker Trinh T. Minh-ha: "Clarity is a means of subjection, a quality both of official taught language and of correct writing, two old mates of power: together they flow, together they flower, vertically, to impose an order." When we demand clarity, we "cannot hear the sounds of difference or strangeness" and we become "oblivious to the rhythm of the eccentric and the offbeat"; we "peremptorily dismiss what cannot be voiced in logical argument and straightforward prose."[21] As I argue in Chapter 10, the religious studies academy has been very influenced by similar currents of thought; as a result, scholars of religion are likely to have considerable sympathy for the critique of analytic clarity.

Transpose this critique into the theological register and it is also very easy to see why some contemporary theologians are wary of the analytic style. If the demand for clear and simple language closes off our ability to recognize difference and strangeness, then Christian theologians should indeed be suspicious of that demand. After all, nothing could be more different or more strange than the object of theological inquiry, the triune God. Here is David Bentley Hart, sounding remarkably like the critical theorists discussed above:

> In the end, analytic philosophy is no purer and no more rigorous than any other style of philosophizing. At times, in fact, it functions as an excellent vehicle for avoiding thinking intelligently at all; and certainly no philosophical method is more apt to hide its own most arbitrary metaphysical dogmas, most egregious crudities, and most obvious flaws from itself, and no other is so likely to mistake a descent into oversimplification for an advance in clarity. As always, the rules determine the game, and the game determines the rules. More to the point, inasmuch as the educated class is usually, at any given phase in history, also the most thoroughly indoctrinated, and therefore the most intellectually pliable and quiescent, professional philosophers are as likely as their colleagues in the sciences

---

[19] Judith Butler, "Values of Difficulty," in Jonathan Culler and Kevin Lamb, eds., *Just Being Difficult? Academic Writing in the Public Arena* (Stanford, CA: Stanford University Press, 2003), 201, 203.

[20] Judith Butler, "A 'Bad' Writer Bites Back," *New York Times*, March 20, 1999.

[21] In Felski, *The Limits of Critique*, 136. The citation is from Trinh T. Min-ha, *Woman, Native, Other* (Bloomington, IN: Indiana University Press, 1989), 16–17. Felski is not giving her own view here—she is not inherently suspicious of clear prose.

and humanities (and far more likely than the average person) to accept a reigning consensus uncritically, even credulously, and to adjust their thinking about everything accordingly.[22]

Another common theological worry also lurks nearby. Many theologians worry less about clarity per se than about its close cousin, predicative assertion. From the patristic period onwards, some Christian theologians have denied that predicative assertion—and especially univocal predicative assertion—is the proper mode of theological speech, preferring instead non-predicative forms like praise, prayer, poetry, and silence.[23] Worries about predication are bound up with worries about idolatry and anthropomorphism: surely, runs the argument, nothing we can describe with ordinary language could really be God.[24] Against this intellectual backdrop, it is easy to see why some theologians might be especially suspicious of theology in the analytic style. If predicative assertions about God are inherently suspect, then the analytic goal of formulating maximally precise, univocal propositions must seem singularly inapt. On this line of thought, analytic precision can only be false precision, and clearly formulated propositions about God are likely to be deceptive, rather than vehicles for theological insight.

I do not endorse the critique of clarity in either its political or theological variants.[25] It is possible to write clearly even about profound and important matters. Analytic philosophers and theologians often succeed in doing so. But even though the critique of clarity is exaggerated, I do think that analytic theologians should take it seriously. By that I mean they should consider the critique in more nuanced and plausible forms, rather than as an unrestricted generalization that is obviously false. When might the demand for clarity be a way to mask superficial thinking? When might sensible, common-sense reasoning inadvertently pick out the easiest path toward a popular conclusion, rather than the right path toward a true conclusion? I would be surprised if the answer to these questions were "never."

---

[22] David Bentley Hart, *The Experience of God: Being, Consciousness, Bliss* (New Haven, CT: Yale University Press, 2014), 47.

[23] In his mystical treatise, *The Life of Moses*, Gregory of Nyssa writes that "the divine word at the beginning forbids that the Divine be likened to any of the things known by men" (2.165), and so the true knowledge of God is "the seeing that consists in not seeing, because that which is sought transcends all knowledge" (2.163). In Gregory of Nyssa, *The Life of Moses*, trans. Abraham Malherbe and Everett Ferguson, Classics of Western Spirituality (New York: Paulist Press, 1978). Similarly, (Pseudo) Dionysius the Areopagite famously claims that God is beyond all affirmative predication and all negation. See *Mystical Theology* 2, in *Pseudo-Dionysius: The Complete Works*, tr. Colm Luibheid (New York: Paulist Press, 1987). Among contemporary thinkers, see Jean-Luc Marion's argument (contra Derrida) that praise and prayer are not disguised predications: Jean-Luc Marion, "In the Name: How to Avoid Speaking of 'Negative Theology'" in John D. Caputo and Michael J. Scanlon, eds., *God, the Gift, and Postmodernism* (Bloomington, IN: Indiana University Press, 1999), 20–53.

[24] I discuss idolatry in detail in Chapter 7.

[25] The alternative view in politics is aptly given by George Orwell, *Politics and the English Language* (Peterborough: Broadview Press, 2006 [1946]). I side with Orwell.

The Characteristic Deformations of Analytic Theology

In the context of this book, however, the best way to pursue this line of thought is by changing to an explicitly theological register. Like all human practices, analytic theology exhibits "characteristic deformations." I take this idea of "characteristic deformations" from Lauren Winner's *The Dangers of Christian Practice*.[26] According to Winner, characteristic deformations are defects that are "proper" to a practice itself. They tell us something about the practice; often they are corruptions of the very qualities that make the practice good in the first place. Winner focuses on fundamental Christian practices like prayer and the Eucharist, but the point generalizes to all human practices, including the practices of academic inquiry. For example, a characteristic deformation of modern science might be *scientism*, the assumption that all meaningful questions have measurable, empirical, repeatable, scientific answers. With scientism, the very methods and habits of mind that make scientific inquiry so valuable in the proper domain have become deformed and inapt, because they have been applied outside of the proper domain. Similarly, a characteristic deformation of poststructuralist literary criticism might involve the shift from aptly emphasizing that literary texts allow multiple competing interpretations to an inapt and untenable relativism, on which literally every interpretation is equally good.

Analytic theology also has its characteristic deformations, and they too are tied to its characteristic virtues. Many of analytic theology's characteristic virtues are also those of analytic philosophy: a concern for linguistic precision, logical rigor, and linear argument, along with a strong commitment to transparent writing. These are genuine virtues, and they are much needed in theology and the study of religion. But it is also easy to see how these same virtues could become deformed. To a hammer, everything looks like a nail. The standard analytic machinery can quickly transform the mysterious and transcendent into the familiar and tractable in a way that misconstrues just how alien and unfamiliar many theological topics really are. This transformation can be valuable: in my view, analytic models of the Trinity usefully and productively transform something unknowable into something familiar and tractable. Such models are valuable precisely because they are simplifications, simplifications that help us see how it could even be possibly true that God is both three and one.[27] But the same practices can also become deformed. Sometimes—not always, but sometimes—when analytic thinkers apply their characteristic virtues to theological and religious questions, the resulting deformation looks like a kind of inadvertent superficiality.

---

[26] See note 1 of this chapter. Her term is "characteristic damage."

[27] Many theologians would disagree, of course. The key point is that analytic models are *models*, and models cannot be identified with the thing itself and may not even resemble it very closely. See Wood, "Modeling Mystery."

Although I am reluctant to offer a concrete example, I recognize that one is required. Alvin Plantinga's critique of divine simplicity is a good example of how analytic philosophy can misfire when applied to theological questions.[28] Given his analytic assumptions, the only way Plantinga can make sense of divine simplicity is by asserting that God is a property. (This is roughly the argument: if God is simple, then God must be identical to all of his own properties. Only a property can be identical to a property. So God must be a property himself.) Whatever we think about divine simplicity, this criticism does not show that divine simplicity is incoherent. It shows that Plantinga's analytic philosophical assumptions and habits of mind have not properly equipped him to understand what the historic Christian tradition has meant by divine simplicity. He has inadvertently fallen victim to some of the characteristic deformations of analytic philosophy. Of course, this is not to say that every analytic thinker inevitably makes the same errors, or that analytic thought is constitutively unable to give an account of divine simplicity.

Analytic theologians may bristle at the suggestion that analytic philosophy has characteristic deformations. They shouldn't. In fact, they should weave this critique into the story of their own recent successes. Recent analytic theology is very much an attempt to mitigate the characteristic deformations of analytic philosophy of religion. Its advocates rightly point to recent analytic theology as evidence that the field is becoming more theologically sophisticated, but these recent treatments stand out precisely because they are atypical. For example, analytic theologians point to Jonathan Jacobs's work as evidence that analytic theology can take the apophatic tradition seriously. But Jacobs's work is so noteworthy because analytic thinkers have mostly ignored the apophatic tradition.[29] The same point holds for issues of ritual and religious practice, and the recent analytic work on those topics.[30] Analytic theologians correctly highlight colleagues who are careful readers of patristic and medieval texts, because in the past, analytic thinkers have not been especially careful readers of patristic and medieval texts. And so on.

For good Christian reasons, analytic theologians should agree that they are vulnerable to characteristic deformations. The Christian faith itself insists that everything, including human reason, has been warped by sin. As Winner puts it, "because nothing created is untouched by the Fall, Christians should not be surprised when lovely and good, potentially gracious Christian gestures are damaged,

---

[28] Alvin Plantinga, *Does God Have a Nature?* (Milwaukee, WI: Marquette University Press, 1980), 47.

[29] Jonathan D. Jacobs, "The Ineffable, Inconceivable, and Incomprehensible God: Fundamentality and Apophatic Theology," in Jonathan L. Kvanvig, ed., *Oxford Studies in Philosophy of Religion* (2015), 158–76; See also Sameer Yadav, "Mystical Experience and the Apophatic Attitude," *Journal of Analytic Theology* 4 (2016): 18–43.

[30] Terrence Cuneo, *Ritualized Faith: Essays on the Philosophy of Liturgy* (New York: Oxford University Press, 2016); James M. Arcadi, *An Incarnational Model of the Eucharist* (Cambridge: Cambridge University Press, 2018).

or when human beings deploy those Christian gestures in the perpetuation of damage."[31] Analytic theology cannot escape this damage, because analytic theologians are not immune from the cognitive consequences of sin and the Fall.

From the analytic point of view, what really rankles is the assumption that analytic theology can *only* exhibit its characteristic deformations, or that every instance of analytic theology must exhibit them from beginning to end. These assumptions are just a way of invalidating analytic theology in advance, without argument, when every form of inquiry—indeed, everything at all—exhibits characteristic deformations as well as characteristic virtues. As is so often the case, there is no way forward other than mutual engagement and respectful argument. But for that to happen, analytic theologians need to agree that they are vulnerable to analytic philosophy's characteristic deformations, even though analytic inquiry remains valuable and important. And from the other direction, its opponents need to agree that analytic theology is a valuable and important form of inquiry, notwithstanding its characteristic deformations. I hope to make both cases in this book.

[31] Winner, *The Dangers of Christian Practice*, 3.

5

What Is Analytic Theology?

A report from the front: even at analytic theology conferences, attended mainly by scholars who present their own work as analytic theology, it is not always obvious what any given person means by the label. When I say that I am writing a book on analytic theology, more than one person has replied with "Great! Maybe you can finally tell us what analytic theology is!" And the number of senior scholars who have given the "Analytic Theology Lecture" at the American Academy of Religion annual meeting who then later jokingly asked me "Does this mean I'm an analytic theologian?" Well, let's just say the number is not zero, and leave it at that.

I have good news and bad news. The good news is that it is fairly easy to define analytic theology to a reasonable level of precision. The bad news is that if we want anything more than a reasonable level of precision—if we want something that approaches an essential definition, which specifies necessary and sufficient conditions—then we want in vain. Although I will not fully argue the point here, I am convinced that there are no absolute, fixed boundaries between philosophy and theology, or, for that matter, between analytic and non-analytic philosophy, from which it follows that there are no absolute, fixed boundaries between analytic theology and other closely related forms of inquiry.

The most promising way to distinguish philosophy from theology is that of Thomas Aquinas. Roughly, theology—what he calls *sacra doctrina*—begins from revelation; the theologian accepts as true certain premises drawn from scripture and tradition and then reasons about their implications.[1] Philosophy, by contrast, begins from generally available premises that are in principle credible to anyone reasoning properly. This distinction between philosophy and theology is helpful, but it is also blurry. One can easily convert theology to philosophy (or vice versa) simply by treating one's supposedly revealed premises as conditional. So I am doing theology if I say: "God exists and became incarnate in Jesus of Nazareth,

---

[1] Thomas Aquinas, *Summa Theologiae* 1.1 as in Brian J. Shanley, O.P., trans, *The Treatise on the Divine Nature* (Indianapolis, IN: Hackett, 2006), 2–17. Several contemporary philosophers of religion make a parallel move, and argue that, on this definition, much analytic philosophy of religion should be classified as theology. See especially J. Aaron Simmons, "Living in the Existential Margins: Reflections on the Relationship between Philosophy and Theology," 147–57; J. L. Schellenberg, "Is Plantinga-Style Christian Philosophy Really Philosophy?," 229–43. At the moment, the best treatment of the relationship between analytic philosophy of religion and analytic theology is Max Baker-Hytch, "Analytic Theology and Analytic Philosophy of Religion: What's the Difference?" *Journal of Analytic Theology* 1 (2016): 1–16.

Analytic Theology and the Academic Study of Religion. William Wood, Oxford University Press (2021). © William Wood.
DOI: 10.1093/oso/9780198779872.003.0005

therefore p, q, and r." But I can always say instead: "Accept for the sake of argument that God exists and became incarnate in Jesus of Nazareth. Then it would follow, conditionally, that p, q, and r." Anyone, Christian or not, can assess whether p, q, and r really would follow, which (by hypothesis) makes this argument an instance of philosophy, not theology.

Distinguishing analytic from continental philosophy is even trickier. My considered view is that notwithstanding frequent reference to the "tools and methods" of analytic philosophy—a reference I make myself—there are no uniquely analytic tools and methods, or any necessary and sufficient conditions for demarcating analytic philosophy from other forms of inquiry. Instead, analytic philosophy is a MacIntyrean intellectual tradition.[2] Analytic philosophy is a distinctive form of inquiry not because it has unique tools and methods, but because it is the product of a distinctive intellectual culture. But that is exactly why it is difficult to demarcate analytic from continental philosophy. Intellectual traditions have porous boundaries, and it is possible for a single thinker to be a member of more than one intellectual tradition at the same time.

So the prospects of an essential definition of analytic theology are dim. But that does not mean that we are utterly in the dark about how to identify it. There are paradigm cases of analytic and non-analytic philosophy: we would never mistake the work of David Lewis for the work of Jacques Derrida. And even if there are no tools and methods used by all and only analytic philosophers, it would be silly to deny that some methods and approaches are seen more commonly in analytic philosophy than in other kinds of philosophical inquiry, let alone in other forms of humanistic inquiry.[3] There are also paradigm cases of philosophy and theology, and even between philosophy about Christian topics and Christian theology: we might usefully contrast Lewis's "Do We Believe in Penal Substitution?" with, say, anything by David Bentley Hart. And regarding analytic and non-analytic

---

[2] According to Alasdair MacIntyre, an intellectual tradition is:

> an argument extended through time in which certain fundamental agreements are defined and redefined in terms of two kinds of conflict: those with critics and enemies external to the tradition who reject all or at least key parts of those fundamental agreements, and those internal, interpretive debates through which the meaning and rationale of the fundamental agreements come to be expressed and by whose progress a tradition is constituted.
> (MacIntyre. *Whose Justice? Which Rationality?* [Notre Dame, IN: University of Notre Dame Press, 1989], 12)

See also Hans-Johann Glock, *What is Analytic Philosophy?*, 204–30.

[3] As discussed in Chapter 4, Michael Rea's widely cited list of analytic desiderata will do as well as any:

> (1) Write as if philosophical positions and conclusions can be adequately formulated in sentences that can be formalized and logically manipulated; (2) Prioritize precision, clarity, and logical coherence; (3) Avoid substantive (non-decorative) use of metaphor and other tropes whose semantic content outstrips their propositional content; (4) Work as much as possible with well-understood primitive concepts, and concepts that can analyzed in terms of those; (5) Treat conceptual analysis (insofar as it is possible) as a source of evidence.
> (Rea in Crisp and Rea, eds., *Analytic Theology*, 5–6; see also 17–26).

theology, it is very clear that Michael Rea is practicing a different mode of inquiry than Graham Ward. So much is obvious.

Furthermore, we should not suppose that analytic theology has no precedents in the Christian tradition. Everyone agrees that Christian theologians have always helped themselves to whatever they regard as the most useful philosophy of their day. So Thomas Aquinas drew on Aristotle, Paul Tillich drew on Heidegger, a whole host of twentieth-century German theologians drew on Hegel, etc. For a variety of reasons, we do not call the resulting work "Aristotelian theology," "Heideggerian theology," or "Hegelian theology," but even though the names are different, the underlying relationship is the same. Analytic theology is just Christian theology that draws on analytic philosophy, analogous to the way Aquinas draws on Aristotle, and so forth.

This suggestion lies behind my own preliminary definition of analytic theology in Chapter 1: "theology—usually constructive, systematic, Christian theology— that uses the tools and methods of analytic philosophy." It also lies behind two additional prominent definitions, one from William J. Abraham, and the other from the Oxford Studies in Analytic Theology Series (in which this book appears):

(Abraham):   Analytic theology...is systematic theology attuned to the deployment of the skills, resources, and virtues of analytic philosophy. It is the articulation of the central themes of Christian teaching illuminated by the best insights of analytic philosophy.[4]

(OSAT):   Analytic theology utilizes the tools and methods of contemporary analytic philosophy for the purposes of constructive Christian theology, paying attention to the Christian tradition and the development of doctrine.[5]

Neither of these is an essential definition, but they are still helpful. They capture most of the work that currently goes under the heading of analytic theology, including paradigm cases like Timothy Pawl and William Hasker (discussed below). They do not suffice for borderline cases and gray areas. For example, they do not really capture the work of scholars who do not use analytic tools and methods directly, but who may be sufficiently steeped in the intellectual culture of analytic philosophy to count as analytic theologians anyway.[6] They also leave out methodological treatments that are *about* analytic theology, rather than instances *of* analytic theology.

In a way, though, these considerations just reinforce the broader point that I am trying to make. The more we pursue something like an essential definition that captures all and only cases of analytic theology, the more we are pushed in

---

[4] William Abraham, "Systematic Theology as Analytic Theology," in Crisp and Rea, eds., *Analytic Theology*, 54.

[5] https://global.oup.com/academic/content/series/o/oxford-studies-in-analytic-theology-osat.

[6] I would say that much of William Abraham's work is like this, for example (which is obviously not a criticism).

the direction of ever longer descriptions with ever more qualifications, to the point where the resulting definition becomes unwieldy.[7] But anyone who understands the sense in which Aquinas borrowed philosophical methods from Aristotle, or the sense in which Tillich borrowed philosophical methods from Heidegger, can grasp what analytic theology is to a reasonable degree of precision. That is all we really need, in my view.

Toward Theological Analytic Theology

To tell the truth, the question that really interests me is not "What is analytic theology?" or even "What makes analytic theology *analytic*?" but "What makes analytic theology *theology*?" Asking this question sets the stage for the specific intervention I want to make in the ongoing debates about how to evaluate analytic theology. I want to push analytic theology in a more explicitly theological direction. I would like to see analytic theology become more historically informed, more sensitive to premodern ways of reading and thinking, and more attuned to mystery and to the limitations of human thought. To pick up the analogy mentioned in the previous section, Aquinas's *Summa Theologiae* is a work of theology—a work of *sacra doctrina*—and Aquinas is first and foremost a Christian theologian, one who appropriates the philosophy of Aristotle in the service of explicitly Christian theological aims.[8] The same is true (believe it or not) of Tillich's *Systematic Theology* and the way he uses existentialist philosophy. The

---

[7] Jonathan C. Rutledge does not attempt an essential definition, but he does try to develop a definition that is more discriminating than the minimal definitions I commend in this chapter. This is the result:

> Analytic theology applies analytic (though not exclusively analytic) concepts and methods to theological issues and applies theological concepts and insights to issues that have traditionally been of interest to analytic philosophers. Although the analytic concepts and methods under question are wide ranging, they include the utilization of logical and linguistic analysis and are read typically, though not essentially, against a background of philosophical literature roughly beginning with the likes of Frege, Russell, Moore, and Wittgenstein. Moreover, analytic theology recognizes the importance of (i) allowing its practitioners to include both non-propositional items in the set of theological data and groups as possible subjects of discourse, as well as (ii) accommodating the social construction of a number of concepts that are important to the theological task with some notable exceptions such as the concepts of truth, objectivity, rationality, justice, and the good.
>
> (Jonathan C. Rutledge, "Analyzing the Muddles of Analysis: (Some of) What Analytic Theologians Can Learn From the History of Analytic Feminism," *Modern Theology* [May 6, 2019], doi:10.1111/moth.12525)

I like this definition, but relative to the more minimal definitions already in the literature, I am not convinced that it improves our understanding of analytic theology enough to justify its additional complexity.

[8] It should be uncontroversial to note that Aquinas considered himself a theologian, not a philosopher. One can accept this point without also saying (as some scholars do) that Aquinas had no use for philosophy or collapsed philosophy into theology. See Wayne J. Hankey, "Why Philosophy Abides for Aquinas," *Heythrop Journal* 43 (2001): 329–48. Hankey's opponents (who take the stronger view just noted) include Mark Jordan, "Theology and Philosophy," in Norman Kretzmann and Eleonore Stump, eds., *The Cambridge Companion to Aquinas* (New York: Cambridge University Press, 1993), 232–51.

analytic theology that I find most interesting, and the kind that I want to flourish, is similarly theological.

I say this for three reasons. First, my own primary academic discipline is theology, and I very much believe that academic theology would benefit from an infusion of analytic thought. But the best way to make that case to theologians is by showing them that analytic theology can be valuable *as theology*. Second, I also think that the more theological analytic theology becomes, the more resistant it will be to some of the characteristic deformations of analytic philosophy (see the discussion in Chapter 4). When analytic theologians are more historically informed and have a greater understanding of premodern ways of reading and thinking, they will not be so quick to transform the mysterious and unknown into the familiar and tractable, and they will be a bit more suspicious about common sense and the transparency of language. Third, I am convinced that Christian theology is a legitimate academic discipline, one that can find a place even in ostensibly secular universities. Although this claim does not apply only to analytic theology, it is especially clear with respect to analytic theology, precisely because analytic theology borrows so many norms of inquiry from philosophy. Note, however, that this claim becomes more provocative when analytic theology seems more like an authentic form of Christian theology. It is comparatively easy to agree that analytic philosophers of religion should be able to think about Christian topics without somehow excluding themselves from the realm of acceptable academic discourse. It is harder, and therefore more interesting, to argue that Christian analytic *theologians* can think about Christian topics *as Christians* while still engaging in properly academic inquiry. That is the argument I want to make in this book.

The argument begins in this chapter with an extended discussion of two paradigm cases of analytic theology, provided by Timothy Pawl and William Hasker. I then look at a recent collection of essays that push analytic theology in new directions, focusing on the contribution from Sameer Yadav, who critiques existing analytic theology from a liberation perspective and calls for an "analytic theology of liberation." Looking at Pawl and Hasker will help clarify what analytic theology is, and what makes it distinctive. But I also read their work as examples of the kind of analytic theology I want to commend. I argue that Pawl's 2016 book *In Defense of Conciliar Christology* is best read as an example of "faith seeking understanding," and Hasker's 2013 *Metaphysics and the Tri-Personal God* is an example of constructive theology. I then turn to Yadav and the collection of essays in which his work appears, *Voices from the Edge: Centering Marginalized Voices in Analytic Theology*. These essays are each important in their own right and also bear directly on my call for more theological analytic theology. Arguably, analytic theology can only become more theological when it takes liberation theology and "marginalized voices" more seriously than it has so far. Yadav makes this case forcefully, and argues that, in a sense, all good theology must be liberation theology. While I am not willing to go this far myself, many theologians will agree with Yadav, and analytic theologians should certainly wrestle with his critique.

Analytic Theology as Faith Seeking Understanding: Timothy Pawl's Defense of "Conciliar Christology"

One of the joys of teaching bright undergraduates is that they don't always know what "everybody" already knows. So when I teach Timothy Pawl's article "A Solution to the Fundamental Philosophical Problem of Christology," my students do not "know" that they should approach Pawl as an analytic theologian, which, of course, can only mean that he is a hyper-rationalist, logic-chopping philosopher with no appreciation for mystery and tradition.[9] On the contrary, my students' objections often run the other way. They accuse Pawl of playing "the mystery card" himself, and go on to criticize him for relying overmuch on tradition-based theological assertions rather than autonomous philosophical arguments. Of course, there are a host of problems with this stock response, and pointing them out is part of the purpose of the ensuing discussion. But I love that they read Pawl this way, because I think they are onto something. Notwithstanding his philosophical apparatus, there really is a sense in which Pawl's argument is fully, robustly theological. Moreover, it is theology of a venerable and traditional sort: theology as *fides quaerens intellectum*, faith seeking understanding.

The phrase "faith seeking understanding" comes from Anselm's *Proslogion*, and points back to Augustine's famous maxim *crede ut intelligas*, "believe so that you may understand."[10] So construed, Christian theology begins with an epistemic posture of assent to scripture and tradition, or, more generally, to whatever theological resources one regards as authoritative. On this account, theology does not seek to prove that faith claims are true; it assumes their truth and then tries to understand them more deeply and elucidate their consequences.[11]

Daniel Migliore's prominent textbook account of faith seeking understanding helps fill out this picture. Though it does not aim to prove its foundational axioms, Christian theology does involve asking questions and "struggling to find at least provisional answers to these questions." (No intellectual discipline proves its own

---

[9] Timothy Pawl, "A Solution to the Fundamental Philosophical Problem of Christology," *Journal of Analytic Theology* 2 (2014): 62–85.

[10] As he writes in its prologue Anselm originally planned to circulate the *Proslogion* anonymously with the title "Faith Seeking Understanding." See Anselm, *Basic Writings*, ed. and trans. Thomas Williams (Indianapolis, IN: Hackett, 2007), 75.

Augustine's maxim is found in Augustine, *Tractates on the Gospel of John*, paragraph 29.6, commenting on Jn 7:17 in *The Fathers of the Church*, vol. 88, trans. John W. Rettig (Washington, DC: Catholic University of America Press, 1993), 18.

[11] Treating scripture and tradition as foundational and authoritative does not mean we can never question them or challenge them. I discuss this issue in Chapter 11.

axioms. That's why they are *axioms*. And every discipline asks questions and looks for provisional answers, so Christian theology is not unusual here.) The questions posed to theology can change as the prevailing culture changes: "The changing, ambiguous, and often precarious world poses ever new questions for faith, and many answers that sufficed yesterday are no longer compelling today."[12] The theological task, therefore, includes more than just elucidation. It can also include argument and counterargument, in an effort to dissolve apparent tensions and contradictions that arise from what one believes.[13] Anselm himself sums up this approach to theology very well. Theological inquirers do not seek explanations:

> in order to achieve faith through reason, but rather so that they can delight in the understanding and contemplation of things they already believe, and so that they may be "always ready," to the best of their ability, "to give an answer to all who demand . . . the reason for the hope that is in" [them].[14]

This is precisely Pawl's own task. I want to develop this claim by looking at the book-length version of Pawl's solution to the fundamental philosophical problem of Christology, as presented in his 2016 monograph *In Defense of Conciliar Christology: A Philosophical Essay*. Pawl's book offers a clear example of analytic theology as faith seeking understanding.

On "Conciliar Christology" and Pawl's Assumptions

"Conciliar Christology" is Pawl's own term of art, but its meaning is straightforward enough. Conciliar Christology is "the Christology put forward by the first seven ecumenical councils of Christendom."[15] More precisely, it is "is the conjunction of all the claims made at these councils concerning the doctrine of the incarnation."[16] This is already a characteristically analytic starting point, and so it is worth flagging some of Pawl's assumptions at the outset. First, he assumes that the proceedings and documents of the first seven ecumenical councils have a

---

[12] Daniel L. Migliore, *Faith Seeking Understanding: An Introduction to Christian Theology*, 2nd ed. (Grand Rapids, MI: Eerdmans, 2004), 3, 4.

[13] See Aquinas, *Summa Theologiae*, 1.1.8.

[14] Anselm, *Cur deus homo*, 1.1, as in Williams, ed., *Anselm: Basic Writings*. The internal quotation is 1 Peter 3:15.

[15] Timothy Pawl, *In Defense of Conciliar Christology* (New York: Oxford University Press, 2016), 1. Those councils are: the First Council of Nicaea (325), the First Council of Constantinople (381), the Council of Ephesus (431), the Council of Chalcedon (451), the Second Council of Constantinople (553), the Third Council of Constantinople (680–81), and the Second Council of Nicaea (787). Pawl has good reasons for choosing exactly these councils, and not more, or fewer (Pawl, *Conciliar Christology*, 1–2).

[16] Pawl, *Conciliar Christology*, 1.

determinate and identifiable propositional content. Second, he assumes that the councils are all mutually consistent. That is, when we join together all the propositional claims these councils make about the incarnation, the resulting conjunction is itself free from internal contradiction. Third, he assumes that conciliar Christology is true. It therefore follows, obviously, that Pawl also assumes the truth of the traditional Chalcedonian account of the incarnation, namely that Christ really is one person who is both fully human and fully divine because he possesses both a complete human nature and also the complete divine nature. Again, Pawl *assumes*, but does not argue for this claim. At no point does he take himself to be offering arguments that conciliar Christology is true or even possibly true. Rather, he assumes its truth and seeks to answer what he regards as the most serious objections to that truth.[17]

Interestingly, conciliar Christology itself includes the claim that some aspects of the incarnation are mysterious. According to various canonized texts, the exact manner of the union between Christ's divine and human natures is ineffable.[18] The technical term for the union of the divine and human natures is "the hypostatic union." Pawl understands these texts to assert that it is not possible for human beings to give an account of the hypostatic union, which means that it is not possible to say exactly how or in what sense it can be the case that Christ has both a human nature and a divine nature. So, in summary, Pawl assumes the truth of all the claims about the incarnation made by the first seven ecumenical councils of the Church, assumes that Christ is both fully human and fully divine because he has both a human nature and a divine nature, and assumes that it is not possible, even in principle, to say how it can be the case that something has both a human nature and a divine nature. I trust that it is becoming more clear why I call his book an instance of "faith seeking understanding."

Pawl's Solution to the "Fundamental Problem"

The "fundamental philosophical problem of Christology" is not new, but this specific way to name the problem entered the analytic literature by way of Richard Cross:

> T]he fundamental philosophical problem specific to the doctrine is this: how is it that one and the same thing could be both divine (and thus, on the face of it, necessary, and necessarily omniscient, omnipotent, eternal, immutable,

---

[17] For all of the above assumptions, see Pawl, *Conciliar Christology*, 2–4.
[18] For some relevant texts, see Pawl, *Conciliar Christology*, 20–22.

impassible, and impeccable) and human (and thus, on the face of it, have the complements of all these properties)?[19]

In short, the fundamental problem (call it "The Problem") is the problem of incompatible properties. Christ seems to be both necessarily omniscient, as the divine Son, the second person of the Trinity, and yet also limited in knowledge, as the human man, Jesus of Nazareth. If Christ is both human and divine, he must have both human and divine properties, and human properties are not (so it seems) logically compatible with divine properties. So nothing can be both human and divine—from which it follows that the traditional, conciliar Christology is false. We can run the same argument using the idiom of "predicates" instead of properties. Pawl prefers this idiom:

> Anything with two natures, one divine, and one human, will have some predicates aptly said of it in virtue of one of those natures, but others apt of it in virtue of the other nature. Some of these predicates will be inconsistent with one another. And so anything with both a divine and a human nature will have inconsistent predicates true of it. No one thing, however, can have inconsistent predicates true of it. Consequently, nothing can have both a divine and a human nature. Thus, Conciliar Christology, since it entails that Christ has both a divine and human nature, is false.[20]

The problem—or should I say "The Problem"—is real and it calls for a response. As Pawl notes, when fully spelled out, The Problem presents a formally valid argument that begins from initially plausible premises and leads to the conclusion that the traditional account of the incarnation is not only false but necessarily false.[21] When confronted with a formally valid argument, there are really only two legitimate ways to respond: either accept the argument's conclusion or find a way to deny one of its premises. Anything else is just changing the subject. Someone who continues to believe that conciliar Christology is true, therefore, must deny a premise, as Pawl does here.

Before presenting his own solution to The Problem, Pawl discusses several other ways one might respond, and argues that they are not as successful, either because they are not consistent with conciliar Christology or because they do not actually resolve the prima facie contradiction it poses. (One of these unsuccessful ways involves the appeal to mystery, which I discuss below.) Pawl's own solution is to deny that the candidate predicates are really incompatible, by revising their

---

[19] Richard Cross, "The Incarnation," in Thomas P. Flint and Michael Rea, eds., *The Oxford Handbook of Philosophical Theology* (New York: Oxford University Press, 2009), 453.

[20] Pawl, *Conciliar Christology*, 75.   [21] Pawl, *Conciliar Christology*, 89.

truth conditions—that is, by revising the conditions under which we can truthfully apply them.

He focuses on passibility and impassibility. Initially, it seems that something is passible when it can be causally affected by some other thing, and it is impassible when it cannot be causally affected by any other thing. Conciliar Christology asserts that Christ is both passible, in virtue of his human nature, and yet also impassible, in virtue of his divine nature. Plausibly, nothing can be both passible and impassible, given the following initial truth conditions[22]:

PASSIBLE: *S* is passible just in case it is possible that at least one other thing causally affect *S*.

IMPASSIBLE: *S* is impassible just in case it is not the case that it is possible that at least one other thing causally affect *S*.

Pawl argues that these truth conditions are incorrect, and that, contrary to our initial assumptions, something can be both passible and impassible at the same time. To soften up the ground, he presents a fanciful thought experiment.[23] He asks us to imagine a world in which everything, absolutely everything, has exactly one arm. Furthermore, each thing's arm can be either bent (say, at 90 degrees or more) or unbent. In such a world, precisely because everything has exactly one arm, we would naturally say that nothing can be both "arm-bent" and "arm-unbent":

ARM-BENT: *S* is arm-bent just in case *S* has an arm that is bent 90 or more degrees.

ARM-UNBENT: *S* is arm-unbent just in case *S* has an arm that is not bent 90 or more degrees.

Now suppose that into this crazy one-armed world, there comes a cheerleader, a two-armed cheerleader. His left arm is bent 90 degrees, but his right arm is straight. Because he has two arms, he can be both arm-bent and arm-unbent. To further the fiction, suppose too that most philosophers and logicians in this world were not convinced of the existence of the cheerleader. (After all, he is literally the only thing in the world that has two arms.) They would probably continue to insist that nothing can be both arm-bent and arm-unbent. Meanwhile, fans of the cheerleader would have to revise the conditions under which the terms "arm-bent" and "arm-unbent" truthfully apply.

Pawl uses this thought experiment to motivate a similar response to the problem of Christ's incompatible predicates. Just as we have to understand the

---

[22] Pawl, *Conciliar Christology*, 154.   [23] Pawl, *Conciliar Christology*, 155–57.

predications "arm-bent" and "arm-unbent" differently when we learn that something can have two arms, so must we understand, e.g., "passible" and "impassible" differently when we learn that something can have both a divine and a human nature. Just as it turns out that "arm-bent" and "arm-unbent" are not contradictory predications after all, so does it turn out that "passible" and "impassible" are not contradictory predications after all. Instead, we need to revise their truth conditions like so:[24]

PASSIBLE: *S* is passible just in case *S* has a concrete nature that it is possible for some other thing to causally affect.

IMPASSIBLE: *S* is impassible just in case *S* has a concrete nature that it is impossible for some other thing to causally affect.

By revising the truth conditions of the candidate predications, and indexing them to concrete natures, Pawl dissolves the logical contradiction posed by The Problem: the predications are no longer contradictory.[25] Because Christ, and only Christ, has a divine and a human nature, Christ, and only Christ, is both passible and impassible.

I have simplified Pawl's argument considerably, but I trust it is clear that he offers a novel and elegant solution to The Problem. To recap: according to Pawl, there is no real contradiction involved in predicating divine and human attributes to Christ so long as (a) it is possible for one thing to have both a divine and a human nature, and (b) the relevant predications are indexed to their respective natures and understood according to the revised truth conditions above. The only real question—given Pawl's assumptions and the way he has set up the problem— is whether his suggestion that we must revise the truth conditions is sufficiently well motivated. Pawl has a variety of ancillary arguments to try to show that his solution is well motivated and not ad hoc, but the bulk of the work is done by the cheerleader analogy. The fundamental intuition is clear enough: when we learn that something previously regarded as impossible turns out actually to exist (a two-armed cheerleader, a God-man), we must revise the way we understand the logical relationships that obtain between predicates we previously regarded as incompatible.[26]

---

[24] Pawl, *Conciliar Christology*, 155–59.

[25] Pawl discusses "concrete natures" in *Conciliar Christology*, 34–46. A "concrete" nature is a concrete particular, rather than an abstract property. Christ's concrete human nature, then, would include both his human body and his human soul (if indeed there are souls).

[26] This seems like just what we should expect. Suppose you are a hardened naturalist: would you really expect all your conceptualizations of the world to remain exactly the same if Christianity were true?

Conciliar Christology as Faith Seeking Understanding

Pawl understands himself as a philosopher, and he calls his own book a "Philosophical Essay" in its subtitle. But I read it as a work of theology, and furthermore a work of faith seeking understanding. I say this not just because Pawl begins from Christian theological assumptions, but because those assumptions structure his whole argument—not only what he includes but also what he omits. Most obviously, he assumes the truth of the first seven ecumenical councils, which entails assuming the truth of the traditional Chalcedonian picture of the incarnation. But the very idea of "Conciliar Christology" presupposes that the first seven ecumenical councils are mutually consistent, which in turn presupposes that they have a determinate, identifiable propositional content. (We cannot be certain that the councils are mutually consistent unless we are able to identify exactly what they teach.) These two assumptions also flow from a posture of faith seeking understanding.

Some historians and historically minded theologians would dispute the suggestion that the first seven ecumenical councils are mutually consistent and present a single, unified Christology.[27] Others, from a different direction, would dispute Pawl's assumption that the councils have an identifiable and determinate propositional content. For my own purposes, I do not need to settle these disputes. What matters is the reason why Pawl assumes that the councils are mutually consistent and can speak with one voice. Pawl assumes that the councils are consistent because he is a committed Roman Catholic who accepts the infallible teaching authority of the Church.[28] If the councils were mutually inconsistent, then by definition they would teach something false. But (on this line of thought) the Church cannot err in matters of doctrine, and therefore the councils cannot teach anything false. So Pawl's assumption does not spring from historical or hermeneutical naivety but from a posture of faithful assent to the magisterial authority of the Church. This posture is also one of faith seeking understanding.

---

[27] Mark DelCogliano presses this and other historical questions in a very informative blog post: https://afkimel.wordpress.com/2017/04/17/the-christ-of-analytic-theology-a-review-essay/.

[28] Pawl chose to submit his manuscript to the Chief Censor of his Archdiocese in order to secure the *nihil obstat* and the *imprimatur* which certify that the book is free of doctrinal error. In the sequel to *Conciliar Christology*, he writes:

> in this book (and everywhere) I am attempting to think with the mind of the orthodox Christian faith; in particular, in consonance with the teachings of the Catholic Church. If, in the end, my interpretation of the councils is incorrect, or if my reasoning, unbeknownst to me, commits me to views contrary to the current or future teaching of the Church, then I renounce those views and the problematic commitments I made which lead to them.
>
> (Timothy Pawl, *In Defense of Extended Conciliar Christology* [New York: Oxford University Press, 2019], 30, n. 30)

The posture of faith seeking understanding also determines what Pawl omits. He regards it as an authoritative teaching of the Church that it is not possible to give a positive account of the hypostatic union, so he does not attempt one. That reticence means that he does not ever *argue* that Christ is both fully human and fully divine—indeed, he does not even argue that this claim is so much as possibly true.[29] (This is why my undergraduate students find Pawl frustrating: by their lights he just assumes the very thing they most want him to prove.) Pawl does not give anyone who does not already believe conciliar Christology any new, positive reasons to accept it. Instead, he tries only to show that the strongest objections against conciliar Christology do not succeed.

For this very reason—whether Pawl intended it or not—there is an apophatic core at the heart of *Conciliar Christology.* This is the case, even though some of what he actually says about mystery will likely strike theologians as tin-eared.[30] (He does a much better job in his next book, a sequel to *Conciliar Christology.*[31]) The story he tells in *Conciliar Christology* is fundamentally a story about the absolute, ontological uniqueness of the God-man. That story is completely compatible with some much-admired, broadly apophatic theological accounts that treat Christological assertions as "non-contrastive discourse" or that posit an "absolute distinction" between the divine and created orders.[32] At the heart of Pawl's argument is the ineffable, unanalyzable hypostatic union of the divine and human natures. As Pawl tells it, what previously seemed impossible—that one person

---

[29]   Pawl, *Conciliar Christology,* 2.

[30]   His main point is that an appeal to mystery does not suffice as a response to a formally valid argument purporting to show that some Christian teaching is false. I fully agree with this point. The Christian tradition has always distinguished between a mystery and a bare contradiction, and the mystery of the incarnation is not the "mystery" of how *P* and not-*P* can both be true. (Here see Robert Sokolowski, *The God of Faith and Reason: Foundations of Christian Theology* [Washington, DC: Catholic University of America Press, 1982], 37–38.) Dissolving contradictions allegedly found in the doctrine of incarnation should, therefore, be seen as a way of preserving its mystery rather than dissolving it. So far so good. The problem is that Pawl sometimes seems to assimilate mystery to mere ignorance, such that something is mysterious just in case we don't happen to understand it (see *Conciliar Christology,* 89). But traditionally, a mystery is something that in principle surpasses all human understanding, not something about which a given person happens to be ignorant.

[31]   There he writes:

> Importantly, from my point of view, I don't think we can go further than defeating defeaters for the central mysteries of the faith. That is, I think that our approach should be one of answering objections to the central mysteries of the faith. I agree with the standard notion of "mystery" employed in Catholic theology, which is put well by de Aldama and Solano: "A mystery in the strict sense [is] a truth that transcends not only human philosophy but also the angelic natural intelligence. Even if it is made known by divine revelation and has been accepted by an act of faith, still regarding its intrinsic possibility it remains impervious to the human intellect." I do not take us to be able philosophically to prove the truth or even possibility of the incarnation. Such is beyond our abilities.
>
> (Pawl, *In Defense of Extended Conciliar Christology,* 5)

The internal quotation is to J. A. Aldama and S. J. Iesu Solano, *Sacrae Theologiae Summa IIIA: On the Incarnate Word on the Blessed Virgin Mary,* trans. S. J. Kenneth Baker (Saddle River, NJ: Keep The Faith, 2014), 97.

[32]   For example, Kathryn Tanner, *God and Creation in Christian Theology: Tyranny or Empowerment?* (Minneapolis, MN: Fortress Press, 2005 [1988]); Sokolowski, *God of Faith and Reason.*

could be both fully human and fully divine—turns out to be actual (though even here we know not how). Since what is actual is possible, it simply follows that it is possible for one and the same person to be omniscient and limited in knowledge, passible and impassible, and so forth. But in order to understand *that*, we have to change the way we understand our very language. Before Christ, we thought that "passible" and "impassible" were contradictory terms; only after Christ can we see that they are not. Language itself bends with the gravitational pull of the God-man. But we cannot, even in principle, explain how the God-man is so much as possible.

Can "Faith Seeking Understanding" Really Describe Academic Theology?

At this point, some readers may be so convinced about the theological credentials of *Conciliar Christology* that they now wonder how it can even count as an academic work at all. How can Pawl be entitled to assume the truth of conciliar Christology? More generally, how can "faith seeking understanding" be a legitimate mode of academic inquiry? I address such questions at length in Chapter 11, so I will give only a brief response here. The question arises because Pawl assumes, but does not argue for, his specifically Christian-theological claims. Yet there is no general academic obligation to prove the truth of one's assumptions before basing a line of inquiry on those assumptions. If there were, most lines of inquiry could never begin. In the philosophy of mind, for example, someone might assume a materialist account of the mind, and then try to respond to objections from mind/body dualists without ever arguing that the materialist assumptions are true. Pawl's argument has exactly the same structure. He is not begging any questions, because he is not actually trying to convince anyone that conciliar Christology is true. Rather, he is trying to show that some initially plausible objections to conciliar Christology do not succeed. If you believe that p, and I then tell you that p is false because it is inconsistent with q and r, you do not suddenly acquire a rational obligation to prove to me that p is true. You are perfectly entitled to point out that, when properly understood, q and r are not actually incompatible with p. That is the deep structure of Pawl's argument.

Analytic Theology as Constructive Theology: William Hasker's *Metaphysics and the Tri-Personal God*

Academic theologians often treat theology as a kind of intellectual history. When I am asked by other theologians what my academic specialty is, the questioner often expects an answer in terms of some historical period: I work on medieval theology, or early modern theology, or twentieth-century Protestant theology, or whatnot. The prevailing assumption is that to do academic theology is just to study the history of theology. On this view, the theologian tries to understand, for example, Martin Luther's account of the Trinity rather than developing her own account of the Trinity. This might also require her to investigate the historical antecedents of Luther's account, or how Luther's account differs from those of his near contemporaries. But it will not usually involve directly assessing whether Luther's account is true, or defending one's own alternative account.

By contrast, analytic theology emerges from analytic philosophy, and analytic philosophy features a very different intellectual culture, one in which it is normal to argue in one's own voice about the fundamental structure of reality—about how things really are, in the world, outside any text. As a result, analytic theology is explicitly, unashamedly *constructive* in a way that many other forms of theology are not. As a rough-and-ready definition, I would say that the constructive Christian theologian tries to offer his or her own account of the meaning or truth of some doctrine or claim of the Christian tradition (as I argued in Chapter 2). Alternatively, on a slightly broader definition, a constructive Christian theologian tries to show how the meaning and truth of some Christian doctrine or claim entails that another Christian interpretation of reality is correct. (For example, I might try to show that one consequence of the doctrine of original sin is that we should affirm some specific theory of politics.) These are, admittedly, self-serving definitions of constructive theology. But they do not apply only to analytic theologians.[33]

William Hasker's *Metaphysics and the Tri-Personal God* is a work of constructive Christian theology. Hasker's book inaugurated Oxford University Press's "Oxford Studies in Analytic Theology" series, and it is one of the first book-length examples of analytic theology. Hasker aims to construct and defend a broadly orthodox, philosophically coherent account of the Trinity that answers the question: How can there be three divine persons—Father, Son, and Holy Spirit—but only one God? He takes as dialogue partners contemporary philosophers of religion, major twentieth-century theologians, and historians and scholars of the early Church. Theologians and historians have almost entirely ignored the trinitarian contributions of analytic philosophers of religion, and analytic philosophers of religion have not really assimilated the insights of theologians and historians. Hasker aims to construct a synthesis that draws on all three camps.

He wants his synthesis to be faithful to the Christian tradition, and consistent with its historic trinitarian creeds. At the same time, his is very much a

---

[33] Here are some theologians who count as constructive on these definitions: Thomas Aquinas, John Calvin, Friedrich Schleiermacher, Karl Barth, Paul Tillich, Karl Rahner, Hans Urs von Balthasar, Rowan Williams, Kathryn Tanner, and Sarah Coakley. My point is that this is not a definition that excludes everyone but, say, Richard Swinburne.

contemporary synthesis, one that draws heavily on contemporary analytic metaphysics, and therefore not one that could have emerged in the fourth century, with the doctrine of the Trinity itself. In other words, Hasker wants to develop a coherent, orthodox Christian account of the doctrine of the Trinity, but he does not argue that any patristic figure ever affirmed the account he develops. The difference between these two goals is the difference between constructive theology and historical theology.

I write for a broad audience, and so it might be useful to lay out briefly what the orthodox doctrine of the Trinity actually is and to say something about how it arose.[34] The doctrine of the Trinity asserts that there is exactly one God, who exists as three concrete, really distinct divine beings, Father, Son, and Holy Spirit. More precisely, according to the creeds promulgated by the early Church's first two ecumenical councils: the Father, Son, and Spirit are three distinct divine *persons* (*personae* in Latin; *hypostaseis* in Greek) who share a single divine *nature* (*substantia* in Latin; *ousia* in Greek). The three persons cannot be distinguished by degrees of divinity: they are all equally, fully, and maximally divine. Furthermore, the Christian God is necessarily and eternally trinitarian, and so "Father," "Son," and "Spirit" do not merely name three different contingent or temporal stages in the life of God. In other words, there can be no time, not even the "time" before creation, at which one divine person existed without the others. Nor are "Father," "Son," and "Spirit" merely different names for the same thing: the three persons are each real, and really distinct, even though they also share a single divine nature. The orthodox tradition specifies that the three persons are distinguished only by their relations of causal origin: the Father alone is "unbegotten," the Son alone is "begotten from the Father," and the Spirit alone "proceeds" from the Father (and the Son).[35] Although the New Testament contains some proto-trinitarian language, the doctrine of the Trinity developed slowly, over the course of the first four centuries of the Common Era, before reaching final, definitive formulation in the ecumenical Councils of Nicaea (in 325) and Constantinople (in 381).[36]

Even from this brief résumé, it should be clear that the doctrine of the Trinity presents some major conceptual difficulties. It is not easy to see how there could be only one God when there are also three distinct, fully divine persons. Alternatively, it is not easy to see how there could be three distinct, fully divine persons who all instantiate the same, numerically identical divine nature. These

---

[34] For standard textbook accounts see J. N. D. Kelly, *Early Christian Doctrines* (London: A&C Black, 1985); Basil Studer, *Trinity and Incarnation: The Faith of the Early Church*, trans. Matthias Westerhoff (Edinburgh: T&T Clark, 1993). The best contemporary scholarly account is Lewis Ayres, *Nicaea and Its Legacy*.

[35] In 1054 the Eastern and Western Churches divided over the Western decision to add the Latin phrase *filioque* [and the son] to the original Niceno-Constantinopolitan Creed of 381.

[36] The normative trinitarian creed is called the "Nicene Creed" because it was initially formulated at the Council of Nicaea, and later augmented at the Council of Constantinople.

conceptual difficulties do not exhaust the questions we might fruitfully ask of the doctrine of the Trinity. Contemporary theologians have been much more interested in examining the implications of trinitarian doctrine for the way we should worship, or do theology, or structure a just society.[37] But even though we might ask other questions of the doctrine of the Trinity, the basic logical problem—what Hasker calls the "three-in-oneness problem"—remains pressing.[38]

Hasker's Constructive Proposal

I turn now to Hasker's own constructive proposal.[39] First, as with Pawl, it is very clear that his project is not an instance of natural theology, or any form of modernist foundationalism. Hasker does not try to prove that God is trinitarian using only neutral premises available to all. He explicitly founds his project on "the revelation of God in Jesus of Nazareth."[40] He further assumes that the New Testament presents a broadly reliable account of the life and teachings of Jesus, and that we are justified in treating the Nicene Creed as a reliable guide to the truth about the Trinity. We can make these assumptions, according to Hasker, because anyone who affirms the orthodox doctrine of the Trinity at all must conclude that "divine providence has been at work in guiding the Church in its understanding, and in preventing it from falling into destructive errors."[41] His is not in any sense "a Cartesian project, in which the objective is to demolish our existing edifice of belief, scour the building site down to the bedrock, and build all over again with imperishable materials."[42] Like Pawl, Hasker assumes without argument certain aspects of the normative Christian tradition, accepts that they are reliable guides to the truth, and seeks to explicate their claims with the best intellectual tools in his possession.

Hasker is a "social trinitarian," which means that he defends an account of the Trinity on which the Father, Son, and Spirit are "distinct centers of knowledge, will, love, and action" as well as "distinct centers of consciousness."[43] To put it another way, on social trinitarianism, the three persons are also three numerically distinct divine agents. When they act together, they act in concert (and

---

[37] One can find examples of all of these approaches, as well as pointers to classic statements of modern Trinitarian theology in Giles Emery and Matthew Levering, eds., *The Oxford Handbook of the Trinity* (New York: Oxford University Press, 2011). See also Khaled Anatolios, ed., *The Holy Trinity in the Life of the Church* (Grand Rapids, MI: Baker, 2014).

[38] William Hasker, *Metaphysics and the Tri-Personal God* (New York: Oxford University Press, 2013), 1.

[39] This discussion below borrows from my published review of Hasker in *Scottish Journal of Theology* 69 (2016): 234–36.

[40] Hasker, *Metaphysics and the Tri-Personal God*, 7.

[41] Hasker, *Metaphysics and the Tri-Personal God*, 9–10.

[42] Hasker, *Metaphysics and the Tri-Personal God*, 10.

[43] Hasker, *Metaphysics and the Tri-Personal God*, 22.

necessarily so, according to Hasker), but their actions also remain numerically distinct. Prima facie, it is especially difficult to see how the three persons, so-construed, nevertheless count as a single God. The special challenge for social trinitarians is therefore to avoid tritheism.[44] Social trinitarianism has antecedents in pre-Nicene Christianity, and it is close in spirit to the patterns of worship found in Eastern Christian thought, but it has never been the dominant Christian account of the Trinity in either the East or the West.[45]

Hasker's social trinitarianism is an example of the constructive way he approaches theology. He recognizes that to describe any ancient, patristic or medieval author as a social trinitarian would be anachronistic, and he agrees that social trinitarianism in its present form "is inescapably indebted to insights drawn from recent philosophy, psychology, and sociology."[46] Many theologians will find his account of trinitarian personhood suspiciously modern, as if a trinitarian person is a typical Cartesian subject that just happens to be divine. This would be a devastating objection if his goal were to elucidate the patristic notion of personhood, but that is not his goal. His goal is to defend a coherent account of the Trinity on which three distinct divine agents nevertheless count as one God. So long as he can avoid tritheism, his modern account of personhood is not inherently problematic. (It isn't as though the creeds anathematize the modern account of personhood, after all.) Furthermore, his account of social trinitarianism is not utterly divorced from historical reflection. He points out that the earliest Christians might well have had a more flexible notion of monotheism than we do now. After all, they seem to have prayed to and even worshipped Christ, while also continuing to regard themselves as monotheists. And Christianity arose from Second Temple Judaism, in which monotheism was primarily a practical doctrine, focused on worship, rather than a metaphysical doctrine.[47] Contemporary social trinitarianism offers the best way to interpret these ancient practices, according to Hasker.

Having made his case that we should understand the three persons along social trinitarian lines—as distinct centers of knowledge, will, love, and action—Hasker turns to the even more challenging task of explaining the divine unity. He has to

---

[44] The sharpest philosophical critic of social trinitarianism is Brian Leftow. See his "Anti Social Trinitarianism," in Stephen T. Davis et al., *The Trinity: An Interdisciplinary Symposium* (New York: Oxford University Press, 1999), 203–50; and "A Latin Trinity," *Faith and Philosophy*, 21 (2004): 304–33. Perhaps here I should add that Hasker did not persuade me to become a social trinitarian myself, but he did convince to take it more seriously as an orthodox option. It is also perhaps worth noting that social trinitarianism has been much more popular with contemporary systematic theologians than with analytic philosophers of religion.

[45] Though not about social trinitarianism per se, see the discussion in Catherine Mowry LaCugna, *God for Us: The Trinity and Christian Life* (New York: Harper Collins, 1991). See also Khaled Anatolios, "Personhood, Trinity, and Communion in Some Patristic Texts," in Anatolios, ed., *The Holy Trinity in the Life of the Church*, 147–64.

[46] Hasker, *Metaphysics and the Tri-Personal God*, 24.

[47] Hasker, *Metaphysics and the Tri-Personal God*, 179.

work especially hard to show that the Father, Son, and Spirit nevertheless count as just one God. Given his philosophical background, he construes this task as one of metaphysical explanation and modeling. His commitment to the creedal formulations of Nicene orthodoxy requires him to say that the three persons all instantiate a single divine nature. His challenge, then, is to show how contemporary metaphysical theories about natures and individuation can contribute to a coherent account of the ancient creedal formulations.

As an initial move, meant to prepare the way for his metaphysical account of the divine unity, Hasker presents an extended comparison that, at first glance, seems deeply problematic. He compares the Trinity, in which one divine nature supports three distinct divine persons, with "split-brain" and "multiple personality" cases in psychology, in which a single human body/mind/soul supports distinct centers of consciousness or distinct human personalities.[48] The comparison may seem troubling, but it is important to be clear about the exact work Hasker means for it to do.[49] Hasker's claim is that split-personality cases provide some indirect evidence that it is possible for one divine nature to support three distinct divine personalities. This is his reasoning: the actual implies the possible, and so if it is true (actual) that one concrete human nature can support multiple distinct human personalities, understood as distinct centers of consciousness and agency, then it follows that this state of affairs is possible. Since the human case is possible, we then have reason to believe that the much more mysterious divine case is also possible.

This analogy does not bear the entire burden of his argument. Hasker ultimately appeals to the metaphysics of constitution as the best philosophical framework in which to understand the way the three persons instantiate a single divine nature. Matters get technical here, and I lack the space to lay out Hasker's account even in abbreviated form. But the basic idea is that the single divine nature *constitutes* the three persons. Constitution does not entail identity, and so the divine nature is not identical to any of the three persons, nor is any of them identical to each other; yet they are one insofar as they are constituted by the single divine nature. A remote analogy: a piece of cloth, for example, can constitute a flag without being identical to the flag (since we could destroy the flag without destroying the cloth—by bleaching it, for example). The constitution relation gives us a way to say that two or more things are the same, without saying that they are identical. The value of this move for trinitarian theology should be clear. Suppose we agree that the divine nature constitutes the three trinitarian persons, without being identical to any of them. Then we can say that Father, Son, and Spirit each

---

[48]   Hasker takes no position on the metaphysics of human persons, and the tern "body/mind/soul" should not be read as committing him to any theory of the relation between mind and body.

[49]   Hasker, *Metaphysics and the Tri-Personal God*, 231.

instantiate a single divine nature, without being identical to that nature, and without any person being identical to any other person.

What does Hasker take himself to have established with his account of the Trinity? He describes his own goal in terms of "epistemic possibility."

> We cannot aspire to prove that the unity of the divine persons in a single con-crete nature is really, i.e., metaphysically possible—and no one should expect this of us...We may, however, attempt to show that the Trinity as we conceive it is *epistemically* possible—i.e., that the doctrine is not inconsistent with anything we know to be the case. This will include rebutting non-question begging argu-ments that have been advanced against the doctrine...We may also attempt to show, so far as possible, that the doctrine is plausible, and that it not merely does not contradict known truths but is consonant with relevant things that we know.
>
> (Hasker, *Metaphysics and the Tri-Personal God*, 226)

Although Hasker does not use it himself, the quasi-scientific idiom of "modeling" is very helpful here. Hasker wants to construct a *model* of the Trinity that is con-sistent with the historic trinitarian creeds, and also consistent with everything else we know from contemporary thought. As Michael Rea puts it, a model of the Trinity "helps us to see how it might be coherent to say that there is one god but three divine persons...The models are heuristic devices aimed at making the doctrine intelligible."[50] Like models in other disciplines, these analytic theological models "are constructed in a way that involves deliberate simplification, or other imaginative modification of reality, in order to make some relationships visible or problems tractable."[51] In my view, this is the best way to understand Hasker's appeal to multiple-personality cases and the metaphysics of constitution. These appeals function as models meant to offer an interpretation of traditional trinitar-ian orthodoxy that shows that the divine "three-in-oneness" is epistemically pos-sible, and consistent with everything else we know.

Metaphysics and the Tri-Personal God as Constructive Theology

Although the first third of his book examines recent historical scholarship on the development of the doctrine of the Trinity, Hasker explicitly describes his own task as primarily constructive rather than historical or exegetical. He tries to ground his project in the patristic tradition, but he does not assume that the

---

[50] Michael Rea, "Introduction," in Michael Rea, ed., *Oxford Readings in Philosophical Theology*, vol. 1, 4.

[51] Peter Godfrey-Smith, "Metaphysics and the Philosophical Imagination," *Philosophical Studies* 160 (2012): 97–113. See also Wood, "Modeling Mystery," and Oliver Crisp, *Analyzing Doctrine* (Waco, TX: Baylor University Press, 2019), 54–55, 86–89.

trinitarian thought of the patristic fathers is unsurpassable; nor does he assume that we must adopt their own exegetical assumptions and philosophical methods as our own.[52] For example, he summarily rejects divine simplicity as incoherent, unhelpful, and "devoid of biblical warrant."[53] He also insists that we must "move beyond simply repeating traditional formulas," and argues that our patristic fore-bears "did the best they could with the philosophical resources that they had at their disposal, and it remains for us to do the same with what is available to us today." In short, "if we are to have a viable and coherent trinitarianism for our own time, *we need to do better*...than they were able to do."[54]

Hasker contrasts his own constructive work with the work of "many patristics scholars," who (in his view) are too reluctant to challenge the philosophical views of the patristic fathers. His contrast nicely encapsulates the distinction between constructive theology and historical theology:

> Their training, naturally enough, focuses mainly on the historical and philo-sophical skills needed if one is to properly interpret ancient documents. Such philosophical training as they have tends to be concerned mainly with the ancient philosophies that constituted the philosophical resources that were available to the early theologians. In interpreting the Fathers, furthermore, they are rightly concerned first of all to make sense of the texts as they stand, giving a sympathetic interpretation to assertions which to us today might seem at first sight to be implausible or even untenable. And finally, many of them develop an attachment and a sense of alliance with at least some of the fathers to whom they devote their careers...All of this, it must be acknowledged, is entirely natural and in many ways commendable, *but it leaves a fundamental question unanswered: are the philosophical assumptions and claims made by the various Fathers in their accounts of the Trinity credible and defensible?* If they are, then there is work that needs to be done in warding off the challenges posed by more recent philosophy. If they are not, then an even more challenging task awaits us: the task of refor-mulating in our own philosophical idiom, the theological claims they set forth in terms of philosophical assumptions we can no longer adopt as our own.[55]

---

[52] "to ignore what we have learned since the fourth century about the interpretation of biblical texts is simply to disregard some of what we know (or with good reason believe) to be the truth, and this cannot be the right way to arrive at further truth" (Hasker, *Metaphysics and the Tri-Personal God*, 168).

[53] Hasker, *Metaphysics and the Tri-Personal God*, 55; 36–39, 55–61. Divine simplicity is the view that God has no parts whatsoever, not even conceptual parts, and so we cannot really distinguish between God and his will, intellect, actions, or attributes. Nearly all patristic and medieval theologians affirmed divine simplicity, but it is fair to say that it is especially hard (though not impossible) to make sense of the doctrine while remaining within an analytic philosophical framework. I discuss simpli-city in passing throughout Part III.

[54] Hasker, *Metaphysics and the Tri-Personal God*, 162, 169, 77.

[55] Hasker, *Metaphysics and the Tri-Personal God*, 170. My emphasis.

This statement might seem like disciplinary chauvinism, but it really is not. Trinitarian orthodoxy does face contemporary philosophical challenges that fourth-century thinkers could never have anticipated. It would be surprising if this were not the case. Critics of analytic philosophical theology often argue that patristic theologians were not especially preoccupied with logical coherence, and did not worry much about the logical problem of the Trinity. As far as I can see, that argument is correct as a matter of historical exegesis, but it does not establish the further point that *we* should not be interested in the logical problem. We do not live in the intellectual milieu of the patristic fathers. The logical problem is a problem for *us*, regardless of whether it was a problem for them. And to address that problem, we should bring to bear the full wealth of our philosophical and theological tools, even when they were not available to our patristic forebears. That is what Hasker does, which is why he presents such a clear example of constructive theology.

Analytic Theology as Constructive Theology

Most analytic theology is constructive theology. Understanding the difference between constructive and historical theology is, therefore, crucial for understanding what analytic theologians are trying to accomplish, and why their work can seem so alien to non-analytic theologians. In my experience, many academic theologians are slightly suspicious of constructive theology. There is a sense that one has to "earn" the right to be constructive, and only sufficiently well-established theologians dare to take the risk of giving their own original account of theological topics. Even theology that claims to be constructive is often only indirectly constructive, or constructive at a one-step remove, because the theologian's own views are so heavily mediated through her exegesis or interpretation of some other target figure or text. (This is not a criticism; my own first book is like this.[56]) By contrast, analytic theology is directly constructive in a way that can seem jarring to other theologians.

Constructive theology is valuable, and the theological academy would benefit if more theologians felt entitled to write in a constructive vein. This point in no way negates the value of historical theology. Indeed, the best constructive theology must still be historically informed and, as the OSAT series puts it, sensitive to "the Christian tradition and the development of doctrine." Compared to previous analytic work on the Trinity, Hasker's *Metaphysics and the Tri-Personal God* represents a step forward. He spends a third of the book discussing patristic sources and contemporary patristics scholarship, and another third discussing

---

[56] William Wood, *Blaise Pascal on Duplicity, Sin, and the Fall: The Secret Instinct* (New York: Oxford University Press, 2013).

major twentieth-century systematic theologians. Historical theologians will likely be dissatisfied with his treatment of these historical sources, but it is clear that the engagement itself has informed Hasker's own constructive thought in a salutary way.

For example, toward the end of his third constructive section, he warns against "the tendency to treat classic theological texts and expressions as if they were formulas in symbolic logic." He criticizes the "insistence on univocal language," in trinitarian discourse displayed by other analytic thinkers, which "flies in the face of virtually the entire theological tradition, which has insisted that *analogical* language is very much to be expected in our assertions concerning the divine; indeed, that it is indispensable."[57] From a theological point of view, this is all to the good.

Hasker concludes with a short chapter on the "grammar" of the Trinity that offers a quick résumé of the rules that govern trinitarian speech.[58] They are not intended as his own constructions; rather, they are meant to summarize the way trinitarian discourse has actually developed in Christian scripture and tradition. For example, the Old and New Testaments standardly use the term "God" to refer to the Father. Even so, it is legitimate for Christians to refer to each of the trinitarian persons as "God," and to worship or pray to them as God. Finally, it is appropriate to refer to the Trinity as a whole as "God." This usage is allowed, but not required; it is not the primary use of the term. As far as I can see, as a descriptive matter, Hasker accurately presents the traditional grammar of "God" in Christian speech. The grammar of "God" is strange; but then, so is orthodox Christianity.

Expanding Conversations in Analytic Theology: Race, Gender, Ability, Class

I hope that my engagement with Hasker and Pawl is illuminating, but I also worry that it gives the wrong impression of analytic theology as a whole. That is, I worry that it reinforces the assumption that analytic theology can *only* address issues of narrow logical coherence, and has nothing to say about wider, more holistic concerns. Accordingly, in this section I will discuss a collection of essays edited by Michelle Panchuk and Michael Rea: *Voices from the Edge: Centering Marginalized Voices in Analytic Theology.*[59] The volume focuses on topics such as race, gender, ability, and class—topics that have recently been at the heart of the humanities as a whole, but comparatively neglected in analytic theology and philosophy of

---

[57] Hasker, *Metaphysics and the Tri-Personal God*, 197.
[58] Hasker, *Metaphysics and the Tri-Personal God*, 246–47.
[59] Michelle Panchuk and Michael Rea, eds., *Voices from the Edge: Centering Marginalized Voices in Analytic Theology* (New York: Oxford University Press, 2020).

religion. With *Voices from the Edge*, Panchuk and Rea hope to establish a new agenda, "for the sake of the health and integrity of the discipline" of analytic theology.[60] I will first give a short description of some of the chapters in *Voices from the Edge*, and say a bit about what they collectively mean for analytic theology as an emerging school of thought. I then discuss one chapter in more detail. That chapter is Sameer Yadav's "Toward an Analytic Theology of Liberation." In my view, Yadav poses the sharpest extant challenge to the dominant paradigm of analytic theology.

Helen De Cruz opens the volume by arguing that philosophers of religion should pursue "epistemic friction" by deliberately seeking out alternative points of view, especially from philosophical and religious traditions other than their own. Her call for epistemic friction reinforces one of my own major claims in Part IV of this book, where I argue that analytic theologians should engage with genealogy, critique, and other non-analytic forms of inquiry. In an essay on the atonement, Kathryn Pogin argues that analytic theologians writing on the atonement have ignored the insights of feminist theology. As a result, their models of atonement valorize suffering and submission to violence, and can be harmful to oppressed groups. As both De Cruz and Pogin recognize, their arguments represent mainstream views in other parts of the academy, but analytic theologians and philosophers of religion have not assimilated them. Two chapters discuss the effects of religious trauma, shame, and epistemic oppression on religious adherents, including lesbian, gay, bisexual, transgender, and intersex Church members: Joshua Cockayne, Jack Warman, and David Efrid consider the social epistemology of deconversion by spiritually violent religious trauma. Dawn Moon and Theresa Tobin discuss the particular forms of shame experienced by LGBTI Christians of color, and argue that racist histories of sexuality and gender generate particular forms of spiritual homelessness. Two chapters discuss "social bodies" and the afterlife: Blake Hereth discusses transgender embodiment in the afterlife, and considers whether (and how) gender dysphoric "mismatches" should be corrected in the eschaton, without also making everyone cisgender. Kevin Timpe's chapter, "Defiant Afterlife: Disability and Uniting Ourselves to God," argues that at least some disabled persons will retain their disabilities in heaven, because their disabilities will not hinder complete union with God. The theology of disability has become an especially vibrant topic among analytic theologians.[61]

---

[60] Panchuk and Rea, eds., *Voices from the Edge*, 1.
[61] Richard Cross, "Disability, Impairment, and Some Medieval Accounts of the Incarnation: Suggestions for a Theology of Personhood," *Modern Theology* 27 (2011): 639–58; Kevin Timpe and Aaron Cobb, "Disability and the Theodicy of Defeat," *Journal of Analytic Theology* 5 (2017): 100–20; Scott Williams, ed., *Disability in Medieval Philosophy and Theology* (New York: Routledge, 2020); Blake Hereth and Kevin Timpe, eds., *The Lost Sheep in Philosophy of Religion: New Perspectives on Disability, Gender, Race, and Animals* (New York: Routledge, 2020).

Even from this brief and incomplete summary, it should be obvious that *Voices from the Edge* presents something other than the usual analytic fare. Collectively, the essays in this volume expand the horizons of analytic theology, both methodologically and substantively. Methodologically, several authors draw on sociological and other empirical data rather than conceptual theorizing. Substantively, most of the essays discuss topics—trauma, disability, race, gender—that so far have not been a part of the analytic theological conversation. The volume invites the analytic theology community to expand its conversation by focusing on these topics, but it remains an open question whether that invitation will be taken up. There is no reason why it *cannot* be taken up—that is, there is no reason to think that analytic theology, understood as theology that draws on the tools and methods of analytic philosophy, cannot also speak to questions about social justice. Analytic philosophy offers many valuable resources for feminist philosophy, the philosophy of race, and other topics that bear on social and economic justice.[62] Just as more traditional analytic theologians draw on the tools of analytic metaphysics and epistemology when considering topics like the incarnation and the Trinity, so too can more "contextual" analytic theologians draw on equivalent analytic resources in their own work.[63]

The sheer existence of this volume is interesting and consequential. First, it shows that analytic theology is capable of moving in new and unexpected directions, and discussing important questions about social justice. Second, the collection shows that analytic theology is capable of generating internal critique. A mature academic discourse needs the capacity to be self-critical, and certainly needs to move beyond the proselytizing and cheerleading stage that has characterized much analytic theology so far. Finally, this volume paves the way for closer links between analytic and non-analytic theology, since many non-analytic theologians also care deeply about similar issues and wish to use their academic work as a vehicle for social justice.

Toward an Analytic Theology of Liberation

I turn now to Sameer Yadav's chapter "Toward an Analytic Theology of Liberation."[64] As Yadav points out, there is "no discernable strand" of analytic

---

[62] Prominent book-length treatments include Sally Haslanger, *Resisting Reality: Social Construction and Social Critique* (New York: Oxford University Press, 2012), Joshua Glasgow, Sally Haslanger, Chike Jeffers, and Quayshawn Spencer, *What Is Race? Four Philosophical Views* (New York: Oxford University Press, 2019). Another important book is Miranda Fricker, *Epistemic Injustice: Power and the Ethics of Knowing* (New York: Oxford University Press, 2007).

[63] "Contextual" theologies like liberation theology, black/womanist theology, and feminist theology all treat concrete, culturally conditioned human experiences as major sources of theological reflection.

[64] Sameer Yadav, "Toward an Analytic Theology of Liberation," in Panchuk and Rea, eds., *Voices from the Edge*, 47–74.

theology that "contributes centrally to the current state of black or womanist theologies, more critical and revisionary feminist theologies, queer theologies, or any other radical social and political theologies."[65] He then argues (correctly, in my view) that the methodological norms appropriate to analytic theology are not incompatible with liberation theology. It follows that an analytic theology of liberation is possible: there can be such a thing.[66] This is already an important point. Yadav then makes the much stronger claim that an analytic theology of liberation is, in a sense, obligatory. According to Yadav, *all* good theology must pursue the emancipatory aims of liberation theology. Much analytic theology does not, at least not obviously. Yadav's essay, therefore, poses a sharp challenge to the dominant paradigm of analytic theology.[67] Yadav's challenge is important in itself, and I suspect that many (non-analytic) theologians will be very sympathetic to it, so it is worth discussing it at greater length.

The core of Yadav's argument is his claim that good theology depends on values other than narrowly epistemic values like truth or warrant.[68] Good theological theories must aim "not merely at truth, but also at justice for the socially and politically oppressed."[69] According to Yadav, theological theorizing is always guided by moral and prudential norms in addition to purely epistemic norms. Not even knowledge about God is valuable for its own sake. He asks us to imagine a research program that studies divine omniscience by compiling an ever longer list of true mathematical propositions that are known by God.[70] This research program would have as its aim the noble goal of increasing our knowledge of God, and each new proposition would indeed add to the scope and coherence of the program's explanatory power. But we should all agree that something would be amiss with such a program. According to Yadav, this (admittedly silly) thought experiment shows that we do, in fact, use non-epistemic values—values other than bare truth—to guide theological inquiry. When analytic theologians choose their research programs and construct their theories, they always draw on some kind of shared background story about what is valuable for human flourishing: what it is valuable to know and what it is valuable to do. This shared background story will in turn depend on a wider story about the social and political conditions of human flourishing, both individually and in community. Whether we are

---

[65] Yadav, "Toward an Analytic Theology of Liberation," 48–49.

[66] Yadav specifically mentions Michael Rea's prominent list of analytic norms. See note 3 of this chapter.

[67] I would go so far as to say that Yadav's essay poses the sharpest critique of analytic theology that I have seen so far, not least because his is an internal critique: Yadav understands analytic theology well, is basically sympathetic to analytic methods, and therefore is well positioned to make criticisms that actually land.

[68] Note that this claim still allows good theology to value truth, just not to value truth to the exclusion of other values.

[69] Yadav, "Toward an Analytic Theology of Liberation," 54.

[70] Yadav, "Toward an Analytic Theology of Liberation," 58.

aware of them or not, these background stories reveal the cognitive and practical goods that we regard as worth pursuing.

Like other liberation theologians, Yadav argues that many theologians, including analytic theologians, do not sufficiently reflect on the non-epistemic values that undergird their projects of inquiry. As a result, they simply assume the values that prevail in the dominant social and political culture. Because these prevailing values are often oppressive, their theological projects often inadvertently reinforce oppressive social structures. He gives the example of analytic perfect being theology as a form of inquiry that can foster oppression because it implicitly identifies divine power with male power.[71]

In order to do Christian theology well, we need to base our projects of inquiry on the values of the Christian Gospel, rather than the values of the fallen world. The Christian Gospel treats freedom from social and political oppression as constitutive, fundamental values. That is why these values must define the subject matter of good Christian theology. Yadav bolsters this claim with an account of creation, fall, and redemption in Christ on which the fall causes a breach in the human relationship with God, which in turn introduces defects in human community that take the form of social and political oppression.[72] The Christian Gospel is constitutively about repairing these defects, which means that it is constitutively about liberation from the forces of social and political oppression. It follows that good Christian theology also ought to be about our present and future liberation from social and political oppression. To the extent that it is about something else, it is bad theology.

The liberative norm for good theology is also a methodological norm. As Yadav puts it, "our ability to evaluate or assess the significance of our explanatory theories for a Christian liberative ambition will depend on our epistemic access to the relevant facts about liberation for the oppressed." Moreover, "epistemic access to facts such as these is not evenly distributed—not everyone is in an equally good position to identify or evaluate them."[73] We need to listen to people who are oppressed, and let them guide our reflections on what counts as good theological theorizing. Conversely, those who belong to privileged social groups are in acute danger of self-deception: "those belonging to privileged groups who benefit from the material disadvantages of oppressed groups are very strongly prudentially motivated to maintain a kind of insensitivity to the relevant facts that would threaten their relative advantages."[74]

Yadav does offer one concession to theology that is not explicitly liberative. Good theologians can still theorize about "matters that seem only distantly related

---

[71] Yadav, "Toward an Analytic Theology of Liberation," 62.
[72] Yadav, "Toward an Analytic Theology of Liberation," 63–66.
[73] Yadav, "Toward an Analytic Theology of Liberation," 66, 67.
[74] Yadav, "Toward an Analytic Theology of Liberation," 67.

to the identification of the oppressed," but theorizing about any non-liberative subject matter "faces a kind of justificatory burden about what makes its putative deliverances worth knowing."[75] In other words—and returning to analytic theology—theorizing about more conventional topics in analytic theology may turn out to be acceptable, perhaps even good, but the burden of proof is on those who pursue those topics to show that they do indeed cohere with the liberative aim of all good Christian theology. This will not be an easy task, for Yadav's concession does not furnish us with a wide-open door. If it were easy to show that, for example, giving a cogent metaphysical account of divine timelessness can be understood as a way of working toward the liberation of the oppressed, then Yadav would have no quarrel with existing analytic theology, and there would be little need for his intervention. So I assume that he would indeed say that much— perhaps most, perhaps even all— existing analytic theology fails to satisfy his desiderata.

Yadav's argument is an important challenge to the current state of analytic theology, and it deserves a full-length response that I cannot now provide. But because the challenge is aimed at forms of analytic theology that I myself commend, I do want to offer at least a preliminary reply. I first note that Yadav's argument is not new; it forcefully re-presents the charges that liberation theologians have long made against other forms of academic theology. I say this not to criticize, but only to make a point that might otherwise be overlooked. Yadav's argument is aimed at analytic theology, but it applies with equal force to all forms of non-liberative theology. He does not argue that analytic theology is especially bad, or especially non-liberative, and many other forms of theology will also fall under the same critique.

I agree with Yadav that theology that constitutively contributes to oppression is, by definition, bad theology. And I agree that theology that directly serves liberative aims is likely to be good theology. I am even sympathetic to the idea that theology that directly serves liberative aims is *better* than theology that does not. But I cannot quite follow Yadav all the way. I am not prepared to say that all theology must directly and explicitly serve liberative aims in order to count as good theology. Sometimes good theology can indirectly and implicitly serve liberative aims.

As Augustine teaches, all good theology fosters love of God and love of neighbor.[76] And theology cannot foster love of God or love of neighbor if it contributes to oppression. But one can accept this point without holding that the *only* way to foster love of God and love of neighbor is by directly focusing on social and political liberation. Another way to foster love of God and neighbor is by showing that

---

[75] Yadav, "Toward an Analytic Theology of Liberation," 65.
[76] Augustine, *De doctrina christiana*, 1.84 in Saint Augustine, *On Christian Teaching*. Oxford World's Classics, trans. R. P. H. Green (New York: Oxford University Press, 1997).

the Christian God is real, and one way to do that is by showing that the creeds are not absurd and the God they reveal is not impossible. Furthermore, on the Christian point of view, God's grace is the ultimate cause of our ability to love God and neighbor at all. But God's grace cannot be constrained. Unlikely as it may seem, it may even be the case that God calls some people to repentance, virtue, and holiness via analytic reflection on divine simplicity, or the Trinity, or the two natures of Christ. I do not see how we could rule that possibility out in advance, or why the Gospel message tells us that we must rule it out.

Even though I cannot follow Yadav all the way to his ultimate conclusion, I am grateful for his intervention in the analytic discussion, and I agree that his challenge must be taken seriously. It would be very valuable indeed if there were more analytic liberation theologies—valuable in itself and even more valuable for the wider theological scene. I have no doubt whatsoever about that.

Conclusion: Analytic Theology Is Good

By now I hope that a reader will have a better idea of what analytic theology is, and at least a preliminary sense that some analytic theology really does count as theology. By discussing the *Voices from the Edge* collection, I also hope to have shown that analytic theology is evolving in unexpected ways. Theologians who might have thought—with good reason—that analytic theology cannot speak to concerns of social justice should at least remain open to the possibility that it can. That is an important conclusion in its own right.

I'd like to end this chapter with a bit of additional reflection on why analytic theology is valuable. (This reflection anticipates my discussion of "rigorous appreciation" in Chapter 14.) I think it is obvious that there are intra-Christian reasons why analytic theology is valuable. Christian theology, even metaphysically inflected analytic theology, is a way of expressing one's love and desire for God. As such, Christian theology is intrinsically good. (I argue for this claim at various points throughout the book, but especially in Chapter 6.) More narrowly, Christians should agree that it is good to try to answer rational objections to key Christian doctrines, and similarly good to try to give positive models for how to understand them in a way that coheres with other things we take ourselves to know. Those tasks are perennial, and analytic theology is one way that Christians today can pursue them fruitfully.

At the same time, however, I also think that there are non-Christian reasons for valuing analytic theology, reasons that anyone might accept. Intellectual inquiry is good. Focused thinking about terrifically difficult problems is good. Watching very intelligent people think as deeply and carefully as they can about things that matter to them more than anything else—that too is good.[77] Analytic theology displays all of these goods, something that anyone can recognize, even without accepting the underlying Christian framework. A parallel suggestion is familiar enough in other intellectual contexts. One can admire Plato without being a Platonist. I can admire the dazzling intellect behind Saadia Gaon's *Book of Doctrines and Beliefs* without being Jewish.[78] So, of course, I do not mean to suggest that analytic theology *alone* displays these intellectual goods, or even that analytic theology displays them to a greater degree than other kinds of inquiry. But anyone who affirms that these are genuine goods at all has a reason to value analytic theology.

---

[77] My own inner pedant compels me to add: of course, I do not mean the claims in this paragraph as unrestricted, exceptionless generalizations. A group of evil people thinking hard about how to be more evil is not particularly good, or admirable, for example.

[78] Saadya Gaon, *The Book of Doctrines and Beliefs*, trans. Alexander Altmann (Indianapolis, IN: Hackett, 2002).

PART III
THEOLOGICAL ANALYTIC THEOLOGY

Part III develops the argument that analytic theology really is theology. Chapter 6 argues that the Christian doctrine of creation furnishes a theological warrant for analytic theology. Chapters 7–9 are a connected response to some of the most common theological objections to analytic theology. Those objections concern idolatry, ontotheology, univocity, and so-called "theistic personalism." I argue that analytic theologians can avoid this contemporary syllabus of errors by preserving the creator/creature distinction and theorizing with an attitude of worship. In order to make this case, I first try to get clear about what is actually wrong with each of these theological errors. Chapter 10 picks up the theme of worship, and argues that analytic theology can be understood as a form of spiritual practice.

6

A Theology of Analytic Reason

Many theologians and scholars of religion find analytic theology alien and indigestible. It seems both immoderately secular and immoderately religious at once. Analytic reasoning emphasizes linear arguments and propositional beliefs, and appeals to common norms of rationality. By the standards of the contemporary humanities, analytic thought can seem not only modern but hypermodern. And even though analytic theologians frequently refuse various historical and critical turns associated with modernity, and defend very traditional forms of religious belief, their theism can still seem, well, grimly rationalistic. It exhibits none of the excess, uncertainty, and extravagance beloved by postmodern and postsecular thinkers.

Analytic theology develops from analytic philosophy of religion, which is a branch of analytic philosophy, which arises in the early twentieth century. It is therefore trivially true, and uninteresting, to say that analytic theology is "a product of modernity" in this narrowly temporal sense. The claim, rather, is that analytic theology is *characteristically* modern; that is, that it exhibits precisely those unwholesome preoccupations and patterns of reasoning that arise only in modernity and that typify the modern age. In the contemporary religious studies academy, this is a devastating charge. Scholars of religion and theologians are divided against each other, and subdivided again within their respective disciplinary guilds; they don't agree about much, but they do agree about this: nobody wants to be *modern*.

In every part of the religious studies academy, we therefore find a sharp critique of modern rationality, sometimes labeled "secular reason" or "autonomous reason." This critique is widely affirmed by both theologians and theorists of religion, because it goes hand in hand with genealogical criticism of the secular as such.[1] According to this "postsecular" critique, secular reason claims—falsely—to be objective, neutral, and disinterested.[2] The norms of secular reasoning only

---

[1] Among scholars of religion, see, for example, Saba Mahmood, "Secularism and the Hermeneutics of Empire," *Public Culture* 18, no. 2 (2006): 345. Talal Asad, *Secular Translations: Nation-State, Modern Self, and Calculative Reason* (New York: Columbia University Press, 2018), esp. 10, 41, 46, 97, 144, 150. Paul Stoller, "Rationality," in Mark C. Taylor, ed., *Critical Terms for Religious Studies* (University of Chicago Press, 1998), 239–55, esp. 244–46, 251–52. Among theologians, see above all John Milbank, *Theology and Social Theory*, 2nd ed. (Malden, MA: Wiley-Blackwell, 2006), and the "Radical Orthodoxy" school generally.

[2] For further discussion of what I call the "postsecular consensus" in theology and the academic study of religion, see the Conclusion.

Analytic Theology and the Academic Study of Religion. William Wood, Oxford University Press (2021). © William Wood. DOI: 10.1093/oso/9780198779872.003.0006

purport to be universal, to bind all rational subjects as such, and to be invariant across cultures. The immediate aim of secular reasoning is propositional belief and propositional knowledge; in other words, an act of reasoning is a purely intellectual act that culminates in assent to a proposition. The more remote aim of secular reasoning is mastery and control: over nature, over other people, over oneself. As such, the modern paradigm of rationality is scientific empiricism, which presents itself as both the most reliable path toward knowledge and the most reliable means of controlling the natural and social world.

The charge, then, is that analytic theology relies too much on modernist patterns of reasoning. The specifically theological version runs like this: because analytic theology is in thrall to "secular reason," or "autonomous reason," it cannot be properly theological at all, not even in principle.[3] Since this is a theological objection to analytic theology, the best way to respond to it is also theological. In this chapter, I argue that analytic theology and analytic reasoning are actually grounded in the Christian doctrine of creation, broadly understood to include the claim that human beings are fallen creatures who, nevertheless, bear the image of God and Christ. The doctrine of creation provides the theological warrant for analytic theology.

The Christian doctrine of creation entails that human inquiry as such is valuable. It also entails a weak form of metaphysical realism, and a thin account of common human reason. These entailments are minimal, but they are enough to ground the project of analytic theology. Against the backdrop of the twin claims that humans are created in the image of God and also fallen, analytic theology has an obvious justification: analytic theology can help us distinguish theological statements that are likely to be true from theological statements that are likely to be false. In the service of this theological aim, analytic theology draws on and extends the God-given tools of common human reason. Analytic theology is not the only way, or always the best way, to try to understand God better. But it is a legitimate and valuable form of theological inquiry.

---

[3] Here the gulf between analytic and non-analytic thinkers looms especially large. In my experience, analytic theologians and philosophers of religion struggle to make sense of the suggestion that there is anything importantly modern about the analytic method or about their own intellectual concerns. By contrast, other theologians and scholars of religion are likely to treat this suggestion as self-evident, in part because they are steeped in the Foucauldian maxim that different eras exhibit different regimes of rationality and truth (Michel Foucault, *Discipline and Punish: The Birth of the Prison* [New York: Vintage, 1991], "Truth and Power," in Paul Rabinow, ed., *The Foucault Reader* [New York: Pantheon, 1984], 51–75). I return to the issue of the modern character of analytic philosophy in the book's Conclusion. Here I will only remind my analytic colleagues that they should not assume that because they make "arguments" and patristic and medieval figures also make "arguments," there are no meaningful differences between analytic theology and premodern theology. Analytic theologians have conceptual tools their predecessors lacked, and also differ from premodern thinkers in the assumptions they take for granted, and the kinds of questions they regard as salient.

The Christian Doctrine of Creation

In this section, I lay out my own account of the Christian doctrine of creation. I believe my account to be quite traditional, but I will not defend it against alternative theological interpretations. Nor will I defend it from scientific, philosophical, or other non-theological objections. The point of this section is to establish common ground with those Christian theologians who also affirm a similar account of creation, but who remain skeptical of analytic theology. I want to show them that analytic theology is warranted by the very doctrine of creation they already affirm. I will also appeal to this account of creation in Chapters 7–9, where I defend analytic theology from a nest of interconnected worries about idolatry, ontotheology, univocity, and so-called "theistic personalism." Of course, I also hope that non-Christian readers will gain something from this chapter—a better understanding of how Christians traditionally understand creation, perhaps, or a greater appreciation for how Christian theologians think and argue. I warmly invite them to listen in as interested outsiders.

Free Creation out of Nothing

The Christian doctrine of creation teaches that the world and everything in it is good because it is freely created out of nothing and continually sustained in existence by the triune God. The claim is complex. I will try to unpack it. The claim that God creates "the world and everything in it" should be understood maximally: everything that is not God is created by God. God does not fall under the scope of his own act of creation, since God does not create himself or cause himself to exist. Everything else does fall under the scope of God's act of creation.[4] From this strict disjunction between created and uncreated, it follows that neither the world nor anything in it is divine. Everything other than God is created, and not divine; only God is uncreated and only God is divine.[5] All too often, we reduce the claim that everything is created to a claim with a much narrower

---

[4] The contemporary scholarly consensus holds that this very strong account of creation out of nothing is not explicit in the biblical texts on creation, but developed over time, and probably did not attain its full scope until the medieval period. For a discussion of early Christian views of creation, and references to important primary and secondary literature, see Markus Bockmuehl, "Creatio ex Nihilo in Palestinian Judaism and Early Christianity," *Scottish Journal of Theology* 65 (2012): 254–70; Paul Gavrilyuk "Creation in Early Christian Literature: Irenaeus against the Gnostics and Athanasius against the Arians," in Janet Soskice, ed., *Creation "Ex Nihilo" and Modern Theology* (Malden, MA: Wiley-Blackwell, 2013), 22–32. Gerhard May, *Creatio Ex Nihilo: The Doctrine of "Creation out of Nothing" in Early Christian Thought* (Edinburgh: Edinburgh University Press, 1994).

[5] "Divine" here does not mean "supernatural" in the modern sense of that term: angels, for instance, are not divine precisely because they are created.

scope, so that it becomes only the claim that all matter is created, or that all substances or concrete particulars are created. Yet on the traditional Christian understanding, God creates more than matter, substances, and concrete particulars. God also creates the fundamental framework in which those substances and particulars arise and interact. So God creates the laws of nature, including the most fundamental laws of physics. Everything that is not God is created by God. "Everything" means everything.[6]

God also conserves, sustains, and preserves the world at all times. This claim is also implicit in the doctrine of creation *ex nihilo*. Creation out of nothing is a metaphysical claim about the constant, absolute dependence of the universe on God. It is not a temporal claim about how the universe began. As Aquinas showed in the thirteenth century, we may coherently hold that the universe is created out of nothing even if we also hold that it is eternal, and has no beginning in time.[7] Creation is not a one-off event after which the universe continues to exist on its own, apart from God's creative action (like a divine kick-off that gets the Big Bang going). That idea is deism, not Christian theism. To use the traditional language, the doctrine of creation and the doctrine of conservation are different descriptions of the same divine activity.

Christians traditionally hold that God *freely* creates and sustains out of nothing. Against various forms of pagan and Gnostic thought, which hold that the universe came into being either by accident or by necessity, the Christian tradition has asserted that God freely chooses to create. Theologians have disagreed about the precise sense in which God is free to create. Defenders of divine freedom have not always understood it in modern fashion, as the libertarian ability to do otherwise.[8] Nevertheless, the historic tradition has been unwilling to impose any kind of external constraint or external necessity on God, and so even those

---

[6] Necessarily existing abstracta pose a unique set of challenges. Christian theists throughout the centuries have offered various accounts of how to reconcile the realm of necessity with the doctrine of creation. (For example, does God create the laws of logic or the necessary truths of mathematics? Does God create perfect triangles in Platonic heaven over and above mundane triangular objects?) Christian theists have usually tried to defend either the view that these too are created or, if they are not created, that they somehow exist eternally in the divine mind, such that they count as an aspect of God. For discussion, see Paul Gould, ed., *Beyond the Control of God? Six Views on the Problem of God and Abstract Objects* (New York: Bloomsbury Academic, 2014).

[7] On the claim that creation is a relationship of metaphysical dependence on God, see *Summa Theologiae* [=ST] 1.45.2, reply obj 2; ST 1.45.3, ST 1.104.1; ST 1.46; Here is a helpful thought experiment (my own): Imagine the arrow of time is a number line with a first point. If time has a beginning, then God creates and sustains every point on the whole arrow, from its first point in the past and forward indefinitely into the future. Now imagine that time has no beginning. We would tell the same story, only with the arrow of time stretching infinitely backward into the past as well as into the future. At every moment of its existence, the universe is created and sustained out of nothing, regardless of whether the arrow of time extends infinitely backward through the past as well as infinitely forward into the future. It is the whole arrow and all its points that are sustained by God.

[8] Anselm seems to deny that God has libertarian freedom not to create, for example, whereas Aquinas holds the contrary view. For discussion, see Katherin Rogers "Anselm on God's Perfect Freedom," *The Saint Anselm Journal* 1 (2003): 1–8.

who hold that God must create regard the "must" as an internal necessity entailed by the divine nature. They therefore continue to regard the act of creation as intentional and free.

Finally, the Christian doctrine of creation affirms that the world is good. Indeed, this affirmation is the central pillar of the doctrine of creation. In the opening chapter of the Genesis creation account, the refrain "And God saw that it was good" occurs multiple times; at the end of the six-day creation, God surveys his work and pronounces it "very good." From the start, then, the biblical creation narrative blocks the perennial temptation to denigrate materiality, embodiment, and change: it is precisely the world as physical and as developing that is affirmed as good. Moreover, the goodness of creation does not belong solely to some primordial past. Despite the Christian narrative of the Fall, the world is still construed as fundamentally good. The doctrine of continuous creation *ex nihilo* re-enters the picture here. Because God continually creates the world and holds it in being, and because (axiomatically) God is good, it follows that the world must be good as well. A wholly good God brings only good things into being.

The Triune God and the Divine Logos

What about this God? What can we learn about God from the doctrine of creation as I have so far presented it? The answer depends on how we construe the question. If we construe it as a philosophical question, then the answer is: something, but not much. So far, I have mostly presented the outlines of a theistic doctrine of creation, one that for the most part does not draw on explicitly Christian axioms. But we must distinguish the Christian doctrine of creation from a merely theistic doctrine of creation, and we must distinguish both from the philosophical claim that the universe has an external cause. If we construe the question "What can we learn about God from the doctrine of creation?" not as a philosophical question, but as a Christian-theological question, then we can—and should—say much more. Christian doctrine is a single, unified tapestry. The doctrine of creation properly includes the full wealth of Christian teaching about God, Christ, and salvation. It also includes the dual claims that humans are made in the image of God and yet have fallen from their original state.

Our creator is triune: Father, Son, and Holy Spirit. The doctrine of the Trinity establishes tight conceptual connections among divine freedom, goodness, love, and wisdom. In traditional Christian theology, it is the doctrine of the Trinity that grounds the claim that creation is not only good but a gracious gift. Because God is triune, God alone is already maximally self-giving, even prior to the act of creation, because God the Father eternally gives the whole of the divine substance to the Son and Spirit. The triune persons are constituted by relations of mutual love and self-diffusive goodness. In a sense, Christian theology affirms the Neoplatonist maxim that goodness is self-diffusive but argues that its requirements are always satisfied by the trinitarian relations. Because God is triune, God is not only perfectly good and loving but perfectly complete and self-fulfilled. The mutual love that the trinitarian persons have for one another overflows into the act of creation, but not as the result of internal or external necessity. Since God does not need to create anything at all, creation is entirely gratuitous.

Christ, the Divine Logos

Creation is entirely gratuitous, and yet it is also rational and intelligible, because the act of creation occurs in and through God's Word, the *Logos*, who is also God the Son, the second person of the Trinity. A pious claim—but what does it mean? In Christian texts, we now translate the Greek word *logos* as "Word," but in pre-Christian Greek, the word *logos* had a range of meanings, all associated with discursive rationality: "reason," "argument," "speech," or "rational account," among others. Christians say that creation occurs in and through the Word in part because the Gospel of John's austere and beautiful opening lines deliberately identify the divine Logos with the Genesis creation narrative:

> In the beginning was the *Logos*, and the *Logos* was with God, and the *Logos* was God. He was in the beginning with God. All things came into being through him, and without him not one thing came into being. What has come into being in him was life, and the life was the light of all people. The light shines in the darkness, and the darkness did not overcome it. (John 1:1–5)

The Gospel of John presents the Logos in personal terms, as an agent of creation, but the Greek word *logos* still carries its original connotations. The claim that "all things came into being" through the Logos, therefore, asserts that the universe is rationally ordered and intelligible because Christ is an agent of creation.

This move was already anticipated by pre-Christian thought. By the first-century AD, certain strands of Hellenistic philosophical thought had already come to regard "the Logos" in quasi-divine terms. For the Stoics, the Logos is an immanent principle of divinity that pervades everything that exists, and the world is intelligible to us because it manifests the divine Logos, which constitutes the rational structure of the universe. The Stoic good life is a life that conforms to the world's rational structure, which is to say, a life that conforms to the Logos. Greco-Roman "Logos theology" begins with Stoic thought but is quickly appropriated by other Hellenistic traditions. Philo of Alexandria, a first-century Jewish philosopher who wrote in Greek, uses the idea of the Logos to synthesize biblical revealed religion and Greek philosophy. Philo's language can seem strikingly similar to later Christian interpretations of the Logos. He calls the Logos "divine reason," "the interpreter and prophet of God," "God's firstborn," and even a "second God."[9] Scholars tend to interpret these expressions as more allegorical and metaphorical than literal; nevertheless, the similarity to Christian thought is striking.[10]

The Christian account of Christ as the Logos emerges from this Hellenistic intellectual milieu. Yet the Gospel of John's claim that "the Word became flesh and lived among us," (1:14) is far more radical than anything found in Philo or the Stoics. In its own way the notion that the Logos—understood as Rationality itself—became a concretely existing human man is no less shocking in its historical context than the claim that the one God of Israel has a divine Son who became a human man. Indeed, from the Christian point of view, they are the same claim. Early Christian apologists embraced this paradox. In discussions with cultured pagans, at a time when philosophy was regarded as a way of life, the early apologists appealed to the doctrine of the Logos to identify Christ as the true source of philosophical wisdom, and to present Christians as the only true philosophers. Justin Martyr writes about "Reason himself, who took form and became man and was called Jesus Christ," and says that all people throughout history who have "lived reasonably" are actually Christians, because they have drawn upon Christ, who is Reason.[11]

Logos theology also contributed to a distinctively Christian doctrine of creation. From the beginning (as it were) patristic and medieval theologians associated the work of creation with the Logos and held that the world is orderly and intelligible because it is created by the Father according to the rational pattern furnished by the Word. To explain this point, Thomas Aquinas, like many others, uses the analogy of a craftsman who first forms a mental concept of the artifact that that he wishes to construct. The concept is the pattern or blueprint according to which the thing is made. When the craftsman finishes his work, and the artifact actually exists, it has a specific structure and order just insofar as it instantiates the pattern that first existed in the mind of the craftsman. Similarly, God the

---

[9] These citations may be found in A. H. Armstrong, ed., *The Cambridge History of Later Greek and Early Medieval Philosophy* (New York: Cambridge University Press, 1967), 143; and James D. G. Dunn, *Christology in the Making: An Inquiry into the Origins of the Doctrine of the Incarnation*, 2nd ed. (London: SCM, 1989), 221.

[10] According to Dunn, Philo does not really construe the Logos as a second, concretely existing divine hypostasis distinct from the Father, but as a way of understanding the Platonic realm of archetypes or forms in light of the Genesis account of God as creator. The Logos is the divine mind, which contain the patterns used to create the universe. "On this analogy then the Logos is 'the reasoning faculty of God in the act of planning to create the universe." (*Christology in the Making*, 224–25).

[11] 1 *Apol* 5; 1 *Apol* 46; 2 *Apol* 10. See Justin Martyr, "First Apology and Second Apology," trans. Marcus Dods and George Reith, eds. Alexander Roberts, James Donaldson, and A. Cleveland Coxe, *Ante-Nicene Fathers*, Vol. 1 (Buffalo, NY: Christian Literature Publishing Co., 1885). Revised and edited for New Advent by Kevin Knight: *First Apology*: http://www.newadvent.org/fathers/0126.htm, accessed July 6, 2020; *Second Apology*: http://www.newadvent.org/fathers/0127.htm, accessed July 6, 2020.

Father creates all things in and through his own unique "concept," the divine Word, the principle of intelligibility for everything that exists.[12]

Imago Dei, Imago Christi: Human Beings in the Image of Christ, the Incarnate Word

The Genesis narratives affirm that human beings are created in the image and likeness of God (1:26–27). The narratives are laconic as to what exactly this means. It is clear from the Hebrew that it is humanity itself that reflects the image and likeness, and that both men and women are included. So the image is not to be identified with biological sex or gender. Beyond this relatively uncontroversial point, there is little consensus about how to interpret the *imago dei* claim. On many traditional interpretations, the phrase "image and likeness" refers to some distinctively human capacity, whatever is highest and best in us, and often further construed as whatever it is that separates us from other animals. Unsurprisingly, then, since ancient times, interpreters have read the "image and likeness" as referring to our reason and our free will. These are the capacities that human beings enjoy which other animals (they thought) seem to lack.[13] These are the capacities that God enjoys in superabundance. On this traditional interpretation of the *imago dei*, therefore, what sets human beings apart, what is highest and best in us, and what most closely approximates the divine is nothing less than our rationality and our freedom.

This is a valuable interpretation, given my own constructive aims. Even so, it must also be heavily qualified. Somewhat paradoxically, the traditional (that is, patristic and medieval) doctrine of the *imago dei* can actually seem too modern, precisely because it valorizes rationality and freedom to such a great degree. The traditional interpretation seemingly reinforces an account of human subjectivity on which we are little more than disembodied, emotionless calculators that also happen to exercise libertarian free will. And a doctrine that locates the image of God in rationality and free will can all too easily become a way to deny the dignity, worth, and humanity of people whose capacities for reason and freedom are more limited.

We can preserve what is best about the traditional account of the *imago dei*, and also take seriously the concerns of its contemporary critics, if we understand the image of God in Christological terms.[14] On this understanding, to be created

---

[12] Thomas Aquinas, *ST* 1.45.6, *ST* 1.34.3.

[13] As will soon become clear, I am not endorsing this traditional interpretation, at least not wholesale, and so I am not myself committed to the view that there is any unbridgeable gulf between the capacities of human beings and non-human animals.

[14] The best recent account of a Christological understanding of the image is Kathryn Tanner, *Christ the Key* (New York: Cambridge University Press, 2010), 1–57.

in the image of God is to be created in the image of Christ, the divine Word incarnate. As divine Word, Christ is the perfect image of God; as a fully human man, Christ also shows us what it looks like for a human being to approximate that image in a created way. Here one must immediately insist: it is the Word's humanity that is soteriologically significant, not the Word's maleness. Yet this is not a novel, trendy account of "embodiment," but one of the Church's earliest teachings.

According to Irenaeus, writing in the second century, human beings are made in the image of God because they have human bodies, and thereby image Christ's human body. Although Adam precedes the incarnate Christ in time, Christ is the pattern according to which Adam is made. God created human beings so that the Word could become flesh. The incarnation is, therefore, the telos of humanity and the reason for our creation.[15] Although it is proper to say that Christ's flesh is Adam's flesh—meaning that Christ is a human man, and therefore a descendent of Adam—it is equally proper to say that Adam's flesh is Christ's flesh. Because this account of the *imago dei* makes Christ's humanity normative for humanity in general, the account is not only properly traditional, but also fully theological.

A Christological account of the image is also multivalent and therefore constructively fruitful. There are many different ways to be in the image of Christ. The diversity of humanity reflects the diversity of ways that we can stand in the image of Christ, our human prototype. A Christological account of the *imago dei*, therefore, provides an important corrective to accounts that locate the image entirely in our rationality and our freedom. Because we image Christ simply by virtue of having human bodies, the Christological account enables us to say that literally every human being is made in the image of God, irrespective of their mental or physical capacities. Moreover, the fact that the Word was genuinely human means that Christ was open to the entire range of human experiences and emotions. It follows that different human beings can imitate Christ differently across the range of those experiences. By understanding the *imago dei* in Christological terms, then, we can go a long way toward addressing legitimate criticisms of the traditional account. On the whole, a Christological account of the *imago dei* is far more satisfactory than an account that focuses only on rationality and freedom, narrowly construed.

Even so, we can still make the traditional (and useful) claim that we image Christ when we exercise our reason. True, Christ is no philosopher, but the incarnate Christ is God's own eternally spoken Word, the very source of the world's intelligibility, living among us as a human being. Recall that Justin Martyr calls

---

[15] Irenaeus *Adversus Haereses* III.22.3, trans. Alexander Roberts and William Rambaut in *Ante-Nicene Fathers,* Vol. 1, eds. Alexander Roberts, James Donaldson, and A. Cleveland Coxe (Buffalo, NY: Christian Literature Publishing Co., 1885). Revised and edited for New Advent by Kevin Knight, http://www.newadvent.org/fathers/0103.htm, accessed July 6, 2020. For discussion and further citations see Denis Minns, *Irenaeus* (London: Geoffrey Chapman, 1994), 83–102.

him "Reason himself, who took form and became man."[16] Contemporary Christians may well regard this ancient depiction as quaint, but they should not regard it as false. As the Word, Christ is indeed God's own reason and God's own wisdom and yet also, somehow, a human being. This is the mystery of the incarnation. To treat human rationality as a reflection—an image—of Christ, the divine Word, is not a reluctant concession to a dubious Hellenistic metaphysic: on the contrary, it expresses one of the Church's most fundamental Christological claims.

Furthermore, a Christological account allows us to see clearly why reason and freedom are so valuable. On this account, the real value of reason and freedom derives from the fact that they enable us to know and love God, in imitation of Christ. That is, we are meant to use our reason and our freedom to imitate Christ, who knows and loves God the Father completely and freely, both as the divine Word and as a human man. Christ shows us why reason and freedom are so valuable, by showing us what they are for. Our highest and best endowments are not reason and free will per se—considered only as bare, formal capacities—but reason and free will considered instrumentally, as the means by which we can fulfill our deepest purpose as creatures, by coming to know and love God.

Because God the Son, the divine Logos, is Reason itself, the doctrine of the Logos is the ultimate Christian-theological ground for any form of rational inquiry, including analytic theology. Since the Logos ultimately grounds the order and intelligibility of creation, even the "natural" and scientific quest for empirical causes is implicitly theological. Rational inquiry as such is a form of reverence for Christ. When we exercise our reason, we imitate and draw closer to God the Son, who is Reason. Any theistic doctrine of creation will appeal to the divine act of creation to explain the order and intelligibility of the universe, but only the Christian doctrine of creation also understands this explanation as an appeal to Christ, the incarnate Word.

The Fall and Its Cognitive Consequences

Would that this were the whole story! On the Christian doctrine of creation, we are good: created rational and free, in the image of Christ. But we are also fallen. The Christian doctrine of the Fall constrains the way we should understand the claim that human beings manifest the image and the likeness of God. On the one hand, we must honor the biblical suggestion that the image and likeness are what makes us human, from which it follows that we cannot lose the image and likeness without ceasing to be human. On the other hand, we must also honor the further claim that, as a result of the Fall, human beings are no longer in the state

---

[16] Justin Martyr, 1 *Apol* 5, see also 2 *Apol* 10.

of their creation, and so the image and likeness are weakened. As Blaise Pascal noted so forcefully in the seventeenth century, the *imago dei* claim and the doctrine of the Fall together constitute a dialectical understanding of human nature that perpetually pushes us from optimism to pessimism and back again. We must always say that we are made in the divine image and yet also fallen; neither statement alone will suffice.

As we have seen, the traditional doctrine has identified the *imago dei* with human rationality and freedom, and so it is not surprising that advocates of that doctrine also hold that the Fall has marred our reason, warped our desires, and deformed our choices. Throughout the ages, theologians have appealed to the cognitive and affective consequences of the Fall to explain the way human beings act and reason now, in our present state.[17] I would like to avoid getting sidetracked by questions about whether Christians can regard the Fall as a discrete historical event. Whatever our views about that question, all Christians can endorse the present-day phenomena of original sin, the noetic effects of sin, and the cognitive consequences of the Fall. We now live in a world thoroughly shaped by the sinful choices of our forebears, and we ourselves are also sinners, down to the very depths of our own subjectivity. After the Fall, our reasoning is often rationalization, because we typically reason under the influence of biased and self-serving desires. That is the key truth that contemporary Christians must accept, regardless of its historical provenance.[18]

The Doctrine of Creation as the Ground of Human Inquiry

With this account of the Fall and its cognitive consequences, I complete my presentation of the Christian doctrine of creation. The doctrine of creation gives us grounds to trust our rational faculties. We live in a universe created by God, with the faculties God created us to have. Because God is the agent-cause of both our cognitive faculties and the environment in which they operate, we have grounds to affirm that our faculties are fit for that environment, that they do aim at truth, and consequently that our concepts do map onto the world as it is.[19] We are also created in the image of Christ, the divine *Logos*, who is Reason itself. So we have further grounds to affirm that our more abstract, higher-order deductive, inferential, and ratiocinative abilities are similarly truth-apt. Even so, although we have

---

[17] For example, the doctrine of the Fall offers theologians a way of explaining why the existence of God is not obvious to all people, and why, even among religious believers, we observe widespread disagreement about the nature of God.

[18] In a previous work, I defended—or, at least, sympathetically exegeted—an account of the cognitive consequences of the Fall based on Blaise Pascal's *Pensées*. See Wood, *Blaise Pascal on Duplicity, Sin, and the Fall.*

[19] Here I pause to note that I see no reason why these claims should be incompatible with the theory of evolution, though I will not argue the case.

been created by God in the image of Christ, we are not divine, nor even especially Christlike. Our cognitive powers are limited. Moreover, we are fallen creatures who bear the noetic effects of sin. We therefore must also admit our own fallibility and recognize that the world surpasses our ability to understand it completely. The doctrine of creation grounds our epistemic optimism, but it also demands a deep epistemic humility about whether we do, in fact, know all that we take ourselves to know.

The doctrine of creation has several important implications for the way we should understand rational inquiry. Rational inquiry is just the project of using our God-given rational faculties for their designed purpose: trying to know and love God more fully, whether directly, in theological inquiry, or indirectly, in other forms of inquiry. Yet our projects of inquiry can only be genuinely rational when we accept the possibility that we might err in our conclusions. (Dogmatic self-certainty is a form of pride, which is inimical to genuine inquiry.) Because loving the truth is a form of loving God, we want to minimize our errors and cognitive biases, and so we need to find ways of distinguishing truth from falsehood. This is the project of rational inquiry, broadly construed. All of this is just to say that the doctrine of creation provides the ultimate theological warrant for all forms of rational inquiry, including analytic theology. Below I discuss some further implications for the doctrine of creation on rational inquiry as such, before turning to theology specifically. I argue that when we accept the doctrine of creation, we should also accept a weak form of metaphysical realism about the natural world, along with a thin account of common human reason and its universally binding normative force.

Scientific Inquiry and Weak Realism about the Created World

It has long been evident that the doctrine of creation provides the theological warrant for scientific inquiry.[20] There is a natural fit between human reason and the intelligible structure of the created world: not only is the universe orderly in itself; it is intelligible *to us*, a genuine marvel that is well explained by the doctrine of creation. By investigating the created world, by attending to it carefully and trying to understand it, we indirectly learn something about God, our creator. Seeking God through his creation is a form of reverence for God and a key element of human flourishing. This is the traditional account of the value of scientific inquiry.

---

[20] See Peter Harrison, *The Fall of Man and the Foundations of Science* (New York: Cambridge University Press, 2007), and *The Bible, Protestantism, and the Rise of Natural Science* (New York: Cambridge University Press, 1998).

Properly understood, the doctrine of creation also implies a specific account of the metaphysical framework within which scientific inquiry occurs. We cannot seek God through his creation unless the natural world is really there for us to know, and unless we really are able to know it as it is. In philosophical terminology, it seems to follow that the doctrine of creation therefore grounds a weak realism about the natural world.[21] As I understand it, weak realism includes these two claims: (1) things in the world really exist, independently of the human mind; and (2) the human mind is capable of knowing things in the world as they really are. These statements are very general, but they do still discriminate weak realism from prominent forms of anti-realism.[22] The scope of "things in the world" includes whatever objects, phenomena, and states of affairs God actually does create and sustain.[23] On the doctrine of creation, it is trivially true that such things do not depend for their existence on human mental activity, and so (1) is straightforward. But because the world is created in and through the *Logos*, there is also an objective rational structure to the world, a "way-that-the-world-is." Human rationality reflects the image of the divine *Logos*, and so human beings can grasp, or fail to grasp, that structure. Claim (2), therefore, adds an epistemological condition to the first. Not only is it the case that there is a real world; it is also the case that we have epistemic access to that world. There are objective truths about the world, and we can know them, or at least some of them. So far so good.

I have called this form of realism "weak" realism to distinguish it not just from anti-realism but also from overly strong forms of metaphysical realism.[24] As far as I can see, these stronger forms of metaphysical realism strengthen claim (2) above by packing in a series of unhelpful intensifiers, so that it becomes the far more extravagant claim that human beings can know things in the world perfectly, or completely, or without distortion, or the claim that there is a single true description of everything, readily discoverable by properly functioning minds. I do not endorse this stronger form of realism, at least not for human beings. True, on the doctrine of creation, there is (obviously) a single "God's-eye view," since God does

---

[21] The term "weak realism" comes from Michael R. Slater, *Pragmatism and the Philosophy of Religion* (New York: Cambridge University Press, 2014), 153–70.

[22] For the present purposes, it suffices to define "anti-realism" as the denial of weak realism so construed. So an anti-realist is just someone who denies either of the claims that constitute weak realism. Merold Westphal correctly notes that condition (2) really does most of the work in distinguishing realists from anti-realists, but most pro-realist arguments focus only on (1). See Merold Westphal, "Theological Anti-Realism" in Andrew Moore and Michael Scott, eds., *Realism and Religion: Philosophical and Theological Perspectives* (Burlington, VT: Ashgate, 2007), 131–32. Anti-realism is not a strawman position. Notwithstanding their many differences, prominent anti-realists who deny either (1) or (2) would include Jacques Derrida, Richard Rorty, Westphal himself, and, behind them all, Immanuel Kant.

[23] To be pedantically explicit: Is God a "thing in the world?" No.

[24] Slater, *Pragmatism and Philosophy of Religion*, 155; see also Westphal's account of the position he rejects in "Theological Anti-Realism." Westphal's own version of anti-realism might actually be compatible with my version of weak realism.

know his creation completely and without distortion. But it is no part of the doctrine of creation, or Christian theism, to insist that human beings can ever occupy the God's-eye view. I want to walk a line between, on the one hand, stronger forms of realism, on which reality is perfectly knowable to us, and, on the other, those forms of idealism on which we have no access to things-in-themselves, rendering reality fundamentally unknowable to us. On the former, we ourselves must (*per impossibile*) occupy the God's-eye view and, on the latter, we cannot be confident that our concepts map onto the world at all. The doctrine of creation and the claim that we are made in the image of Christ, the divine *Logos*, together give us the resources to walk the needed line.

Common Human Reason: Limited but Universally Binding

Christians who affirm the doctrine of creation and agree that it implies a weak metaphysical realism should take a further step. They should agree that human reason is, in some sense, universal. In other words, the Christian doctrine of creation also grounds a thin account of common human reason. By "common human reason," I mean methods and norms of reasoning that are common to all human beings, in virtue of the fact that they are human. There may be other, non-theological ways to ground a thin account of common human reason—an appeal to our common evolutionary inheritance, for instance. But by grounding common human reason in the doctrine of creation, I make an explicitly theological appeal: anyone who affirms the Christian doctrine of creation should also accept the following thin account of common human reason.[25]

There are formal norms of reasoning that are valid across all cultures, and in all times and places. Consider, for instance, the basic rules of logical inference or the basic patterns of mathematical reasoning. The proposition "2+2=4" is true everywhere, and the inference "If p then q; p, therefore q" is always truth-preserving. These logical norms are universally valid. To these simple examples I would add similarly basic forms of causal reasoning: whatever the right philosophical analysis of causation turns out to be, causal reasoning is universal, and when a basic instance of causal reasoning is correct, it is universally correct. We observe (for example) that water boils when it gets hot enough, and we correctly reason that the heat has caused the water to boil. This basic causal inference is not locally, temporally, or culturally conditioned: "Enough heat causes water to boil" is universally true. All human beings also engage in a similar form of reasoning known as inference to the best explanation. They might disagree about what the best

---

[25] It may also be the case that the doctrine of creation grounds a much stronger account of common human reason, but for my own constructive purposes, I have no need of a stronger account. The thin account will suffice.

explanation for a given phenomenon actually is, but they do not dispute the value of the method itself, since it is ubiquitous in ordinary life.[26]

These forms of reasoning are universal because their *normative* force is universal. Thus, I make no empirical claims about how often people actually do reason well or badly; my argument rests on a normative claim about what counts as good reasoning, always and everywhere. As Thomas Nagel puts it:

> we test our reasons partly by asking whether they are applications of principles that are generally valid...Unless we think that anyone should draw the same conclusion from the same premises, we cannot regard the conclusion as justified by reason. Reasons are by definition general, and we aim always to extend their generality.[27]

Whether or not Nagel's point holds for every form of human reasoning, it does seem to hold for the very basic forms I discussed above. This is what I mean by saying that the doctrine of creation grounds a thin account of common human reason. Christians, at least, should agree that human reason is universal, in the sense I have outlined, because our rational faculties all aim at, and are measured by, a common standard, the divine Word, Reason itself. On the doctrine of creation, we should expect it to be the case that at some very basic level, the norms of reasoning are universally valid. And that is, in fact, what we do observe.

This view is entirely compatible with the existence of widespread rational disagreement, especially in moral and theological matters. From a Christian theological perspective, we can attribute such disagreement to the cognitive consequences of the Fall. Yet the cognitive consequences of the Fall manifest differently in different domains of inquiry. We experience them more vividly in those areas of inquiry that are closest to our fundamental purpose of knowing and loving God. So the cognitive consequences of the Fall will be especially devastating for theological inquiry, and also for moral and ethical inquiry. They will probably also have a strong impact on metaphysical and epistemological inquiry too. (It is no surprise, then, that we see persistent, fundamental, widespread disagreement in exactly these areas of inquiry.) At the other end of the spectrum, there is no good reason to suppose that the Fall has drastically affected our ability to draw basic logical and causal inferences, or to do mathematics. This is not to

---

[26] Consider: you come home from work one day only to discover that the box of chocolates you had been saving is empty. You conclude that the best explanation for this lamentable state of affairs is that while you were out, your shiftless, chocolate-loving housemate ate the whole box. Of course, other explanations are possible. Your landlord could have used his master key to enter your apartment and eat your chocolates. Or a particularly crafty thief could have broken in and eaten them without leaving any other trace. But all in all, the best explanation is that your housemate is the culprit. (This example is taken from https://answptest2.dreamhosters.com/2014/09/30/how-can-we-increase-theological-knowledge-in-the-same-way-we-increase-scientific-knowledge/).

[27] Thomas Nagel, *The Last Word* (New York: Oxford University Press, 2001), 79.

say that everyone is equally good at logic and math, or that there are no persistent disagreements in these areas, only that those disagreements seem less likely to be due to the noetic effects of sin.

Many theologians are committed to some (broadly MacIntyrean) account of tradition-bounded inquiry.[28] My account of common human reason is also compatible with the claim that, in order to reason well, we must be socialized into intellectually virtuous traditions of inquiry. This need will be especially acute in those domains of inquiry that are most affected by the Fall: theological, moral, and ethical inquiry. Accordingly, it is useful to regard tradition-bounded inquiry as a continuum, with philosophical, moral, and religious inquiry at one end and mathematics and logic at the other end. On the former, more tradition-bounded end of the continuum, we need to be socialized into an intellectual tradition in order to learn what goods (intellectual and otherwise) we should value. Common human reason may tell us what counts as a valid inference from a premise to a conclusion, but it often cannot tell us what premises we should accept in the first place. At the other end of the spectrum, purely formal kinds of inquiry such as logic and mathematics are much less dependent on substantive norms that can only be passed on by virtuous intellectual traditions in the MacIntyrean sense. Scientific inquiry occupies the contested middle ground of the continuum, and scholars argue about whether it is closer to one extreme or the other.

The most important point for my own emerging defense of analytic theology is that argument across traditions of inquiry is possible precisely because the basic core of common human reason is universal.[29] This point holds even for moral and religious inquiry. On my account, the norms of reasoning can be highly tradition-dependent, just not entirely tradition-dependent. Some norms, like the most basic forms of logical and causal inference, are universal. This account also coheres with what we do, in fact, observe: widespread, persistent disagreement about substantive philosophical, moral, and religious questions, less disagreement about empirical questions, and even less about purely formal questions.

Theological Inquiry

The Christian doctrine of creation should lead us to value inquiry as such, including scientific inquiry; it should also lead us to accept weak realism about the natural world, and to endorse at least a thin account of common human reason. I now use these same same building blocks to construct a theological defense of analytic theology, one that is similarly grounded in the doctrine of creation.

---

[28] Alasdair MacIntyre, *Whose Justice? Which Rationality?* is a *locus classicus* for this view.
[29] It is also the case that traditions overlap—rival traditions can still share some premises and axioms.

First, recall the purpose of inquiry as such. From the Christian point of view, all inquiry aims at God, whether indirectly or directly. In scientific inquiry, we try to learn more about God's creation, and in this way, we come to learn about God the creator. In theological inquiry, we try to learn more about God himself. In so doing, we imitate—very remotely, to be sure—Christ's perfect knowledge and perfect love of God the Father. We have the ability to imitate Christ in this way because we are made in his image.

As a form of theological inquiry, analytic theology aims to help us know and love God more deeply. All human inquiry about God must reckon with the dialectic of optimism and pessimism that arises from the fact that we are both created in the image of Christ and yet fallen from our ideal state. God is both revealed and hidden, and so we arrive at theological knowledge only with great difficulty and in the face of many errors. Within this theological context, analytic theology has a clear purpose, and an obvious rationale: analytic theology can help us distinguish theological statements that are more likely to be true from theological statements that are more likely to be false.

The very distinction between true and false theological statements seems to require some suitable analogue to the weak metaphysical realism outlined above. Finding the right analogue proves tricky, however. Certainly we want to say that God really exists and would have the same essential attributes even if there were no human beings. It seems to follow that:

(1a) There are theological objects, properties, and truths that really exist, independently of the human mind.

This claim seems a suitable analogue to the realist ontological claim (1) in the section "Scientific Inquiry and Weak Realism about the Created World" above. Some might want to put scare quotes around "objects," and "properties," in (1a), but the basic realist point that God exists and does not depend on human minds seems clear enough.[30] After all, to say that God is triune is to say that God is necessarily and essentially triune, not triune only for us.

What about the second, epistemic condition? Recall that (2) asserts that human minds can know the world as it is. Many theologians would deny that human beings are capable of knowing God as God really is, whether in this life or the next. Indeed, this denial has been the dominant view throughout the Christian tradition. If analytic theology constitutively excludes the dominant view of the Christian tradition about whether God is knowable, then that is a problem for analytic theology. But all Christians should agree that God has revealed himself to us in Christ, and through the scriptures, and has therefore allowed himself to be

---

[30] Slater speaks of "religious objects, facts, or properties which exist independently of the human mind" (*Pragmatism and Philosophy of Religion*, 157).

known by us to some degree. Even the most austere apophatic theologian would have to agree that there are *some* theological truths that we should affirm, including some truths about God. "God creates all things out of nothing" seems like a plausible candidate, for example. Instead of the very optimistic claim that we can know God as God really is, then, I propose:

(2a) Human beings can make true statements about God and other theological matters.[31]

One advantage of (2a) is that it establishes what we can truthfully say about God, rather than what we can know. I intend for this shift toward assertion to be agnostic about the relationship between truthful assertion and knowledge. In other words, the shift itself does not take any position on what we can know about God.[32] Even an orthodox Barthian can affirm (2a), though she might add the further proviso that we can only make true statements about God when God grants us this ability. Similarly, a diehard Swinburnian rationalist can affirm (2a) without any such proviso. Thus, as I have formulated it, (2a) is sufficiently capacious that theologians who differ sharply about theological method can still affirm it. Analytic theology requires (2a); it does not require anything stronger.

The doctrine of creation serves as the theological warrant for (1a) and (2a). However valuable and important it is to learn about the created world, our creation has a deeper purpose. Most fundamentally, we have been created with the desire to know and love God. We can be sure that this desire is not empty, and that God wants us to know and love him, because he has revealed himself to us in Christ. This fact alone assures us that (1a) and (2a) are true.

As discussed above, the doctrine of creation gives us some reason for optimism about theological inquiry, but it also gives us a reason for deep epistemic humility. Because of God's sheer transcendence, knowing God would be unlike knowing anything else, even if our cognitive faculties were functioning properly, and on the Christian story, our cognitive faculties are not functioning properly. We are worse than fallible: we are fallen, wracked by the noetic effects of sin. In theological inquiry, we have especially strong grounds to be skeptical about the seductive deliverances of our own reason. After the Fall, we may still love the truth, but we love ourselves, and our own private versions of the truth, even more. When we consider the whole picture of creation and Fall, we find that we have the desire to

---

[31] If we can make true statements about God (the most problematic case), then it seems straightforward to agree that we can make true statements about other theological "objects, properties, and truths."

[32] Furthermore, for all I have said so far, (2a) is also compatible with the claim that all positive predications about God are analogous, a claim more commonly held by theologians, as well as the claim that some positive predications about God are univocal, a claim more commonly held by philosophers of religion. So for now I can bypass that perennial debate as well.

seek God, and some capacity for knowing God, joined to a deep-seated tendency to claim for ourselves a certainty and a grasp of truth that are not really on offer. Given both aspects of this picture, we need some way to distinguish theological statements that are likely to be true from those that are likely to be false.

Analytic Theological Inquiry

Analytic theology can help. Analytic theology is one way that we can use our God-given rational faculties to try to distinguish theological truth from theological error. Everyone can accept this claim, regardless of their views about the broader relationship between faith and reason. Suppose we take a traditional "faith seeking understanding" approach to theology, and hold that theology must begin from a perspective of faithful assent to revelation. Advocates of this approach should still agree that God wants to be known by us, since he revealed himself in Christ. They should also agree that the sheer fact that God has revealed himself in Christ does not itself suffice to answer every question that can arise about how to understand what has been revealed. The history of the Church, especially in its first few centuries, is a testament to the point that fundamental questions about how to understand revelation will always arise. So even if we do think that theology requires an attitude of faithful assent to revealed truths, we can still legitimately wonder exactly what truths have been revealed, what they mean, and how they can be true, or at least consistent with everything else we take to be true. We can also wonder about the further truths that are entailed by those that have been revealed. Analytic tools and methods are well suited to addressing such problems. The problems are perennial.

So the Church has always been faced with exactly the kinds of questions that analytic theology is good at addressing. This point already suggests that analytic theology is a legitimate form of theological inquiry. To reinforce it, we need only establish that we can legitimately use our common human reason to try to understand God better. (Below I will argue that the "tools and methods" of analytic theology are really just systematic extensions of common human reason.) Grant that revelation can seem unclear or conflicting. Yet when revelation seems unclear or conflicting, surely those with faith can legitimately "seek understanding" by using their common human reason—especially since their common human reason is an image of the divine Logos. Anyway, what else would they use? Sometimes our reason might tell us that we should defer to a legitimate authority, and nothing that I have said entails that we must use *only* our reason to address *all* theological questions. But suppose someone denies that we can ever legitimately use our common human reason to try to understand God better. What does that view even amount to? Perhaps we should simply repeat the ancient creedal formulae without rationally assessing them, or perhaps we should always defer to some

Church authority, without ever asking any questions of our own. Someone who takes that kind of view simply denies the value of *all* theological inquiry, not just the value of analytic theology. That person is not my interlocutor.

So long as we agree that it is possible and desirable to use our common human reason to try to distinguish theological truth from theological error, we should agree that analytic theology is a legitimate form of theological inquiry. The distinctively analytic "tools and methods" that feature in analytic theology should not be regarded as weird esoteric practices that are guilty until proven innocent. Rather, they are systematic extensions of ordinary forms of reasoning, analogous to the way that properly scientific methods are also systematic extensions of ordinary forms of reasoning. In each case, because the doctrine of creation authorizes the ordinary practices, we have reason to believe that it also authorizes the systematic extensions.

Consider scientific inquiry first. Imagine a premodern forager trying to determine whether a newly encountered fruit is safe to eat. The forager might first examine the fruit, and compare its smell and appearance with other fruits that he knows are safe. He might then try to feed the fruit to a nonhuman animal and observe whether the animal will eat the fruit, and what happens to the animal if it does. Perhaps then he might try a small taste himself, and then a larger taste, and so on, until he determines that the fruit is safe to eat, at which point he feels free to give the fruit to other people. This investigation is not properly "scientific" in the more precise, contemporary sense of the term, but it is certainly on a continuum with properly scientific inquiry.[33] The forager formulates a very basic hypothesis and then runs some simple experiments as a way of gathering evidence to support or disconfirm it. The doctrine of creation surely authorizes this kind of very basic inquiry into the natural world, which is, after all, God's creation. But properly scientific inquiry is simply a systematic extension of exactly this kind of rudimentary inquiry. If the doctrine of creation authorizes the former, it seems reasonable to hold that it authorizes the latter. True, it does not simply follow, as a matter of logical entailment, that the doctrine of creation authorizes the systematic extension just because it authorizes the rudimentary starting point. But it is difficult to see why inquiry into the natural world would become less theologically permissible as it becomes more precise, more systematic, and more successful. At the very least, I think the burden of proof falls on those who affirm that the doctrine of creation authorizes empirical inquiry in general but does not authorize scientific inquiry. Scientific inquiry is really just a more systematic way of trying to use our common human reason to understand the natural world.

---

[33] According to the physicist and popular-science writer Chad Orzel, the scientific method is really a systematic extension of basic human practices that we all use to understand the world: "Look, Think, Test, Tell," as he puts it. Chad Orzel, *Eureka: Discovering Your Inner Scientist* (New York: Basic Books, 2014), x.

I now make the same point with respect to the tools and methods of analytic theology. Analytic theology is just theology that draws on analytic philosophy. Despite its formidable technicality, logical machinery, and occasionally outlandish thought experiments, analytic philosophy is really just a systematic extension of ordinary forms of reasoning, analogous to the way that properly scientific inquiry is an extension of ordinary efforts to understand the natural world.[34] Analytic philosophy began as a kind of "common-sense philosophy" in distinction from the more esoteric philosophical systems found in German idealism.[35] Its chief methods include formal logic, concern for linguistic precision, counterfactual reasoning to determine what is possible, and the use of thought experiments to facilitate such reasoning. These methods all require skill and training to use well, but they are extensions of the ordinary forms of the common-sense reasoning that we use in daily life. The hyperprecision that features in analytic thought is different in degree but not in kind from ordinary "person in the street" demands to say exactly what we mean (no more, no less!). And one need not be a philosopher to engage in speculative, "what-if" style thought experiments. We do something similar every time we wonder about the future. Finally, it is obvious that we all value logical consistency, if for no other reason than that we so frequently accuse others of being inconsistent.

At this point, my argument is vulnerable to a serious misunderstanding. I can well imagine someone who objects: "Wait! If we redefine analytic theology as nothing more than 'using our reason in theological inquiry,' doesn't it become trivially true that analytic theology is legitimate, and doesn't everyone become an analytic theologian?" Not quite. Return again to the analogy with natural science. To say that properly scientific inquiry is a systematic extension of ordinary empirical investigation does not mean that the ordinary investigation is also properly scientific. Not every kind of empirical inquiry counts as properly scientific inquiry—interpreting texts is empirical but not scientific, for instance. Similarly, to say that analytic theology draws on philosophical tools and methods that systematically extend ordinary forms of reasoning does not entail that every instance of reasoning counts as "analytic." The two extended forms (science, analytic theology) are not *methodologically* equivalent to their respective non-extended forms. But the theological warrant that accrues to the non-extended forms also transfers to the extended forms.

---

[34] See Timothy Williamson, *Doing Philosophy: From Common Curiosity to Logical Reasoning* (New York: Oxford University Press, 2018).

[35] See Jack Reynolds, "Common Sense and Philosophical Methodology: Some Metaphilosophical Reflections on Analytic Philosophy and Deluze," *Philosophical Forum* 41 (2010): 232:

> On the question of what role common sense should have in reining in the possible excesses of our philosophical methods, the continental answer to this question, for the vast majority of the usual suspects associated with this tradition, would be something like "as little as possible," whereas the analytic answer, for the vast majority, would be "a reasonably central one."

To consolidate and conclude: the doctrine of creation gives us good reason to value theology as such, traditionally understood as faith seeking understanding. So the only real question is whether analytic theology counts as a legitimate way for those with faith to seek understanding. This question resolves into the practical question of whether analytic theology really can help us distinguish theological truth from theological falsehood. The answer to this question is *sometimes, but not always*—an answer that is boring, pedantic, and true. Defenders and critics of analytic theology alike often treat it as more unique than it actually is, but in terms of its overall value, analytic theology is really no different from most other forms of theological inquiry. Sometimes it is useful, but not always, and whether it is useful or not depends on one's theological task. Boring, pedantic, and true.

Analytic Theology and Autonomous Reason

Analytic theology inherits the same theological warrant that accrues to inquiry in general, along with any additional theological warrants that accrue to Christian theology in general.[36] There is no reason to single out analytic theology as especially problematic from a Christian theological point of view—all forms of theology are at risk of anthropomorphism, idolatry, self-serving biases, and similar errors, because all theology occurs in the wake of the Fall. Still, just because all forms of theology are vulnerable to these errors, that does not mean that they are all equally vulnerable to them. No doubt some theological readers will worry that analytic theology is especially vulnerable to certain very grave errors. Considering one such worry returns us to the theme of "secular reason," or its more theological variant, "autonomous reason." Notwithstanding its grounding in the doctrine of creation, perhaps analytic theology does assume a theologically unacceptable notion of autonomous reason. To assess this worry, we need a deeper understanding of what "autonomous" reason is supposed to be. Once we have this understanding, it is clear that analytic theology is no more autonomous than any other form of theological reasoning.

Three Views of Autonomous Reason

It is not always obvious what any given critic means by "autonomous reason." Sometimes, the target seems to be an exaggerated version of Enlightenment rationality. On this construal, autonomous reason aims to be entirely self-determining,

---

[36] A friendly reminder that the purpose of this chapter is to give a Christian theological justification for explicitly Christian analytic theology. Some, but not all of the argument would also apply to other forms of theology, including non-Christian and non-analytic forms.

and free from all external influences, including authority, tradition, and culture. The twin paradigms of this version of autonomous reason are the Cartesian *cogito*, on the one hand, and modern empirical science, on the other. The *cogito* abstracts away from everything other than a subject's own act of thinking, assuming that a priori human reason must support the entire edifice of knowledge. Scientific inquiry aims at universally valid, transcultural truths, by subjecting its claims to empirical criteria of verifiability or falsifiability. As we valorize it more and more, science becomes *scientism*, such that scientific reasoning becomes the only acceptable paradigm for inquiry.

It is easy to see why theologians should resist this exaggerated picture of autonomous reason. If we take the Christian doctrine of creation seriously, there can be no autonomous reason—not like the version presented above, anyway. Nothing can be *entirely* self-determining or free from *all* external influences, for the simple reason that nothing whatsoever can exist without the continuous creative activity of God. Yet analytic theology does not presuppose this exaggerated construal of autonomous reason. As I argued in Chapter 2, analytic theology is not an a priori project, and as I argued in Chapter 5, leading analytic theologians understand their work as "faith seeking understanding." Recall the way Pawl assumes the truth of "Conciliar Christology" or the way Hasker begins from scripture and tradition. In general, the idea that philosophers, let alone theologians, must prescind from their deep values and intellectual commitments has very little currency among contemporary analytic thinkers. Few, if any, analytic theologians would agree that they should bracket their religious commitments before they begin to theologize. So analytic theology does not exhibit this version of autonomous reason.

Alternatively, critics of "autonomous reason" sometimes mean to attack the assumption that theology is beholden to philosophy, such that that all theological claims stand in need of philosophical justification in order to count as rational. (This is a typical Barthian critique of autonomous reason.) For example, this construal seems to be what Andrew Moore criticizes under the headings of "apologetic reason" and "inferential reason" in his chapter on "Reason," in the *Oxford Handbook of Systematic Theology*. On the view that Moore rejects, "the task of reason is…to demonstrate at the bar of neutral, universal reason the rationality of [Christian] doctrines in their authoritative forms." The problem, according to Moore, is that "apologetic reason risks creating the impression that the doctrine has an independent standing as a problem to be solved or that the logic of trinitarian discourse is at risk unless and until Christians can show that it is not subject to philosophical objections."[37] In other words, in the grip of

---

[37] Andrew Moore, "Reason," in Kathryn Tanner, John Webster, and Iain Torrance, eds., *The Oxford Handbook of Systematic Theology* (New York: Oxford University Press, 2007), 399.

autonomous (apologetic) reason, theology wrongly subjects its claims to the tribunal of putatively neutral and universal philosophical justification.

I can understand why opponents might think that analytic theology depends on autonomous reason in this sense. Compared to other theologians, analytic thinkers do tend to focus heavily on challenges to the logical coherence or general plausibility of Christian doctrines. Yet we should be very cautious about treating this focus as evidence that they also think Christian doctrines are "at risk" without "neutral" philosophical justification. They might think that it is *good* to be able to show that Christian doctrines are coherent or generally plausible without also thinking that we *must* show this in order to be rational in affirming the doctrines. (I take it that this is Timothy Pawl's view, for instance.[38]) After all, analytic theology grows out of analytic philosophy of religion, and analytic philosophy of religion is decisively anti-foundationalist in its epistemology.[39] So we should not assume that the default view among analytic theologians is that everyone must hold their Christian beliefs in suspension until those beliefs are backed up by philosophical arguments. In fact, analytic theologians are far more likely to hold the opposite view. So analytic theology does not exhibit this version of autonomous reason either.

There is a third construal of "autonomous reason," this one associated especially with Radical Orthodoxy, *nouvelle théologie,* and other contemporary theological opponents of neo-scholasticism.[40] This view is difficult to summarize in a short space, but the following claim lies at its heart: on a properly Christian view, there can be no autonomous reason, because there can be no real distinction between reason and revelation, or between philosophy and theology; to suggest otherwise is a modern, secular fiction. Thus John Milbank:

> The very notion of a reason–revelation duality, far from being an authentic Christian legacy, itself results only from the rise of a questionably secular mode of knowledge. By contrast, in the Church Fathers or the early scholastics, both faith and reason are included within the more generic framework of participation in the mind of God: to reason truly one must be already illumined by God, while revelation itself is but a higher measure of such illumination, conjoined intrinsically and inseparably with a created event

[38] See the discussion in Chapter 5.

[39] Nicholas Wolterstorff, "How Philosophical Theology Became Possible within the Analytical Tradition of Philosophy," 155–70.

[40] *Nouvelle théologie* began as a movement in mid-twentieth-century Catholicism. Over against neo-scholastic formalism, it emphasized spiritual exegesis, art, literature, and mysticism and called for a deeper engagement with patristic thought. For a helpful introduction to the influence of *nouvelle théologie* on Radical Orthodoxy, see Simon Oliver, "Henri de Lubac and Radical Orthodoxy," in Jordan Hillebert, ed., *T&T Clark Companion to Henri de Lubac* (London: TT Clark, 2017), 393–418.

which symbolically discloses that transcendent reality, to which all created events to a lesser degree also point.[41]

Here so-called "autonomous" reason belongs in a secular, deist thought-world where God sets the universe in motion and then leaves it alone. But that is not the Christian story. On the Christian story, God freely creates the world out of nothing and continues to hold it in existence. Without constant divine activity, the universe would fall back into nothingness and cease to exist. Furthermore, on the Christian story, the act of creation is gracious: the whole of creation is a divine gift. Human reason is itself a gracious gift of God, a gift continually given, and so it can never be autonomous in the relevant sense.

At such a high level of generality, this critique of autonomous reason seems entirely compatible with analytic theology. It expresses a view about the ultimate source of rationality. On its own, it passes no judgment at all on individual acts of reasoning, and takes no position on what good arguments in theology should look like.[42] Faced with this critique, the analytic theologian could simply agree that rationality always has its ultimate source in divine illumination. That is, the analytic theologian could simply agree that whenever she reasons truthfully about God, her act of reasoning is a participation in the divine *Logos*, or a product of divine illumination, or something that otherwise depends on God's grace. Why not? It seems to me that the burden of proof falls on someone who insists that the analytic theologian is never entitled to such a view. When we collapse the distinction between reason and revelation, it actually become harder, not easier, to charge analytic theologians with relying too much on autonomous reason. If everything is revelation, faith, and grace, why not analytic theology too? Does God *hate* modal logic?

The whole theological debate about "autonomous reason" occurs at a very high level of abstraction. When we push the debate down to a more concrete level, it starts to look quite different. Instead of focusing on hypostasized "reason," it is better to look at individual acts of reasoning. When we look at individual acts of reasoning, it becomes apparent that analytic theology is no more "autonomous" than any other form of theology. Analytic thinkers make logical inferences, just like other theologians. They interpret texts, just like other theologians. They

---

[41] John Milbank, in John Milbank, Catherine Pickstock, and Graham Ward, eds., *Radical Orthodoxy: A New Theology* (New York: Routledge, 1999), 24. See also John Milbank, *The Suspended Middle: Henri de Lubac and the Debate Concerning the Supernatural* (London: SCM, 2005).

[42] This is not to say that *Milbank* expresses no further views on these questions, of course. My point is that the very high-level claim that all reasoning depends on divine illumination does not, in itself, tell us anything one way or the other about whether any specific act or style of reasoning is sound. *Nouvelle théologie*'s critique of scholastic formalism is not entailed by the critique of autonomous reason, and so they do not stand or fall together.

explore tensions and apparent contradictions in the tradition, again, just like other theologians. In other words, analytic theology, like other forms of theology, proceeds by way of ordinary acts of reasoning. This is the case even if we agree that all "ordinary" acts of reasoning are also grace-infused participations in the divine *Logos*. So long as we agree that good theology can proceed by way of ordinary acts of reasoning, then analytic theology seems to be in the same position as its non-analytic counterparts. The critique of autonomous reason does not have any special implications for analytic theology in particular.

Conclusion: The Tragedy of Analytic Theology

Analytic theology is a valuable, but limited form of theological inquiry. Other kinds of inquiry, and other ways of knowing, may indeed be more valuable, but this fact does not undermine the genuine and abiding value of analytic theology. The premodern Christian tradition regarded human reason as one of God's greatest gifts. Patristic and medieval theologians held this view notwithstanding their keen sense of the limitations of human reason after the Fall. At the same time, compared to their modern descendants, they also had a wider conception of rationality. On the premodern understanding, rationality included not only empirical observation and linear, discursive reasoning, but also immediate intuition or insight, what Aquinas calls *intellectus*. *Intellectus* is a higher form of knowing: it is how the angels know, and how we humans will know God in the afterlife, when we receive the beatific vision.[43] *Intellectus* most resembles God's own knowledge, which is not discursive. So while it is indeed very traditional, and very Christian, to laud the power of reason, we must be careful not to overvalue discursive reasoning and ratiocination. Analytic theology, and the analytic philosophy on which it depends, may seem to do just that.

But we are not God; nor are we angels; and we do not yet enjoy the beatific vision. In this life, as fallen creatures in a fallen world, we must reason discursively. We have no alternative. To be sure, we do grasp some truths by immediate intuition and insight. And the more we learn about embodied rationality, the more we realize that our emotions can also be vehicles of knowledge.[44] Any sufficiently capacious account of human rationality must embrace these facts. Some people might even know God and the saving truths of the Christian faith immediately and intuitively. I am prepared to concede that they have an epistemic advantage over the rest of us, who must reason our way toward those same truths.

---

[43] Thomas Aquinas, *Summa Contra Gentiles*, 3.60.
[44] Jesse Prinz, "Emotions Embodied," in Robort Solomon, ed., *Thinking about Feeling* (New York: Oxford University Press, 2004), 44–60; Rebecca Sachs Norris, "Examining the Structure and Role of Emotion: Contributions of Neurobiology to the Study of Embodied Religious Experience," *Zygon* 40 (2005): 181–99.

But at least for me, and for those like me, the alternative to discursive reasoning about God is not intuitive knowledge or mystical insight, but muddle and confusion.

God is not a thing in the world, and one might suppose that we can only reason discursively about things in world. It is true that God is not a thing in the world, but it is not true that we can only reason discursively about things in the world. We can reason discursively about God, because God has revealed himself to us. In so doing, he has accommodated himself to our cognitive limitations. It is God who ensures that we can reason discursively about God. This is a supremely gracious act of divine condescension. But God's gracious act does not entail that we can reason about God skillfully. We must seek to understand God—that is a divinely given imperative—and for most of us, that means reasoning discursively. Human reason remains one of God's greatest gifts, but we are not very good at discursive reasoning, and we are rarely in a position to be confident of our own conclusions, especially when it comes to matters divine.

This claim sets up a novel and potentially quite fruitful way to regard analytic theology. Behold the tragedy of analytic theology: we must reason discursively about God, *even though* discursive reasoning is not an especially good way to understand God. (It is far inferior to worship, prayer, and immediate insight, for example.) After all, the much-vaunted "tools and methods" of analytic philosophy are just the tools and methods of discursive reasoning. Those tools are blunt and often nearly unusable, but we must use them anyway, because, for some theological tasks, they are still the best tools we currently have.

7

How to Avoid Idolatry

The very first verse of scripture tells us that God is our creator; the first Commandments forbid idolatry and instruct us to worship God alone. In the New Testament, Christ offers the *Shema* as the foundation of the Law (Mark 12:29–30): "Hear, O Israel: The Lord our God, the Lord is one. And you shall love the Lord your God with all your heart and with all your soul and with all your mind and with all your strength." All these lessons are inextricably linked. It is because God is our creator that we owe God, and God alone, the honor of loving worship.

Contemporary theology is haunted by the specter of idolatry.[1] Yet, for many people, the word "idolatry" conjures up little more than the golden calf scene in Cecil B. DeMille's over-the-top epic *The Ten Commandments*. On this picture, we can agree that idolatry is very bad, but wonder how it could ever be tempting. Who would worship a human artifact, no matter how shiny? But like the serpent, idolatry is subtle; it takes many forms, not all of them so crude. In its subtler forms, idolatry is a perennial human temptation, and so we would expect theologians in every age to critique it. But that critique also takes a different form in every age. Right now, a very specific discourse on idolatry has taken root in contemporary academic theology. This discourse emerges from the unexpected nexus of French and German phenomenology, Kantian idealism, and classical (Thomist) metaphysics. It is rhetorically extravagant and occasionally excessive. Often it obscures more than it reveals.

The foundational figure of this contemporary discourse on idolatry is Jean-Luc Marion.[2] Marion is not worried about worshiping literal graven images. Consider his succinct definition of idolatry as "the subjection of God to human conditions for the experience of the divine."[3] Note first the word "subjection": somehow human beings are able to claim mastery over God. Note, too, the emphasis on "experience": much of the contemporary discourse on idolatry is less about

---

[1] Despite the theme's prominence, one of the only book-length treatments of idolatry is Moshe Halbertal and Avishai Margalit, *Idolatry* (Cambridge, MA: Harvard University Press, 1998).

[2] See especially Jean-Luc Marion, *The Idol and Distance*, trans. Thomas A. Carlson (New York: Fordham University Press, 2011), *God without Being*, trans. Thomas A. Carlson (Chicago: University of Chicago Press, 1995). Other leading exemplars include such philosophers and theologians as David Bentley Hart, Merold Westphal, and John Caputo; Thomists like Brian Davies and David Burrell, and various figures associated with the "Radical Orthodoxy" movement, as well as those they have influenced, such as Denys Turner.

[3] Marion, *Idol and Distance*, 6.

Analytic Theology and the Academic Study of Religion. William Wood, Oxford University Press (2021). © William Wood. DOI: 10.1093/oso/9780198779872.003.0007

wrongly worshiping God than about assimilating God to something that can be an object of conscious experience. Since *thought* is a form of conscious experience, even thinking about God threatens to "subject" God to finite human conditions. Elsewhere, Marion writes:

> The advent of something like "God" in philosophy therefore arises less from God himself than from metaphysics..."God" is determined starting from, and to the profit of, that of which metaphysics is capable, that which it can admit and support. This anterior instance, which determines the experience of the divine starting from a supposedly unavoidable condition, marks a primary characteristic of idolatry.[4]

The claim here is that philosophy—in the form of metaphysics—cannot investigate God at all, but only "God," a human construct, and an idol. Consider now Gavin Hyman's *Short History of Atheism*. Like Marion, Hyman associates idolatry with metaphysical reasoning about God, but adds the proviso (which Marion shares) that such reasoning inevitably treats God as "a being," by which he means a discrete individual, a thing in the world:

> God is therefore not only not a "being," he is also not subordinate to, nor contained by, the Being of beings. The whole panoply of metaphysical procedures—rational argument, empirical evidence, experiential inference and so forth—simply cannot apply to God. If they are, they are treating God as an "object" or "thing" within the realm of Being, and the conclusion of such an investigation will inevitably be that such an "idol" does not exist.[5]

Hyman's point—the conclusion of his entire book—is that metaphysical reasoning about God not only leads to atheism but is in fact a form of atheism, precisely because it is a form of idolatry.

These representative quotations show why contemporary theological discourse on idolatry seems constitutively opposed to analytic theology. If ordinary reasoning in the form of "rational argument, empirical evidence, [and] experiential inference" simply cannot apply to God at all, and in fact can yield only idols, then the project of analytic theology seems doomed. This is not to say that every

---

[4] Marion, *God without Being*, 34.

[5] Gavin Hyman, *A Short History of Atheism* (New York: Tauris, 2010), 179. This passage exhibits some of the rhetorical extravagance noted earlier in this section: it seems unlikely that Hyman really means that rational argument, empirical evidence, and experiential inference do not "apply to God" *at all*. (I bet he would agree that God is not identical to Genghis Khan, for example, or a turnip.) He probably means to say something considerably more restrained, that we cannot use "metaphysical procedures" to prove the truth of positive, substantive theological claims. Also, to be clear about what is going on here: Hyman writes these words as a Radically Orthodox Christian, not an atheist who denies the reality of God.

participant in the discourse on idolatry explicitly labels analytic theology or analytic philosophy of religion as idolatrous—though several do.[6] Yet the level of cross-disciplinary argument in this discourse has been low. Contemporary theologians tend to be steeped in an internal, specialized, continental discourse, or, alternatively, an equally internal and equally specialized Thomist discourse. Analytic theologians have their own internal discourse and do not seem to understand the force of the continental critique. We need to do better. Analytic theology is not uniquely vulnerable to idolatry, but it is entirely fair to wonder whether analytic theology takes divine transcendence seriously enough. In comparison with their continental counterparts, many analytic theologians do affirm a less transcendent God. But is the analytic God transcendent *enough*? There is room for sincere disagreement about this question, and the argument itself is well worth having. Yet the polarized rhetoric around the idolatry charge has actually made it harder to have this more fundamental argument.

Across Chapters 8–10 I defend analytic theology from various versions of the idolatry charge, but most of all, I want partisans on all sides to understand their counterparts better. In this chapter, I try to uncover what idolatry really is, and what it is not. The core concept of idolatry involves worshiping something other than God, even when we extend the notion of "worship" to include modern variations like "treating something other than God as ultimate." Because idolatry involves false worship, it cannot be assimilated to mistaken believing: idolatry is more than a cognitive error. Much of the contemporary theological discourse on idolatry concerns so-called "conceptual idolatry." Yet conceptual idolatry only makes sense within the context of contemporary phenomenological thought and its Kantian inheritance. Insofar as conceptual idolatry is anything more than a cognitive error, it is about thinking about God in the wrong way, with an impious or prideful attitude. But there is no reason to think that analytic theology uniquely fosters such an attitude. I conclude by offering some suggestions for how to avoid idolatry: by maintaining the creator/creature distinction, and by thinking about God with an attitude of reverence.

What Is Idolatry?—Toward a Core Concept of Idolatry

We first need to get a better sense of what idolatry is and what counts as idolatrous. The quotations from Marion and Hyman in the preceding section clearly show that in contemporary theological discourse, the meaning of the term "idolatry" has expanded. (Metaphysical reflection on God is not obviously identical to

---

[6] See, for example, N. N. Trakakis "Does Univocity Entail Idolatry?" *Sophia* 49 (2010): 535–55, Andrew Gleeson "The Power of God," *Sophia* 49 (2010): 603–16, Brian Davies, "A Timeless God?" *New Blackfriars* 64 (1983): 217, Hyman, *Short History of Atheism*, 57, 140.

worshiping a created artifact.) For now, I want to focus on the core concept, before turning to the more recent expansions like "conceptual idolatry." The core concept of idolatry is the notion of wrongly directed worship. Idolatry entails worshiping something other than God. Because anything other than God is, by definition, a creature, idolatry entails worshiping a creature instead of God. Idolatry therefore inverts the creator/creature relationship. At bottom, that is why it is wrong.

This definition of idolatry presupposes an understanding of worship. But exactly what counts as "worship" is not an easy question to answer. In its focal meaning—the sense in which we would say that Christians, but not Jews, worship Christ—worship features:

(i)   certain more or less formal, and often communal, ritualized practices
(ii) directed at some intentional object
(iii) that are meant to convey attitudes like reverence, obedience, awe, adoration, gratitude, or unrestricted love.[7]

This sense of worship captures what, for example, Augustine calls *latreia*—"the kind of service [*cultus*] we owe to the Deity."[8] Idolatry would then be directing *latreia* to something other than God. For the earliest Christians, when polytheism was still a live option, idolatry usually meant venerating the emperor or worshiping the false gods of the Greco-Roman pantheon.[9]

This initial account of idolatry depends on construing "worship" according to its focal meaning. This account is useful, but on this understanding of idolatry, idolatry becomes vanishingly rare: in the focal sense of "worship," few contemporary Christians are actually tempted to *worship* some created thing instead of God. Even within the core concept of idolatry, however, there is an extended sense of "worship" with an equally venerable pedigree. This extended sense of worship drives a more expansive account of idolatry. On this account, idolatry involves treating something other than God as ultimate, as the center and source of all value. In this sense, we "worship" whatever we regard as most important and most valuable, as the highest and best good of all, the good around which we order our lives and orient all our subsidiary goals. When the object of our

---

[7] See Jeroen de Ridder and Rene van Woudenberg, "Referring to, Believing in, and Worshipping the Same God: A Reformed View," *Faith and Philosophy* 31 (2014): 51. See also Jason Lepojärvi, "Worship, Veneration, and Idolatry: Observations from C. S. Lewis," *Religious Studies* 51 (2015): 543–62; Tim Bayne and Yujin Nagasawa, "The Grounds of Worship," *Religious Studies* 42 (2006): 300–302. I say "some intentional object" because the act of worship requires an object, even if that object does not really exist. We cannot worship without worshiping *something*, however ill-defined.

[8] Augustine, *City of God* 10.1, trans. Henry Bettenson (New York: Penguin, 1972), 372.

[9] Interestingly, on the most common early Christian understanding these false gods and idols were actually demons: 1 Cor 8:5-6,1 Cor 10:20–22; Tertullian, *De idololatria* [On Idolatry], trans. J. H. Waszink and J. C. M. van Winden (Leiden: Brill, 1987), Augustine, *City of God* Books 6–9.

worship is something other than God, that thing becomes our idol.[10] So, for instance, if I orient my life around the pursuit of wealth, then money is my idol; likewise for my nation, my race, physical pleasure, and so on. As Karl Barth puts it:

> a god is that in which human beings place their trust, in which they have faith, from which they expect to receive what they love and to protect them from what they fear. A god is that to which one gives one's heart...Wherever the human heart is, in other words, wherever the foundation of our real confidence and hope, the *primum movens* of our vitality and the basis of the security of our lives, there also, in all truth, is our god.[11]

Similarly, John Calvin asks: "For what is idolatry if not this: to worship the gifts in place of the giver himself?"[12] Every good thing comes from God, and when we love some good thing in a disordered way, without also loving the God who created it, we fall into idolatry.

In summary, idolatry is wrongly directed worship, the act of worshiping something other than God. In its initial, focal meaning, "worship" is construed narrowly, and so the objects of idolatry are things like false gods and the physical artifacts meant to represent them. Yet there is also an extended sense of "idolatry" that results from analogously extended senses of "worship" and the "gods" that are the objects of worship. On the extended sense, idolatry entails treating something other than God as the center and source of all value. In both its initial and extended senses, idolatry inverts the creator/creature relationship because it involves treating something created as if it were ultimate. With this brief account of idolatry in place, we are in a better position to understand what idolatry is not.

---

[10] This extended sense of idolatry has become more prominent in the modern period, but even the early church had a notion of idolatry broader than that of worshiping human artifacts. See, for instance, Origen's *Homilies on Jeremiah* 5:2 (on Jer. 3:22): "For we confess no other god, as the gluttonous do the belly...nor silver as do the lovers of money, nor greed, which is idolatry, nor do we make anything else God and divinize it, as the multitude do." In Origen, *Homilies on Jeremiah and 1 Kings 28*, trans. John Clark Smith. Fathers of the Church (Washington, DC: Catholic University of America Press, 1998), 43. Tertullian's treatise on idolatry opens with an argument that every sin involves idolatry and idolatry includes every sin, for instance (Tertullian, *De idolatria*, 1). The extended sense is also implicitly present in Augustine's distinction between the love of enjoyment and the love of use (in *De doctrina christiana*). It is a sin to love god with the love of use, and to love anything else with the love of enjoyment.

[11] Karl Barth, "The First Commandment as an Axiom of Theology," in H. Martin Rumscheidt, ed., *The Way of Theology in Karl Barth: Essays and Comments* (Eugene, OR: Pickwick, 1986), 69. See also *Catechism of the Catholic Church*, 2113–14.

[12] John Calvin, *Institutes of the Christian Religion* (1559), ed. J. T. MacNeill, trans. F. L. Battles (London: S. C. M. Press, 1961), 4.17.36. Calvin is talking about the practice of Eucharistic adoration, but the question is helpful whether it hits or misses its target here.

Idolatry Isn't Just Being Wrong about God

We need to preserve the distinction between being wrong about God and wrongly worshiping something other than God. In this life, both may be inevitable, but only the latter is idolatry. We need to preserve this distinction even if we accept the extended senses of "idolatry" and "worship." Someone who is very mistaken about God—who holds many false beliefs about God—may be much more likely to treat something other than God as the center and source of value, and to organize his life around pursuing that other thing. Being mistaken about God may well dispose one to idolatry, in this sense. But the two are not identical.[13]

It might be tempting to think that there is no real distinction between being wrong about God and wrongly worshiping something other than God. Surely we must be able to identify the God we want to worship in order to orient our worship correctly. After all, if we cannot identify God correctly, then we cannot successfully worship God. And if most of our beliefs about God are false, then surely we cannot identify God correctly. So the distinction between being wrong about God and worshiping the wrong God seems to collapse. This line of thought is tempting, but it is also misguided. It implies that we need a correct definite description of God in order to worship God—something like "the Creator of heaven and earth" or "Father, Son, and Holy Spirit." The term "definite description" is a bit of philosophical jargon, but the idea is straightforward. First, a definite description is supposed to pick out just and only the one unique object that satisfies the description. So the definite description "author of Hamlet" picks out just and only William Shakespeare, assuming that Shakespeare is indeed the author of Hamlet. Second, a definite description always refers to whatever it is that uniquely satisfies that description. So if it turns out that Shakespeare did not write Hamlet, then "author of Hamlet" would refer to whoever did, in fact, write Hamlet—even if that person is otherwise unknown to us.

On this understanding of reference, if we try to worship God under a false definite description, then our acts of worship would misfire, because they would not refer to God at all. If we add to this account of reference a sufficiently expansive account of idolatry, then we might even think that our false definite descriptions are themselves akin to idols, such that our false worship becomes idolatry, just because we hold false beliefs about God. Yet this is not a good account of reference, nor a good account of worship, nor a good account of idolatry. We can successfully refer to God and worship God using false definite descriptions. It follows that being wrong about God does not entail wrongly worshiping something other than God.

---

[13] For a similar argument, see Richard Cross, "Idolatry and Religious Language," *Faith and Philosophy* 25 (2008): 190.

A mundane example first: Suppose you and a friend are at a party and you see a man across the room who is drinking what appears to be champagne from a champagne flute and who appears to be wearing a nice watch. You say to your friend "That guy drinking champagne has a nice watch!" Now, suppose your friend happens to know that the man in question is drinking water, not champagne, from his flute. What if your friend then says to you "Ha! No one over there is drinking champagne! As a result of your false beliefs, your expression is empty and you have not referred to anyone at all!" Your friend is being a jerk. You did refer to the man. You had a false belief about him, to be sure, but it was a false belief about *him*, that guy, the guy to whom you successfully referred.[14]

Now a more theological example: Suppose the Thomists are correct, and God's essence and existence are identical. But suppose too that for a variety of reasons, this proposal just makes no sense to you, and so you deny it. What's more, not only do you deny the proposal; you regularly publish academic articles attempting to refute it. But you are motivated throughout by a sincere and pious desire to understand the God of Abraham, Isaac, and Jacob—the God of Jesus Christ—as well as you can, and you also recognize (indeed, feel very keenly) how limited your ability to understand God really is. Although the differences are stark, you respect your intellectual opponents and treat them with humility and Christian charity: you are all engaged in the same noble project of theological inquiry after all. By hypothesis, you are mistaken about God. But are you guilty of idolatry because you have failed to refer to God at all? I submit that the answer is no. To say otherwise is to collapse idolatry into being wrong about God.

To avoid confusion down the line: I have argued that we can successfully worship God even when many of our definite descriptions of God are incorrect. But this claim does not entail that correct definite descriptions are useless. Free from jargon, the point is obvious: we can successfully refer to God even with a false description, but, of course, we can also refer to God with a true description. In fact, a correct definite description of God really would uniquely refer to God. (On the assumption that God really does create everything else *ex nihilo*, then the description "Creator *ex nihilo* of the universe" really does refer to God.) So a correct definite description of God can indeed help us worship God and avoid idolatry, even though affirming false definite descriptions does not entail that we do fall into idolatry.

[14] This example is adapted from Keith Donnellan, "Reference and Definite Descriptions," *Philosophical Review* 75 (1966): 281–304. Without going too far afield, let me say summarily that according to the best contemporary accounts of reference, we can successfully refer to an object even when we hold many false beliefs about that object, so long as we intend to refer to that object. In addition to Donnellan (above), a foundational source for this view is Saul Kripke, *Naming and Necessity* (Cambridge, MA: Harvard University Press, 1980). See also William Alston, "Referring to God," *International Journal for Philosophy of Religion* 24 (1988): 113–28; John Allen Knight, "Descriptivist Reference and the Return of Classical Theism," in Jeanine Diller and Asa Kasher, eds., *Models of God and Alternative Ultimate Realities* (Dordrecht: Springer, 2013), 207–23.

For consider the alternative: if we cannot worship God under false definite descriptions, then many—perhaps most—acts of worship would misfire. I would venture to say that most ordinary Christians throughout history have probably worshiped God under some very anthropomorphic (and therefore false) descriptions, even though they have intended to worship the God of their ancestors and the God of the Christian tradition. Even a minimally accurate description like "Creator of heaven and earth" or "the Supreme Being" is probably not what many religious adherents actually have in mind when they worship, for example. The point is even stronger for anything more theologically sophisticated, like "one substance in three persons" or "metaphysically simple." Intuitions will vary here, but if our theory of idolatry requires that most Christians throughout history have accidentally failed to worship God at all, then our theory comes at too high a cost, especially when better alternatives are available. Furthermore, given my target audience (contemporary theologians who are skeptical of analytic theology), it is important to emphasize that someone with a strong account of divine transcendence and a highly apophatic theology actually has even more reason to reject the idea that we need a correct definite description in order to worship God. If you think that finite human beings cannot form any correct concept of God, but you still want to say that we must praise and worship God, then you should welcome an account of reference that does not require worshipers to have correct definite descriptions of God. On the narrow construal of "worship" and "idolatry," it therefore seems that we must distinguish between worshiping the wrong God (idolatry) and being wrong about God (cognitive error).

Extended Idolatry: Still Not Just Being Wrong about God

Even in its extended sense, idolatry is meant to be a kind of wrongly directed worship and so we still must distinguish idolatry from merely holding false beliefs about God. Consider these two scenarios:

(A) I have been very badly catechized, and so I believe that God—the God of Jesus Christ, and the God of Abraham, Isaac, and Jacob—wants me to make as much money as possible and live the most lavish lifestyle I can manage. But in spite of myself, I take a low-paying job so that I will have more time to care for sick family members, I volunteer at a homeless shelter, and I live modestly. By my own lights, I'm a bad Christian.

(B) I explicitly consider myself a devout Christian, and nod piously whenever someone tells me that Christ calls us to love the poor, but I act as though money is the ultimate good, and I organize my life around the pursuit of wealth. So, in a way, money is my real "God," despite my own self-understanding.

In scenario (A), I hold a false belief about God, but even in the extended sense of worship it does not seem that I worship something other than God. In scenario (B), even though my explicit beliefs about God are true, I still count as an idolater because my worship (in the extended sense) is thoroughly misdirected.

This is just a toy example, but it gets at an important point. We are trying to understand whether analytic theology leads to idolatry because of the distinctively analytic approach to thinking about God. I suspect that some critics of analytic theology might say that analytic theologians fall into idolatry because they somehow elevate their own reason above God. But in order to make this case, we would have to show that (many? most?) analytic theologians look like the person in scenario B, and treat their own reason as the ultimate good, as the center and source of value, and organize their lives around their own reason. I am prepared to accept that this scenario is possible: deifying one's own reason in this sense seems to be a species of the sin of pride, and every Christian should agree that the sin of pride is an ever-present temptation. But we cannot just assume that this form of self-deification uniquely pervades analytic theology.

The distinction between being wrong about God and worshiping the wrong God is also important because the two errors call for very different responses. The right response to philosophers and theologians who inadvertently arrive at mistaken conclusions about God in the course of their research is to show why those conclusions are mistaken, not to demand that they repent of the sin of idolatry. In other words, the proper response is further argument. The proper response to idolaters is prophetic denunciation, moral exhortation, and a call to repentance. The sin of idolatry is very grave, and so we must be careful not to see it where it does not exist. Nor should we offer prophetic denunciation as a way of sidestepping the intellectual demand for rational argument. To accuse intellectual opponents of idolatry is to say that as a result of their views they fall so far outside the boundaries of acceptable Christian discourse that they worship another God altogether. If they have *that* problem, then it would be otiose to argue with them. An idolater does not even succeed in being wrong about the Christian God, since he does not successfully refer to that God at all. But when someone is wrong about God, even massively wrong, the right theological response is to show why they are wrong, with arguments.

Conceptual Idolatry

Contemporary theology may indeed be haunted by the specter of idolatry, but the anxiety does not seem to be about idolatry in its initial or even extended senses. Rather, the anxiety concerns another, relatively recent form of idolatry—"conceptual idolatry."[15] The anxiety arises from a heightened sense of divine

---

[15] The contemporary critique of conceptual idolatry does have some grounding in the patristic tradition. See, for example, Gregory of Nyssa, *Life of Moses*, 81: "The divine word at the beginning

transcendence filtered through French phenomenology by way of Martin Heidegger and Immanuel Kant. Jean-Luc Marion succinctly expresses the key worry: "When a philosophical thought expresses a concept of what it names 'God,' this concept functions exactly as an idol."[16] The claim is straightforward, and rests on a prior account of God's absolute transcendence: we cannot form any concept of God, and so whatever we take ourselves to be thinking about when we think about "God" is not really God at all, but an idol. The line of thought here, I take it, is something like this: God is absolutely transcendent. So, when we think about God, and especially when we make predicative assertions or ascribe properties to God, we necessarily fail, because we simply cannot grasp God with our creaturely concepts. Instead, we construct for ourselves mental simulacra, false concepts of "God" that we can grasp, precisely because we have constructed them ourselves. Sometimes this act of construction can even be described as violent. John Caputo writes:

> we must not do violence to God; we must respect God's transcendence. We must take every means to avoid compromising God, reducing God to something less than God is. We do not want to turn the creator into a human creation; to make God the image and likeness of man; to worship an idol, a graven image.[17]

In short, someone falls into conceptual idolatry when his own concept of God takes the place of the real God as the object of his inquiry and worship. This error can even be regarded as an act of violence against the real God. Here many analytic philosophers, who are perhaps too literal-minded, will object: surely no one, ever, in the whole history of the human race, has actually mistaken his own *concept* of God for the real God and accidentally worshiped it. ("Oh glorious concept, I bow down before you as the omnipotent creator of the universe.") The whole idea is indeed ridiculous—which is, of course, a reliable sign that this overly literal objection must have missed the point. Something else must be going on.

One possibility is that "conceptual idolatry" is just a baroque formulation of the same problem discussed above, the problem of being wrong about God. It seems inarguable that God surpasses our cognitive grasp. So, when we think about God, or try to describe God, it therefore seems certain that we will often miss the mark. Perhaps this is all that is meant by conceptual idolatry: we falsely

forbids that the Divine be likened to any of the things known by man, since every concept that comes from some comprehensible image, by an approximate understanding and by guessing at the Divine nature, constitutes an idol of God and does not proclaim God." Note, however, that even here the worry is specifically about concepts that come from "some comprehensible image" of God, whereas the contemporary worry seems to concern any form of thinking about God with concepts.

[16] Marion, "God without Being," 16.
[17] John Caputo, "How to Avoid Speaking of God: The Violence of Natural Theology," in *The Prospects for Natural Theology*, ed. Eugene Long (Washington, DC: Catholic University of America Press, 1992), 129.

believe that we can explain God or represent God comprehensively to ourselves, when we cannot. If this is all there is to conceptual idolatry, then it is merely a cognitive error, the error of being mistaken about God and about our own limitations. In that case, it would not really be a form of idolatry at all. Yet it certainly seems as if there is more to the charge of conceptual idolatry: the very rhetoric of "idolatry," let alone the rhetoric of violence (discussed below), suggests that conceptual idolatry is a sin, something for which we are morally culpable.

From Conceptual Idolatry to Conceptual Violence

To that end, it is useful to set Jean-Luc Marion's critique of conceptual idolatry in its wider context:

> The concept consigns to the sign what at first the mind grasps with it...but such a grasp is measured not so much by the amplitude of the divine as by the scope of a *capacitas*, which can fix the divine in a specific concept only at the moment when a conception of the divine fills it, hence appeases, stops, and freezes it. When a philosophical thought expresses a concept of what it names "God," this concept functions exactly as an idol.

Marion portrays concepts both as the agents and as the objects of the actions of others. The concept itself "consigns" the object of our cognition to a sign; the resulting conception then "fills," "appeases," "stops," and "freezes" our capacity for thought. Perhaps this is metaphorical language, but it is also quite revealing: for Marion, our concepts are active barriers that prevent God from appearing to us. Alternatively, concepts are also like containers, containers that can only hold so much. When they are full, when they have expanded to their full capacity, they become rigid and frozen, and so fix before the mind's eye something that, again, cannot be God, precisely because it has been successfully contained. He continues directly:

> It [a concept of God] gives itself to be seen, but thus all the better conceals itself as the mirror where thought, invisibly, has its forward point fixed, so that the *invisible* finds itself, with an aim suspended by the fixed concept, disqualified and abandoned; thought freezes, and the idolatrous concept of "God" appears, where, more than God, thought judges itself.[18]

The language is opaque, but the point is straightforward—although the metaphor has changed once again. Now, concepts have become mirrors. This change in

---

[18] Marion, "God without Being," 16.

metaphor makes it even more difficult to conceptualize God. Barriers can sometimes be porous, and containers can sometimes hold something. Conceptual mirrors can never reveal God. They can only present us with ourselves.

We should be wary of such metaphors. If we construe concepts differently, then perhaps the contemporary problem of conceptual idolatry will not loom so large. There is no single generally agreed-upon account of concepts. Depending on how one understands concepts, one may or may not face the problem of conceptual idolatry. Suppose that we take a Wittgensteinian view of concepts and say that "to have a concept of X" is just to be able to use the word X skillfully as a speaker of a natural language.[19] Or suppose we take Robert Brandom's pragmatist view and say that a concept is a norm of reasoning and judgement, such that to have a concept of X is to have the ability to use X correctly when drawing inferences.[20] On both accounts, having a concept is a kind of ability, and on either account, it is trivially easy to think *about* God—though, of course, we might still be very mistaken in what we think.

Marion has taken some common Kantian metaphors about concepts and intensified them. Kant distinguishes between the phenomenal world, the empirical world of appearances, and the noumenal world, the world of "things in themselves" that by definition cannot be objects of sensory experience. In Kant, concepts are like filters that stand between our conscious experience and the sensory manifold that constitutes the phenomenal world. Whatever the world is like in itself, we can only experience the world as always already filtered through our concepts. Noumenal objects—like God—that cannot pass through our conceptual filters cannot be objects of experience or knowledge. By definition, God transcends the world of sensory experiences, so we cannot have any empirical concept of God. But God is not like an abstract mathematical object either, and so we do not grasp truths about God a priori, the way we might grasp that a triangle is a figure with three angles and three straight sides. Because Kant thinks that knowledge can only be sensory/empirical or conceptual/a priori, he concludes that we therefore cannot have any *knowledge* of God, but he does not conclude that we cannot even think about God or refer to God.[21] Marion takes this further step. According to Marion, by trying to think about God using concepts that cannot apply to God, we are trying to turn God into the kind of thing we *can* think about, which is an attempt to constrain and confine God. This is akin to an act of violence. After all, it is an act of violence to try to force something to fit through an

---

[19] See M. R. Bennett and P. M. S. Hacker, *Philosophical Foundations of Neuroscience* (Malden, MA: Blackwell, 2003), 339–40.

[20] See Robert Brandom, *Articulating Reasons* (Cambridge, MA: Harvard University Press, 2000). Kevin Hector develops Brandom's idea into a theological semantics in his *Theology without Metaphysics* (Cambridge: Cambridge University Press, 2011), 103–47.

[21] See Andrew Chignell, "As Kant Has Shown: Analytic Theology and the Critical Philosophy," in Crisp and Rea, *Analytic Theology*, 117–35.

unsuitable filter, and no less an act of violence to try to force something into an insufficiently capacious container.

If human concepts are like containers, and if thinking about things with the wrong concepts is a way of violently confining them, then it is easy to see how being wrong about an object can equate to doing violence to that object. Likewise, if concepts are like mirrors, then thinking about the Other entails forcing the Other to be like the Self, another kind of violence. This may all sound very puzzling to analytic ears, but the assumption that thinking can be a form of violence is well established in the continental tradition; here Marion joins a philosophical lineage that includes Nietzsche, Heidegger, Levinas, and Derrida.[22] Indeed, Marion's sharpest theological critics do not convict him of rhetorical excess but of failing to go far enough. According to Caputo, Marion "does not escape the violence he wants to avoid," and indeed "provokes an even greater violence"; he is "not innocent of the originary ontological violence" associated with language itself.[23] In plain language, and in a somewhat different context, Kevin Hector helpfully shows what is at stake:

> The danger is obvious: if one thinks that one's preconceived ideas correspond to an object's fundamental reality, one may be tempted to force the object to fit one's conception of it, whether because one fails to see anything beyond one's conception or, worse, because one tries to make it conform to that conception. We see this sort of violence at its most graphic when human persons are its object—when, for instance, a woman or a person of color is allowed to "show up" only insofar as he or she fits within one's prior conception of femininity, blackness, and so on, and when his or her attempts to transcend these conceptual boundaries are met with implicit or explicit resistance.[24]

The danger, in short, is the danger of denying the otherness of the other—of forcing an object to conform to what we assume must be the case, rather than allowing the object to be what it truly is. With this account before us, it is easy to see why the rhetoric of "conceptual idolatry" brings with it the language of sin and moral opprobrium. Because we cannot cognize the incomprehensible God, we turn God

---

[22] SeeDavid Bentley Hart, *The Beauty of the Infinite* (Grand Rapids, MI: Eerdmans, 2004), 2:

> A certain current within contemporary philosophy, however, asserts that violence is—simply enough—inescapable: wherever Nietzsche's narrative of the will to power has been absorbed into the grammar of philosophical reflection, and given rise to a particular practice of critical suspicion, a profound prejudice has taken root to the effect that every discourse is reducible to a strategy of power, and every rhetorical transaction to an instance of an original violence,

Hart rightly adds that Christian theologians cannot simply ignore the challenge that every discourse is violent, because the Christian narrative of sin and fall makes the same challenge.

[23] Caputo, "How to Avoid Speaking of God," 131, 142.

[24] Hector, *Theology without Metaphysics*, 11.

into something we can cognize, and reduce God to the "God" of our thoughts, a human artifact: an idol.

Reformulating Conceptual Idolatry

But again—these are only metaphors. Concepts are not literal barriers or filters, and even if Kant is right and there is a "real" world of uncognizable things-in-themselves, there is no reason to believe that we are literally containing, constraining, or acting violently toward its denizens when we think about them or refer to them. People can form concepts *about* violence, or act violently as a result of their concepts, but their *concepts* cannot literally be violent. To be sure, there are those who think otherwise. But a picture holds them captive—another metaphor—the picture of concepts as barriers, or filters, or distorting lenses, or even as violent border guards.

Kant's Copernican revolution purports to establish that we actively construct our first-personal experiences, as the mind imposes concepts on the non-conceptual sensory manifold. Conscious experience, then, is something we *do*, not just something that just washes over us. However much they may disagree with aspects of the Kantian program, phenomenologists like Marion follow Kant in taking subjective thinking and experiencing as the objects of their inquiry.[25] Phenomenology is the study of human consciousness as experienced from the first-person point of view. For those steeped in contemporary phenomenology, the central theological question therefore becomes: How can we represent God to ourselves, when God is unrepresentable by human concepts?

By and large, analytic theologians do not ask this question, because they do not endorse Kant's account of concepts, or his broader epistemological idealism, and because they do not take subjective experience as the object of their inquiry. To be clear: the mere fact that analytic theologians differ on these fundamental matters does not entail that they are correct and their phenomenological colleagues are misguided. But the questions that preoccupy contemporary phenomenologists are simply unasked by many analytic philosophical theologians. So a fruitful dialogue between analytic and non-analytic theologians about the problem of conceptual idolatry must step back and first try to come to terms with the legacy of Kant.

The rhetoric of conceptual violence and conceptual idolatry makes some sense in the thought-world of contemporary phenomenology, which remains deeply Kantian. But its moral force relies on a subtle equivocation between two different senses of what it is to be an "object." If we construe "object" in phenomenological

---

[25] For a good survey of the influence of Kantian epistemology on later phenomenology, see Tom Rockmore, *Kant and Phenomenology* (Chicago: University of Chicago Press, 2011).

terms, as "intentional object," that is, as something that exists in the mind, then it is easier to treat thinking as a kind of violence. Intentional objects are constituted through our concepts.[26] Thinking about an intentional object with the wrong concepts in turn constitutes that object wrongly. Perhaps this could be a kind of "phenomenological violence." But phenomenological violence does not itself entail any act of real-world violence against any extra-mental object. Hence the subtle equivocation: what really matters is extra-mental violence, but the critique aims only at phenomenological violence. We should not overstate this point—the two are related. (Thinking violent thoughts might lead someone to engage in real-world violence against a real-world object.) But they are not the same—especially not when the object of our thought is God. We cannot literally do violence to God, or harm God, or even, really, dishonor God. We can think about God wrongly, perhaps even violently, but that has no impact whatsoever on God.

Thinking about God in the Wrong Way

This point suggests a way forward, and a better way to understand conceptual idolatry. Conceptual idolatry is not just being wrong about God. Conceptual idolatry also requires thinking about God *in the wrong way*. From a Christian-theological perspective, it is certainly possible to think about God in the wrong way. God is our creator and redeemer, and surpasses our comprehension. Accordingly, we should think about God with reverence, gratitude, and humility. To think about God in the wrong way would be to negate these attitudes. Such a negation would not harm God, but it would harm *us*, because it would orient us away from God, and prevent us from treating God as the center and source of value. It would prevent us from worshiping God. But this means that, like other forms of idolatry, conceptual idolatry is determined more by the *way* we think about God than by *what* we think about God. Conceptual idolatry is finally an affective and attitudinal error and not just a cognitive error. This is not surprising, since idolatry is always a kind of wrongly directed worship, and worship is more affective and attitudinal than cognitive.

How to Avoid Idolatry

These reflections suggest what we must do to avoid idolatry. First and foremost, we must not worship anything other than God. We can understand "worship" here in both its narrow, explicitly religious sense, and in its extended sense: we

---

[26] In this sense, Pegasus is an intentional object when I think about Pegasus, regardless of whether Pegasus exists outside the mind.

must not treat anything other than God as ultimate, or as the center and source of value, that around which we order our lives. At the same time, the discourse on conceptual idolatry has shown that there is another component to idolatry: we must not worship God (the real God) in the wrong way. But worshiping God in the wrong way is not primarily a matter of holding false beliefs about God but about one's affective and attitudinal response to God. We must approach God with love, reverence, gratitude, and humility. In short, we must approach God as creatures before their Creator.

To reiterate a point I made above: idolatry inverts the creator/creature distinction because it involves treating something created as if it were ultimate. But when get the Creator creature/distinction right, we are more likely to avoid idolatry. So even though idolatry is not fundamentally a matter of having false beliefs about God, it is still important to get the creator/creature distinction right. Robert Sokolowski has formulated a nearly canonical version of this distinction:

> Christian theology is differentiated from pagan religious and philosophical reflection primarily by the introduction of a new distinction, the distinction between the world understood as possibly not having existed and God understood as possibly being all that there is, with no diminution of goodness or greatness.[27]

I endorse this formulation without reservation.[28] At the risk of redundancy, I would now like to quote several other, more or less equivalent formulations from Sokolowski and David Burrell. Like the charge of idolatry itself, the "creator/creature distinction" has been weaponized in contemporary theological polemics. Critics of analytic theology frequently claim that leading analytic theologians fall into idolatry precisely because they misunderstand this distinction.[29] Given this fact, I want to be especially clear about what the distinction is, using the exact words of those who commend it:[30]

> But in the Christian distinction, God is understood as "being" God entirely apart from any relation of otherness to the world or to the whole. God could and would be God even if there were no world. Thus the Christian distinction is appreciated as a distinction that did not have to be, even though it in fact is. The

---

[27] Sokolowski, *God of Faith and Reason*, 23.

[28] Sokolowski calls this "the Christian distinction," but David Burrell adds the helpful point that Judaism and Islam also affirm a maximally sharp distinction between creator and creature. See his *Faith and Freedom: An Interfaith Perspective* (Malden, MA: Blackwell, 2004), 3–19.

[29] For example, David Burrell, "Creator/Creatures Relation: 'The Distinction' vs. 'Ontotheology,'" *Faith and Philosophy* 25 (2008): 177–89; Brian Davies, *The Reality of God and the Problem of Evil* (New York: Continuum, 2006), 52–54; Trakakis, "Does Univocity Entail Idolatry?," 543–46; David Bentley Hart, *The Experience of God*, 126–34.

[30] The following quotations are all from Sokolowski, *God of Faith and Reason*, 32–33.

most fundamental thing we come to in Christianity, the distinction between the world and God, is appreciated as not being the most fundamental thing after all, because one of the terms of the distinction, God, is more fundamental than the distinction itself...

It is not just that things could have been very different from the way they are; we are now to speak of things, and of the whole, as possibly not having been at all...

In Christian faith God is understood not only to have created the world, but to have permitted the distinction between himself and the world to occur. He is not established as God by the distinction (whereas pagan gods are established by being different than other things). No distinction made within the horizon of the world is like this, and therefore the act of creation cannot be understood in terms of any action or any relationship that exists in the world.

All of these quotations, in various ways, make the same point: the Christian concept of God entails that God is metaphysically ultimate. God might have been all that is; everything other than God has been created and might not have existed. Furthermore, the act of creation—understood as creation *ex nihilo*—is not like any form of intra-worldly causation. *Creatio non est mutatio*: creation is not a change, as the Thomists put it.[31] Exactly so.

Burrell makes more or less the same points in a 2008 *Faith and Philosophy* symposium on the creator/creature distinction and "ontotheology."[32] (I address the question of ontotheology in Chapter 8. For now, let it mean simply "treating God as a being among beings."):

a coherent characterization of the creator must highlight the unique and ineffable relation between creatures and creator...

"The distinction" then becomes a way of gesturing towards what indeed distinguishes those who believe the universe to be freely created by one God from anyone else. For the God in question would be God without creating all-that-is, so much so that everything-that-is adds nothing to the perfection of being of such a One. (To use a familiar abstract descriptor, that is what "monotheism" entails; not a simple reduction of the number of gods to one.) What makes this so significant philosophically is that it forbids any ordinary brand of "onto-theology" wherein a notion of being can be stretched to include the creator as well as creation...

Any piece of writing which proceeds to talk about "God" without adverting to this "distinction" cannot help but speak about an item in the universe, better called "god."

---

[31] Thomas Aquinas, *Summa Theologiae* 1.45.2 ad 2.
[32] The following quotations are all taken from David Burrell "Creator/Creatures Relation," 178–80.

Sokolowski and Burrell both argue that we can avoid idolatry only by preserving the creator/creature distinction. That distinction, in turn, arise from the basic Christian claim that God creates out of nothing, so that everything other than God depends on God for its existence, and God depends on nothing whatsoever for his existence. Furthermore, on this view, God would not be diminished in any way if God had not created.

For the sake of economy and easy reference, and not out any conceptual sleight of hand, I would like to distill the previous quotations into two related claims. On my reading, in order to preserve the creator/creature distinction, and as an aid to avoiding idolatry, one's theological views must be consistent with both claims:

(Divine Uniqueness): God is ontologically distinct from everything other than God. If there are "modes" or "manners" or "ways" of existing, then God and creatures do not have the same mode, manner, or way of existing.

(Divine Ultimacy): God and only God is ultimate. God depends on nothing else for his existence, causal powers, or real attributes; everything other than God depends on God for its existence, causal powers, and attributes.

Theological views that are consistent with (Divine Uniqueness) and (Divine Ultimacy) successfully preserve the creator/creature distinction and repudiate the cognitive errors that are likely to lead to idolatry. As I read it, (Divine Ultimacy) captures what is at stake in the extended sense of idolatry: someone who affirms (Divine Ultimacy) will also affirm that God is the center and source of all value. (Divine Uniqueness) and (Divine Ultimacy) also rule out the suggestion that God is a "thing in the world" or "a being among beings" in the sense deprecated by contemporary theological opponents of idolatry.[33]

Even so, by themselves (Divine Uniqueness) and (Divine Ultimacy) are not enough to ward off idolatry. Idolatry is fundamentally a matter of false worship and, as discussed above, false worship is more than false believing. It follows that we cannot avoid idolatry solely by affirming views consistent with (Divine Uniqueness) and (Divine Ultimacy). We need a third condition, one that requires us to approach God worshipfully. I propose:

(Worship): When thinking about God, think only with an attitude of worship, i.e., with adoration, reverence, awe, love, obedience, humility, and gratitude. Direct attitudes of worship only to God.

---

[33] Some analytic theologians and philosophers of religion would want to qualify my (Divine Ultimacy) so that necessarily existing abstract objects do not depend for their existence on God. I take it that this is Peter van Inwagen's view, for example. See Peter van Inwagen, "God and Other Uncreated Things," in Kevin Timpe, ed., *Metaphysics and God: Essays in Honor of Elenore Stump* (New York: Routledge, 2009), 3–20. That is not my own view, but I acknowledge that the question is a difficult one.

(Worship) is a bit vague, I admit, and its list of worshipful attitudes is not meant to be exclusive or exhaustive. But I hope it still conveys enough about what it would be like to approach God in a non-idolatrous way. When we add (Worship) to (Divine Uniqueness) and (Divine Ultimacy), we have a full picture of how to avoid idolatry: we can avoid idolatry by maintaining the creator/creature distinction and by regarding God, and only God, with a worshipful attitude. So when we want to know whether any general form of theology or any individual instance of theology is idolatrous, we should look for violations of the creator/creature distinction and negations of the attitude of worship.

I want to be completely transparent about where I have ended up. According to some theologians, the creator/creature distinction logically entails a variety of additional controversial theological views: divine simplicity, for example, or the Thomist account of primary and secondary causation, or that divine and creaturely attributes are incommensurable.[34] As a result, those theologians will likely insist that anyone who does not affirm these further views *ipso facto* violates the creator/creature distinction and falls into idolatry. For instance, advocates of divine simplicity argue that only a simple God could be metaphysically fundamental in the way required by (Divine Uniqueness) and (Divine Ultimacy).[35] They may be right. But they are not *obviously* right. In other words, it is not simply obvious that either the doctrine of divine simplicity or the other views mentioned above are true, still less that they are logically entailed by the creator/creature distinction.[36] Someone who thinks they are so entailed owes the rest of us some good arguments to that effect. In the wake of the Fall, it is not easy to grasp all the subtle entailments of the doctrine of creation. More to the point, it is highly uncharitable to assume that anyone who denies these further views also denies the creator/creature distinction and falls into idolatry—not least because idolatry is not finally a matter of false believing at all, but wrongful worship. What matters for avoiding idolatry is affirming the creator/creature distinction as captured by (Divine Uniqueness) and (Divine Ultimacy) and approaching God with an attitude of (Worship).

---

[34] On the claim that divine and creaturely attributes are incommensurable, see Chapter 9. On the distinction between God's primary causation and secondary creaturely causation, see W. Matthews Grant, *Free Will and God's Universal Causality: The Dual Sources Account* (London: Bloomsbury, 2019); Brian J. Shanley, "Divine Causation and Human Freedom in Aquinas," *American Catholic Philosophical Quarterly* 72 (1988): 99–122.

[35] David Bentley Hart, *The Experience of God*, 134–42. Edward Feser has defended this view at length across several blog posts. See especially "Why Is There Anything at all? It's Simple," http://edwardfeser.blogspot.com/2013/10/why-is-there- anything-at-all-its-simple.html, accessed May 15, 2019.

[36] The same goes for the univocity thesis (see Chapter 8) as well any particular account of the metaphysics of participation (the claim that created things participate in God's uncreated being and goodness).

Analytic Theology and the Creator/Creature Distinction

Do analytic theologians avoid idolatry? I think they do—or at least most of them do, most of the time. Certainly, there is nothing about the analytic method that entails idolatry. My full defense of this claim stretches across Chapters 8 and 9, which together discuss ontotheology, univocity, and so-called "theistic personalism." But the bedrock of that defense adverts to the claim that God creates and sustains everything out of nothing. Leading analytic theologians all explicitly affirm *creatio ex nihilo*, and along with it, the claim that everything that exists depends entirely upon God. Indeed, they often sound remarkably similar to their non-analytic counterparts on this point. Here, for instance, is Thomas V. Morris:

> Absolutely everything distinct from God depends on God for its existence. This is a foundational claim for any thoroughly theistic ontology. If God is the greatest possible being, a maximally perfect source of existence, then he is not just one more item in the inventory of reality. He is the hub of the wheel, the center and focus, the ultimate support, of all. The difference between theism and atheism is thus not just a disagreement over whether one entity of a certain description exists or not. It is a disagreement over the origin, and thus the ultimate nature, of everything.[37]

Here is T. J. Mawson, making the same point in a slightly more analytic idiom:

> God's creatordom amounts not simply to his being that without which the world could never have started...The world depends ultimately on God's will for its existence and its character...I am using the concept of creatordom here in a sense rather more restricted than it would be used in everyday life, one which might be captured by the phrase "ultimate creatordom." For X to be the ultimate creator of Y is for Y to be dependent on X and on nothing else more ultimately for its existence and character...any non-ultimate creator must depend ultimately on God for his or her existence and character and in particular for the "creative" powers that he or she has; and thus nothing is ultimately created by anything other than God—in the sense of dependent for its existence and character on something other than God and on nothing else more ultimately.[38]

Mawson concludes that God himself "is dependent on nothing for his existence and character; a fortiori, he is dependent on nothing else more ultimately for his existence and character."[39]

---

[37] Thomas V. Morris, *Our Idea of God* (Downers Grove, IL: InterVarsity Press, 1991), 155.
[38] T. J. Mawson, *Belief in God* (New York: Oxford University Press, 2005), 71.
[39] Mawson, *Belief in God*, 71.

Brian Leftow, perhaps the leading contemporary defender of analytic "perfect being theology," explicitly affirms *creatio ex nihilo* and endorses the continuous, metaphysical dependence of everything that exists on God:

> Now the Bible treats creating as criterial, as making the distinction between false and true deity: "the gods of the nations are but idols, but the Lord made the heavens." Creating everything is central to the Biblical picture of God. That He is the Creator of all is literally the first thing the Bible tells us about Him.[40]

Leftow is even careful to distinguish creating *ex nihilo* from other forms of causation:

> for all x, if x is not God, a part, aspect or attribute of God or an event, God makes the creating-*ex-nihilo* sort of causal contribution to x's existence as long as x exists.[41]

He goes on to argue that it is because God is our creator that we owe God love and obedience, and he offers a rich discussion of philosophical and biblical reasons to call God "*the* ultimate reality."[42] Finally, here is Timothy Pawl:

> According to Traditional Christian Theism, God is the author of all that exists— all besides God, that is. Nothing exists without originating from God as its source. Furthermore, Traditional Christian Theism also affirms that God was under no compulsion to create; the divine might have created nothing at all. Creation, Traditional Christianity teaches, is a gratuitous act.[43]

Even Richard Swinburne, the chief whipping boy of the "analytic theology is idolatry" crowd, holds that God creates and sustains all substances, properties, and laws of nature, and is therefore metaphysically ultimate:

> God is the creator and sustainer of any universe there may be in the sense that any substance that exists apart from himself exists because God causes it to exist as long as it exists or permits some other being to do so...If the universe (of substances other than God) had a beginning, God caused that beginning; and if it has always existed, God continually sustains it in being. Likewise substances have the properties, including their causal powers and liabilities, that they do because God keeps them in being having those properties, or allows some other being to do so. Laws of nature, that is, mundane substances having the causal

[40] Brian Leftow, *God and Necessity* (New York: Oxford University Press, 2012), 413.
[41] Leftow, *God and Necessity*, 20.   [42] Leftow, *God and Necessity*, 3.
[43] Timothy Pawl, "Traditional Christian Theism and Truthmaker Maximalism," *European Journal for Philosophy of Religion* 4 (2012): 198.

powers and liabilities that they do, operate because God causes them to operate (or allows some other being to do so).[44]

Some might think that Swinburne has an overly restricted notion of creation out of nothing since he repeatedly introduces concessions like "causes it to exist… *or permits some other being to do so.*"[45] These locutions might suggest that, according to Swinburne, things other than God also have the power to create, which might imply that Swinburne does not maintain the creator/creature distinction. Yet even though Swinburne does not regard the act of creation as a *sui generis* form of causation (as Thomists do), it does not follow that he thereby denies the creator/creature distinction altogether. So even though he does not think that the term "creation" just means "creation out of nothing," he is very clear that only God can create out of nothing, and that things other than God only have causal powers at all because God grants them such powers. Moreover, Swinburne also describes God's causality as "so pure, so great, and tied so essentially to one individual that *no other thing can be except as dependent on it.*"[46] From the wider context, it is clear that Swinburne holds that God creates out of nothing, sustains all things in existence, and—most importantly—functions as the only metaphysically ultimate cause of everything that is not God. This is still a picture of (Divine Ultimacy) and (Divine Uniqueness). These are the key claims that one needs to establish to maintain the creator/creature distinction. And, of course, even if it did turn out that Swinburne is a viable target of the "analytic idolatry" charge, then critics who make that charge should aim it at Swinburne alone, and not tar all analytic theologians with the same brush.

The fact that these analytic theologians so emphatically affirm the doctrine of creation out of nothing is strong evidence that they also affirm (Divine Uniqueness) and (Divine Ultimacy) and thereby avoid the cognitive errors associated with idolatry.[47] Of course, even strong evidence is defeasible, and it could be the case that each of these very careful thinkers accidentally endorses some further position that is incompatible with their own stated views about creation out of nothing, and therefore incompatible with (Divine Uniqueness) and (Divine Ultimacy). But at the very least, I think I have successfully placed the burden of proof on those who still want to pursue the idolatry charge against analytic theology. It falls to them, the critics, to show exactly where the inconsistency lies. Otherwise, hermeneutical charity demands that we take analytic theologians at their word, and regard them as innocent of the charge of idolatry.

---

[44] Richard Swinburne, *The Christian God* (New York: Oxford University Press, 1994), 128.

[45] My italics. Brian Davies criticizes Swinburne on this point in his *An Introduction to the Philosophy of Religion* (New York: Oxford University Press, 2000), 11–12.

[46] Swinburne, *The Christian God*, 152. My italics.

[47] On the question of whether they can maintain the attitude of (Worship), see Chapter 10.

8

The Real Trouble with Ontotheology and Univocity

Someone once asked Alvin Plantinga whether God is a being. "Of course, what else is there to be?" he replied.[1] For the good St. Alvin, to deny that God is a being is to deny that there is a God, that is, to affirm atheism. But when I mention this remark to theological colleagues, they tend to roll their eyes (or worse). They think that by calling God a being, Plantinga is turning God into an ordinary empirical object, like a plant or a table. In their view, if God is a being, then God can only be a thing in the world—in effect, an idol. Contemporary theologians are more apt to speak of God as "beyond Being" or as "the ground of Being" rather than as "a being." They understand "being" or "existence" to mean "creaturely being" or "created existence," and so they think, not unreasonably, that since God is the creator, God cannot exist in the same way that other things exist.

This chapter continues and extends the argument of Chapter 7. Like the broader discourse on idolatry, contemporary theological anxiety about whether God is "a being" emerges from an unexpected confluence of sources: continental phenomenology, Thomism—in both its classical and Wittgensteinian variants—and even grand-narrative style genealogies of modernity itself.[2] Whatever its sources, this theological anxiety has a name. In fact, it has two names: "ontotheology" and "univocity." As terms of theological opprobrium, they are coextensive, perhaps even equivalent. Ontotheology is the error of treating God as a being among beings; univocity affirms that Creator and creatures all fall under a single concept of *being*. Both seemingly lead to the same theological fault: the sin of idolatry. As Nick Trakakis helpfully puts the charge: "univocity entails a strong form of anthropomorphism that in effect treats God as a creature and thus succumbs to idolatry."[3] Ontotheology, therefore, presupposes univocity, and univocity entails ontotheology. Both are forms of idolatry. Or so it would seem.

---

[1] As reported in C. Stephen Evans, "On Taking God Seriously," in William J. Wainwright, ed., *God, Philosophy and Academic Culture* (New York: Oxford University Press, 1996), 64.

[2] "In other words, the proposition 'God is a being' itself appears as an idol, because it only returns the aim that, in advance, decides that every possible 'God,' present or absent, in one way or another, has to be" (Marion, *God without Being*, 44). See also John F. Wippel, *The Metaphysical Thought of Thomas Aquinas* (Washington, DC: Catholic University of America Press, 2000), 544, 560; Herbert McCabe, *God Matters* (New York: Continuum, 1987), 2–9; Hart, *The Experience of God*, 30; Brad Gregory, *The Unintended Reformation* (Cambridge, MA: Harvard University Press, 2012), 38.

[3] Trakakis, "Does Univocity Entail Idolatry?," 540.

Analytic Theology and the Academic Study of Religion. William Wood, Oxford University Press (2021). © William Wood.
DOI: 10.1093/oso/9780198779872.003.0008

To spell out the worry more fully: suppose we say that God exists and Socrates exists and that the word "exists" has the same meaning in both statements. To say that the word "exists" has the same meaning in both statements means that God and Socrates can both be grouped together under a single concept—perhaps the concept *existing things* or *beings*. But if God and Socrates can both be grouped together under a single concept, then (so the argument runs) that concept must refer to some real, extra-mental attribute that they both have in common. But God and Socrates cannot have any real attributes in common without either turning God into a creature or turning Socrates into God. Either way, univocity leads to idolatry.

Although the discourse on ontotheology and univocity tends to focus on the attribute of "being," the underlying worry generalizes to all divine attributes and all theological predications. The real problem is denying divine transcendence by reducing God to the level of a creature. We reduce God to the level of a creature when we treat God as a being among beings, but also (so runs the worry) when we say that the word "good" in "God is good" means the same thing as the word "good" in "Socrates is good." Once again, we seem to be picking out some real, extra-mental property that God and Socrates both share.[4] And once again, if God and Socrates can share properties, then God cannot be unique enough or transcendent enough to be anything other than some item in the world—an idol.

At first blush, analytic theology and philosophy of religion seem profoundly at odds with the contemporary hostility to ontotheology and univocity. As far as I can tell, most analytic thinkers are perfectly happy to agree that God is a being, and just as happy to say that "exists" can be used univocally of God and creatures.[5] They are similarly untroubled by other univocal predications like "is good" or "is wise." In fact, they find continental worries about ontotheology and univocity quite baffling. Yet, as discussed in Chapter 7, representative analytic thinkers also affirm creation out of nothing and endorse the creator/creature distinction. We should, therefore, try to understand the analytic commitment to univocity on its own terms, as something that makes sense given analytic presuppositions. This means understanding it as something other than an inexplicable fall into obvious idolatry. The alternative is to attribute gross inconsistency to thinkers who famously prize philosophical consistency.

---

[4] This worry is one reason why some contemporary theologians are keen to distinguish "divine names" from "divine attributes." Treating "goodness" as a divine name, rather than a divine attribute, is understood to be a way of avoiding univocity and ontotheology. Unlike attributes, "names of God" are "pre-eminently important for prayer, for praise, and for calling upon...the Lord. Names are important for being in relation...Names of God are not, in the first instance, the fruits of natural theology, but are disclosed in scripture," Janet Martin Soskice, "Names of God: Or Why Names Are Not Attributes," *New Blackfriars* 101 (2020): 184.

[5] Thomas Williams, "The Doctrine of Univocity Is True and Salutary," *Modern Theology* 21 (2005): 575–85; Marilyn Adams, "What's Wrong with the Ontotheological Error?" *Journal of Analytic Theology* 2 (2014): 3–8.

At the same time, few analytic thinkers have really taken the trouble to try to understand what motivates theological worries about ontotheology and univocity. The few published responses from analytic theologians and philosophers on these questions have too often looked like cheerleading aimed at the home team rather than serious efforts to understand and persuade their opponents.[6] Ontotheology is not some newly fashionable postmodern heresy, but the very same worry about idolatry already discussed in Chapter 7. It follows that analytic theologians should indeed worry about ontotheology, but as long as they avoid idolatry, they avoid ontotheology too.

With respect to univocity, nothing about the analytic method requires it, and there are important analytic thinkers who defend analogical predication.[7] But overall, it is fair to say that most analytic theologians do hold that positive terms can be predicated univocally of God and creatures.[8] Their commitment to univocity is not a commitment to ontotheology, however, because ontotheology and univocity are not actually equivalent.

Univocity can be understood in two ways. It can be understood as a semantic thesis, about the meanings of words, or as an ontological thesis, about sharing the same really existing, extra-mental properties. I call the latter "ontological sameness." When it comes to God and creatures, only the latter thesis is worrying, and only the latter is a form of ontotheology. Semantic univocity does not entail ontological sameness—not in general, and not with respect to "being" and "exists." Even though many analytic theologians do affirm semantic univocity, and do say that God is "a being," it does not follow that they endorse ontological sameness between God and creatures, violate the creator/creature distinction, or fall into ontotheology or idolatry.

---

[6] I would say that both Williams and Adams (note 4, above) fall into this trap. Williams defends Duns Scotus's account of univocity from contemporary misinterpretations, and argues that analogy collapses into either equivocation or univocity. He also points out that we can only formulate deductive arguments for God's existence with univocal terms. But he does not really try to understand why so many contemporary theologians (and not just the Radically Orthodox) continue to worry about univocity. For her part, Adams—unsurprisingly—is good on Plotinus, Augustine, Aquinas, and Scotus, but not so good on Heidegger and ontotheology. Her rhetorical strategy is to accept what she regards as Heidegger's wholesale identification of ontotheology with philosophical theology, further accept that Anselm, Aquinas, and Scotus are ontotheologians, and finally argue that ontotheology is not actually bad, because it can really be "a form of prayer" (12). I would run her argument in reverse: rightly understood, ontotheology actually is bad, but none of the aforementioned figures falls into ontotheology (though I do not attempt to exonerate them in the discussion below).

[7] Daniel Bonevac, "Two Theories of Analogical Predication," *Oxford Studies in the Philosophy of Religion* 4 (2012): 20–42; other analytic philosophers of religion who question univocity include Lorraine Juliano Keller, "Semantics for Divine Intrinsic Predications" (forthcoming) and "Defending Divine Ineffability" (forthcoming). See also Jonathan Jacobs, "The Ineffable, Inconceivable, and Incomprehensible God: Fundamentality and Apophatic Theology," *Oxford Studies in Philosophy of Religion* 6 (2015): 158–76.

[8] Everyone, even diehard Thomists—even Thomas himself—agrees that negations can be predicated univocally of God and creatures, so I restrict my argument to positive predications. I am also not considering incarnational predicates: everyone also agrees that, for example, when applied to the incarnate Word, "Christ is thirsty" and "Peter is thirsty" are univocal.

Ontotheology as Ontological Sameness

The real problem of ontotheology is the problem of "ontological sameness." Ontological sameness violates the creator/creature distinction because it ignores the difference between God and creatures. God and all of God's properties are uncreated; creatures and all of their properties are created. What is created cannot also be uncreated, so it follows that God and creatures cannot be ontologically the same, because they cannot share any really existing, extra-mental properties. Analytic thinkers do not always face this issue squarely. Too often they seem content to assume that God and creatures can share properties.[9] But this is a troubling view. Consider again the two theses from Chapter 7:

(Divine Uniqueness): God is ontologically distinct from everything other than God. If there are "modes" or "manners" or "ways" of existing, then God and creatures do not have the same mode, manner, or way of existing.

(Divine Ultimacy): God and only God is ultimate. God depends on nothing else for his existence, causal powers, or real attributes; everything other than God depends on God for its existence, causal powers, and attributes.

If we affirm (Divine Uniqueness) and (Divine Ultimacy), then to maintain consistency, we must also deny that God and God's creatures are ontologically the same with respect to their modes, manners, or ways of existing, and also with respect to any properties they instantiate. The challenge for analytic theologians is to show that they do not treat God and creatures as ontologically the same even if they hold that God is "a being," or claim that "exists" has the same meaning in "God exists" and "Socrates exists." Though they have mostly ignored this challenge so far, I am confident that they have the resources to meet it.

Heidegger's Critique of Ontotheology

Although my own argument is primarily constructive rather than genealogical or exegetical, it is useful to take a short detour into the historical origins of the contemporary anxiety about ontotheology. Many contemporary theologians think that metaphysics as such inevitably becomes idolatrously ontotheological, and a

---

[9] For example, in an article on divine transcendence, Jonathan Kvanvig writes, almost as an aside:

I shall simply assume, and not argue, that religious language must sometimes be univocally predicated of God and other beings...As I mean 'univocal predication', the fact that God has some of the same properties that other things have is sufficient for some religious language to be univocal. Thus, all I am assuming is that God and other things share some properties.   (Jonathan Kvanvig, "Divine Transcendence," *Religious Studies* 20 [1984]: 378).

fortiori any form of explicitly theistic metaphysics. Since theistic metaphysics is the bread and butter of analytic theology, a defense of analytic theology must also answer these charges. But the worry that metaphysics inevitably becomes ontotheological has a specific history, and understanding that history actually goes a long way toward dispelling the underlying worry.

The source, the ur-text, for the contemporary theological anxiety about ontotheology is a 1957 essay by Martin Heidegger called "The Ontotheological Constitution of Metaphysics."[10] This essay nicely encapsulates Heidegger's broader critique of metaphysics, which many contemporary theologians simply take for granted. It matters, therefore, quite a lot, that Heidegger's famous essay is actually the product of an academic seminar on Hegel. Whatever life the problem of ontotheology may now have among contemporary theologians, it began as a set of specific worries about *Hegel's* account of Being. Heidegger's critique of ontotheology really only generalizes to the degree that other metaphysical systems resemble Hegelian idealism. Of course, Heidegger himself thinks that Hegelian idealism is the high point of Western metaphysics, and so he thinks that critiquing Hegel is equivalent to critiquing metaphysics as such. But this is a highly contentious claim, to say the least.

Hegel is not a pantheist, but treating him like a pantheist is a useful fiction for those who know next to nothing about Hegelian idealism and only want to be able to make sense of Heidegger's critique. According to Hegel, God is the Absolute Mind, or Absolute Spirit (*Geist*). Furthermore, God can be identified with reality itself: God is the totality of everything that exists, understood as a teleological process. The teleological process of reality aims at God's own complete self-knowledge. The whole of reality is the process by which God, understood as the Absolute Mind, comes to know itself perfectly and completely *as* the whole of reality. Human consciousness is a moment in the Absolute Mind's own unfolding process of coming to understand itself. In this sense, "absolute truth" is a label that properly applies only to the Absolute Mind's own self-knowledge, and more precisely to the Absolute Mind's self-knowledge as devoid of all difference and particularity, since the Absolute knows itself truly only when it knows itself as the whole of reality.[11] Thus construed, the perspective of absolute truth is one that by definition effaces all real difference.

Hegel's system is a kind of immanent theistic monism: in the final analysis, everything that exists is God, who is identical to the world in flux, and who gradually comes to know itself (himself?) as the totality of existence. It is very easy to see why Hegel's metaphysics is ontotheological. Hegel's account of God as Absolute Mind (*Geist*) seems to erase every ontological distinction, not just the distinction between God and creatures. If *Geist* is all, then all is *Geist*, and so

---

[10] The essay may be found in Martin Heidegger, *Identity and Difference*, trans. Joan Stambaugh (New York: Harper and Row, 1969).

[11] Heidegger, *Identity and Difference*, 43.

everything collectively becomes identical to God. Yet, interestingly, on this scheme, God as *Geist* is still an individual being, a thinking subject—the only individual being, perhaps, but certainly not apophatically beyond being. God as *Geist* causes the whole of reality to exist, not via a transcendent act of creation, but through the immanent unfolding processes of intra-worldly causes and effects. In no sense does Hegel posit a radical distinction between creator and creature.

Heidegger's critique of metaphysics aims at Hegel in the first instance, but soon expands. All metaphysics is ontotheological, because all metaphysics tries to explain, and thereby erase, the difference between Being and beings. Here "beings" are concretely existing things, and Being is whatever it is that grounds their existence, akin to the way Goodness or the Good might ground the goodness of individual things.

To emphasize more perspicuously the distinction between universals and properties, on the one hand, and the individual bearers of those universals or properties, on the other, throughout the rest of this chapter I will use small capitals to denote universals, properties, and things that play the same causal and explanatory role as universals and properties (for example BEING and GOODNESS). I will also use italics to denote concepts (the concept of *being*, for example). According to Heidegger, Western metaphysics since its inception "has eminently been both ontology and theology."[12] Metaphysics, the study of the most general features of existence, seeks to explain why things exist. Metaphysics proceeds in one of two ways: Either it searches for the BEING that all beings have in common, analogous to the way all red things might be said to have REDNESS in common. This is ontology. Or metaphysics searches for the ground of BEING understood as the primary cause of BEING: that from which the BEING of beings derives, the Supreme Being. This is theology.[13]

"How does the deity enter into philosophy, not just modern philosophy, but philosophy as such?" asks Heidegger.[14] Western philosophy seeks answers, theories, and explanations. The deity enters philosophy as an explanation, as the answer to a question about the cause and ground of beings. Because philosophy sets the terms of the question, philosophy also predetermines the answer. The result is God as *causa sui*, the God of philosophy who is the self-caused cause of all BEING: "This is the metaphysical concept of God."[15] Yet this God, the God of metaphysics, is no God at all. "Man can neither pray nor sacrifice to this god. Before the *causa sui*, man can neither fall to his knees in awe nor can he play music and dance before this god."[16]

---

[12] Heidegger, *Identity and Difference*, 54.

[13] For Heidegger's understanding of the ancient Greek roots of ontotheology, see Iain Thomson, *Heidegger on Ontotheology* (Cambridge: Cambridge University Press, 2005), 31.

[14] Heidegger, *Identity and Difference*, 55.   [15] Heidegger, *Identity and Difference*, 60.

[16] Heidegger, *Identity and Difference*, 72. We should not assimilate the idea of God as *causa sui* (a being that causes itself) to God as "first cause" (a being that causes everything other than itself). Heidegger probably conflates the two, but Merold Westphal does not (see *Overcoming Ontotheology*

Fortunately, according to Heidegger, the God of metaphysics is now dead—killed by Nietzsche, who brought the whole explanatory tradition of Western metaphysics to a close. Heidegger believes that Nietzschean will to power is the ultimate conclusion of Western metaphysics. Nietzsche shows that *nothing* ultimately grounds and explains the nature of individual beings, and nothing explains reality as a whole. Rather, what metaphysicians call a "ground" or a "fundamental explanation" is simply the contingent result of their own all too human interpretive choices. There is no God and no deep explanation of reality—self-serving human beings interpret the world in self-serving ways and then call the result "God" or "metaphysics." After Nietzsche, all that is left of metaphysics is the will to power, or what Heidegger calls "the will to will."[17]

Technology is the "metaphysics of the atomic age," according to Heidegger, because metaphysics and technology each seek dominance, mastery, and control.[18] Metaphysics arises from a desire for intellectual mastery; it is an attempt to know the ultimate foundations of things so that we can classify them, order them, control them, and use them for our own purposes. Technology is the specific form that this general desire for mastery takes in our own era. It is both a way of manipulating the world and a way of seeing the world. Technology allows us to treat unique beings as undifferentiated cogs in an impersonal process. (Heidegger has in mind the technologies of the modern state bureaucracy and the automated factory assembly line.) Metaphysics and technology are both expressions of the same will to power. Both aim to eradicate genuine differences among beings and turn the other into the same. Furthermore, they both achieve this aim by categorizing and classifying beings. But these explanatory schemes are imposed. They are not innate or natural.

How to Avoid Ontotheology

Heidegger's critique of ontotheology seems uncompromising. But it is precisely here—with his portrait of metaphysics as will to power, dominance, mastery, and control—that we should seek a rapprochement with analytic theology. It is not surprising that contemporary theologians have turned Heidegger's critique of ontotheology into a critique of the sin of idolatry. Heidegger explicitly portrays

---

[New York: Fordham University Press, 2001], 4–7), and so Marilyn Adams's riposte to Westphal misses the mark: "Westphal's idea that we cannot sing and dance before the first cause fails to take seriously Who the first cause really is." (Adams, "What's Wrong with the Ontotheological Error?," 12). The substantive point is that analytic metaphysics does not presuppose the claim that everything that exists has a cause, and so analytic theism does not assume that because God exists, God must have a cause, from which it would follow that God could only be self-caused.

[17] Heidegger, *Identity and Difference*, 66.   [18] Heidegger, *Identity and Difference*, 52.

ontotheology in ethical terms, as an immoral bid for power and domination. But we can understand the moral valence of this critique in two ways. We can distinguish between ontotheology as an attitude or outlook, on the one hand, versus ontotheology as a set of false conclusions, on the other. From Chapter 7, it seems clear that only the former is akin to idolatry.

First, let us say that someone exhibits the "ontotheological attitude" when they unjustifiably and hubristically seek to control other beings and to erase real differences among them, and when they do this with an immoderate certainty about their own conclusions. In explicitly theological terms, we can say that ontotheology is an attempt to claim the divine perspective for oneself, or to appeal to God to advance one's own projects of dominance. As Merold Westphal puts it, "ontotheology consists in the pride that refuses to accept the limits of human knowledge." The critique of ontotheology "is directed not at *what* we say about God but at *how* we say it, to what purpose, in the service of what project."[19] So defined, the ontotheological attitude is incompatible with the attitude of (Worship) defined in Chapter 7:

(Worship):   When thinking about God, think only with an attitude of worship, i.e., with adoration, reverence, awe, love, obedience, humility, and gratitude. Direct attitudes of worship only to God.

So the way to avoid the ontotheological attitude, at least with respect to God, is to theorize with an attitude of worship. But we can still do metaphysics, even theistic metaphysics, with an attitude of worship. Some attempts to understand God better or theorize about God might be contrary to the attitude of worship, but there is no reason to assume that they all are.[20]

Second, from a Christian-theological point of view, ontotheological inquiry can lead to false conclusions about God in either of two ways. On the one hand, ontotheological inquiry might dissolve creaturely being into God's own being, the way Hegel seems to do. Here the divine BEING would function as something like a Platonic universal that other existing things instantiate in the way that (let's say) red things instantiate REDNESS.[21] On the other hand, ontotheological inquiry might offer the same explanation for God's being and for the being of other things. (Or, if you prefer, offer the same explanation for the fact that God exists and the fact that other things exist.) This move would portray God as "a being among beings" or "a thing in the world." It might also make God depend on BEING for his own existence, and thereby deny that God is metaphysically

---

[19] Merold Westphal, *Overcoming Ontotheology*, 7.   [20] See the argument in Chapter 10.

[21] Even theologians who defend a participatory ontology (see the discussion below) would not agree that creatures instantiate the divine attributes in the way that concrete particulars instantiate universals.

ultimate. In either case, ontotheology construed as set of false conclusions is not consistent with (Divine Uniqueness) and (Divine Ultimacy):

(Divine Uniqueness):   God is ontologically distinct from everything other than God. If there are "modes" or "manners" or "ways" of existing, then God and creatures do not have the same mode, manner, or way of existing.

(Divine Ultimacy):   God and only God is ultimate. God depends on nothing else for his existence, causal powers, or real attributes; everything other than God depends on God for its existence, causal powers, and attributes.

But theological views that *are* consistent with (Divine Uniqueness) and (Divine Ultimacy) successfully preserve the creator/creature distinction and, when combined with an attitude of (Worship) successfully avoid idolatry, and therefore also avoid ontotheology. As I concluded in Chapter 7, there is every good reason to think that leading analytic theologians do affirm (Divine Uniqueness) and (Divine Ultimacy) because they explicitly hold that God creates and sustains out of nothing. So there is every good reason to think they also avoid idolatry and ontotheology.[22]

Analytic theologians typically misunderstand the anxiety about ontotheology because they lack the intellectual background to see it as a genuine challenge at all. Yet it is very unlikely that any analytic theologian holds the self-evidently absurd view that God is "a thing in the world" in the sense of "an object in the created universe." Nor does any analytic theologian think that God depends on BEING for his own existence, or hold that BEING is somehow ontologically or causally prior to God. (As I discuss below, for the most part, they deny that there is any really existing property of BEING at all. If there is no such property at all, then God cannot depend on it for his existence.) Interpretive charity demands that we recognize these points. Unless they explicitly argue otherwise, we should assume that analytic theologians accept the creator/creature distinction and accept that there is a fundamental ontological difference between God, who is uncreated and uncaused, and everything other than God. Of course, they differ among themselves, and with non-analytic thinkers, about how to spell out this distinction, but this is not troubling, since there is no scriptural or creedal requirement that the creator/creature distinction must be spelled out in only one way.

---

[22] And as I also noted there, some analytic thinkers would qualify (Divine Ultimacy) so that God does not create necessarily existing abstract objects. Whether this qualification amounts to ontotheology is a question that I cannot pursue here, except to say that, of course, I am not committed to the claim that *every* analytic theologian or philosopher of religion avoids ontotheology.

Semantic Univocity and Ontological Sameness

Contemporary theologians may be riddled with anxiety about ontotheology, but they have been positively obsessed with univocity. In some respects, the contemporary focus on univocity merely carries on a long debate between followers and critics of Thomas Aquinas that began in medieval times and never really abated. Aquinas famously denied univocity: he held that all positive predications of God and creatures must be analogical, and can never be univocal. (So in the statements "God is good" and "Socrates is good," the word "good" has different, though analogous meanings, according to Aquinas.) Aquinas grounds this view about theological predication in a broader metaphysical account of analogous existence in which God's simple, uncreated existence is analogously related to heterogeneous created existence as its cause—in an analogous sense of "cause," of course.[23] Since Aquinas's own day, people have been arguing about how to interpret his account of analogy and whether it is finally coherent.

In our day, debates over univocity have moved far beyond exegetical arguments about the proper interpretation of Aquinas. The charge of univocity has been weaponized to such a degree that prominent theologians now blame univocity for the rise of secularism, atheism, Protestantism, and even modernity itself. More precisely, they blame the thirteenth-century friar John Duns Scotus for infecting Christendom with the virus of univocity and thereby destroying the glorious medieval synthesis of faith and reason. Although my own argument is constructive, not genealogical, it is important to understand the nature and scope of the vituperation heaped upon Scotus in order to understand why contemporary theologians condemn univocity in such strong terms. Moreover, some defenders of analytic theology also defend Scotus on univocity, which further contributes to the suspicion about analytic theology.

John Duns Scotus: History's Greatest Monster (The Scotus Story)

It is no exaggeration to say that Scotus gets blamed for all the travails of modernity. John Milbank calls Scotus's theory of univocity "the turning point in the destiny of the West."[24] When Scotus treats "being" as a univocal term, "at a stroke, [he] anticipated transcendental philosophy, idolized God, obscured the ontological difference, and...set us on the intellectual course to modernity."[25] According to Milbank's colleague Catherine Pickstock, "the Scotist shift towards a univocal ontology is more fundamental for modern thought than the shift to the subject

---

[23] Thomas Aquinas, *Summa Theologiae*, 1.12–13.
[24] John Milbank, *The Word Made Strange* (Malden, MA: Blackwell, 2007), 44.
[25] John Milbank, *The Future of Love* (Eugene, OR: Cascade, 2009), 159.

and to epistemology."[26] This is the "Scotus Story" promulgated by advocates of Radical Orthodoxy, and it is impossible to overestimate how far its influence has spread.[27] Roman Catholic Bishop Robert Barron offers an especially clear formulation:

> The trouble began with Duns Scotus's option for a univocal conception of being in contradistinction to Thomas Aquinas's analogical understanding…In an effort to make the "to-be" of God more immediately intelligible, Duns Scotus proposed a univocal conception of existence, according to which God and creatures belong to the same basic metaphysical category, the genus of being. Though God is infinite and therefore quantitatively superior to any creature or collectivity of creatures, there is nevertheless no qualitative difference, in the metaphysical sense, between the supreme being, God, and finite beings. Whereas Aquinas insisted that God is categorizable in no genus whatsoever, Scotus held that God and creatures do belong together to a logical category that in a real sense transcends and includes them. The implications of this shift are enormous and, to my mind, almost entirely negative.[28]

The Scotus Story has even seeped into the work of ostensibly secular historians like Brad Gregory, and it plays a key role in Charles Taylor's magnum opus *A Secular Age*.[29]

Although the Scotus Story has now permeated the ambient intellectual culture, medievalists and Scotus specialists have consistently argued that, as an interpretation of Scotus, it is untenable, even flat-out false.[30] And it does seem very unlikely that all the travails of modernity can be laid at the footsteps of a single thirteenth-century Franciscan friar and his commentary on the *Sentences*, even if Scotus really did hold the views attributed to him. Happily, however, for my own constructive purposes, I can bypass historical questions about Scotus's own views. What matters to me is the contemporary critique of univocity, because I want to show that analytic theologians are not proper targets of that critique. We do not need to get Scotus right in order to get univocity right, and if univocity really does

---

[26] Catherine Pickstock "Duns Scotus: His Historical and Contemporary Significance," *Modern Theology* 21 (2005): 544.

[27] The term "Scotus Story" is taken from Daniel P. Horan, *Postmodernity and Univocity* (Minneapolis, MN: Fortress Press, 2014).

[28] Robert Barron, *Priority of Christ: Towards a Postmodern Catholicism* (Grand Rapids, MI: Brazos, 2007), 12–13.

[29] See the discussion in Horan, *Postmodernity and Univocity*, 74–89.

[30] The leading voice here has been Richard Cross. See his "Where Angels Fear to Tread: Duns Scotus and Radical Orthodoxy," *Antonianum* 76 (2001): 7–41, and *Duns Scotus on God* (Burlington, VT: Ashgate, 2005), 249–59. See also Scott M. Williams "John Duns Scotus," in William J. Abraham and Frederick D. Aquino, eds., *The Oxford Handbook of the Epistemology of Theology* (New York: Oxford, 2017), 423–25; Stephen Dumont, "The Univocity of the Concept of Being in the Fourteenth Century: John Duns Scotus and William of Alnwick," *Medieval Studies* 49 (1987): 1–75.

have such deleterious theological consequences, we should reject it now, no matter what Scotus thought. In fact, however, even from the figures quoted above, it is clear that the real problem with univocity is what I have called "ontological sameness." Pickstock criticizes Scotus's "univocal ontology," and Barron criticizes Scotus's (alleged) claim that God and creatures "belong to the same basic metaphysical category"[31] Milbank worries that Scotus has "obscured the ontological difference" between God and creatures.[32] Brad Gregory says that for Scotus, God "belongs to a more encompassing reality with creatures."[33] These are all worries about ontological sameness, not semantic univocity. For the analytic theologian, this is good news. Analytic theologians have a variety of ways to avoid ontological sameness, even if they do endorse semantic univocity.

Distinguishing Semantic Univocity from Ontological Sameness

Although they are often conflated, it is crucial to distinguish between semantic univocity and ontological univocity, or, as I prefer to say, between semantic univocity and ontological sameness. Semantic univocity pertains to the order of language and thought: it is a thesis about the meaning of terms in a spoken or written language and, by extension, the mental concepts those terms express. In the sentences "Diamonds are hard" and "Stones are hard," the word "hard" is used univocally, because it has the same meaning in both. (Compare "Diamonds are hard" and "Metaphysics is hard," where the word "hard" has different, but related meanings.) We could make the point using the idiom of concepts by saying that both diamonds and stones fall under the extension of a single univocal concept *hardness*. (A reminder: I will italicize words that denote concepts, and I will continue to use small caps for words that denote universals or properties.) Ontological univocity, or ontological sameness, pertains to more than sameness of meaning. It pertains to the order of extralinguistic, extra-mental reality. It concerns what really exists. To continue with the example above: perhaps diamonds and stones are hard because they share the same really existing property, HARDNESS. Then the semantic univocity of the word "hard" reflects an underlying ontological sameness in diamonds and stones. We call them both "hard" because they are the same with respect to their hardness: they each instantiate the same real property, HARDNESS.

There is no single, generally agreed-upon account of properties, or whether there even are any at all.[34] On some accounts, properties are multiply realizable,

[31] Barron, *Priority of Christ*, 13; Catherine Pickstock, "Duns Scotus: His Historical and Contemporary Significance," 544.
[32] John Milbank, *The Future of Love*, 159.   [33] Gregory, *Unintended Reformation*, 37.
[34] For a helpful overview, see Francesco Orilia and Chris Swoyer, "Properties," in *The Stanford Encyclopedia of Philosophy* (Summer 2020 edition), Edward N. Zalta, ed. https://plato.stanford.edu/archives/sum2020/entries/properties/, accessed July 8, 2020.

abstract universals. For example, Platonic realism holds that properties exist independently of their bearers—so REDNESS is construed as a Platonic form. On Aristotelian realism, the form REDNESS really exists, but not independently; rather, it only exists insofar as it inheres in red things. On still other accounts, properties are not multiply realizable universals at all, but particulars, known as "tropes": the individual, distinct REDNESS of this apple, the individual, distinct REDNESS of that apple, and so on. On still other accounts—nominalist accounts—there are no real, extra-mental properties at all, but only individual things, grouped together by a mental concept: no REDNESS, just a collection of things that all fall under the concept *red*.

Because I understand ontological sameness in terms of sharing the same property, I need to say a bit more about what it is, on my understanding, to share a really existing, extra-mental property. The crucial point is that properties (if they exist) serve as part of the ontological grounds (or truth-makers) for true predications. If there is a property of REDNESS, for example, then what makes "The apple is red" true is that the property of REDNESS is exemplified by the apple. The property of REDNESS, as exemplified by the apple, serves as the ontological ground (or truth-maker) for the predication "is red" when said of the apple. Note that it is the property of REDNESS (as exemplified by the apple) that plays this role, and not, for example, the apple itself, or its skin, or anything like that. Precisely what it is to hold that there is a really existing property of REDNESS is to insist that only such a property could play the necessary role. Similarly, if I say both "The apple is red" and "The stoplight is red," then—if there is a property of REDNESS—these statements are true just in case the apple and the stoplight both exemplify the same property of REDNESS. In that case, in my terminology, they are ontologically the same with respect to their REDNESS. Whether or not two items share a property is an ontological fact about the world and not just a fact about how we speak or think.

But what, precisely, is it for two things to exemplify the same property of REDNESS? If two things only count as ontologically the same when they share a *numerically* identical property, then ontological sameness is only possible on Platonic or Aristotelian realism. I do not want to take any position on what properties are, and I also do not want to make things too easy for myself. So I will just stipulate that if properties are particulars—that is, tropes—then two instances of the same trope suffice for ontological sameness. Intuitively, this seems right: two red apples do seem to be ontologically the same with respect to their REDNESS, even if it turns out that the individual REDNESS of this apple is numerically distinct from the individual REDNESS of that apple.

In the discussion below, I argue that semantic univocity can be theologically innocent. Semantic univocity does not entail ontological sameness, and so it is possible to say that God and creatures "exist"—and furthermore that God is "a being" and "an individual"—in a semantically univocal sense without violating the creator/creature distinction or falling into idolatry. (The same goes for the locution "a person," but I discuss that term in Chapter 9.) When I say that semantic univocity does not *entail* ontological sameness, I mean the word "entail" in its strict logical sense. If *p* entails *q*, then it should not even be possible to find even a single case, real or imagined, in which *p* obtains but *q* does not obtain. So if semantic univocity entails ontological sameness, then every statement whatsoever in which we assert that *a* is *F* and *b* is *F* also posits a real, extra-mental property of F-NESS shared by *a* and *b*. Conversely, to say that semantic univocity does not entail ontological sameness is to say that there is at least one case in which we can assert that *a* is *F* and *b* is *F* without positing a real, extra-mental property of F-NESS shared by *a* and *b*. Finding even one case, real or imagined, is a significant result: once it is clear that semantic univocity does not entail ontological sameness, we can no longer assume that every case of semantic univocity is also a case of ontological sameness, and so we have to look at each case individually, including cases about God and creatures.

One more bit of ground-clearing: my discussion here is entirely defensive. I aim to answer the plausible but misguided worry that semantic univocity entails deleterious theological consequences on its own, apart from ontological sameness. I do not positively endorse semantic univocity or claim that, without univocity, analogy resolves into equivocation.[35] Nor do I take any position of my own on more fundamental meta-ontological questions about the existence, nature, or modes of BEING, except to stipulate that Christian orthodoxy requires an ontology that is consistent with (Divine Ultimacy) and (Divine Uniqueness). For their part, most analytic philosophers would deny that there is any such property as BEING, which means that they would cheerfully agree that God and creatures do not share that property. But given my target audience, I need to work up to this position, not just assert it and move on. Finally, people who are convinced that nominalism is the road to theological ruin will worry that I am smuggling a nominalist metaphysics in through the back door of semantics. I'm really not—I promise.

Univocity: What's the Real Worry?

When it comes to God and creatures, the real worry is about ontological sameness. Semantic univocity is worrying only if it entails or presupposes ontological sameness. Here is the pertinent worry: given a suitably strong doctrine of divine transcendence, it seems idolatrous to claim that God and creatures can have any properties or attributes in common. This worry is especially acute with respect to

---

[35] For such an argument, see Williams, "The Doctrine of Univocity Is True and Salutary."

what many regard as the most fundamental attribute of all, BEING. God is the uncaused creator of everything other than God, and so God and creatures cannot exist in the same way without reducing God to the level of creatures or elevating creatures to the level of God. Ontological sameness with respect to God and creatures threatens to commit us to a flattened ontology on which God and creatures exist on the same ontological plane, with the result that God has become merely one more existing thing among others.

It is ontological sameness, not semantic univocity, that threatens the "participatory ontology" so beloved by many contemporary theologians.[36] On this account, all created perfections—including, for some, BEING or EXISTENCE—"participate" in God's unlimited and uncreated perfection. To say that all created perfections participate in God is to say both that they are caused to exist *ex nihilo* by God and that they resemble God, however remotely, in virtue of being so caused. Whatever perfections created things have, they have as a result of their participation in God. This claim is utterly unrestricted: even the goodness of a delicious piece of chocolate cake (for example) is ultimately a participation in the unlimited, uncreated goodness of God the creator. For my part, I find the notion of a participatory ontology deeply appealing. But note that from beginning to end, this is a metaphysical story about the nature of value. It is not a semantic story about the meanings of words.

Semantic univocity on its own would only be worrying if semantic univocity entailed ontological sameness. That is, semantic univocity would only be worrying if attributing a term univocally of God and creatures presupposed that God and creatures actually share some real, extra-mental property. Suppose we say that God "exists" or is "a being" in the same univocal sense that Socrates "exists" or is "a being." If that univocal assertion commits us to the further claim that God and Socrates share a real property of EXISTENCE or BEING, or have the same mode of existence, or that they otherwise exist in the same way, then semantic univocity would entail ontological sameness. In that case, on the assumption that affirming ontological sameness between God and creatures is really a form of ontotheology or idolatry, it would follow that semantic univocity must be rejected.

But suppose—provisionally, for now, in advance of the argument to follow—that semantic univocity does not entail ontological sameness. That is, suppose the word "exists" can have the same meaning in "God exists" and "Socrates exists," but this lexical or semantic fact does not commit us to any metaphysical claims about the mode, manner, or ontological basis of their respective existences, and so does not commit us to ontological sameness. In that case, it is hard to see why semantic univocity by itself would amount to idolatry, even if it turned out to be

---

[36] See, for example, the theologians who promulgate the "Scotus Story," above.

the wrong theory of theological predication. Adopting the wrong semantic theory is not a sin at all, so it cannot be the sin of idolatry.

Semantic Univocity Does Not Entail Ontological Sameness

If semantic univocity entails ontological sameness, then it should not be possible to identify even a single case of semantic univocity, real or imagined, that is not also a case of ontological sameness. In the search for such a case, instead of going straight to the difficult matter of theological predication, it is useful to look first for counterexamples among more mundane matters. The easiest way to see that semantic univocity does not entail ontological sameness is to consider disjunctive predicates. A disjunctive predicate picks out one or more properties, but it does not always pick out exactly the same property every time. Here is a story about a made-up disjunctive predicate, just to illustrate what I mean.

Suppose that two children have a big box full of toys, and for some reason they want to sort them all by color. But they want to sort them in a special way: every toy that is either blue or green goes into one pile, and every other toy, those that are neither blue nor green, go into another pile. When the children finish, they have one big pile of blue and green toys and another big pile of toys that are neither blue nor green. Now suppose they make up a new category word, just to amuse themselves, and they say, "We have a big pile of 'bleen' toys and a big pile of toys that are not 'bleen.'" Suppose they start using this term regularly within their own household, and soon enough everyone in their family uses the word "bleen" to mean "something that is either blue or green." So they will say things like "The sky is bleen," or "The grass is bleen," and so forth.[37]

In this story, the predicate "is bleen" has a univocal meaning in the statements "The sky is bleen" and "The grass is bleen." It means "either blue or green." But it is not necessary—and, in fact, very implausible—to suppose that this univocal meaning picks out a really existing extra-mental property of BLEENNESS. The children have made up a new predicate, but they have not summoned into existence a new, extra-mental property that was not there before. There is no single property that grounds the truth of "The sky is bleen" and "The grass is bleen." Instead, the predicate "is bleen" picks out things that have either the property of BLUENESS or the property of GREENNESS. Formally, where a is the sky, and b is the grass, and F is BLEEN, we have a case in which a is F, and b is F, but there is no property of F-NESS shared by a and b. This is a case of semantic univocity without ontological sameness.

---

[37] Here I am drawing on Nelson Goodman (*Fact, Fiction, and Forecast*, 4th ed. Cambridge, MA: Harvard University Press, 1983) but making a different point than the one he makes with "grue" and "bleen."

This is a made-up story about a made-up predicate, but some natural language predicates seem to be disjunctive predicates, just like "bleen." For example, consider the predicate "is primary-colored." The primary colors are red, yellow, and blue.[38] We can say "That apple is primary-colored" and "That sapphire is primary-colored" and the predicate "is primary-colored" has a univocal meaning across both statements. But there is no need to posit a real, extra-mental property, PRIMARY-COLORED, to explain why the apple and the sapphire are both primary-colored. The predicate "is primary-colored" is a disjunctive predicate that is satisfied either by the apple's property of REDNESS or the sapphire's property of BLUENESS. This is another case of semantic univocity without ontological sameness.

These examples already suffice to show that semantic univocity does not *entail* ontological sameness. Some philosophers think that many ordinary predications follow the same logic. Many "higher-level" predicates pick out one or more lower-level properties, and do not pick out a single property shared by everything to which the predicate truthfully applies. The philosopher John Heil makes this case with respect to the predication "is red":

As it happens, however, objects can be red without—in any sense—sharing a property in virtue of which they can be said to be red. A tomato, a stoplight, and a head of hair can all be red. We say that they are different *shades* of red. Perhaps a property corresponds to each of these shades of red. Then, the predicate 'is red' truly applies to tomatoes, stoplights, and redheads, and it applies to these things in virtue of their possessing certain properties, but it does not apply to each of them in virtue of their possessing the *very same* property.[39]

And Richard Cross makes a similar argument with the predicate "is an animal," which can be satisfied by BEING A CAT, BEING A DOG, BEING A MOUSE, etc.:

For example, cats and dogs fall under the extension of the concept *animal*—but there is no reason to suppose that there is something real, ANIMALITY, common to them. The concept *animal* is…[an] abstraction. Nothing is just an animal. Things are animals in virtue of being particular kinds of thing—cats and dogs, for example—and the fact that cats and dogs fall under the extension of the concept *animal* is explained simply by the fact that they are cats and dogs: anything which is a cat is an animal, and anything which is a dog is an animal.[40]

[38] Or red, green, and blue. Or cyan, magenta, and yellow. It's complicated. See https://science.howstuffworks.com/primary-colors.htm, accessed July 9, 2020.

[39] John Heil, "Levels of Reality," *Ratio* 16 (2003): 211.

[40] Cross, "Idolatry and Religious Language," 191. I added the small caps to be consistent with my own usage.

According to Cross, the concept *animal* is a mental abstraction that we use to talk in a general, nonspecific way about things that are (either cats or dogs or mice or rabbits, or...). So even though we predicate "animal" univocally of cats and dogs, we do not need to posit the existence of some really existing extra-mental property of ANIMALITY that inheres in both cats and dogs. This is another case of semantic univocity without ontological sameness.

Some readers will not be persuaded by all of these examples, but the "bleen" case on its own suffices to show that semantic univocity does not strictly *entail* ontological sameness. My goal so far has been only to establish this very narrow point. We cannot always infer ontological sameness from semantic univocity. Because we cannot, we must argue about specific cases. This point holds even for the much more lofty case of God and *being*. We cannot conclude, a priori and in advance of any argument, that the univocal statements "God exists" and "Socrates exists" entail that God and Socrates both share a common property of EXISTENCE.

Interlude: Semantic Univocity and Explanatory Sameness

Critics of semantic univocity sometimes argue that, for example, "God is wise" and "Socrates is wise" must be analogical predications, rather than univocal predications, because we cannot give the same account of God's wisdom and Socrates's wisdom. This argument treats sameness of account—or, as I call it, "explanatory sameness"—as a necessary condition of semantic univocity, and then concludes that because we cannot give the same account of (e.g.) God's wisdom and Socrates's wisdom, we cannot predicate "is wise" univocally.[41] It is true that we cannot give the same account of God's wisdom and Socrates's wisdom. God's wisdom is uncreated and essential, and Socrates's wisdom is created and contingent, among other differences. But we can still predicate "is wise" univocally of both God and Socrates, for semantic univocity does not entail explanatory sameness.

Once again, it is easy to see this point in general by considering a fairly trivial example. Take the two statements "Bullet trains are fast" and "Olympic sprinters are fast." It should be clear that the predicate "is fast" has the same univocal meaning in both statements: something like "moving or capable of moving at a high speed relative to others of its kind." But we would not give the same account or explanation of what makes the bullet train fast and what makes the sprinter fast. When we explain why trains are fast and why sprinters are fast, we appeal to very different facts in each case: different physical structures, different chemical

---

[41] The idea that "sameness of account" is a criterion of univocal predications was a commonplace in medieval semantics. See, for example, Aquinas, *ST* 1.13.5, Ralph McInerny, *Aquinas and Analogy* (Washington, DC: Catholic University of America Press, 1996), 53. But our own semantics should not be medieval.

reactions, different causal origins, etc. True, trains and sprinters differ far less than God and creatures. But they still differ quite a lot. But the predicate "is fast" remains univocal across both statements, notwithstanding these differences in explanation.

So we should distinguish between (i) predicating a term univocally in two statements and (ii) giving the same explanation for what makes the predication true in both statements. Condition (i) can obtain, even when condition (ii) does not. And so from the denial of (ii), we cannot infer the denial of (i). Opponents of univocity frequently blur semantic univocity, ontological sameness, and explana-tory sameness in an unhelpful way. For example, consider this passage from Nick Trakakis, with my own boldface labels inserted in brackets:

> Recall that the univocity thesis holds that there are some words that we use of God and creatures that have the same meanings [**positing semantic univocity**]. When we say, for example, that God is good, the goodness we predicate of God shares at least something in common with the goodness we predicate of a human being when we call Francis of Assisi or Mother Teresa "good people" [**inferring ontological sameness**]. The problem is that human goodness, even at its best and purest, is no match for God's goodness. But this is…more importantly, a qualitative difference: God's goodness is unique in that it has qualities or proper-ties not had by any form of creaturely goodness [**denying ontological same-ness**]. For example, on some theories (those that accept divine simplicity), goodness is not a part of God, but is God himself, whereas the same does not hold of any human being: Francis of Assisi, although an exceptionally good and saintly person, is not identical with goodness itself, but only contingently bears the property of 'goodness' [**denying explanatory sameness**]. On other theories (such as those advocating the free will theodicy) God's goodness entails not intervening to prevent the Holocaust during WWII, whereas any human being who acted in this way would (correctly) be charged as callous, if not evil [**deny-ing explanatory sameness**]…But what is important for our purposes is how the univocity thesis minimises or even denies many of these differences. For if the univocity thesis is true, then we mean precisely or essentially the same thing by "goodness" when describing God as "good" and when talking of some human person as "a good person" [**denying semantic univocity**].[42]

Trakakis starts out by criticizing semantic univocity, but he assumes that semantic univocity entails ontological sameness: his list of problems with semantic univocity are all problems with saying that God and creatures exemplify the same properties. He continues with two examples meant to show that we cannot give the same

---

[42] Trakakis, "Does Univocity Entail Idolatry?," 545.

explanatory account of God's goodness and human goodness: unlike human beings, God is identical to his goodness, and unlike human beings, God cannot be held to ordinary moral standards. He assumes these examples give us a reason to deny semantic univocity. But as a matter of logic, his argument does not go through, because semantic univocity does not entail either ontological sameness or explanatory sameness. For all he has said, the word "good" could still have the same meaning in "God is good" and "Francis is good," even though what makes each statement true is radically different.

"God Exists" and "Socrates Exists": Semantic Univocity without Ontological Sameness

Now to the real issue. Is there a way to say that "God exists" and "Socrates exists" with a univocal sense of "exists" without violating the creator/creature distinction and falling into idolatry? We need a way of denying that semantic univocity about "being" or "exists" implies ontological sameness about BEING or EXISTENCE. The first way to deny the implication would be to deny that there is any real, extra-mental property of BEING or EXISTENCE at all. If there is no such property at all, then God and creatures cannot share it. The second way to deny the implication would be to agree there can be a real, extra-mental property of BEING or EXISTENCE, but deny that everything that exists shares a *single* real property of BEING or EXISTENCE. There could be two or more such properties that are distinct and logically disjunctive, all of which are picked out by the completely general univocal term "exists." In either case, we can assert "God exists" and "Socrates exists" univocally without implying any ontological sameness with respect to the property EXISTENCE and without violating the creator/creature distinction.

Most contemporary analytic philosophers hold roughly the first view. First-order logic—the backbone of analytic philosophy—does not treat existence as a property at all, and so whatever contemporary analytic philosophers are saying when they say "Socrates exists" and "God exists," they are probably not saying that God and Socrates share the property of EXISTENCE, for they typically deny that there is any such property to share.[43] According to his expert defenders, Duns Scotus, the original medieval univocity theorist, holds roughly the second view.[44] Whether he actually did or not, the view is certainly available to contemporary thinkers. Suppose that the concept *being* is an abstraction that does not refer to any single real property common to God and creatures. Instead it picks out, in a general way, two logically distinct and non-overlapping properties, UNCREATED

---

[43] See discussion below: "God Exists, God is One".   [44] See n. 30, above.

BEING (God's being) and CREATED BEING (creaturely being). This suggestion is parallel to the example of "is primary-colored" (above), which does not refer to a single really existing property common to all colored objects, but to the logically distinct and non-overlapping properties REDNESS, YELLOWNESS, and BLUENESS. UNCREATED BEING is not just an accumulation of more and more CREATED BEING, just as REDNESS is not an accumulation of more and more BLUENESS: in both cases, the properties are disjuncts. This view is not just of interest to Scotus specialists. In fact, some of the most interesting recent work in analytic metaphysics has argued that existence is not unitary but divides into logically disjunctive modes. These disjunctive modes are ontologically distinct, but they can still be referred to by a (semantically) univocal concept of existence or being.[45]

Some philosophers and theologians worry that when we use the word "being" or "exists" univocally, we commit ourselves to the claim that BEING—construed as something like a Platonic universal—is causally or ontologically prior to God, such that God depends on BEING for his own existence.[46] Or, to say the same thing, we might worry that when we use the word "being" or "exists" univocally of God and creatures, we implicitly claim that they both fall under the genus Being. These worries are confused, because they conflate two very different forms of dependence. Our ability to use the term "being" univocally does require us to have a univocal concept, *being*, that applies to God and creatures. So as speakers of a language, our ability to make univocal assertions depends on our having univocal concepts. But this kind of conceptual dependence does not entail that our univocal words and concepts depend on an underlying univocal ontology. Nor, obviously, does it entail that God himself somehow depends on our concepts for his own real, extra-mental existence and attributes. Just because we predicate a term univocally of two items, or have a univocal concept with which we mentally group both items together, we cannot infer that the two items share any real, extra-mental properties or belong together as members of a really existing genus or natural kind—recall the "bleen" case. Semantic facts do not perfectly mirror ontological facts, because semantic univocity does not entail ontological sameness.

Virtually all analytic theologians would deny that there is a really existing, extra-mental property of BEING shared by God and creatures. They would also deny that God and creatures depend on BEING for their existence. Most analytic theologians take a Kantian or Fregean view of existence, on which existence is "thin," because there is no real attribute of EXISTENCE or BEING at all. Ironically,

---

[45] See especially Kris McDaniel, *The Fragmentation of Being* (New York: Oxford University Press, 2017).

[46] For example, Brian Davies, "Are Names Said of God and Creatures Univocally?" *American Catholic Philosophical Quarterly* 92 (2018): 324–25; David Bentley Hart, *The Experience of God*, 118, 128; Hyman, *Short History of Atheism*, 68–70; John Milbank, "Intensities," *Modern Theology* 15 (1999): 454–55; Barry Miller, *A Most Unlikely God*, 77.

"ontological plane?" No again, for the same reason. Would it commit them to the view that God and Socrates are both "things in the world?" Well, if by "in the world," we mean "in the created, spatiotemporal world," then still no. The numerical sense of "existence" is silent about that too.

In my view, instead of any of these questions, we should ask "Is it the case that only created beings can be counted?" This question really gets at the heart of the issue. The numerical sense of "exists" asserts that whatever exists can be counted—whether created or uncreated. Throughout the long history of trinitarian and Christological debates, we see efforts to reconcile the claim that there is one God with the claim that there are three divine persons, or to understand how there can be one Christ who is, nevertheless, fully human and fully divine. Those debates presuppose the ability to count—that is, individuate—divine natures and divine persons. Similarly, the very notion that there is an "absolute distinction" between God and creatures presupposes that we can distinguish between them, which in turn presupposes that we can count them. Even advocates of divine simplicity insist that God alone is absolutely simple, and this statement is semantically and extensionally equivalent to the statement that exactly one thing is absolutely simple. There are, indeed, venerable strands of Christian apophaticism that go so far as to deny even a univocal sense of the divine unity.[54] But these accounts are unusually strong even within the apophatic tradition. They are not inherently more traditional than the ubiquitous, and straightforwardly biblical, exhortation that God is one.

What about "God is a Being" or "God is an Individual"?

The previous discussion also shows how to understand the claims that God is "an individual" or "a being." (And again, both claims are related to the claim that God is "a person," which I discuss in Chapter 9.) Contemporary non-analytic theologians are deeply skeptical of such claims, because they think that calling God "a being" or "an individual" is tantamount to treating God like a thing in the world or an idol.[55] Analytic philosophers struggle to understand their skepticism: from an analytic point of view, both claims are completely innocuous. The numerical interpretation of "exists" provides a way forward. On this account, it is, indeed, the case that God and Socrates are both "beings" and "individuals," but this fact has no real ontological freight. To say that they are both individuals is just to say

---

[54] Pseudo-Dionysius, "The Divine Names," 13.2–3, in *Pseudo-Dionysius: The Complete Works*, 128–29.
[55] Davies, "Are Names Said of God and Creatures Univocally?" 325. Hart, *Experience of God*, 30:

God…is not something posed over against the universe, in addition to it, nor is he the universe itself. He is not a "being," at least not in the way that a tree, a shoemaker, or a god is a being; he is not one more object in the inventory of things that are, or any sort of discrete object at all.

---

however, some contemporary theologians argue that the thin analytic conception of existence is precisely the problem.[47] Because the existential quantifier does not denote a rich, substantive account of BEING or EXISTENCE, they think that analytic philosophy as such cannot express the claim that God's BEING radically differs from creaturely BEING. Thus David Bentley Hart:

> In analytic terms, existence is often no more than the instantiation of some concept or other, and so everything that exists must exist in precisely the same sense: as a conceptual possibility that happens to have at least one instance out there somewhere…The most curious aspect of this approach to "existence" language, as should be obvious, is that it has absolutely nothing to do with *real* existence at all…Only if the difference between God and creatures can be contemplated as the difference between absolute *actual* being and contingent *actual* being can the word "God" illuminate the mystery of existence in the way classical theism assumes it does.[48]

Hart's prose is sometimes opaque, but here he seems to be saying that because analytic philosophy has a thin notion of existence, analytic philosophers cannot distinguish between a divine mode of being and a creaturely mode of being. Here the problem with analytic thought is not precisely the usual ontotheological worry outlined above, that God and creatures exist in the same way because they both share the same attribute of EXISTENCE or both fall under the genus of BEING. Rather, the problem with analytic thought is now that God and creatures exist in the same way precisely because analytic thought posits no attribute of EXISTENCE or BEING at all.

This seems to be Hart's line of argument: Without any real attribute of EXISTENCE, we do not have the resources to distinguish God's divine, non-contingent mode of existence from the ordinary contingent creaturely mode of existence.[49] We therefore cannot say that God's unique, uncreated, unlimited hyper-existence differs absolutely from ordinary limited, contingent creaturely existence. Since we cannot distinguish God and creatures with respect to their EXISTENCE, we must conclude that they exist in the same manner, mode, or way.

If I have interpreted Hart correctly, he has made a bad inference. He seems to assume that because analytic thinkers do not posit any rich attribute of BEING or EXISTENCE, then they cannot distinguish God and creatures with respect to their mode, manner, or way of existing. We should more charitably conclude only: if a given analytic thinker denies that there is an attribute of EXISTENCE, he or she must find some other way to distinguish God from creatures with respect

---

[47] Barry Miller, *From Existence to God* (New York: Routledge, 1991).
[48] David Bentley Hart, *The Experience of God*, 126–27.
[49] Hart may not like analytic "property-talk," so I have switched to talk of "attributes."

to their ontological status. In fact, analytic thinkers do distinguish divine and creaturely modes, manners, and ways of existing, and they do draw the required ontological distinctions between God and creatures, just by different means. I discuss some of those ways below, and others in Chapter 9, on theistic personalism.

God Exists, God Is One

Given the defensive character of the argument so far, we might still legitimately wonder what we *are* asserting when we say that God and creatures exist with the same sense of "exist." Simply denying that there is a common property of existence seems to dodge the theological problems with univocity rather than face them squarely. We need to say more. So here is a way to understand the claim that "being" is univocal, and that God and creatures both fall under the univocal concept *being*. It does not posit ontological sameness or violate the distinction between God and creatures.

Peter van Inwagen has argued that "exists" is really a number word: to say that something exists is to say that the number of those things is greater than zero.[50] So "Cats exist" means that the number of cats is greater than zero, and "Unicorns do not exist" means that the number of unicorns is zero. Number words are plainly univocal. (The word "three" has exactly the same meaning in "I will give you three chances to surrender" and "There are three books on the table," even though chances and books are very different kinds of things.) So "exists" and related words like "being" are also univocal. Van Inwagen also points out that "exists" is inter-definable with the univocal terms "all"/"every" plus logical negation. To say that "There exists a *g*" is just to say "It is not the case that all things are not a *g*" or "It is not the case that everything is not a *g*." Since "all" and "every" are univocal terms, as is the logical negation sign, van Inwagen concludes that "exists" is univocal as well.

On this account, then, to say "Socrates exists" is just to say "At least one thing is Socrates" and to say "God exists" is just to say "At least one thing is God."[51] (At this point, do not get hung up on the word "thing," which is being used here as a content-free term, like a variable.) From the univocal sense of "exists" we cannot infer that God and Socrates have anything whatsoever in common except the fact that they can be correctly counted by a number greater than zero. Moreover, the statement "At least one thing is God" does not tell us anything whatsoever about what God is like. It makes no reference to created being or uncreated being. It does not tell us that God is powerful, wise, and good, or that God created the heavens and earth. It does not tell us that God is (or is not) triune. It tells us just and only this: that there is at least one thing that is identical to God, without saying more about what that means. The statement "God exists" is neutral about how to fill out the content of the concept *God*. So when we assert only the bare statement "God exists," we are not saying much at all—no more, and arguably even less, than Aquinas was saying at the end of the Five Ways with his statement *et hoc dicimus deum*: "and this [singular thing] we call God."[52]

If this account of "exists" succeeds as an interpretation of the existential quantifier in first-order logic, then it can also successfully preserve the creator/creature distinction and steer clear of idolatry.[53] At this point, some theologians might find their trinitarian antennae twitching. They might even regard the doctrine of the Trinity as the perfect theological counterexample to van Inwagen's account of "exists." For there is a sense in which God is one, but there is also a sense in which God is three. Christians are not "mere monotheists," and so perhaps it is not the case that there is "one" God in the same sense in which there might be "one" table in a room. This is a fair reply, but it does not succeed as a counterexample. It merely pushes the underlying univocity of "exists" (or "there is") back either to the level of the trinitarian persons or to the level of the divine nature. For Nicene Christians must say that there is exactly one Father, exactly one Son, and exactly one Spirit. It is not permissible to say that there is "a sense in which there is more than one Father, or no Fathers," and so on for the other divine persons. Similarly Nicene Christians must say that there is exactly one divine nature, not "a sense in which there is one divine nature and a sense in which there is more than one or zero." So there is a univocal sense of "exists" at the trinitarian level too.

This account of existence is very thin, but that is exactly why it can suit theologically. If "exists" is really a number word, then the semantic univoc "exists" does not in any way imply that there is (or is not) a real attribute o ence or being common to both God and creatures. Do Christians agree th is one God? Then, they can also agree that "exists" means the same thing exists" and "Socrates exists." Wouldn't that commit them to the view th existence is the same "kind of existence" as Socrates's existence? No it w for the numerical sense of "existence" says nothing whatsoever about existence." Alternatively: wouldn't it put God and creatures on

[50] Van Inwagen takes himself to be developing W. V. O. Quine's meta-ontology: see "On What There Is" in *From a Logical Point of View* (New York: Harper, 1953), 1–19. In the discussion below, I am summarizing van Inwagen's *Existence: Essays in Ontology* (Cambridge: Cambridge University Press, 2014), 60–71.

[51] It is worth noting that someone committed to the numerical sense of "exists" is not thereby committed to the further thesis that all names are disguised definite descriptions and that all singular terms must be eliminated and turned into predicate variables. We could treat "God" as a disguised definite description—a word that stands in for some set of definite descriptions like "creator of heaven and earth"—but we do not have to. We could treat it as a proper name.

[52] The phrase *et hoc dicimus deum* concludes the Fourth and Fifth ways. The first similar expressions. *ST* 1.2.3.

[53] For an interesting discussion of the way that van Inwagen's account of "exists" d with the suggestion that there are multiple ways of existing, see McDaniel, *F Being*, 22–27.

that they can both be counted. This claim does not entail that they are both created individuals or limited individuals or that they exist in the same way, or on the same plane, or anything like that. Furthermore, this account does not posit Being as a genus of which God and creatures are species, another common worry about univocity. Nor does it claim that God and creatures depend on BEING (still less on the word "being" or the concept *being*) for their existence. To clear up another potential confusion: although this account presupposes that we can use numbers in order to say that whatever exists is countable, it does not commit us to the claim that numbers are ontologically prior to God, or uncreated, and it does not suppose that God himself depends on numbers for his existence (whatever that would mean). The account is entirely neutral on all these questions.

Analytic philosophers and theologians struggle to understand the problem with calling God "a being" or "an individual" because they typically regard atheism, pantheism, or polytheism as the only alternatives to these locutions. On atheism, God is not a being because there is no God; on pantheism, God is not a being because every individual being is really a constituent of God; on polytheism there are multiple gods. None of these options is acceptable, from the Christian point of view. Conversely, opponents of univocity would say that God cannot be "a being" or "an individual" in the same way that Socrates is "a being" and "an individual" unless both God and Socrates exist in the same way or have the same mode of existing, which would effectively turn God into a creature. The numerical sense of identity outlined above can address this worry because it does not posit any modes, ways, or manners of being at all.

Even so, there is another common version of the worry that might still have some purchase on analytic theologians. This version has to do with whether God is "a member of a kind." Gerald Hughes clearly lays out the problem:

> Since there is no kind of thing to which God belongs, God is not an individual either. To be an individual is to be *an* individual, one among possibly many individuals... To be a member of a kind is to satisfy the description by which that kind is defined. Since kind-terms are universals it is logically possible for there to be indefinitely many individuals which satisfy that description, and equally, it is logically possible for there to be none.[56]

The key assumption seems to be that anything that counts as "an individual" must be either one of several possible individuals of the same kind ("it is logically possible for there to be indefinitely many individuals which satisfy that description") or a contingent individual ("it is logically possible for there to be none"). So by calling God "an individual," we are saying that he is a member of the kind, *deity*

---

[56] Gerard Hughes, *Nature of God* (New York: Routledge, 1995), 50.

(let's say), which just entails that God is either one among many possible individuals of that kind, or contingent, or both. The resulting God then seems far less transcendent than the God of classical Christian theism.

Analytic theologians can respond to this worry in a variety of ways. First and foremost, they can argue that God exists necessarily and thereby deny that God is contingent—and, indeed, they all do argue exactly this.[57] Second, they can deny the underlying interpretation of what it is to be "an individual." For example, they might argue as follows: Why assume that calling something "an individual" implies that there might be other things that have the same essential attributes? To say that something is "an individual" is just to say that there is at least one such thing, making no reference at all to whether it is necessary or contingent, to whether it is member of a kind, or to whether there are, or might be, any more instances of that item. There is no inherent a priori reason to prefer Hughes's account of the meaning of "an individual" to the numerical account. If anything, the numerical account seems to cohere better with the way we use the term "individual" in ordinary language. Third, analytic theologians can use the resources of analytic perfect being theology to preserve the creator/creature distinction by distinguishing the God of Christian theism from other conceivable but non-actual "gods." I discuss this third option at length in Chapter 9, on so-called "theistic personalism." Here I will say summarily that analytic theologians have a variety of strategies to preserve (Divine Uniqueness) and (Divine Ultimacy) and so the worry that analytic theology treats the Christian God as "just another god" is not tenable.

Semantic Univocity: Not an All-or-Nothing Affair

I have argued that in positive statements about God and creatures, semantic univocity does not entail ontological sameness. Moreover, semantic univocity is not an all-or-nothing affair: semantic univocity about any given term does not entail semantic univocity about all terms. We might well accept the univocal use of one term—for example, "being"—without committing ourselves to the univocity of any other term, or to the sameness of any property. Suppose you hold that all positive predications of God and creatures are analogical. (This is Aquinas's view.) So you think that in the statements "God is wise" and "Socrates is wise," the word "wise" is being used analogically. You also affirm divine simplicity and with it the suggestion that God is *ipsum esse subsistens*, subsisting being itself. You have a variety of reasons for denying that God and creatures can share any properties.

[57] See the discussion of so-called "theistic personalism" in Chapter 9.

Great! You can continue to affirm the very same underlying metaphysical framework and semantic theory of analogical predication. You can continue to hold that the word "wise" is predicated analogically of God and Socrates. Nothing that I have said requires you to reject analogical predication at all, let alone reject it wholesale. Should you also (contra Aquinas) endorse the univocal, numerical sense of "exists" along with your other views, you would simply affirm all of the following claims:

(1) There is exactly one God (or, if you prefer, exactly one x such that x lacks all composition).
(2) There is exactly one Socrates.
(3) The word "exists" has the same meaning in "God exists" and "Socrates exists."
(4) The word "wise" does not have the same meaning in "God is wise" and "Socrates is wise."
(5) The word "wise" in "God is wise" is analogously related to the word "wise" in "Socrates is wise."

I see no reason to think that (1)–(5) are inconsistent. Univocity about "exists" does not entail univocity about any other term, so it is compatible with analogical predication. And as long as it is possible to count metaphysically simple objects, then the numerical sense of "exists" is compatible with divine simplicity. And we have to be able to count metaphysically simple objects in order to say that they number exactly one, and we need to be able to say *that* in order to distinguish God from everything other than God.

Semantic Univocity, the Ontotheological Attitude, and the Attitude of Worship

According to Merold Westphal, the critique of ontotheology "is directed not at *what* we say about God but at *how* we say it, to what purpose, in the service of what project."[58] In my own phrasing, we exhibit the ontotheological attitude when we claim the divine perspective for ourselves, or attempt to use God as something that serves our own projects of dominance. So understood, it is hard to see how semantic univocity about "exists" inherently presupposes the ontotheological attitude. Is counting something an act of dominance? I suppose it could be, in some circumstances, but it does not have to be. Merely counting something—the sheer act of counting, in itself, apart from why one is counting—seems entirely neutral. Suppose you are convinced that some terms can be used univocally of God and

---

[58] Westphal, *Overcoming Ontotheology*, 6–7.

creatures, and you hold this view because you think that semantic univocity is required in order for human beings to be able to speak meaningfully about God at all. And suppose you further hold that we must speak meaningfully about God, since we are under a divine imperative to try to understand God better in order to praise and worship God more fully. This view seems like the very opposite of the ontotheological attitude.

Conclusion

Opponents of univocity do not adequately distinguish between semantic univocity and ontological sameness. For their part, analytic theologians do not always take the worry about ontological sameness as seriously as they should. Nor have they tried to understand why their non-analytic counterparts worry about calling God "a being" or "an individual." Neither side has engaged charitably with the other. By now I hope it seems very clear that semantic univocity does not entail ontological sameness, and that semantic univocity, on its own, is nothing to worry about. As discussed above, most theological opponents of univocity actually target a "univocal ontology," or what I call ontological sameness. Strikingly, even when they do explicitly set out to criticize semantic univocity, they simply assume that it entails ontological sameness. It does not. There may, indeed, be legitimate worries about supposing that God and creatures exist in the same way, or imagining that they could each instantiate the same properties. But there are no theological worries about saying that words can have the same meanings in statements about God and creatures, provided that we also guard against ontological sameness.

One might wonder why critics of univocity have not recognized this point. Part of the reason, I suspect, is that debates about univocity and analogy have tended to be historical and exegetical disputes about how to interpret medieval figures like Aquinas or Scotus. Both thinkers—and especially Scotus—are notoriously difficult for non-specialists to interpret, and so it is not easy to determine what they actually meant. But regardless of what Aquinas meant or what Scotus meant, with the resources of contemporary philosophy, we ourselves can see that semantic univocity does not entail ontological sameness, and that ontological sameness between God and creatures is the real problem.

At the same time, however, my defense of semantic univocity is limited. In fact, I have not argued that philosophical theology needs semantic univocity; nor have I argued that semantic univocity is better than its alternatives, including the Thomist doctrine of analogy. All of these further debates about univocity and analogy remain unaffected by anything I have said here. My hope, however, is that we can now treat them as matters of reasonable theological disagreement, rather than as crypto-creedal questions that must be answered "correctly" in order to remain within the boundaries of genuinely Christian speech.

9

On "Theistic Personalism"

Is the God of analytic theology more like Zeus than like the God of Abraham, Isaac, and Jacob? More like Odin than the God of Jesus Christ? Some kind of "invisible, super-duper superman"?[1] Plenty of critics think so. This is the latest version of the idolatry charge aimed at analytic theologians. This version of the charge is not directly about ontotheology or univocity but about a newly discovered, latter-day heresy called "theistic personalism." The charge itself is really just a less sophisticated version of the same worries about ontotheology and transcendence. Unlike the dense and impenetrable problem of ontotheology, however, "theistic personalism" is easy to understand. The worry about theistic personalism is the worry that God is "a person, like you and me, only much better and without our human deficiencies," writes Roger Pouivet. He continues: "When you read some philosophers of religion, including Richard Swinburne, Alvin Plantinga, or Open Theists, God appears as such a person, in a sense closer to Superman than to the Creator of Heaven and Earth."[2]

Analytic theists do not endorse or self-ascribe the label of "theistic personalism," which is only ever used pejoratively, by critics. The more immediate target of the theistic personalism charge is analytic "perfect being theology" (PBT), here understood as analytic reflection on the nature of God and the divine attributes. More precisely, PBT is the broadly Anselmian project of trying to articulate a concept of God by asking: What properties must be instantiated by God in order for God to count as the perfect being? (Or, alternatively, the greatest conceivable being, the greatest possible being, the maximally great being, or as the only being worthy of worship?[3]) The maximally great, worship-worthy being would be not just powerful, but omnipotent, not just knowledgeable but omniscient, not just good, but perfectly good, and so on.[4] So the worry about theistic personalism is the worry

---

[1] Andrew Gleeson, "The Power of God," 603.

[2] Roger Pouivet, "Against Theistic Personalism," *European Journal for Philosophy of Religion* 10 (2018): 1.

[3] I do not assume these are all equivalent. The list is only meant to present some common analytic terminology. I also use "perfect being theology" with an expansive sense. It encompasses PBT narrowly construed: the project of deriving an overall concept of God via rational reflection on the divine attributes, as well as attempts to elucidate individual divine attributes without building up an overall concept of God.

[4] Leading PBT theorists include Brian Leftow (*God and Necessity*, 7–23, 184–208, "Why Perfect Being Theology?," *International Journal for Philosophy of Religion* 69 [2011]: 103–18), Richard Swinburne (*The Coherence of Theism*), T. J. Mawson (*The Divine Attributes* [Cambridge: Cambridge University Press, 2019]), Katherin Rogers (*Perfect Being Theology* [Edinburgh: Edinburgh University

Analytic Theology and the Academic Study of Religion. William Wood, Oxford University Press (2021). © William Wood.
DOI: 10.1093/oso/9780198779872.003.0009

that the God that emerges from PBT is still too limited and anthropomorphic to be the God of the Christian faith. In other words, the worry is yet another version of the same anxieties about idolatry, ontotheology, and univocity that I have discussed in Chapters 7 and 8.

This term "theistic personalism" was originally coined in a textbook by Brian Davies, who presented it as a contrast to "classical theism":

> according to classical theism, God is not a person. When we speak of persons, we are normally referring to human beings. For classical theists, however, God should be sharply distinguished from these. Human beings have bodies and are parts of a changing and changeable universe. According to classical theism, however, God is incorporeal, unchanging, and not part of the universe...Some philosophers have thought that human persons are really non-material. But even these philosophers take persons to be distinct individuals belonging to a kind so that one person added to another makes two things of the same sort. For classical theism, however, God is not an individual belonging to any kind. You and I are both human beings. Neptune and Mars are both planets. According to classical theism, however, there is nothing of the same kind that God is.[5]

So "theistic personalism," according to Davies, is simply the view that God is literally a person, which he understands as being a "distinct individual" or a "member of a kind" and therefore a "part of the universe." This original worry about theistic personalism is very similar to the worry about whether God is "a being," or "an individual," discussed in Chapter 8. There I argued that we can call God "a being" and "an individual" without committing ourselves to any underlying ontological sameness with respect to God and creatures. The same form of argument also pertains to the question whether God is "a person." We should, therefore, note the many controversial metaphysical assumptions baked into Davies's seemingly innocent line of argument: that anything we call "a person" is also a member of a natural kind ("Persons"); that being a member of a kind implies the possibility of

---

Press, 2000]), and Edward Wierenga (*The Nature of God* [Ithaca, NY: Cornell University Press, 1989]). For analytic criticism of PBT, see Jeff Speaks, "The Method of Perfect Being Theology," *Faith and Philosophy* 31 (2014): 256–66, "Perfect Being Theology and Modal Truth," *Faith and Philosophy* 33 (2016): 465–73. Yujin Nagasawa's *Maximal God* (New York: Oxford University Press, 2017) offers a new defense of perfect being theism, but does not actually argue that God possess perfect power, knowledge, or goodness. Instead of the traditional "omni-properties," Nagasawa argues that it suffices for a maximally great God to instantiate the best consistent combination of great-making properties. Nagasawa's approach—whatever its other merits—renders him more vulnerable than other PBT theorists to the theological worries that motivate the theistic personalism objection.

[5] Davies, *An Introduction to the Philosophy of Religion*, 11. Even Davies's account is somewhat tendentious, since he says that theistic personalists "frequently reject almost all the tenets of classical theism." No doubt many of his targets would regard themselves as classical theists, and so would not recognize themselves in this description.

other members of that kind; that any member of a kind must share really existing properties with other members of that kind; and that, consequently, nothing that is "a person" could be ontologically unique.[6] Yet the bare claim that God is a person does not presuppose any of these controversial assumptions. Without them, the theistic personalism worry evaporates, even on Davies's own terms.

Although Davies's initial discussion is fairly restrained, in both scholarly and popular critiques of analytic theism, the term "theistic personalism" has recently taken on a life of its own. Often it becomes a vehicle for outright mockery. One can get a sense of the level of discourse from this passage by David Bentley Hart:

> Many Anglophone theistic philosophers...reared as they have been in a post-Fregean intellectual environment, have effectively broken with classical theistic tradition altogether, adopting a style of thinking that the Dominican philosopher Brian Davies calls theistic personalism. I prefer to call it monopolytheism myself (or perhaps "mono-poly-theism"), since it seems to me to involve a view of God not conspicuously different from the polytheistic picture of the gods as merely very powerful discrete entities who possess a variety of distinct attributes that lesser entities also possess, if in smaller measure; it differs from polytheism, as far as I can tell, solely in that it posits the existence of only one such being. It is a way of thinking that suggests that God, since he is only a particular instantiation of various concepts and properties, is logically dependent on some more comprehensive reality embracing both him and other beings. For philosophers who think in this way, practically all the traditional metaphysical attempts to understand God as the source of all reality become impenetrable.[7]

So, in summary, theistic personalists supposedly regard God not just as "personal" but literally as a person—the greatest conceivable person, to be sure, but still a person in more or less the same sense as an ordinary human person. According to critics, treating God as a person, even the greatest conceivable person, is equivalent to treating God as a very exalted creature. It is just another form of ontotheological idolatry. Instead of the metaphysically ultimate, absolutely transcendent God of the Christian faith, we get...something else. God becomes merely the biggest, best, most powerful thing there is—Zeus on steroids, but nicer—and so, once again, God has become too similar to creatures.

As Hart's quotation makes clear, the theistic personalism charge is really just an excitable version of the same worries about ontological sameness discussed in Chapter 8. Insofar as I have already addressed those worries, I have already

---

[6] See the discussion in Chapter 8 on God as "a being" and "an individual."
[7] Hart, *Experience of God*, 127–28.

responded to the theistic personalism charge.[8] And to be honest, I do think that "theistic personalism" is more a public relations problem for analytic theology than a substantive theological worry. In informal conversations, I have regularly observed that younger theologians have so thoroughly internalized the "theistic personalist/classical theist" dichotomy that they are surprised when I tell them that virtually all analytic theists affirm creation out of nothing and accept the creator/creature distinction. So while I very much doubt that there is any plausible sense in which the God of analytic theology is like Zeus and Odin, there is still some value in showing exactly why not.

Analytic Perfect Being Theology and the Creator/Creature Distinction

Admittedly, at first glance, it can be hard to see what all the fuss is about. Analytic PBT theorists say that God is "a person" because God exhibits personal characteristics like knowing, willing, and loving.[9] Their opponents agree that God exhibits characteristics like knowing, willing, and loving, and even agree that God is personal, but still deny that God is "a person." So both sides agree that the very same characteristics make God either "a person" or "personal," depending on their preferred terminology. Insofar as this is anything other than a lexical difference, the worry, once again, seems to be that calling God "a person" commits us to various forms of ontological sameness between God and creatures. To respond to this worry, PBT theorists need to show that the divine attributes and activities are sufficiently different from their correlative creaturely attributes and activities. More precisely, PBT theorists need to show that divine knowing, willing, and loving (etc.) differ sufficiently from creaturely knowing, willing, and loving. Suppose we could articulate a concept of God on which God is "a person," but still sufficiently different from any created thing, such that we preserve the distinction between divine, uncreated persons and human, created persons. In that case, I do not think there would be any worry about whether we can call God "a person." We would simply have semantic univocity without ontological sameness, once again.

---

[8] Note Hart's conflation of logical and ontological dependence in the quoted passage. Our statements about God, or our concepts of God, might logically depend on, in the sense of presuppose, our concept of this or that property. But that does not mean that God himself, the creator of heaven and earth, stands in a relation of dependence on those properties. Hart's indictment is actually another case of conflating semantic univocity and ontological sameness.

[9] In fact, leading analytic PBT theorists already accept that the term "person" must take on an extended meaning when applied to God, For example, Swinburne agrees that God is a person only in an analogical sense (*A Christian God*, 156) and claims that there are some respects in which on his view God is not a person (*The Coherence of Theism*, 105). T. J. Mawson concurs: according to Mawson, God is "more of a person than any of us" (*Belief in God*, 19). For discussion of these points, see Ben Page, "Wherein Lies the Debate? Concerning Whether God Is a Person," *International Journal for Philosophy of Religion* 85 (2019): 307–8.

PBT theorists, therefore, need to show that God is not just a very exalted creature. Happily, when properly understood, this just is the project of analytic perfect being theology. Analytic perfect being theology is a way of drawing the creator/creature distinction, not a way of effacing it. The method is cataphatic rather than apophatic, but the intended outcome is the same: to distinguish God from everything that is not God, and to make it clear that everything that is not God depends entirely on God.

Creation out of Nothing, Again

The best way to preserve the creator/creature distinction is by affirming a strong doctrine of creation out of nothing. As discussed in Chapter 7, leading PBT theorists explicitly affirm creation out of nothing, including the claim that everything that exists depends entirely upon God for its continuing existence. Here, again, is Thomas V. Morris, one of the contemporary founders of analytic PBT:

> Absolutely everything distinct from God depends on God for its existence. This is a foundational claim for any thoroughly theistic ontology. If God is the greatest possible being, a maximally perfect source of existence, then he is not just one more item in the inventory of reality. He is the hub of the wheel, the center and focus, the ultimate support, of all. The difference between theism and atheism is thus not just a disagreement over whether one entity of a certain description exists or not. It is a disagreement over the origin, and thus the ultimate nature, of everything.[10]

Recall David Bentley Hart's claim that on the analytic "way of thinking," God becomes "only a particular instantiation of various concepts and properties," and is, therefore, "logically dependent on some more comprehensive reality embracing both him and other beings."[11] But PBT theorists like Morris, Mawson, Leftow, and Swinburne all explicitly argue that God is metaphysically ultimate, the fundamental source of the existence of everything other than God. They all explicitly deny that God depends on any "more comprehensive reality." They all explicitly affirm that God creates and sustains *ex nihilo*. Furthermore, their views are not atypical of analytic theologians.[12] The insinuation that analytic

---

[10] Morris, *Our Idea of God*, 155.   [11] Hart, *Experience of God*, 125–26.

[12] Some prominent analytic theists do deny that God creates all abstract objects: see, for example, Peter van Inwagen, "God and Other Uncreated Things," Nicholas Wolterstorff, *On Universals* (Chicago: University of Chicago Press, 1970). For useful discussion and rebuttal, see Michelle Panchuk, "Created and Uncreated Things: A Neo-Augustinian Solution to the Bootstrapping Problem," *International Philosophical Quarterly* 56 (2016): 99–112; Paul Gould, ed., *Beyond the Control of God?*, Leftow, *God and Necessity*, 510–35.

theologians turn God into some kind of Greco-Roman deity is simply false. Their views about creation already suffice to rebut the "theistic personalism" charge.

God and Metaphysical Modality

Perfect being theology can sharpen the creator/creature distinction. PBT proceeds by way of conceptual reflection on the divine nature and divine attributes. This kind of reflection is itself a method for distinguishing God from creatures. The method becomes even more powerful when we bear in mind the modal status of God's existence and attributes. It is a foundational claim of PBT that God exists necessarily—God cannot fail to exist—whereas creatures exist contingently, precisely because they depend on God. This difference establishes a sharp distinction between creator and creature. No created thing exists necessarily.

Analytic theists explicate divine necessity using modal logic and the idiom of "possible worlds." The claim that God exists necessarily is equivalent to the claim that God exists in all possible worlds. The easiest way to understand this idiom is by thinking about alternative ways this world, our world, could have developed. Here "world" should be understood maximally: not just the Earth, but the entire universe (or multiverse, should there be such), including everything contingent—everything that a Christian theist would regard as created. In the actual world, Paris is the capital city of France, but that does not seem like a necessary truth: we can imagine various ways in which history happened differently, with the result that Toulouse (let's say), rather than Paris, is the capital of France. In the actual world, the closest star to the Earth, other than the Sun, is 4.22 light years away, but it might well have been 5.22 light years away instead, so that is not a necessary truth either. So in contrast with these contingent truths, the claim that God exists necessarily can be understood as the claim that there is no way the world could have gone such that there is no God. God's existence is not contingent: it is not the case that there just happens to be an almighty creator, but there may well not have been.[13] Rather, God exists necessarily.

Critics of analytic PBT and theistic personalism sometimes argue that even a necessarily existing God might not be metaphysically ultimate. Often, such critics are committed to some account of divine simplicity. On their view, a composite God that necessarily exists still cannot serve as the absolute, ultimate, most fundamental explanation, because we would still be left with questions about *why* God exists necessarily, and why God is "composed" in this way and not that. The

---

[13] As I briefly discussed in Chapter 4, one of the advances of modern modal logic is that we now have sensible ways to speak of entities and objects as necessarily existing, whereas on previous understandings of modality, necessary existence seemed nonsensical, because the realm of necessity was restricted to statements, and associated with analytic truths ("All bachelors are unmarried males").

doctrine of divine simplicity—that God has no parts at all, not even conceptual parts—is thought to provide a final answer to such questions.

It is not my task in this book to defend or criticize divine simplicity, but it is worth emphasizing that the analytic "necessary existence account" is logically compatible with divine simplicity. That is, there is no reason why one could not affirm both. I can also concede that, providing we can make sense of it, the doctrine of divine simplicity might provide a further explanation why God exists necessarily: God exists necessarily because God is simple, and therefore his essence is identical to his act of existing. But even without simplicity, the necessary existence account sufficiently distinguishes God from creatures, and successfully establishes that God is metaphysically ultimate, which is, after all, what we are trying to do.

Now consider the modal status of the divine attributes. God is not just very powerful, but omnipotent, as powerful as it is possible to be. Furthermore, God is *essentially* and *necessarily* omnipotent—which means that God cannot fail to exemplify omnipotence, whether in our world or in any alternative possible world. Defining omnipotence precisely is a tricky philosophical task, but as a rough-and-ready definition, let's just say that God has the maximum possible power to bring about states of affairs.[14] Arguably, there cannot be two omnipotent beings, since they would each have the power to bring about states of affairs unwanted by the other, which is impossible.[15] So necessary existence and omnipotence already secure (Divine Uniqueness) and (Divine Ultimacy) and distinguish God from creatures. I suspect, though will not argue, that we could make parallel moves with other divine attributes: no creature could be essentially and necessarily omniscient, no creature could be perfectly good, and so forth. The "God of perfect being theology" could never be a creature, not even a very exalted creature, because no creature could instantiate the divine attributes, and certainly no creature could instantiate them in all possible worlds. This is what I mean when I say that PBT is a cataphatic way of drawing the creator/creature distinction.

Here I think it is worth dwelling on a very real difference in the way that analytic and non-analytic thinkers use modal terminology. In non-analytic discourse, modal terms—terms like "essential/accidental," or "possible/impossible," or "contingent/necessary"—are often used loosely. One sometimes sees expressions calling Christ "the impossible possibility," for example, which seems to be a way of saying that the incarnation is "very unlikely" or "unexplainable" or "completely unpredictable" or "miraculous," or some such. But this is not the way analytic theologians use modal terms. Analytic thinkers use modal terms like "impossible," "possible,"

---

[14] For a (much) fuller account, see Brian Leftow, "Omnipotence," in Thomas P. Flint and Michael C. Rea, eds., *The Oxford Handbook of Philosophical Theology* (New York: Oxford University Press, 2009), 167–98.

[15] I recognize that matters get tricky here, and not everyone would agree that there cannot be more than one omnipotent being.

and "necessary" in their strictest sense, such that the first term is logically contradicted by both of the others. Impossible states of affairs can never obtain, period. Possible states of affairs can obtain. Necessary states of affairs must obtain.

When we bear this point about modal terminology in mind, it is easier to appreciate what analytic theologians are trying to do with perfect being theology. When analytic theologians give an account of divine omnipotence, for example, that account is supposed to spell out what it would be for God to have the greatest possible power in all possible worlds. They therefore find it puzzling when opponents accuse them of limiting or reducing God. For what is the alternative to saying that God has the greatest possible power? That God has more than the greatest possible power? Logical space divides exhaustively into the possible and the impossible. Once we find ourselves saying that God has "more than the greatest possible power," contradiction looms. Suppose God really could do something impossible. But if God can do it, then it would be possible, by definition. And if something is impossible, then not even God could do it, by definition. If the statement "God has more than the greatest possible power" is meant literally, it expresses not a paradox, but a contradiction. A contradiction cannot express a deep and important truth about divine mystery, because it cannot express any truth at all. Of course, one might legitimately wonder whether finite humans are really in a position to *identify* what is possible for God. This is an important question, and I return to it below.

Limits, Limit Cases, and Barry Miller's "Most Unlikely God"

In summary, analytic PBT is really a way of drawing, not erasing, the creator/creature distinction. I would now like to test this claim against a genuinely sophisticated critique of analytic PBT. Barry Miller's *A Most Unlikely God* offers one such critique. According to Miller, analytic PBT theorists erase the creature/creature distinction because they treat divine attributes as the logical maxima of created attributes rather than as altogether "off the scale" of created attributes. According to Miller, the divine attributes and creaturely attributes are different in kind, rather than merely in degree. On the analytic view, by contrast, "God is like some of his creatures in being powerful, knowing, good, and so on. He is unlike them, however, in having each of these properties to the maximum degree." Miller faults this view "not because it attributes too much to God, but because it attributes far too little." In effect, Miller is accusing analytic PBT theorists of theistic personalism before the term itself was actually in vogue. He continues:

> For the creator of the Universe, even the maximum degree of all the great-making properties is not enough... All these might well be more than enough for a perfect human being, and they might even be exactly right for any creature that was

a perfect pure spirit. They are far from right, however, for the perfect being who created the Universe. He is simply not like that at all; and perfect-being theology does him a great disservice in suggesting that he is.[16]

Soon Miller reaches the by now familiar conclusion: "As conceived of by perfect-being theologians, therefore, God turns out to be simply the greatest thing around, some kind of super-being that would be quite capable of evoking admiration and wonder, but who could scarcely be described as being absolutely transcendent, or as being worthy of worship."[17]

Miller's alternative to analytic PBT is ingenious, and trades on the distinction between a "limit *simpliciter*" and a "limit case." A limit *simpliciter* is a member of the series it concludes; for example, the speed of light is the limit *simpliciter* of the speed of moving bodies, since nothing can move faster than the speed of light. A limit case, by contrast, is not even a member of the series for which it is a limit case, but is outside that series; nevertheless, the limit case is that to which the series points. For example, consider a series of regular polygons with sides n, $n+1$, $n+2$, and so on. The limit case of this series is a circle, which is not a member of this series because it is not an n-sided polygon at all.[18] Nevertheless, the series points to the circle as its limit case. Miller's ingenious idea is that the divine attributes are *limit cases* of creaturely attributes, rather than mere limits. God's power is off the scale of creaturely power, in the way that a circle is off the scale of n-sided polygons. Analytic PBT treats the divine attributes as different only in degree from creaturely attributes, and thereby turns the divine attributes into mere limits.

So much for Miller's critique. Let us turn to his positive account. What is the "limit case" of creaturely power, according to Miller? An interesting question, as it turns out: according to Miller, the utterly transcendent, off-the-scale limit case that absolutely distinguishes God's unique hyper-power from ordinary creaturely power is...creation out of nothing.[19] So, according to Miller, the fact that God creates out of nothing is what shows that divine power is fundamentally different from created power. But, as we have seen, all the leading PBT theorists also hold that God creates and sustains out of nothing. So both sides agree about the nature of God's power, and even agree about the first-order question of what distinguishes God's power from creaturely power (God's power does not require anything else to operate on). They disagree only about the second-order, semantic issue of whether to call God's power to create out of nothing a "limit case" of power, like Miller, or "the greatest conceivable" power, like analytic PBT theorists. So why are analytic PBT theorists guilty of turning God into "the greatest thing

---

[16] Miller, *Most Unlikely God*, vii–viii.   [17] Miller, *Most Unlikely God*, 3.
[18] Miller, *Most Unlikely God*, 7–10.
[19] Miller, *Most Unlikely God*, 87–88. "Hyper-power" is my term, not Miller's. Miller's view that creation out of nothing is a limit case and not a limit *simpliciter* is ad hoc: he just stipulates that exercising power presupposes that something already exists to exercise power *on* (88). But why assume that?

around, some kind of super-being," when Miller himself is not? Another interesting question—and one for which Miller offers no answer.[20]

Miller apparently finds major differences between his own project and the project of analytic PBT, such that he gives us a God whose power is "off the scale" of created power, when PBT gives us only an exalted creature. But both sides agree that there can be no power greater than the power to create out of nothing, and both sides agree that only God has that power. If Miller preserves the creator/creature distinction, then so do his analytic opponents, since their substantive conclusions are identical. I take this convergence to be evidence, contra Miller, that analytic PBT can serve as a way of drawing the creator/creature distinction, and a way of avoiding idolatry.[21]

Analytic perfect being theology treats God as the perfect being, and it tries to understand what it would be to possess (e.g.) perfect goodness, wisdom, and power. Critics like Miller think that the divine perfections sought by PBT are too similar to created properties. In fact, however, the logic of perfection may well be such that analytic notions of "perfect goodness" or "perfect power" implicitly function more like limit cases (in Miller's sense) anyway, even within the project of analytic perfect being theology.[22] Consider perfect knowledge, omniscience. Just as the first infinite cardinal number is not simply "one more than the next biggest number," so, plausibly, perfect knowledge is not just "knowing the final true proposition," and so on for the other divine attributes. Suppose there is a being, Zod, who is almost omniscient: Zod knows every true proposition but one, p. As it turns out, this is not a coherent scenario. For there are uncountably many other true propositions that imply p, and (by hypothesis) Zod knows all of those propositions without knowing p itself. So Zod would not know p, but would know such propositions as:

(1) I have evidence sufficient for knowledge that p.
(2) Anyone who fails to believe p is making a mistake.
(3) I am making a mistake in failing to believe p.
(4) If only I knew p, I would know all truths.
(5) I know q and I know that q entails p but I do not know p.
(6) I know r and I know that (r entails q and q entails p) but I do not know p.

---

[20] Nowhere does he note that his chief named opponents, including Swinburne and Plantinga, also affirm creation out of nothing.

[21] I hate to break it to Miller, but by my lights he is himself an analytic perfect being theorist. He is an analytic Thomist, who gives his own constructive account of God as the greatest possible reality in dialogue with Aquinas (with whom he agrees) and analytic philosophers of religion (with whom he does not agree). The fact that he criticizes what he takes to be the dominant analytic approach to PBT does not make his own constructive project any less analytic.

[22] Miller considers and rejects this possibility (wrongly, in my view), in *A Most Unlikely God*, 85.

And so on.[23] We could iterate such propositions at will. The takeaway point is this: there can be no Zod, because nothing can really be "almost omniscient." The gap between "omniscient" and "not omniscient" seems more like the gap between the first infinite cardinal and "a really big number." In other words, it seems like a gap that cannot be bridged by successive addition: more like a qualitative than a quantitative gap. Despite his own protestations, in fact, it seems more like Miller's limit case than like a limit *simpliciter*. Miller's point is that there is a radical discontinuity between a limit case and the series for which it is the limit case. Yet there is a similar radical discontinuity between omniscience and almost perfect knowledge. I am confident that the same point would hold for the other divine attributes.[24] The difference between perfection and imperfection cannot be bridged by successive addition: nothing can really be almost perfect. One is even tempted to say that there is an "absolute distinction" between perfection and imperfection, even in analytic perfect being theology.

Are God and Creatures "On the Same Scale of Value"?

Miller worries that the God of analytic PBT is "anything but ineffable," and "discomfitingly anthropomorphic" as a result of the "assumption that greatness in any respect is to be understood in terms of a scale of more and less, with the greatest being at the maximum on that scale."[25] This is a legitimate worry. Many critics do hold that PBT errs precisely because it places God and creatures on the same scale of value, and, to be fair, many analytic thinkers do little to dispel the worry.[26] In order to dispel the worry, however, we must distinguish between two different ways that God and creatures could be "on the same scale" of value. They could be on the same conceptual scale, or they could be on the same quantitative scale. The real worry seems to be about putting them on the same quantitative scale: that would mean that the more of some value God has, the less is available for

---

[23] This list is a modification of Edward Wierenga, "Augustinian Perfect Being Theology and the God of Abraham, Isaac, and Jacob," *International Journal for Philosophy of Religion* 69 (2011): 149. Wieregna directs this criticism against Nagasawa's argument that God does not have to be maximally perfect in order to be worthy of worship: Yujin Nagasawa, "A New Defense of Anselmian Theism," *Philosophical Quarterly* 58 (2008): 577–96.

[24] Consider: suppose God had all possible power except the power to cause a single leaf on a single tree to move. But then God couldn't make the wind move the leaf, or make the tree fall over, thereby moving the leaf, and he couldn't make any creature move the leaf, etc. The point still holds if we leave out intermediary causes. If God can't move the leaf immediately, (by ceasing to create it in one location and then creating it again in another location), then God cannot be creating and sustaining the leaf out of nothing, and plausibly, if God cannot create the *leaf* out of nothing he cannot create *ex nihilo* at all.

[25] Miller, *A Most Unlikely God*, 2–3.

[26] Nagasawa, *Maximal God*, is explicit that God and creatures are on the same scale of value. Other PBT theorist do not so much explicitly endorse this suggestion as assume it, without considering whether it might be theologically problematic.

creatures, and vice versa. For example, if God and creatures were on the same quantitative scale of value with respect to power, then there would be some total aggregate amount of power that exists and that includes the power of both God and creatures. On this scenario, if the percentage of total power held by God is X, then the percentage held by creatures would have to be $100-X$. I agree that this is the wrong picture, no matter how closely X approximates 100. Because God creates out of nothing, God's power and goodness are the source of all created power and goodness and so we should not say that God's power and goodness come at the expense of creaturely power and goodness. They cannot be measured on the same quantitative scale.[27]

By contrast, putting God and creatures on the same conceptual scale of value just means that we can make comparative judgments about their power, goodness, and knowledge. We can say, for example, that God is more powerful than Socrates, without trying to reduce their power to a common underlying measure. Likewise, we can make general comparisons like "A God who creates out of nothing is more powerful than a God who cannot create out of nothing." It seems obvious that we can make these kinds of comparative judgments. We can make them even if God's power is the transcendent source of Socrates's power and not an instance of creaturely power. The same goes for goodness and the other divine attributes. (God really is better than Socrates, after all: God is better than Socrates *because* God's uncreated goodness is the source of Socrates's goodness.) When we go on to posit that God instantiates the logical maxima of values like power, goodness, and knowledge, we do put God and creatures on the same *conceptual* scale, but this does not entail that they are on the same *quantitative* scale. Nothing about analytic PBT requires us to assume that divine power, goodness, and knowledge come at the expense of creaturely power, goodness, and knowledge. Again, the substantive convergence between Miller and analytic PBT theorists discussed above provides evidence for this conclusion, as does the suggestion that there is an unquantifiable gulf between perfection and imperfection.

Absolute Transcendence or Sufficient Transcendence?

We should also distinguish between absolute transcendence and sufficient transcendence. I agree that as long as God and creatures can be measured on the same conceptual scale of value, God cannot be absolutely transcendent—at least not if we construe the word "absolutely" in its literal sense. And so I agree that, in this respect, the God of analytic perfect being theology is not absolutely transcendent. Yet no Christian should hold that God is *absolutely* transcendent, at least not

---

[27] Mark Murphy makes a similar suggestion about divine and creaturely goodness in *God's Own Ethics* (New York: Oxford University Press, 2017), 79–83.

when speaking literally. The absolutely transcendent is unknowable, and the unknowable is unknown: not just unknowable by natural reason but unknowable full-stop. A God who is absolutely transcendent cannot also be revealed, not even revealed as an inexhaustible mystery. If "absolutely transcendent" really means "absolutely transcendent unless revealed," then Christians should agree that God is not actually absolutely transcendent now, since he has, in fact, revealed himself to us. And if your response to this suggestion is to insist that God is so absolutely transcendent that he can still reveal himself *while remaining* absolutely transcendent, then I can only conclude that you are using the word "absolutely" (or perhaps the word "transcendent") with a different meaning, much as someone who calls Christ the "impossible possibility" is using the word "impossible" with a different meaning. Taken literally, the absolutely transcendent is unknowable and the unknowable is unknown. Absolute transcendence is the death of Christian piety.

What really matters is that God is *sufficiently* transcendent. To say that God is *sufficiently* transcendent is to say that God is not a part of creation and does not in any way depend on creation. So long as we preserve the creator/creature distinction and affirm both (Divine Uniqueness) and (Divine Ultimacy), we can be confident that we regard God as sufficiently transcendent. Everyone who wants to remain in the broadly orthodox Christian tradition should agree that God is sufficiently transcendent. Beyond that, there is room for fraternal (and sororal) disagreement about the scope of divine transcendence. The Christian tradition offers us many options besides the binary choice between absolute transcendence and idolatry. So long as analytic perfect being theology gives us a God who is sufficiently transcendent, the question of idolatry need not arise.

Conceivability and Possibility: How Could We Ever Determine What Is Possible for God?

Even if my defense of PBT succeeds, a final worry remains. I can well imagine someone replying as follows: "OK, I will grant that God cannot be more powerful (etc.) than it is possible to be. But finite, limited human beings are in no position to say what the limits of divine power, knowledge, and goodness really are. That is the real problem with PBT." In other words, the real problem is epistemological: when I say that God has "the maximum possible power," I can only mean "as much power as I, a very limited creature, am able to conceive," which, for all I know, is not very much power at all. The anthropomorphism and idolatry do not stem from the purely formal claim that God has the greatest possible power, knowledge, and goodness, but from our substantive attempts to specify what counts as the greatest possible power, knowledge, and goodness. So the objection is: These substantive attempts are why PBT is guilty of theistic personalism. They seem like prideful hubris. They evince the onthotheological attitude, they are contrary to the attitude of (Worship), and therefore they are idolatrous. This is a very important objection, and one worth taking seriously.

The first point to note in response, however, is that this objection has no unique purchase on analytic PBT or even on analytic theology more generally. All theological discourse is vulnerable to this worry, because all theology is the product of finite human efforts to understand a transcendent God. In a way, this point is the same as the point about absolute transcendence above: if we cannot make true statements about God at all, then PBT is indeed pointless. But to be consistent, someone who holds this view would have to reject every other form of constructive theology as well. On this objection, literally every theologian is a "theistic personalist," simply because every form of theology uses human language and is vulnerable to human error.

Second, the project of PBT is completely compatible with having a healthy sense of one's own epistemic fallibility. In other words, we can engage in PBT even though we also recognize that we are often wrong—even about mundane matters, let alone about the nature of God. PBT theorists do take themselves to be articulating what would count as having the greatest possible power, knowledge, goodness, and so forth. But this project need not display the prideful assumption that its conclusions cannot possibly be wrong. So a PBT theorist can consistently say "I am a fallible, limited human being, and so, of course, I might be wrong about what counts as the greatest possible power. Here is my best attempt. If I have gone wrong—and I agree that that is likely—show me where."[28] In this respect, they are in exactly the same position as every theologian, and, indeed, every other scholar. So while it is certainly possible that an individual theologian might be guilty of a prideful, ontotheological attitude when doing PBT, there is no reason to think that the method itself presupposes such an attitude.

Conclusion

The outcome of analytic PBT is a God who creates and sustains everything else *ex nihilo*, and who is as powerful, good, wise, etc. as it is possible to be; a God, moreover, who bears these attributes necessarily and essentially, who cannot not exist, and who therefore exists in all possible worlds. Nothing other than God could have all these attributes. So the idea that perfect being theology erases the distinction between God and creatures does not really hold up. Instead, perfect

---

[28] Recall again Brian Leftow's words, cited in Chapter 2:

> I give many perfect-being arguments in what follows. As I give them, I have a nagging fear that I am just making stuff up. This is not due to uncertainty about God's being perfect. Rather, our ideas of what it is to be perfect are inconsistent and flawed, and there is no guarantee that they match up with what God's perfection really is.
>
> (Leftow, *God and Necessity*, 11–12)

being theology establishes that distinction, systematically and precisely. The idea that the God of perfect being theology is equivalent to a Greco-Roman "god" is laughable. In fact, it would be quite instructive to lay out all the ways in which the "God of PBT" differs from, say, Zeus—who comes into existence, has a spatiotemporal location, is regularly thwarted (even by humans), who often seems quite ignorant, and who, by the way, occasionally commits various forms of sexual assault. I leave this instructive comparison as an exercise for the reader.

True, the God of PBT is not absolutely transcendent. But as long as we preserve the creator/creature distinction, and do not regard God as something that we can manipulate to serve our own ends, then it seems to me that there is scope for rational disagreement about the nature of divine transcendence. To be sure, there are bedrock Christian presuppositions that we must preserve: that God creates out of nothing and is the sole, metaphysically ultimate source of everything else, including the source of all creaturely goodness, power, and wisdom; that God is the absolute standard by which those qualities are measured; that (e.g.) creaturely goodness only imperfectly and remotely resembles divine goodness; and above all, that God's goodness, power, and wisdom do not depend on anything other than God. These are the really fundamental claims. Questions about the full scope of divine transcendence are secondary, and should be understood as potential points of reasonable disagreement, rather than fixed boundaries that divide orthodoxy from heterodoxy. Our philosophical and theological intuitions pull us in multiple directions here.

The heresy of "theistic personalism" has always been labile. Even in Davies's original statement, one can already detect a certain characteristic slippage. The term sometimes seems to be a proxy for idolatrous anthropomorphism, but just as often, it functions as a label for anyone who denies that God is simple, immutable, or atemporal. If a "theistic personalist" is anyone who disagrees with any part of the broadly Thomist conception of God, then many contemporary analytic theologians are indeed theistic personalists, but that by itself does not make them idolaters.[29] The world does not divide into Thomists and idolaters. And if "theistic personalist" just means "not a Thomist," then the label loses much of its theological frisson.

When we look beyond the rhetoric, it often does seem as though much of the *argument* about "theistic personalism" concerns divine simplicity.[30] There is a

---

[29] I am, of course, aware that Thomists are not the only ones who affirm that God is simple, immutable, or atemporal, and not everyone whom I have criticized in this chapter is a Thomist. (Hart is not, for example.) But much of the animus against theistic personalism does seem to be driven by a particular kind of late twentieth-century "Blackfriars Thomism" which traces back to the thought of Herbert McCabe. One can recognize the abiding value of this form of Thomism while still rejecting the rhetoric of "theistic personalism" that emerges from it.

[30] Page makes the same point in "Wherein Lies the Debate?" 311–13. See, for example, Brian Davies, "Divine Simplicity," in Charles Taliaferro and Chad Meister, eds., *The Cambridge Companion to Christian Philosophical Theology* (Cambridge: Cambridge University Press, 2010), 38–39; Hart, *Experience of God*, 134–42.

large literature on simplicity, and I have no wish to add to it here except to say that if simplicity is the real issue, opponents of analytic PBT should say so, and argue about that, and drop the charge of theistic personalism altogether. Is affirming divine simplicity the only way to preserve divine transcendence, avoid idolatry, and distinguish God from creatures? Even as an advocate of simplicity myself, I find this suggestion implausible, but the underlying argument is certainly worth having. Yet this kind of cross-disciplinary discussion becomes less likely, not more likely, so long as opponents of analytic PBT are content to indulge in empty, self-soothing rhetoric about "mono-poly-theism" and "super-duper superman." We need more arguments, not more anathemas.

10

Analytic Theology as a Spiritual Practice

In order to avoid idolatry, we must think about God with an attitude of worship. Theologians are right to worry about ontotheology and idolatry because both are incompatible with the attitude of worship. I have said that we exhibit the "ontotheological attitude" when we exhibit immoderate certainty about our theological conclusions, when we attempt to claim the divine perspective for ourselves, or when we appeal to God to advance our own projects of dominance (see Chapters 7–8). Analytic theologians, like other theologians, can think about God either with an attitude of reverence and adoration or with an ontotheological attitude of mastery and control. While any individual theologian, analytic or otherwise, might fall into idolatry by exhibiting the ontotheological attitude, analytic theology *as a method* is no more vulnerable to idolatry and ontotheology than any other form of systematic theology.

This conclusion on its own suffices as a defense of analytic theology, but in my view, we can go considerably further: there is a sense in which analytic theology may be understood as a spiritual practice. This claim is counterintuitive, and in some quarters, likely to be met with disbelief that borders on incredulity. To explain what I mean, I will first specify what counts as a spiritual practice, by drawing on Pierre Hadot. I then discuss Anselm and Aquinas, who present two historical examples of theology that is theoretical, but also practical in the relevant sense. These brief historical case studies pave the way for the main argument. It is possible to treat analytic theology as an authentically Christian spiritual practice because certain specific features of analytic argumentation can be regarded as spiritual exercises that cultivate virtue. The task of the intellectual, Christian or otherwise, analytic theologian or otherwise, is to see things as they are rather than as we want them to be. Thus, the intellectual life is also a life of virtue insofar as it requires us to engage in a disciplined and patient search for truth, and to subdue the prideful ego so that we will recognize the truth when we see it.

Before continuing, however, I want to be very clear that I do not mean to imply any invidious contrasts. I do not argue that analytic theology is more spiritually nourishing than other kinds of theology. I do not think that everyone would be better-off intellectually—let alone spiritually—if they converted to the one true method of analytic theology. My argument is narrow, and is aimed only at the assumption that analytic theology is especially spiritually sterile. That assumption is false.

Analytic Theology and the Academic Study of Religion. William Wood, Oxford University Press (2021). © William Wood.
DOI: 10.1093/oso/9780198779872.003.0010

Spiritual Practices

I first need to say more about what it could even mean to call analytic theology a "spiritual practice." The place to begin is with the French scholar Pierre Hadot. Hadot has argued that much ancient Hellenistic philosophy should be read as a series of spiritual exercises, through which would-be philosophers grow in virtue, and are progressively taught how to live and how to die.[1] According to Hadot, ancient philosophical schools resemble religious sects much more than they resemble the warring intellectual camps of modern philosophy departments. Schools were judged on the kinds of lives their adherents led as much as on matters of theory. Hadot presents two sets of "Stoic-Platonic" spiritual practices preserved by Philo of Alexandria:

> One of these lists enumerates the following elements: research (*zetesis*), thorough investigation (*skepsis*), reading (*anagnosis*), listening (*akroasis*), attention (*prosoche*), self-mastery (*enkrateia*), and indifference to indifferent things. The other names successively: reading, meditations (*meletati*), therapies of the passions, remembrance of good things, self-mastery (*enkrateia*), and the accomplishment of duties.[2]

I do not propose to rehearse Hadot's own analysis of these practices, but speaking summarily, we can say that intellectual practices are also spiritual exercises when they (1) aim at self-improvement or liberation, instead of simply the acquisition of knowledge; (2) discipline the passions, since unchecked passions and immoderate desires are the enemy of both the spiritual life and the life of the mind; (3) help us see the world as it really is, rather than as we imagine or wish it to be; and (4) help us cultivate specific virtues that are at once intellectual and moral, like attention or concentration.

All four of these aims hang together: changing the way we see the world is the first step toward changing the self, but we cannot change the way we see the world as long as we are in thrall to the passions and lack the virtues of attention and concentration. Some of the practices enumerated by Philo seem more direct (meditations, disciplining the passions, training the memory), and others seem more indirect (research, investigation, listening). Others occupy a middle ground between the two (attention and concentration). The overall point is that philosophical practices that look like metaphysical theorizing can also have spiritual effects for those who read and think with the right attitude. In other words, the practice of philosophy can be spiritually nourishing, even when it is also aimed at constructing better theories. The purpose of retrieving the ancient sense of

---

[1] Pierre Hadot, *Philosophy as a Way of Life: Spiritual Exercises from Socrates to Foucault* (Malden, MA: Blackwell, 1995).

[2] Hadot, *Philosophy as a Way of Life*, 84.

"philosophy as a way of life" is to show that philosophical writing can be both theoretical and practical at once.

Christian Philosophical Theology as a Way of Life: Anselm and Aquinas

There is a clear tradition of "philosophical theology as a way of life" in the Christian tradition. Analytic theology is an authentic development of that tradition. In order to set contemporary analytic theology in its historical context, I next examine Anselm of Canterbury and Thomas Aquinas. They furnish two quite different examples of Christian philosophical theology that is broadly theoretical and also broadly practical. Their theology features deductive, linear arguments aimed at propositional assent, but their arguments may also be read as an itinerary for spiritual growth. Among theologians, it is now fashionable to emphasize the spiritual and practical aspects of the theology of Anselm and Aquinas. By contrast, most philosophers of religion downplay those aspects or ignore them outright. So this section is another exercise in bridge-building, aimed at convincing both sides to see the value of a rival tradition of interpretation. Anselm and Aquinas present theoretical arguments that are also embedded in wider Christian spiritual practices, with the result that their theology as a whole is both theoretical and practical. Analytic theology is not a direct imitation of either Anselm or Aquinas, but a further stage of development in the tradition to which both belong. By looking at Anselm and Aquinas, we gain a better sense of what it means to say that philosophical theology as such may be regarded as a spiritual practice, and a better sense of the argumentative bar that I must clear in order to show that analytic theology should be so regarded.

Anselm: Dialogue, Mediation, Prayer—But Also Argument

Anselm of Canterbury is justifiably regarded as a forerunner of analytic theology. Contemporary analytic theologians and philosophers of religion draw inspiration from Anselm's perfect being theology, his arguments for the existence of God, and his defense of the necessity of the incarnation. They rarely attend to the literary devices and rhetorical forms he uses in his writing, however. Instead, they typically abstract a series of propositional claims from Anselm's text in order to reconstruct what they take to be his real arguments, and then go on to assess those reconstructions.[3] This method is almost constitutive of a certain style of analytic engagement with historical sources, and I have no wish to criticize it.

---

[3] See, for example, Brian Leftow, "Anselm on the Cost of Salvation," *Medieval Philosophy and Theology* 6 (1997): 73–92.

Yet the mere fact that analytic exegetes find it necessary to reconstruct and re-present Anselm's arguments shows that he himself offers something other than linear arguments available for easy inspection. Rather, Anselm's own texts take the form of mediations, prayers, and dialogues—literary forms reminiscent of the ancient spiritual exercises discussed by Hadot.

Consider, for example, the *Proslogion*.[4] It certainly contains one or more a priori arguments for the existence of God (*Pros* 2–4), as well as something very like a decision procedure by which we may derive the divine attributes ("God is whatever it is better to be than not to be" [*Pros* 5]). At the same time, in its prologue, Anselm tells us that he wrote the *Proslogion* "adopting the role of one who strives to raise his mind to the contemplation of God" and describes the often frustrating process by which he arrived at its central argument as a spiritual struggle that culminates in a joyful spark of insight.[5] And, of course, Chapter 1 (entitled "A Rousing of the Mind to the Contemplation of God") is a direct address to God that includes a long meditation on divine hiddenness and the cognitive consequences of the Fall. Even Chapters 2 and 3, which contain the so-called ontological argument, are directly addressed to God. They are, in other words, prayers.

Because it takes the form of an extended prayer, the *Proslogion* is also implicitly an extended dialogue with God. Some of Anselm's other great works explicitly take the form of dialogues. Hadot has argued that ancient philosophical dialogues are actually intended as spiritual exercises, in which the reader is meant to mimic the student's journey from ignorance to insight.[6] Marilyn McCord Adams finds a similar motivation in Anselm's dialogues: "The reader is meant, not merely to pass his/her eyes over the text, but actively to meditate the *Monologion*, to pray the *Proslogion*, to identify in the dialogue with first one speaker and then the other."[7]

Some readers have so emphasized the prayerful and meditative aspects of the *Proslogion* that they have gone on to deny that Anselm makes any properly philosophical arguments at all in that text. On this reading, Anselm writes within the context of faith, for an audience of believing Christians, and so cannot be trying to prove with philosophical arguments that the object of his faith is real or has a particular character. Only within the context of faith is it possible to understand

---

[4] I cite from *Anselm: Basic Writings*, ed. and trans. Thomas Williams (Indianapolis, IN: Hackett, 2007).

[5] Anselm, *Proslogion*, Prologue, 75:

> Sometimes I thought I could already grasp what I was looking for, and sometimes it escaped my mind completely. Finally, I gave up hope. I decided to stop looking for something impossible to find. But when I tried to stifle that thought altogether...it began to hound me more and more, although I resisted and fought against it. Then one day, when my violent struggle against its hounding had worn me down, the thing I had despaired of finding presented itself in the very clash of my thoughts, so that I eagerly embraced the thought I had been taking such pains to drive away.

[6] Hadot, *Philosophy as a Way of Life*, 89–93.

[7] Marilyn McCord Adams, "Anselm on Faith and Reason," in Brian Davies and Brian Leftow, eds., *The Cambridge Companion to Anselm* (New York: Cambridge University Press, 2004), 41–42.

the all-important phrase "that than which no greater can be conceived," a phrase that functions more like a divine name revealed by God than like the premise in a philosophical argument. The fact that the "argument" of the *Proslogion* takes the form of an extended meditation interspersed with direct prayers to God only seems to strengthen this interpretation.[8]

If this interpretation of Anselm is correct, it would furnish valuable ammunition to those who would sharply separate theoretical arguments from practical spiritual exercises. In my view, however, this interpretation is untenable. To be sure, Anselm does not hold in suspension his own belief in God, or imply that Christian faith requires a conclusive proof that God exists in order to be reasonable. Similarly, we can also grant that the "fool" addressed by Anselm in *Proslogion* 2–4 is not a modern atheist or a skeptic who sharply opposes faith and reason. One can grant all this and more and, nevertheless, hold that Anselm offers the argument in *Proslogion* 2–4 as a proof that God exists, and that he further offers many additional philosophical, theoretical arguments in the *Proslogion* and elsewhere.

Anselm offers an a priori argument that God exists using premises that (he believes) any rational person ought to accept, and he *also* sets this argument in the context of an extended meditation designed to elevate the mind toward the contemplation of God. As McCord Adams recognizes, the *Proslogion* is meant to do more than communicate propositional truths. It is meant to help bring about an affective and volitional change in the wills of his readers, and reorient them toward God. In this sense, the *Proslogion* resembles a spiritual exercise, like those discussed by Hadot. By virtue of reading Anselm's argument and identifying with Anselm's desire to understand the God in whom he believes, the reader is step by step led closer to that very same God.

Aquinas: *Sacra Doctrina* as Theoretical and Practical

When we turn from Anselm to Aquinas, we are immediately struck by a clear difference in the style of writing and method of arguing they each employ.[9] Aquinas does not write dialogues or meditations; nor does he pepper his writings

---

[8] The source of this line of interpretation is Karl Barth, *Fides Quaerens Intellectum: Anselm's Proof of the Existence of God in the Context of His Theological Scheme* (London: SCM, 1960).

[9] My interpretation in this section is guided especially by Mark Jordan, *Rewritten Theology: Aquinas after His Readers* (Malden, MA: Blackwell, 2006), Peter M. Candler Jr., "Reading Immemorially: The *Quaestio* and the Paragraph in the *Summa Theologiae*," *American Catholic Philosophical Quarterly* 78 (2004): 531–57; Wayne Hankey, "Philosophy as Way of Life for Christians? Iamblichan and Porphyrian Reflections on Religion, Virtue, and Philosophy in Thomas Aquinas," *Laval théologique et philosophique* 59 (2003): 193–224, and Bruce Marshall, "*Quod scit unda uetula*: Aquinas on the Nature of Theology," in Rik Van Nieuwenhove and Joseph Peter Wawrykow, eds., *The Theology of Thomas Aquinas* (Notre Dame, IN: University of Notre Dame Press, 2005), 1–35.

with prayers and exhortations. He treats theology—*sacra doctrina*—as a deductive Aristotelian science, and explicitly argues that it is more theoretical than practical (*ST* 1.1.1, 1.1.4).[10] To be sure, a large percentage of his corpus is composed of commentaries on authoritative texts, especially the Bible. As Hadot recognizes, the commentary is a venerable genre associated with ancient spiritual practices. And we must note that Aquinas himself explicitly distinguishes *sacra doctrina* from philosophy, understood as metaphysics (*ST* 1.1.1, 1.1.8). Yet the science of *sacra doctrina* employs philosophical reasoning, and its arguments are meant to persuade us to assent to various propositional truth claims. Even Aquinas's biblical commentaries offer controlled exercises in theoretical argument rather than the digressive, allegorical interpretations of, say, Origen or Bernard of Clairvaux. It is not an accident, and not without reason, that contemporary analytic theologians look to Aquinas as a forerunner. Yet Aquinas also regards theology as a spiritual practice. He can, therefore, serve as a forerunner of analytic theology in this respect as well, by showing us how theoretical reasoning can also serve the life of Christian virtue.

It is true that Aquinas does not write theology in the classic genres of prayer, meditation or pedagogical dialogue—the very genres that we most associate with philosophy or theology as a practically oriented "way of life." Yet the key genre in which he does write, the disputed question, is very much a kind of implicit dialogue. Indeed, the written *quaestio* purports to summarize an earlier oral public disputation, in which students and masters presented the best arguments for and against the question at issue.[11] The written *quaestio* does not offer the constant back-and-forth between student and teacher that characterizes an Anselmian pedagogical dialogue. But it does formally and explicitly introduce rival voices and arguments, and thereby encourage the reader to "learn by doing," as he finds himself entertaining and critiquing first one set of arguments, then another, before the question is resolved. When the student reads his teacher's words, he learns to think as his teacher thinks. The text of a disputed question does more than commend the specific propositions that Aquinas himself endorses. Reading a disputed question teaches us to imitate the way Aquinas thinks and reasons about God, the ultimate object of contemplation. In this sense, the disputed question presents an authentic development of the earlier Anselmian spiritual practice of writing and reading Christian pedagogical dialogues. The disputed question is not a dialogue, but it does serve a similar pedagogical function: it trains the mind in the techniques of rigorous thinking about God.

---

[10]   *ST* = *Summa Theologiae*.
[11]   For a brief account of the nature of the medieval disputation, see Brian Davies's introduction to Aquinas's *De malo* in Thomas Aquinas, *On Evil*, ed. Brian Davies (New York: Oxford University Press, 2003), 9.

In its microstructure, each individual article of Aquinas's capstone work, the *Summa Theologiae*, is a miniature disputation that also presents an abbreviated pedagogical exercise for its reader. When one reads an article of the *Summa*, one first encounters a series of objections, attributed to great teachers of the past. The reader thereby finds himself immediately situated amid an ongoing debate among rival authorities that stretches back to antiquity. The *sed contra* ("on the other hand") presents a single sharp and equally authoritative alternative view. To consider carefully both the objections and the *sed contra* requires mental flexibility and a holistic vision of the question at hand. Similarly, only after the reader has grasped the truth—as his teacher sees it—in the *responsio* (response) can he return to the original objections and understand how they have gone wrong. The reader learns to grasp all sides of an issue while he considers Aquinas's own argument, because Aquinas's argument developed in dialogue with those same alternative positions. The further implication is that Aquinas's own position will be challenged, perhaps by the very student reading his text, and will thus become fodder for future disputations, as the ongoing debate continues.

Accordingly, each article of the *Summa* trains its readers in the virtue of humility. The objections testify to the fact that even great authorities can err, which reminds readers that they too can err. The objections and replies together require the reader to consider rival positions carefully and respectfully before dismissing them. Even Aquinas himself, the master, positions himself less as a decisive and infallible guide to the truth than as one inquirer among others, stretching backward and forward through time. Among modern thinkers, one sometimes encounters the claim that there is something inherently prideful about asserting propositional truth claims in theology, and that to do so somehow reduces God to human categories of thought. The *Summa* shows that this charge is false. To reason well about God presupposes the virtue of intellectual humility, but intellectual humility does not require that we abandon assertion or argument altogether.

In its macrostructure, the *Summa* can be read as a spiritual itinerary, as we follow the trajectory of Aquinas's own reasoning about God. We progressively learn to understand God as metaphysical first cause, Trinity, creator, and governor of the world (in Part One); then we consider the nature of virtue and the happy life (in Part Two), before Aquinas finally leads us to Christ and the sacraments (in Part Three). Aquinas deliberately chose to treat his topics in this order, of course; it is also well known that his chosen order was innovative.[12] He wrote primarily for an audience of Dominican preachers, and—once again—he meant for the specific progression of articles and questions in the *Summa* to teach them *how* to think about each of the topics he treats, and not just *what* to think about those topics. Aquinas's deliberately chosen order has a pedagogical point: if we want to

---

[12] Jordan, *Rewritten Theology*, 116–35.

think properly about how to act, we must first learn to see our actions in a wider theological context. As we read through the *Summa* in order, we are trained to see that all questions, even the most seemingly practical, point forward, toward God as our final end, and backward, to God as our ultimate origin.

The *Summa* habituates its readers into a tradition of inquiry, a tradition that is also salvific because its object is God. Theology always has a salvific purpose, according to Aquinas. Reasoning about God is valuable because it prepares us for the beatific vision, the final goal of human life, and the fulfillment of our rational and intellectual capacities (*ST* 1.12.1). In other words, when God grants us the beatific vision, God also perfects the very same intellectual faculties we use when we practice *sacra doctrina*. Theology is a spiritual practice for Aquinas both because its goal is union with God and because its techniques are a creaturely way of seeking that final perfection. When we reason about God, we seek the beatific vision.

Aquinas, no less than Anselm, belongs squarely in the tradition of Christian philosophical theology as a spiritual practice. That tradition develops and changes in the intervening centuries, to be sure. The scholastic disputed question is like a dialogue, but it is not a dialogue. The *Summa* can be read as a meditative spiritual itinerary but this interpretation is far from obvious on its face. Still, in the *Summa* and elsewhere, Aquinas means to commend specific techniques of reasoning about God, in addition to arguments and truth claims. To use those techniques successfully, the inquirer must already have reached an appropriate level of intellectual and moral virtue; moreover, those same techniques also serve to foster intellectual and moral virtues in the inquirer, especially the virtue of humility.

I should now say a word about a distinction that I have to this point intentionally left vague. There is a difference between *doing* and *reading* philosophy or theology; that is, there is a difference between thinking and reasoning for oneself versus reading the work of another. Perhaps it makes sense to say that the former is a spiritual practice, but the latter is not. It is not hard to imagine that Anselm and Aquinas found themselves drawing closer to God as they carefully and prayerfully ruminated and wrote. When we imitate them, when we actually do what they did, it makes sense to say that we also engage in their spiritual practices. On the other hand, when we merely read the derivative product of their practices, perhaps we do not imitate them, and do not engage in any spiritual practice at all.

This distinction between doing and reading is real, but it is not absolute. Certainly, it is possible to read any text whatsoever, however explicitly meditative, without spiritual insight or profit. The mere act of reading does not summon up the presence of God. There are no magic spells. On the other hand, as discussed above, when we read even a very technical, theoretical text in the right spirit, the distinction between doing and reading starts to blur. When we read an author's words in the right spirit, we do imitate her, in a sense, because we learn to think as she thinks and see as she sees. Reading becomes doing. When a theologian intends for her text to be read in such a way as to draw her readers closer to God, that theologian may be said to write a spiritual exercise explicitly. But it is also possible that an author might write a spiritual exercise unintentionally: Who can say, after all, just which texts will lead readers closer to God?

I have argued that both Anselm and Aquinas did intend for their theology to be read as spiritual exercises, but, in fact, that claim is stronger than I actually need. It would suffice to say that their texts can be read as spiritual exercises, whether or not they intended them as such. Furthermore, even if it were the case that the intellectual practices of Anselm and Aquinas were spiritually fruitful only in the first, "doing," sense, and utterly sterile in the second, "reading," sense, they would still furnish examples of the practices of Christian philosophical theology as a spiritual practice in Hadot's terms.

Analytic Theology as a Spiritual Practice

I return now to the central argument. I do not claim that analytic philosophical theologians typically intend that their work be read as spiritual exercises. Even so, reading analytic theology might well be spiritually fruitful for its readers, when they approach it in the right way. (At least, it would be very difficult to argue that this is not possible even in principle.) It seems even more plausible to say that *doing* analytic theology can be a spiritual practice, even if reading it is not. It is this option, actually doing analytic theology, that I pursue here, though much of what I have to say also applies, *mutatis mutandis*, to reading analytic theology. The explicit goal of any piece of analytic writing is to present the truth as the author sees it. This single-minded focus on truth, when combined with the specific techniques of analytic argument, allows analytic theology to become a spiritual practice. It is an authentic development of the earlier tradition of Anselm and Aquinas.

For a Christian, the spiritual warrant for analytic theology is derived from the more general spiritual warrant for inquiry as such (see Chapter 6). Intellectual inquiry as such presupposes a certain level of virtue, and it is always, at least implicitly, oriented toward God as the cause and final end of all things. As Christians, we believe that God created us as intellectual creatures, with an innate desire to know that is itself essentially good and healthy, even though it can be corrupted. Moreover, the innate desire to know is nothing other than a desire for truth, and in order to desire the truth, we must first love the truth. Indeed, in order to seek the truth in earnest, we must love the truth more than we love the self. We must subordinate our other desires, including our desire for intellectual glory, to the desire for truth. We must let the desire to *be* right displace the desire to *seem* right, because the desire to seem right without being right is merely the intellectual version of *libido dominandi*, the will to dominate.

Some might go still further and embrace the ancient and medieval claim that the desire for truth is the desire for God because God is truth itself.[13] On this understanding, when we seek the truth, we also, by that very fact, seek God. Even if we are not prepared to go that far, we may still say that when we seek the truth, we imitate God, who knows all truths. Seeking the truth is a way of conforming our desires to God's plan for us as intellectual creatures: God wants us to know reality as it is, to know ourselves as we are, and, insofar as it is possible, to know God as he is, and not just as we wish him to be. Insofar as inquiry as such features the patient, disciplined pursuit of truth, it is an attempt to see the world as it really is, to live in the Real, and thereby to depart from the shadowland of illusions and fantasies. To seek the truth, in any form, is implicitly to seek God—surely the very essence of any Christian spiritual practice.

From the point of view of the central argument, this is already a useful result. As I noted above, many opponents of analytic theology treat it as a form of inquiry that is almost uniquely spiritually sterile. Yet few would deny that analytic theology features an almost relentless focus on assessing truth claims. This result is important in itself, because it makes the playing field more friendly. Analytic theology inherits the moral worth of inquiry as such, because it is a way of seeking and loving the truth.

At this point, one might object that much of what I have said so far would apply equally to any form of inquiry—whether the "disciplined" study of history, biology, or whatnot. I agree. My aim so far has been merely to establish that analytic theology is not on a worse footing than other forms of inquiry. In fact, however, a Christian can hold that analytic theology is actually on a better footing, because it inherits not just the virtues of inquiry generally, but of theology specifically. Analytic theology features the disciplined pursuit of truth that is common to all sincere inquiry, but, as theology, it is actually a higher form of inquiry because it has a higher object. Analytic theology—like all good theology—features the disciplined pursuit of truth about matters divine: about God, Christ, and salvation. The general pursuit of truth, itself inherently virtuous, is made more virtuous in analytic theology because of its subject matter: God, God's plan for us, the content of the creeds, the meaning and coherence of revelation, and so forth.

Much like the theology of Aquinas, analytic theology is both directly theoretical, in that it is explicitly concerned with presenting and defending propositional truth claims, and indirectly practical, because it can also have practical, spiritual effects. I admit that this claim seems dubious at first blush. One thinks of the shopworn criticism that analytic philosophy, and therefore analytic theology, is no more than "logic chopping." On this critique, analytic inquiry might feature the "pursuit of truth," in some minimal sense akin to mindlessly doing rote

---

[13] For a study of this claim in the thought of Aquinas, see William Wood, "Thomas Aquinas on the Claim That God is Truth," *Journal of the History of Philosophy* 51 (2013): 21–47.

arithmetic problems, but it could not be an authentic spiritual practice in Hadot's sense.

Yet the old Augustinian maxim holds here too: knowledge of God and knowledge of self are mutually entailing, and both have implications for how we should live.[14] Suppose we agree with Aquinas that the contemplation of God is the purpose of human life, and that theoretical reasoning about God can train the intellect to receive the beatific vision. On what basis would we grant this claim for Aquinas, but refuse to grant a similar claim for contemporary analytic theologians? Like Aquinas, analytic theologians use the best philosophical tools to reason about the central claims of the Christian faith. Like Aquinas, the analytic theologian can rightly insist that reasoning well about God is a way of drawing closer to God. By elucidating the contents of revelation, removing objections to Christian belief, and offering possible models of coherence for disputed Christian claims, analytic theologians pursue a theoretical task that is also indirectly practical. We must be guided by the truth about God in order to understand how to live rightly. Analytic theology is a tool that can help us to be good people and to live good lives.

So far I have argued that analytic theology inherits the spiritual worth of inquiry as such and of theology in particular. But some specific features of analytic argumentation are especially conducive to the life of virtue. I now wish to identify five such features: cultivating attention; wonder and attachment; argumentative transparency; imaginative identification with interlocutors; and passively waiting for insight. All are ordinary intellectual practices, but they can also have the effect of fostering the virtue of humility and of cultivating a desire for truth, which in the Christian tradition may be understood as a desire for God.

Attention

Consider first the concentrated attention required to read, understand, and develop very technical analytic arguments. The French mystic Simone Weil holds that attention can be an implicit form of Christian prayer because it requires one to detach oneself from one's goals and biases in order to be fully receptive to the objects of one's attention. She specifically describes the effort of working out a difficult proof in geometry as a kind of prayer, a way of worshiping God, the source of truth.[15] Hadot makes a similar point about Stoic spiritual exercises. He discusses "reading, listening, research, and investigation" as spiritual exercises, and he similarly presents speculative metaphysics as a spiritual practice that helps

---

[14] See, for example, Étienne Gilson's study of "Christian Socratism" in Étienne Gilson, *The Spirit of Mediaeval Philosophy* (Notre Dame, IN: University of Notre Dame Press, 1991 [1936]), 209–29.

[15] Simone Weil, *Waiting for God* (New York: Harper and Row, 1951), 105–16.

us see the world correctly, as a "cosmic Whole," and thereby orient ourselves properly within it.[16] Similarly, many different religious traditions, both ancient and modern, also commend contemplative practices that cultivate attention and focused awareness. So there can be little dispute about the general claim that developing one's powers of attention can be a spiritual practice.

Given that this general claim is beyond dispute, and given that it is also beyond dispute that analytic theology requires considerable attention and concentration, my path seems clear. I merely need to point out that one can intentionally practice analytic theology in order to cultivate those same virtues. Weil and Hadot are both held in very high regard by many contemporary theologians. Presumably, theologians who are happy to agree that geometry (Weil) and stoic metaphysics (Hadot) can function as spiritual exercises should be similarly inclined to say the same thing about intricate analytic proofs and metaphysical arguments.

Wonder and Attachment

Plato says that philosophy begins in wonder, and his student Aristotle agrees.[17] I would say the same thing about theology, including analytic theology. There is a narrow sense of "wonder," synonymous with "puzzlement" or "perplexity." Analytic theology certainly exhibits wonder in this sense. Yet we should be careful not to dismiss as dry and uninteresting even this narrow sense of wonder. Solving puzzles can be delightful, and besides, the narrow sense of "wonder" is the sense that Plato and Aristotle themselves had in mind. But there is another sense of "wonder," one that is closer to "amazement," "astonishment," and "awe." Analytic theology can also exhibit this sense of wonder.

Granted, the norms of contemporary academic writing make it hard for analytic theologians to express this sense of wonder openly. In *Proslogion* 9, when Anselm begins to wrestle with the problem of reconciling God's mercy and God's justice, he is moved to exclaim: "O God, how exalted is your goodness! We can see the source of your mercy, and yet we cannot discern it clearly. We know whence the river flows, but we do not see the spring from which it issues." Anselm's philosophical inquiry into the coherence of the divine attributes is motivated by his sense of wonder and awe at the mystery of God. We don't often see such effusive writing in contemporary analytic thought, but it would be a mistake to assume that analytic theologians do not have similar motivations. They, too, are often motivated by a sense of awe and wonder at the divine. That is why they want to understand their faith more deeply.

---

[16] Hadot, *Philosophy as a Way of Life*, 86.
[17] Plato, *Theaetetus*, 155c–d; Aristotle, *Metaphysics*, 982b.

I group together "wonder" and "attachment," because this deeper sense of wonder is a way of expressing one's desire for God, which is itself the desire for loving attachment to God. When we think about inquiry as *askesis*, it is tempting to overemphasize the virtues of self-denial and detachment. Yet in theological inquiry, self-denial and detachment are only valuable to the degree that they promote deeper and stronger forms of loving attachment: to God above all, but also to other human beings, who are all made in the image of God, to the whole creation, construed as the theater of God's glory, and even to oneself, rightly understood. Those forms of loving attachment in turn nourish a love of truth, the desire to see things as they really are. Objectivity should never be reduced to apathy or indifference. Real objectivity is simply the ability to see things as they really are, but, sometimes, things really are wonderful.

Transparency

I turn next to what may be regarded as the paradigmatic analytic virtue: argumentative transparency. The culture of analytic philosophy is a culture of argument, and so is the culture of analytic theology. I freely grant that the argument culture of analytic philosophy often seems aggressively hostile, a culture that rewards prideful displays of dominance, or even something that might be called intellectual violence: glory in defeating an opponent in argument, and the peculiarly intellectualized form of self-love that results. So there is a real temptation here, but pride and will to power are perennial temptations—found in all forms of human activity.

Hidden within the argument culture of analytic philosophy, however, one finds something that also looks like an inoculation against intellectual pride. Consider, again, my suggestion in Chapter 4 that analytic philosophy prioritizes transparency in argument—my own version of the analytic claim to be especially "clear." An author is transparent just in case she makes it very easy to understand the claims she wants to make, and the reasons she offers in support of those claims. But this means that part of what it is to offer a good analytic argument is to make that argument maximally easy for intellectual opponents to criticize or refute. This is actually a way of choosing to make oneself intellectually vulnerable, and a check against intellectual pride. In the proper spirit, it is a way of implicitly saying to the intellectual community, "If I am wrong, I am wrong in ways that I myself cannot see. Please help me to see them."

Similarly, good analytic reasoning often proceeds very slowly and cautiously, making tiny advances and almost micro-level critiques. This kind of narrow argumentation can sometimes be frustrating for "outsiders" to read, but it can also exhibit real epistemic modesty. One makes the small contribution rather than the grand totalizing claim, and so one is less tempted to regard oneself as the source of any kind of essential wisdom. Here I am reminded of another excellent quotation from Weil. She writes:

> It is perhaps even more useful to contemplate our stupidity than our sin. Consciousness of sin gives us the feeling that we are evil, and a kind of pride sometimes finds a place in it. When we force ourselves to fix the gaze upon a school exercise in which we have failed through sheer stupidity, a sense of our mediocrity is borne in upon us with irresistible evidence. No knowledge is more to be desired.[18]

It does not seem far-fetched to me to say that good analytic philosophy—and therefore good analytic theology—makes it especially easy to have this kind of experience. Even the most successful philosopher is so often shown by his peers to have missed some obvious error that he might be considered a spiritual athlete of stupidity, in Weil's terms.

Once again, someone might well object that all good academic writing aims at argumentative transparency, and so it is not a virtue of analytic theology in particular. And once again, my reply is similar: I make no invidious contrasts. I am prepared to grant that other forms of inquiry may also be regarded as spiritual practices, especially when they foster the intellectual and moral virtues that I here associate with analytic theology. At the same time, it does not seem like special pleading to say that analytic writing *maximizes* argumentative transparency, and prizes it above almost every other rhetorical virtue, in a way that goes beyond what we find in other disciplines.

Imaginative Identification with Interlocutors

The third feature of analytic argument that I want to highlight is the ability to identify imaginatively with interlocutors and intellectual opponents. While very little present-day philosophy and theology takes the form of an explicit dialogue, much of it does still retain an implicit dialogical structure that serves a similar pedagogical purpose. Almost all good philosophy—indeed almost all good inquiry—proceeds by way of an engagement with real and imagined interlocutors. A good piece of philosophical writing presents the views of one's opponents fairly and in their strongest form. It is not uncommon for a philosopher to try his or her best to make an opponent's argument stronger and better before criticizing it, and in the unlikely event that one finds no good counterarguments in the literature, the right thing to do is to try to imagine good counterarguments and present them oneself. At its best, analytic theology displays the same efforts.

---

[18] Weil, *Waiting for God*, 109.

This is an utterly ordinary practice, but it can have profound implications. To do it well, one has to be able to inhabit, at least for a time, not only an alternative point of view, but often a hostile point of view. The more easily one can inhabit the viewpoint of one's intellectual opponents, the better one can argue. By contrast, consider what it would be like to be completely unable to do this: one would be so locked in the certainty that one's own views are correct that one could not even imagine what it would be like for them to be wrong. Surely this is a kind of pride, a glorification of the self and its private projects. Conversely, when one can internalize and inhabit the voices of one's critics, the fixed, prideful self becomes unstable. In order to make this move at all, one must try to free oneself from one's own biases and assumptions in order to see the real force of the arguments. One must put oneself in a "truth-seeking" attitude. As I have argued above, for the Christian, adopting a truth-seeking attitude is a way of loving and honoring God.

Passively Waiting for Insight

I conclude with an aspect of analytic philosophy, and therefore analytic theology, that is quite common, even though it is rarely discussed in print. Frequently, a philosopher working on a tricky problem experiences a sudden flash of insight, an *aha* moment. Such moments seem to strike unexpectedly from "outside," as it were. They do not seem like a predictable result of one's own willful efforts. I am sure these flashes of insight are found in all kinds of intellectual inquiry—indeed, they are part of what makes the intellectual life so pleasurable—but more than most disciplines, successful analytic philosophy must cultivate these spontaneous experiences of insight. A philosopher must adopt an attitude of patient openness toward the truth, because that attitude is a necessary condition of doing good philosophy. It is an attitude that both presupposes and cultivates intellectual humility. A philosopher who is overly enamored with his own argument, and with himself for having devised it, blocks himself from such moments of insight. Successful analytic philosophy, and therefore successful analytic theology, requires us to cultivate an attitude of "active waiting." We wait for insight, remain open to the truth, and patiently hope to receive it, but we wait actively, expectantly. Contrary to stereotypes, philosophers do not merely lie on the couch looking at the ceiling or spend all day watching television while "waiting" for the truth; rather, they read, think, turn ideas over in their minds: this is hard work, to be sure, but it is also a form of waiting, and a form of passivity.

It seems to me that this attitude of active waiting is especially valuable for the Christian to cultivate. We spend much of our lives, maybe all of our lives, actively waiting: for God, for grace, for Christ. On some construals, active waiting just is the Christian vocation. When we actively wait for intellectual insight, we participate in a pedagogical practice that is quasi-sacramental. Waiting for insight and cultivating an attitude of openness toward truth is also a way of training the mind and the will to wait actively for God's grace.

Conclusion

Analytic theology does not wear its spiritual dimension on its sleeve, but neither does the theology of Anselm or Aquinas. Despite the fact that Anselm moves seamlessly from prayers and mediations to technical philosophical arguments, contemporary readers find it all too easy to focus on the latter at the expense of the former. It is even more clear that few contemporary readers appreciate the practical and spiritual aspects of Aquinas's *Summa*. It is very easy—indeed, common—to regard Aquinas's work as utterly devoid of spirituality. Yet, according to many of his leading theological interpreters, the *Summa* is a theoretical treatise that also functions as a set of spiritual exercises. Readers must be taught to see the practical aspects of the *Summa*. They must similarly be taught to see the practical aspects of analytic theology. The fact that they are not obvious to the casual reader does not mean that they are not there. Analytic theology, like the theology of Anselm and Aquinas, is both theoretical and practical. When undertaken in the right spirit, analytic theology can become a spiritual practice: a way of seeking God, and of training the mind and the will to be open to grace. Moreover, the specific techniques of analytic inquiry both presuppose and cultivate the virtue of humility.

I have said that analytic theology becomes a spiritual practice "when undertaken in the right spirit." This qualification is important, but it does not really bear the weight of the argument. I mean only to say that the right attitude is a necessary condition for appreciating the spiritual value of any practice whatsoever. One can treat any practice, even first-order religious practices like the Eucharist, in a closed-off way, and thereby ensure that they will seem spiritually barren. One can treat analytic theology in a similarly closed-off way, but one need not so treat it. There are resources within analytic theology that allow one to treat it as a spiritual practice.[19]

---

[19] This chapter is drawn from William Wood, "Analytic Theology as a Way of Life," *Journal of Analytic Theology* 2 (2014): 43–60. You will notice the change in title from that article to this chapter. I originally wanted the article title to suggest very obviously the comparison with Hadot on philosophy, but in hindsight I think I got carried away. Calling the second-order discipline of theology a "way of life" might imply that it suffices on its own, or renders the sacraments unnecessary. I have never thought that. But I do think analytic theology can be a spiritual practice.

PART IV

ANALYTIC THEOLOGY AND THE ACADEMIC STUDY OF RELIGION

Having argued that analytic theology really is theology, I turn in Part IV to the academic study of religion and argue that analytic theology can flourish in the secular academy as a valuable dialogue partner for scholars of religion. In order to argue that analytic theology counts as "properly academic" inquiry, I first try to understand what the norms of academic inquiry and argument really are (Chapter 11). I then draw on my own background in analytic theology to intervene in three debates that currently preoccupy the academic study of religion. The first debate concerns naturalism and reductionism. While individual scholars of religion can, and often should, practice methodological naturalism, attempts to justify methodological naturalism as a global, field-defining norm inevitably presuppose controversial metaphysical claims, and thereby collapse into ontological naturalism—a position that I call "ontological naturalism on the cheap" (Chapter 12). The second debate concerns the role of "critique" in the academic study of religion, where "critique" is understood as a specific discourse—something more than mere criticism. Critique remains valuable, but in the contemporary religious studies academy, it has become hegemonic, to the point where it threatens to crowd out other equally legitimate methods of inquiry (Chapter 13). This engagement with critique sets the stage for the third debate, which concerns the vexed role of normative inquiry in the academic study of religion (Chapter 14). I endorse normative inquiry, and argue that analytic theology is a form of post-critical, normative inquiry that prizes attachment and "rigorous appreciation." As such, analytic theology can contribute to the study of religions while also maintaining its own distinctive focus on evaluating Christian truth claims and practices. I conclude the chapter with a modest proposal on behalf of comparative analytic theology.

11

Inquiry and Argument in the Secular Academy

I sometimes wonder what exclusivist scholars of religion really mean by "theology."[1] Whatever they are imagining, it does not seem to bear much resemblance to anything I recognize as theology. For example, I doubt it bears much resemblance to the kind of work I discussed in Chapter 5, or, for that matter, to my own argument in Chapters 6–10. How could it, when the attacks are so over the top? Theology "cannot complement the academic study of religion but can only 'infect' it," says Donald Wiebe, as if theology is a contagious disease.[2] According to Russell T. McCutcheon, nothing less than "the future of the human sciences is at stake" when considering whether religious "insiders" actually count as scholars. He presents us with a stark choice: "scholars of human behavior could either be seen as observers capable of making novel claims about the causes of human action or as participants making autobiographical claims of no necessary analytic consequence."[3] Here theology simultaneously seems like an all-powerful force that can bring about the collapse of the human sciences, and yet—somehow, also—like something trivial, a harmless vehicle for self-reporting. And then there is Willi Braun. In his introduction to the highly regarded *Guide to the Study of Religion*, Braun makes it all the way to the fifth paragraph before he finds himself comparing theology to the study of ghosts and insisting that scholarly work on religion must be purged of theology in order to remain "credible" in the modern university.[4]

These worries about theology are not just short-sighted. They are also provincial, in a very literal sense. They really only have any purchase at all in North America, or at least in those places that aspire to reproduce the sharp North American-style separation between Church and state. The best universities in the

---

[1] Recall what I mean by "exclusivist scholars of religion," as defined in Chapter 3. Exclusivists claim, either implicitly or explicitly, that theology is not a legitimate academic subject. This is stronger than just the claim that theology and the study of religions are different forms of inquiry. Not all scholars of religion are exclusivists. I should also emphasize again that by "theology" I mean Christian theology, though most of what I say would generalize to other kinds of theology.

[2] Donald Wiebe, *Politics of Religious Studies*, 155.

[3] Russell T. McCutcheon, ed., *The Insider/Outsider Problem in the Study of Religion: A Reader* (New York: Continuum, 2005), 19. McCutcheon is explicitly writing about "the insider/outsider problem," but it is clear that he understands this as the problem of whether theology counts as legitimate academic work.

[4] Willi Braun and Russell T. McCutcheon, eds., *Guide to the Study of Religion* (New York: T&T Clark, 2000), 5.

Analytic Theology and the Academic Study of Religion. William Wood, Oxford University Press (2021). © William Wood.
DOI: 10.1093/oso/9780198779872.003.0011

UK are all state-funded and public, but they also offer explicitly Christian theology alongside other courses, usually in some kind of hybrid department of theology and religious studies. A similar situation obtains in other European countries, and in Australia. As far as I can tell, the human sciences have not yet collapsed in any of these institutions. Nor, for that matter, have they collapsed in the many private universities in the United States that also offer Christian theology.

The truth is that the kind of theology I am talking about—*academic* theology, the kind of theology that has its own journals, and conferences, and book series— that kind of theology looks quite a lot like the rest of the humanities. The main thing that most academic theologians do is argue with other theologians about how to interpret texts. So most academic theology looks like a mixture of history and literary theory. The main thing that analytic theologians do is argue with other analytic theologians about the logical structure, presuppositions, and entailments of Christian doctrines. So most analytic theology looks like philosophy. In other words, academic theology, including analytic theology, looks like an intervention in an existing scholarly conversation, one that follows the same broad norms of inquiry and argument that apply in other disciplines.

In this chapter, I want to say more about what those norms of inquiry and argument really are, because we need to get clear on the nature of academic inquiry before we can say whether theology counts as properly academic in the relevant sense. But at the outset, I should point out that not all theology is academic theology.[5] And that is perfectly fine. I do not argue that academic theology is the only legitimate form of theology. Instead, I make the much narrower point that academic theology should not be excluded from the contemporary university. Nor do I argue that analytic theology is the only—or even the best—form of academic theology. But it does follow the same broad norms of inquiry found in other academic disciplines, especially philosophy. It is good that there are forms of theology that can flourish in the contemporary university, a setting that remains largely secular. Analytic theology is one such form. But to make that case, we first must understand what characterizes academic inquiry more generally.

On Academic Inquiry and Argument

Stefan Collini wrote a widely praised book, *What Are Universities for?*, that never quite managed to answer its title question.[6] It is hard to blame him, though: the contemporary university has many conflicting purposes. Without taking

---

[5] Some theology explicitly understands itself to speak only within personal or confessional contexts: for example, devotional literature, or some forms of practical theology; similarly, some theology is explicitly aimed at popular rather than academic audiences.

[6] Stefan Collini, *What Are Universities for?* (London: Penguin, 2012).

refuge in platitudes and high-level abstractions, it is not easy to identify a single overarching aim that unites them all. So instead of asking what the contemporary university is for, I ask a slightly different question: What is distinctive about academic inquiry and argument? Whatever else it is, a university is a community of scholars collectively engaged in various projects of specialized inquiry. Whether theology belongs in the contemporary university depends in part on whether theological inquiry counts as a form of properly academic inquiry, and that depends on some prior grasp of what counts as academic inquiry and argument in general.

The qualifier "academic" matters, because the university setting matters. In a sense, scholars in a university are "professional inquirers," analogous to professional musicians. Professional musicians are rightly held to higher standards of technical competence and creativity than nonprofessional musicians. Similarly, scholars in a university are rightly held to higher standards of reasoning and argument than nonprofessional inquirers. As professional inquirers, scholars in a university draw on extensive disciplinary training and expertise, and in the first instance, they think and write for their similarly trained academic peers. They voluntarily accept norms that would be too strict when construed as general norms binding all rational inquirers. An academic scientist asserting a claim to fellow scientists can expect a level of rational scrutiny that would be excessive in other less formal contexts, and so she should assert the claim only if she believes that it can stand up to such scrutiny.

The qualifier "academic" matters for my own purposes as well. In a discussion about whether theology can find a home in the contemporary university, it is important not to blur two sets of questions. On the one hand, there are questions about the rationality of religious belief in general, and when, in general, we are justified in reasoning on the basis of theological assumptions. In my view, recent work in epistemology and philosophy of religion overwhelmingly points toward permissive, theologically favorable answers to these questions. In most contexts, someone can believe in God or appeal to scripture and still be fully rational, even when they cannot defend their views with any further arguments or publicly available evidence. On the other hand, the academic context is different, and more restrictive. Even if there are no epistemological barriers to theological reasoning in general, without further argument it does not follow that theological reasoning counts as a valid form of *academic* inquiry. Theology might fare poorly with respect to the norms of academic inquiry, even if it fares well with respect to the norms of general rationality, because we expect higher standards of evidence and argumentation in a university setting.[7]

---

[7] We would rightly reject the argument of a scholar who appeals to private religious experiences as evidence for his own academic views, for example. ("It turns out that Gettier was wrong! Justified true belief really is knowledge! Jesus told me so in a dream last night.")

Academic inquiry is not just distinctive because of its additional epistemological strictness. At its best, compared to inquiry in other contexts, academic inquiry also allows very great degrees of intellectual freedom, creativity, and risk-taking.[8] Like so much in the contemporary university, "academic freedom" has become a political battleground, but the core concept is straightforward. Academic freedom is simply freedom of inquiry. In its most basic sense, to say that scholars enjoy freedom of inquiry is just to say that they cannot be punished for researching unpopular topics or reaching unwelcome conclusions. Genuine inquiry is impossible when someone works under the threat of reprisal, or when they face political and economic pressure to reach predetermined conclusions.

So far I have presented the university as a community of scholars engaged in specialized research. But the university is a place of teaching as well as learning. Nearly all academics teach, and many understand themselves as teachers first and foremost, regardless of whether they also work in a research-intensive context. Teachers, too, are professional inquirers. The college classroom is a university in miniature, and in its own way, each classroom instantiates the norms of the university at large. Teachers model academic inquiry for their students: they show what it looks like to care deeply about a topic of inquiry, to construct good arguments and challenge them respectfully, and to follow the evidence wherever it leads. Like researchers, teachers and their students are jointly engaged in a project of collective inquiry aimed at expanding the community's knowledge and deepening its understanding. The classroom is a university in miniature because teaching and learning are also forms of academic inquiry.

Scholars in a university understand themselves to have wide latitude to research the topics they like and to teach in the ways that seem most effective to them. In research, this latitude is especially crucial, because what counts as a fit subject for academic inquiry changes as knowledge grows and as cultural understanding develops. Because of the dynamic nature of knowledge and understanding, it is not possible to specify a priori exactly what counts as a legitimate subject for academic inquiry. Alchemy was a legitimate subject in the early modern university, but is not any longer; quantum mechanics was not a legitimate subject in the early modern university, but it is now, and so on. I am inclined to say, even on pain of circularity, that professional academics determine for themselves what constitutes a legitimate topic for academic inquiry. In most cases, the fact that there is a community of scholars who want to research a given topic suffices to render that topic legitimate. In any event, there should be a bias toward openness.[9]

---

[8] Obviously, the qualifier "at its best" is doing a lot of work here. This is a regulative ideal, rather than an empirical description. Sometimes inquiry must change or cease due to practical considerations. Real inquiry does not take place in an idealized, frictionless academy that is free of budgetary constraints and external interference.

[9] Again, this chapter presents a deliberately idealized version of academic inquiry. My question is what counts as a legitimate topic for academic inquiry *in principle*, apart from pragmatic and

Scholars should have wide latitude to push against existing boundaries and move into novel areas of inquiry. Without that latitude, the intellectual life of the university would eventually stagnate, since fewer people would be willing to question established orthodoxies and received opinions.

"Wide latitude" does not mean "utterly without limits," of course. The university as a community of scholars rightly regards some topics and methods as unacceptable, although—naturally enough—academics are free to argue about that too. But, in general, scholars in a university should enjoy the same presumption of trust that other highly trained professionals enjoy in their own institutional contexts. The university provides an institutional context in which academics can explore controversial questions and honestly assess the reasons and evidence that bear on those questions. Without such a context, it is far less likely that anyone would explore controversial questions properly, or indeed at all: in ordinary life, most of us seem quite content with the default received view of things. We all have our favored orthodoxies, and we all enjoy our own dogmatic slumbers.

The Structure of Academic Argument

Academic inquiry is broader than academic argument, but argument is an essential element of inquiry, and not a wholly separate activity. The norms of academic argument govern the kinds of assumptions scholars are allowed to make in their work, how they reason to conclusions and marshal supporting evidence, and how they respond to counterarguments. Making arguments is what academics *do*, and we need to get a grip on what good academic argument looks like in order to determine what counts as a legitimate line of academic inquiry. Only then will we be able to assess the academic status of theological inquiry.

In the context of the perennial battles between theology and religious studies, Thomas A. Lewis offers a succinct indictment of what *bad* academic argument looks like. According to Lewis—reasonably enough—some moves are simply not allowed in legitimate academic argument, at least not in the field of religious studies: "The moves that exclude one from the discipline are appeals to an authority that is claimed not to require justification, appeals to an authority conceived as unquestionable, and appeals to private forms of justification for which, in principle, no argument can be given."[10] I agree that these moves should not be allowed in the academic study of religion, or anywhere else in the academy. But it would

---

funding-based considerations. In the real, non-idealized world, such considerations often determine decisions about whether to pursue a given line of inquiry. I do not dispute that fact, but it is not my concern here, and responding to it would involve very different arguments.

[10] Lewis, *Why Philosophy Matters for the Study of Religion*, 46.

also be useful to have a positive account of what *good* academic argument looks like.

I present such an account in the next section. I offer six norms that collectively establish what good academic argument looks like. As norms, they are regulative ideals, not exceptionless empirical generalizations. As every working academic will recognize, we do not always follow these norms. But precisely because they are norms, they remain binding, since they express ideals that all scholars qua scholars ought to affirm. I take these norms to be internal norms, implicit in the practice of academic inquiry itself: they describe how the best scholars actually do argue, because they describe the way that all scholars should argue. They are imposed, as it were, from within, when we learn how to practice academic inquiry.

A Normative Framework for Academic Argument

My normative framework for academic argument depends on the notion of "discursive commitments," taken from the pragmatist philosophy of Robert Brandom and Jeffrey Stout.[11] This framework is neither especially favorable nor especially hostile to theology, and it captures the nature of academic argument very well. To be clear: neither Brandom nor Stout understands himself to be offering a theory of academic argument per se. Brandom understands his own account of discursive commitments as a theory of semantic content—i.e., a theory about what makes it the case that sentences mean what they do—and Stout draws on Brandom to devise a pragmatic account of truth and epistemological justification. I am not convinced that Brandom and Stout offer viable theories of semantic content, truth, or epistemic justification. But we can still use their basic vocabulary— discursive "commitments," "entitlements," and "challenges"—to construct a fine theory of academic argument. Contra Brandom and Stout, then, I regard the norms below as too strict to govern every discursive context, and I do not defend them as the norms of argument or communication *simpliciter*. I am concerned only with the specific discursive context of the contemporary university, and so all that matters for my purposes is that they can function as the norms that govern legitimate academic argument.

---

[11] See especially Jeffrey Stout, *Democracy & Tradition* (Princeton, NJ: Princeton University Press, 2004), 209–13; Jeffrey Stout, "Radical Interpretation and Pragmatism: Davidson, Rorty, and Brandom on Truth," in Nancy Frankenberry, ed., *Radical Interpretation in Religion* (New York: Cambridge University Press, 2004), 25–52; Robert B. Brandom, *Making It Explicit: Reasoning, Representing, and Discursive Commitment* (Cambridge, MA: Harvard University Press, 1994), 105–11, 130, 141–98, 176–78, 180–98. See also A. P. Norman, "The Normative Structure of Adjudicative Dialogue," *Argumentation* 15 (2001): 489–98. It is worth noting that the fact that I draw on Brandom and Stout does not commit me to their general "pragmatism," understood as a philosophical method. Nor am I committed to Brandom's understanding of faith claims as commitments to which one is not entitled (Brandom, *Making It Explicit*, 105).

Here is the central insight: when we engage in academic argument, we are obliged to support our claims with reasons and evidence, and to respond with reasons and evidence when our claims are appropriately challenged. To tease out the full implications of this insight, I formulate six maxims that collectively establish what it is to engage in academic argument. When we engage in academic argument, we thereby accept these norms and hold ourselves accountable to them:

1.   *We commit ourselves to our <u>claims</u> and to their logical entailments. Our claims and their entailments become our <u>commitments</u>.*

The *claim* is the basic unit of academic argument. Paradigmatically a claim is an assertion or a declarative sentence about what is the case, though other speech acts can also express claims. Claims have a truth value—they are either true or false—though, of course, we may not know what that truth value is. The notion of *commitment* is no less fundamental. Commitment is both an epistemic and an ethical notion. As scholars, when we make claims, we commit to them: we not only assert them; we avow them as our own. When we claim that p, we do more than assert p. We also accept that we can be held responsible for the fact that we assert p. We authorize others to attribute p to us, and, on the basis of our own scholarly testimony, we authorize them to use p in their own reasoning. We also accept the logical consequences of p. (If I claim p, and p entails q, then I implicitly claim q.) A scholar who asserts a claim but then refuses to accept its logical consequences, or denies that he asserted it at all, would not be engaged in legitimate academic argument.

2.   *When we make a claim, we imply that we are <u>entitled</u> to that claim. To be entitled to a claim is to have good reasons and evidence for it.*

We are entitled to our claims when they are based on good reasons and evidence. (I discuss what I mean by "reasons and evidence" below.) Within the confines of the university, it is legitimate to assume that scholars intend to base their own claims on reasons and evidence. They may be wrong about whether their reasons and evidence really do support their claims, but at the very least, when a scholar makes a claim in the context of an academic argument, it reasonable to assume that she takes herself to have reasons and evidence for that claim. If she does not even take herself to have any reasons or evidence for her claims, then she should not assert them at all. Thus, in virtue of claiming that p, she implies that she at least regards herself as entitled to p. A scholar who says "I claim p, but I have no evidence for p" or "I claim p, but I have no reason to believe that p" would place herself beyond the boundaries of academic discourse, even if this form of assertion were allowable in other contexts.[12] She would not really be making an academic claim at all.

None of this requires that every claim be held with certainty or that every claim amounts to a claim of knowledge, period. Academic discourse must allow for provisional claims and hypothetical assertions. In those cases, the relevant claim would be something like "plausibly, p" or "to the best of my current knowledge, p" or "for all anyone knows, p." All of these claims are perfectly normal and legitimate—the point is merely that we should be transparent about our own confidence in our assertions. This point is related to, but not quite the same as, the evidentialist maxim that we must proportion our belief to the evidence. The evidentialist maxim is about the ethics of rational belief, rather than the ethics of warranted assertion. The relevant maxims here would be: do not assert a claim for which you take yourself to have no evidence, and do not assert a claim with more confidence than your evidence warrants.

3. *We should try to support our claims with reasons and evidence that are maximally accessible to others*

I should now say something about what I mean by "reasons and evidence." Formally, reasons and evidence are what make it the case that we are entitled to our claims, that is, justified in believing them. Reasons and evidence are what one gives when one is asked, "Why do you believe that?" Some theories of argumentation sharply distinguish reasons from evidence. They might say that reasons are abstract and conceptual, and exist "in the head," whereas evidence is public and exists "in the world."[13] I do not need to take a position on this question. For my purposes, the formal definition given above suffices, and it does not really matter how, if at all, we distinguish the two.

I do want to say a word about another controversial matter, however. In a book about academic theology, I need to say something more about what counts as a reason, or as evidence, for an academic claim. Specifically, I need to say something about whether, in an academic context, we are obligated to give reasons and evidence that are "public" or "universally accessible" or "universally shared," or whether our reasons and evidence can be relative to some more limited community

[12] Jonathan E. Adler makes the much stronger argument that this form of assertion is conceptually incoherent in his *Belief's Own Ethics* (Cambridge, MA: MIT Press, 2002). For perspicuous criticism see Earl Conee's review in *Notre Dame Philosophical Reviews* (October 15, 2002), https://ndpr.nd.edu/news/belief-s-own-ethics/, accessed July 10, 2020.

[13] Wayne C. Booth, Gregory G. Colomb, and Joseph M. Williams, *The Craft of Research* (Chicago: University of Chicago Press, 2003), 116–18. On this usage, a reason for the claim "The Odyssey is better than the Iliad" might be "Because Odysseus is a more interesting character than Achilles," which is something conceptual or abstract—a view, a fact, a thought, a proposition, or whatnot. By contrast, the evidence for that claim would be actual passages from both epics that we can find on the page.

of inquirers, like members of a religious tradition. As a Christian, speaking to Christians, I am entitled to appeal to the Bible or to Church tradition in support of my claims, but am I similarly entitled as an academic speaking to other academics? The answer is not obvious. Some reasons really do seem too inaccessible to count as legitimate academic reasons. "God told me so last night," does not seem like acceptable evidence for an academic claim—even if God did tell me so last night. At the same time, a strong requirement that academic reasons and evidence must be *universally* shared or accessible seems untenable. We need some middle ground.

It is instructive to change the subject, and ask equivalent questions about (let's say) cutting-edge theoretical physics. Are cutting-edge physicists required to support their claims with reasons and evidence that are "universally shared?" As an empirical description of what is actually the case, the answer is no. Most other academics, to say nothing of most human beings, do not understand the evidence that bears on debates in theoretical physics and so do not "share" that evidence in any meaningful sense. The same point holds if we modalize the requirement to "universally accessible" instead of "universally shared." Most human beings, including most academics, cannot even acquire the specific set of intellectual skills—in mathematics, above all—necessary to evaluate the evidence in cutting-edge theoretical physics.[14] Specialist-level mathematics is a "public" language only in the tautologous sense that anyone who is capable of understanding it can understand it. Theoretical physics is "universally accessible" only in the tautologous sense that anyone who is capable of becoming a theoretical physicist is also capable of understanding theoretical physics. But that is not everyone, not even everyone in the university. The point generalizes: for those of us outside of a given specialist guild, it is not always easy to distinguish between absolutely "inaccessible" reasons (which are therefore disallowed) and relatively inaccessible reasons that seem inaccessible only because we lack the ability, inclination, and expertise to access them. Much academic discourse is really only accessible to other highly trained specialists and inaccessible to everyone else. Instead of demanding "universally" accessible reasons, it makes more sense to require only that one's reasons and evidence should be accessible in principle, and to other specialists.

One might counter that what makes physics and the other empirical sciences "universal," or "public" or "accessible" in the relevant sense is not that anyone is capable of understanding them, but that under the right conditions, their results are verifiable or reproducible by anyone. That is a fair point, and it marks a real disanalogy with theology. But it also marks a disanalogy with every humanistic discipline, even those that are not regarded as suspect by exclusivist scholars of religion. Unless we want to revert to a modernist, empiricist epistemology that

---

[14] Good practice compels me to admit that this is an empirical assertion for which I have sought no evidence, but it seems extremely plausible to me.

treats every kind of inquiry as a more or less deficient version of empirical science, there is no reason to fault theology for not having reproducible results. We should not hold theology to arbitrarily strict intellectual standards.

At the same time, we should not give up on the demand for universally accessible reasons too quickly. Instead of abandoning it altogether, I propose to reframe it as a demand for *maximally* accessible reasons. That is, we should regard the demand for universally accessible reasons as another regulative ideal, rather than as a necessary condition for all legitimate academic inquiry. It does seem right to say that we *ought* to construct arguments that aim at universality, insofar as we can. This point follows from the logic of persuasion. We all hope that our current, actually existing colleagues will accept our conclusions, but we also hope that our potential future colleagues will accept them as well. Thus, an ideal academic argument will appeal to premises and inferences that our future colleagues are likely to share, whoever they turn out to be. It follows that we ought to support our claims with reasons and evidence that are widely, even maximally, accessible. The better we can approximate this ideal, the better our argument will be.

4. *We invite criticism and challenges to our own claims, and when our claims are <u>appropriately challenged</u>, we are obligated to justify them with reasons and evidence.*

Academic inquiry is communal by definition. Some kinds of intellectual work can proceed in secret, in isolation from a wider community of fellow inquirers. Academic work is not like that, since it takes place in the context of the university. To join the university is, *ipso facto*, to join a community of fellow inquirers who are collectively engaged in the pursuit of truth. That community cannot function when its members do not share their work with one another. The act of sharing our work with fellow scholars—whether by publication, formal lecture, or informal conversation—implies that we affirmatively invite their questions and challenges. We invite criticism as a way of trying to identify our own errors, and to mitigate our inevitable blind spots, prejudices, and cognitive biases. We invite criticism so that our own work will improve.

As scholars, we take ourselves to have good reasons and evidence for our claims. Because we have chosen to pursue our intellectual work in a university setting, we also invite appropriate challenges to those claims. We therefore acquire an obligation to present our reasons and evidence when our claims are appropriately challenged. Brandom speaks of "the dimension of responsibility" characteristic of asserting: "In asserting a claim, one...undertakes a responsibility, for one commits oneself to being able to vindicate the original claim by showing that one is entitled to make it."[15] Regardless of whether this dimension of responsibility is

---

[15] Brandom, *Making It Explicit*, 171.

implied by assertion as such, as Brandom believes, it does seem to be implied by assertion in an academic context.

A scholar who refused to share his reasons and evidence when appropriately challenged would not be engaged in academic argument at all. "I claim that p, but I won't tell you why I believe p" is not a legitimate response to a scholarly challenge. (This point holds even if I do, in fact, have good reasons and evidence for p.) The university as an academic institution exists so that scholars will have a community of epistemic peers who are entitled to challenge each other's claims in the service of the collective pursuit of truth. By voluntarily joining that community, we acquire the responsibility of accepting and responding to such challenges.

Because academic inquiry is communal, however, often a scholar can respond to a challenge by appealing to the work of others, or even to a general scholarly consensus. When asked, "Why do you believe p?," it will often be the case that one can only respond, "I have no direct evidence for p, but Jones argues that p." This response is perfectly legitimate. Depending on the nature of the argument, this response could suffice, or it could lead to further arguments about Jones's reasons for accepting p. My real point is that challenges and responses do not occur in isolation from the rest of the scholarly community. The mere fact of a challenge does not obligate a scholar to defend her views foundationalist-style, without recourse to the work of others.

I have said that we invite "appropriate challenges." I also need to unpack what counts as an "appropriate" academic challenge. Not all challenges are appropriate. When someone is entitled to challenge our claims, they impose on us an obligation to respond with our supporting reasons and evidence. This obligation should not be taken lightly, and so the bar for an appropriate challenge should be neither too high nor too low. Not every challenge is appropriate. That much is clear. I cannot legitimately wander into a specialist lecture on Ugaritic philology and start demanding answers to very basic questions about its morphology and syntax. (They would be very basic: I don't know the first thing about Ugaritic.) However much we value free and open inquiry, if every challenge were regarded as appropriate, and if every challenge generated an obligation to present one's reasons and evidence, then academic inquiry would grind to a halt. Pseudo-intellectuals and sophists would constantly challenge everything, and annoying epistemologists could stop any conversation by demanding recursive explanations for how we know that we know that p.

It is also clear that what counts as an "appropriate" challenge is highly contextual, and that the same challenge might be inappropriate in one context but appropriate in another. "How do you know we are not all brains in vats?" might be a legitimate challenge in an epistemology seminar, but not in a lecture about Roman numismatics, for instance. Because what counts as an appropriate challenge will vary according to context, it is not possible to demarcate in advance the necessary and sufficient conditions of appropriateness. Formally, and somewhat vacuously: a challenge is inappropriate in a specific context if someone in that context can legitimately say "I am not obliged to answer this challenge right here and right now." Suppose someone challenges Pawl's book on Christology by demanding that Pawl defend his reasons for accepting the truth of Conciliar Christology (see Chapter 5). In most cases, Pawl could legitimately respond with "I have my reasons, but that question is not what this book is about. Let's focus on the argument of the book itself." Similarly, suppose I am giving a conference paper on a new way to understand the Christian doctrine of the Fall. In that context, it would not be appropriate for someone to demand that I first prove that the Christian God exists, next that God created, and finally that there was a Fall, etc. Yet in other contexts—certain philosophy of religion seminars, for example—those might be perfectly appropriate questions.

5. *We are entitled to treat our commitments as rationally innocent until proven guilty.*

What claims, commitments, and assumptions can legitimately ground a line of academic inquiry? In principle, any claim that we do not already know to be false. Provided that we take ourselves to have good reasons for our claims, and provided that we do invite and respond to appropriate challenges, we can assume that we are entitled to our rational commitments until we learn otherwise. This norm is quite permissive. Its permissiveness trades on the distinction between "taking oneself to have good reasons and evidence for p" and "actually having good reasons and evidence for p." The norm requires only the former, not the latter.

In practice, this means that some scholars will take themselves to be entitled to commitments that actually turn out to be false or unsupported, just because those commitments happen not to have been successfully challenged yet. This result is not ideal, but it is also unavoidable. A more restrictive norm would be far worse. Any interesting line of inquiry begins with contestable assumptions, and if every scholar had a positive obligation to prove the truth of her assumptions to the satisfaction of the wider community from the outset, then scholarship would rarely be able to proceed beyond arguments over first principles. If we do not treat our commitments as innocent until proven guilty, the only alternatives seem to be a relentless, Pyrrhonian skepticism, or an equally untenable classical foundationalism. Both would devastate fruitful inquiry.

Although it is permissive, this norm is not utterly unrestrictive. We are never entitled to assert claims that we know to be internally inconsistent, inconsistent with other known truths, or already empirically falsified. For example, astrology claims that we can predict human events by looking at the movement of celestial objects. This claim is inconsistent with what we know about the nature of celestial objects and the laws of motion, and we can also empirically show that astrology lacks predictive power. Young Earth creationism is inconsistent with what we know about geology and evolution. Claims about parody deities like the Flying

Spaghetti Monster, while often hilarious, are also internally inconsistent. And so on.[16] This norm is a far cry from "anything goes."

6.   *We should withdraw from commitments to which we are not rationally entitled.*

The final norm goes hand in hand with its predecessors. When academic inquiry functions well, we maximize the likelihood that other scholars will successfully challenge our commitments. A successful challenge shows that we are not entitled to our commitments, by showing that they are not sufficiently supported by reasons and evidence. When that happens, we should withdraw from the commitments. We should stop avowing them, and stop using them as premises in our arguments. This is not quite the same as saying that we should stop believing them. The act of belief is not entirely under our direct control, and we cannot usually change our beliefs by fiat. But the act of asserting a claim, and committing ourselves as scholars to that claim, is under our direct control. In an academic context, no one can ever legitimately assert "You have shown that I am not entitled to *p*; nevertheless, *p*." The same point holds for more qualified claims and challenges. A successful challenge might aim at something less than full-blown falsification. A successful challenge might show that our confidence in *p* is too high, or that *p* is less probable than we had previously thought. In that case, we should reduce our confidence in *p* accordingly.

Analytic Theology as Academic Theology

With these general norms of academic inquiry in view, we are now in a position to ask more focused questions about whether analytic theology follows those norms—that is, whether it counts as properly academic work. To make this question even more manageable, I propose to narrow it even further, and to focus on William Hasker's *Metaphysics and the Tri-Personal God*, discussed in Chapter 5. Of the works I discussed in Chapter 5, Hasker offers the most interesting mixture of explicitly theological and philosophical claims, and therefore provides the most challenging case study.

It should come as no surprise that, in my view, Hasker does follow the general norms of academic inquiry. It would be tedious to march through all six of the general norms, one by one, asking whether Hasker passes the relevant test.

---

[16]   What about properly Christian claims like "Christ rose from the dead"? In my view, no one has established that this claim is empirically false, internally inconsistent, or inconsistent with other known truths, including those of the natural sciences. For what it's worth, I would offer the same response with respect to many other miracle reports from other religious traditions. My view rests more on philosophical considerations about what it takes to rule out miraculous claims than on Christian-theological considerations about what miraculous claims happen to be true.

Fortunately, we can dismiss most of them very quickly. Even on a superficial reading, it is obvious that Hasker make claims, takes himself to be entitled to those claims, and takes himself to have good reasons for them (norms 1–2); like all scholars, he is entitled to treat his commitments as rationally innocent until proven guilty (norm 5), and like all scholars he should withdraw from commitments to which he is not entitled (norm 6). So that really leaves only norms 3 and 4. Does Hasker try to support his claims with maximally accessible reasons and evidence (norm 3), and does he invite criticism and challenges, and respond to appropriate challenges with reasons and evidence (norm 4)? Answering these questions suffices to answer the broader question about whether Hasker's work conforms to the general norms of academic inquiry.

How Hasker Argues

It is obvious that Hasker invites and responds to appropriate academic criticism: he chose to publish his book with a respected university press, he agreed to send it out for review to leading journals, and so forth. He has also replied in print to published criticism, by providing additional reasons and evidence for his views.[17] This is all very straightforward. Of course, like most academics, in his published replies, Hasker does not fully agree with his critics; he remains convinced that his own views are sound, and his critics remain similarly convinced of their own rectitude. This standoff raises the issue of persistent disagreement, which I discuss below.

Hasker also supports his claims with appropriately accessible reasons and evidence. To be sure, his whole line of inquiry begins from specifically Christian theological assumptions that not everyone shares. I discuss this issue separately below. But it should be clear that he does not regard himself as a religious authority figure, nor does he regard his own book as a sermon, or a work of divine revelation. His work is not presented as beyond challenge. It is composed of arguments— some philosophical, some exegetical, some historical—none of which is put forward as infallible, unquestionable, eternal, or transcendent. The book is very obviously an academic intervention in an ongoing scholarly conversation. As such, it is utterly ordinary.

Take, for example, chapter 22, "Monotheism and Christology."[18] The argument of that chapter is entirely historical: it makes the case that early Christian monotheism emerged from Second Temple Jewish monotheism, which treated monotheism

---

[17] For example, William Hasker, "God's Only Begotten Son: A Reply To R. T. Mullins," *European Journal for Philosophy of Religion* 9 (2017): 217–38; "Can Social Trinitarianism Be Monotheist?: A Reply to Dale Tuggy," *Faith and Philosophy* 30 (2013): 439–43.
[18] Hasker, *Metaphysics and the Tri-Personal God*, 177–84.

not primarily as a metaphysical doctrine but a form of worship practice. Right or wrong, the case rests on historical evidence, which anyone with the right expertise can dispute. Alternatively, consider a more challenging example, chapter 23, "Each of the Persons Is God."[19] In this chapter, Hasker argues that Christians should interpret the "is" of Trinitarian claims like "The Father is God" or "The Son is God" as predications instead of as assertions of identity. Briefly, according to Hasker, the right way to understand "The Son is God" is to treat it as formally equivalent to the claim "Socrates is wise." They should understand themselves to be attributing a property, the property of divinity, to the Son, just as when they attribute a property, the property of wisdom, to Socrates, in the claim "Socrates is wise."

Whether one agrees with Hasker about all this is irrelevant for now. What matters is how he argues for his favored interpretation. His argument has two prongs. The first is logical. According to Hasker, all other interpretations are ruled out because they are either internally inconsistent or inconsistent with the historic Christian creeds. These judgments are purely philosophical—one need not actually accept the truth of the creeds oneself in order to agree or disagree about whether an account of trinitarian assertions coheres with them. The second, interestingly, is exegetical. He appeals to the opening verse of the Gospel of John: "In the beginning was the Word, and the Word was with God, and the Word was God" (John 1:1, NRSV). When the Gospel says "the Word was God" (*theos ēn ho logos*), the word *theos* (God) is in the predicate position. Following the lead of various New Testament scholars, Hasker reads *theos* as a predicate adjective; on his reading of the passage, the Gospel therefore asserts "that the Logos has the property of *Godhood* or *deity*." He concludes that the Gospel furnishes us with "as good a precedent as could be imagined" for his own proposal, and so his proposal to treat "is God" in the relevant creedal statements as predicative has a biblical warrant.[20]

At first blush, this move might seem like a smoking gun: an academically illicit appeal to the "transcendent and eternal authority" of scripture as evidence in an academic argument.[21] But that is not really what Hasker is doing. There is a significant difference between these two claims: "The Gospel of John says that *deity* is a property; therefore, *deity* is a property" and "The Gospel of John attributes the property *deity* to the Son; therefore, a source regarded as authoritative by Christians effectively treats 'is God' as predicative." Only the former is a naked assertion of biblical authority, and even if this kind of assertion is academically illegitimate, Hasker asserts only the latter, and the latter is certainly legitimate. Hasker wants other Christians to accept his own favored interpretation of

[19] Hasker, *Metaphysics and the Tri-Personal God*, 185–92.
[20] Hasker, *Metaphysics and the Tri-Personal God*, 192.
[21] The reference to "transcendent and eternal authority" is to Bruce Lincoln's second thesis on method, as found in Bruce Lincoln, "Theses on Method," *Method and Theory in the Study of Religion* 8 (1996): 225–27.

Trinitarian assertion, and so he needs to show that his interpretation has roots in the Christian tradition. Yet his appeal to the Gospel of John may be challenged by anyone with the right expertise. Anyone with the right training in Greek can disagree with his interpretation of *theos*. Hasker's real appeal, then, is not to revelation as such but to philology.

Across the book as a whole, the method is similar. Hasker weaves together some (impressive) technical metaphysics along with some (less impressive) interpretations of historical texts, and constructs his own solution to a tricky conceptual problem. Overall, *Metaphysics and the Tri-Personal God* reads like what it is—a dry, carefully argued, academic work that will persuade some but by no means all of its readers. When considered as an instance of academic writing, it is hard to see how it could be regarded as in any way unusual, let alone as a scandalous outlier beyond the scholarly pale—notwithstanding its cheerful self-description as "theology."

Is Hasker Entitled to His Theological Assumptions?

It is time to investigate whether Hasker's Christian commitments invalidate his otherwise legitimate academic work. For all its philosophical pyrotechnics, *Metaphysics and the Tri-personal God* is avowedly a work of theology, understood as faith seeking understanding. Hasker does not disguise the overtly theological assumptions from which he begins[22]:

(a) God revealed himself in Jesus of Nazareth.
(b) The New Testament is a broadly reliable guide to the life and ministry of Jesus, including his resurrection.
(c) Divine providence guided the early church in its formulation of the trinitarian creeds, culminating in the Niceno-Constantinopolitan Creed of 381.

Hasker also says that he explicitly writes for readers who share these assumptions, and admits that those who do not will find his book of little interest. The question before us, then, is: Given that Hasker's constructive project begins from these assumptions, does it really count as scholarship?

Someone who insists that *Metaphysics and the Tri-Personal God* is not properly academic must think that Hasker's Christian commitments somehow effect a kind of inverted alchemy—they transform his book from a dry and technical work of analytic metaphysics into something else, something so deformed that it no longer counts as scholarship at all. What are the principles of this alchemy? They must be very subtle indeed if they pertain only to controversial *theological*

---

[22] These propositions are all found in Hasker, *Metaphysics and the Tri-Personal God*, 7–9. To avoid confusion with the numbered norms of inquiry (above), I label these propositions alphabetically.

assumptions but not, for example, to controversial philosophical, political, aesthetic, economic, or ideological assumptions.

Suppose that instead of a book on the Trinity, Hasker wrote an (almost) identical book about Plato's theory of the Forms. In that hypothetical book, Hasker defends Plato's theory of the Forms as a surprisingly coherent and plausible metaphysical system. According to hypothetical Hasker, many of the most common objections against the theory do not succeed. He begins by laying out the ontological, axiological, and historical assumptions that underlie the theory of the Forms. He then says a few words about why those assumptions are plausible, but he does not defend them at any great length. Next, he offers several chapters critiquing Plato's earliest interpreters, followed by several more chapters critiquing various contemporary readings of Plato. Finally, hypothetical Hasker presents own constructive proposal about how best to make sense of the Forms. To the extent that his argument succeeds, readers become much more sympathetic to the theory of the Forms. Perhaps they even become Platonists themselves.

A book like that would be utterly mundane. It might be done well or poorly, it might be persuasive or not, but no one would doubt for a moment that it was a scholarly intervention into a genuine academic debate. What makes Hasker's book on the Trinity so different? Is it simply that Hasker *believes* the controversial metaphysical assumptions that he lays out? Suppose, then, that the first chapter of Hasker's hypothetical book on the Forms included the sentence "As a matter of fact, I am a committed Platonist and I thoroughly embrace the theory of the Forms." Does that single sentence change the book from a work of scholarship into something else? It is hard to see how. Alternatively, suppose that Hasker's actual book on the Trinity included the sentence "Like all right-thinking people, I myself am a diehard atheist, but I intend to explore whether it is possible to construct a plausible doctrine of the Trinity from the following Christian assumptions (which I myself reject, of course)." Does that alternative book on the Trinity count as a work of scholarship when the actual one does not? Again, it is hard to see how.

This thought-experiment is only meant to soften the ground, not settle the question once and for all. But it does suggest that analytic theologians like Hasker have an easy solution available when opponents claim that they are not entitled to their theological commitments. They can always reformulate their arguments as giant conditionals, so that the "controversial" assumptions are no longer affirmed or commended as true.[23] Thus, Hasker's argument would merely become a large conditional of the following form:

If divine providence guided the early church in its formulation of the canon and the trinitarian creeds, and *if* the New Testament is a broadly reliable

---

[23] Martin Kavka makes a similar point in his "Profane Theology," *Method and Theory in the Study of Religion* 27 (2015): 109; see also Alvin Plantinga, *Warranted Christian Belief* (New York: Oxford University Press, 2000), 419.

guide...(etc.), *then* here is a way that Christians could construct a consistent doctrine of the Trinity.

Anyone could then assess, accept, or reject the argument as a whole, even on the strictest grounds of "neutral" reason, because no one would be asked to endorse the antecedent theological premises as true. Hasker's Christian theological commitments would merely establish the parameters of his inquiry, by identifying the logical space in which he looks for potential answers.[24] This kind of hypothetical or conditional reasoning is ubiquitous, and it is also quite similar to the way scientists construct "models" to guide their inquiry.[25]

So much for the easy solution. Let us now sharpen the dispute. There is no real doubt that Hasker positively affirms these assumptions as true. Let us further assume—in the idiom of Brandom and Stout—that he regards himself as entitled to draw on them in disputes with other scholars. Furthermore, according to the fifth norm of inquiry (above), he is also entitled to regard these assumptions as "innocent until proven guilty." Still, should another scholar appropriately challenge these assumptions, Hasker would acquire a rational obligation to defend them with further arguments, and should it ever become apparent that Hasker is not entitled to them, he should withdraw from them.[26]

At this point, a clash of intellectual cultures looms. Many scholars will take it as a given—as the most obvious thing in the world—that Hasker is not entitled to these theological commitments. So they will insist that he already bears a high burden of proof, and must first show that these assumptions are justified before using them as premises in an academic argument. I disagree. There simply is no general epistemic obligation to begin proper academic arguments with demonstrably true or even uncontroversial premises and hypotheses. There is no such obligation in the natural sciences, let alone in the humanities. If there were such an obligation, inquiry would rarely advance beyond settled platitudes.

Appropriate Challenges Revisited

Matters would be different, however, if Hasker's assumptions have already been falsified. No one is entitled to affirm demonstrably false premises. I turn to this question now. If Hasker's assumptions are indeed demonstrably, evidently false, then he is not entitled to them. Those assumptions, once again, are:

[24] Timothy Pawl's *In Defense of Conciliar Christology* explicitly takes this form, for example.
[25] On the subject of scientific modeling and theological inquiry, see William Wood, "Modeling Mystery."
[26] Though we should also bear in mind that many challenges will be contextually inappropriate. As with the example of Pawl and *Conciliar Christology*, in many cases Hasker could reply to challenges to his underlying theological premises by saying, e.g., "That kind of question really isn't what this book is about."

(a) God has revealed himself in Jesus of Nazareth.
(b) The New Testament is a broadly reliable guide to the life and ministry of Jesus, including his resurrection.
(c) Divine providence guided the early church in its formulation of the trinitarian creeds, culminating in the Niceno-Constantinopolitan Creed of 381.

If it is so obvious that Hasker is not entitled to these assumptions, then it should be easy to show that they are false. Yet what would it take to show that (a)–(c) are false? Well, contra (a), we would have to show either that there is no God or no Jesus of Nazareth or that revealing himself in Jesus of Nazareth is not the sort of thing that God would do. Similarly, contra (c), we would have to show that God did not providentially guide the early church—perhaps by showing (again), that there is no God, or that God exercises no providential governance whatsoever, or at least that God did not exercise such governance over the early Christian church.

It should be evident that (a) and (c) are not strictly empirical historical claims. It follows that someone who wishes to counter them cannot argue against them by appealing only to historical or empirical evidence. It would not suffice, for instance, to argue like this: *Historical data shows that the Council of Nicaea was summoned in order to serve the political purposes of Constantine, and so (c) is false.* The council might well have served the political purposes of Constantine, but that fact is perfectly compatible with the truth of (c). In order legitimately to infer the falsehood of (c) from facts about the history of the council, one would also have to affirm some additional claim such as: *If the council served the political purposes of Constantine, it was not guided by divine providence.* But that is another theological claim about the kinds of historical instruments that God uses to carry out divine plans. So in order to argue against (c) one must engage with the claim at its own level, the level of first-order theology or metaphysics.

The same pattern of argument also applies to putative challenges from religious diversity. I have in mind something like: *Many religious traditions say they are grounded in divine revelation, and therefore Hasker's claims are false.* The conclusion does not follow. It is an empirical fact that many religious traditions say they are grounded in divine revelation, and, for that matter, it is a fact that religious traditions also make mutually incompatible claims. We can conclude from the fact of religious disagreement that all religious claims cannot be true. But we cannot conclude that no religious claims are true. And in other spheres—politics or economics, for example—we do not infer the falsity of p from the fact that some people disagree about p.[27] So, once again, an appeal to empirical evidence cannot, by itself, falsify (a) or (c). We would have to add some additional, non-empirical

[27] The *locus classicus* of this view as applied to the philosophy of religion is Peter van Inwagen, "It Is Wrong, Everywhere, Always, for Anyone, to Believe Anything upon Insufficient Evidence," in Jeffrey Jordan and Daniel Howard-Snyder, eds., *Faith, Freedom and Rationality* (Savage, MD: Rowman and Littlefield, 1996), 137–54.

premises about how we should expect a god to behave. In other words, we would have to engage in theology to undermine theology.

Even Hasker's (b), which comes closest to being an ordinary historical claim, is much less vulnerable to empirical disconfirmation than one might think. Certainly, it is possible in principle that new evidence could establish that there was no Jesus of Nazareth, or that his followers faked the resurrection, either of which would successfully overturn (b). We already know that the Gospels are incorrect in many points of historical detail, and that they took their present form by means of complicated and (seemingly) historically contingent processes. But the relevant question for Hasker is: Do these historical errors and contingencies disconfirm any of his central theological claims about Christ? One cannot really answer *that* question by adducing further historical evidence about (say) first-century Palestine. That question is not an empirical question at all, but another properly theological question about the nature of God, God's purposes, and the forms that divine revelation can take.

To make this point even more explicit, consider the following conditional: *If the Gospels contain historical errors, were not written by eyewitnesses, draw on common Greco-Roman tropes about divinity, and took their final form only after a long period of fermentation, then they are unlikely to be a vehicle for divine revelation.* Many people apparently hold that modern New Testament scholarship has undermined traditional Christian beliefs. I suspect that they implicitly affirm this conditional, or something very close to it. But, again, when we try to determine whether the conditional as a whole is true, rather than just focusing on whether its antecedent is true, we quickly find that we are engaged in theology, not history. If there really is a God who has chosen to reveal himself in Jesus of Nazareth, and who guided Jesus's followers so that they eventually produced the Gospels in their current form, then it is very likely that the Gospels are reliable guides to the most important theological teachings about Christ, even if those teachings are also embedded in a historical narrative that is occasionally inaccurate. This conditional expresses a theological claim about the nature of revelation, and any attempt to assess it must be theological, not historical.

We cannot show that Hasker's theological assumptions are false unless we engage them at the proper level. They express determinate, propositional claims that must be engaged at a similar level of specificity. Broad generalizations about what "everyone" knows will not do. Hand-wavy appeals to "modernity" or "science" will not do. I am reminded of Rudolph Bultmann's famous remark that "it is impossible to use electrical light and the wireless... and at the same time to believe in the New Testament world of spirits and miracles."[28] Really? I have heard this

---

[28] This paragraph draws on William Wood, "On the New Analytic Theology, or: The Road Less Travelled," *Journal of the American Academy of Religion* 77 (2009): 957. The internal citation is to Rudolph Bultmann, *Kerygma and Myth* (New York: Harper and Row, 1961), 5.

statement quoted approvingly many times. It captures the sort of sentiment that academics often accept without question, as an unarticulated background belief about what it means to be appropriately modern. But as a descriptive empirical claim, Bultmann's assertion is obviously false (many people understand contemporary physics very well and still have very traditional religious beliefs) and as a normative philosophical claim that modern science is incompatible with traditional Christianity, it is radically undersupported by argument. Opponents of analytic theology should not imitate Bultmann's breezy dismissal. Someone who wants to challenge Hasker's theological commitments must actually do the hard work of showing why they are misguided.

On Higher-Order Disagreements

Hasker's theological commitments should be treated like any other academic commitment, as innocent until proven guilty. This is not a protective strategy designed to immunize him from criticism. In many circumstances, Hasker may indeed be called upon either to defend those commitments or to withdraw from them. Suppose, then, that someone does mount an appropriate challenge to his theological commitments. What happens next? He should respond by giving the reasons and evidence that support those commitments. Furthermore, he should strive to offer reasons and evidence that are maximally accessible to his interlocutors. If Hasker were to respond to a challenge to (a)–(c) by saying *only* that the evidence for his premises consists in divine revelation, we would rightly judge that he is no longer engaged in academic inquiry. Suppose, however, that Hasker actually says more than this. Suppose he first agrees that his assumptions are drawn from scripture and the Christian tradition, but then makes the following claim: "Actually, it is rationally permissible to trust scripture and tradition, and so it is permissible to hold that scripture and tradition offer evidence that supports (a)–(c). Furthermore, I can defend this claim on generally accessible philosophical grounds."

In other words, suppose Hasker initiates a metalevel argument about what counts as a legitimate source of evidence. This new argument is no longer about whether Hasker is entitled to (a)–(c). Now the argument concerns the second-order claim: *Sometimes we are justified in using [supposedly] authoritative religious sources as evidence in academic arguments.* Suppose that in defense of that metalevel claim, Hasker offers a philosophical account of the nature of rational belief and legitimate appeals to authority.[29] His account is purely philosophical and features

---

[29] Examples of such accounts include Samuel Fleischacker, *Divine Teaching and the Way of the World: A Defense of Revealed Religion* (New York: Oxford University Press, 2011), and Linda Zagzebski, *Epistemic Authority: A Theory of Trust, Authority, and Autonomy in Belief* (New York: Oxford University Press, 2012). See also C. A. J. Coady, *Testimony: A Philosophical Study* (New York: Clarendon, 1992).

rational arguments that are, in principle, open to anyone. If successful, they entail that his original first-order appeals to scripture and tradition are epistemologically legitimate. This second-order argument would not be a historical-empirical argument. Yet it would still be entirely accessible in the relevant sense. It would be an argument that, in principle, anyone could join, because anyone could criticize the underlying epistemology and suggest a better alternative. At the same time, if the metalevel argument succeeds, Hasker's rational commitment to (a)–(c) seems to rest on solid ground, even though—crucially—his interlocutor need not ever accept (a)–(c) himself.

Recall Thomas A. Lewis's point about the moves that exclude one from the discipline of religious studies: "The moves that exclude one from the discipline are appeals to an authority that is claimed not to require justification, appeals to an authority conceived as unquestionable, and appeals to private forms of justification for which, in principle, no argument can be given."[30] It should be clear that in my (admittedly imaginary) scenario above, Hasker has not violated this dictum. He entertains and replies to challenges to his original theological commitments. He also entertains and replies to challenges about whether he is entitled to his supporting reasons and evidence. At no point does anyone appeal to unquestionable authority or forms of justification that are inherently private. As the argument ramifies, it becomes philosophical and epistemological, but still appropriately accessible, even according to very strict standards of accessibility.

This kind of higher-order argument is very common across the academy. Jones asserts p on the basis of evidence E. Smith replies that Jones is not entitled to appeal to E. Jones counters that she is indeed entitled to appeal to E for reasons x, y, and z. Smith may or may not accept x, y, and z. If she doesn't, then the argument may shift upward again to whether x, y, and z really do support the appeal to E. And so forth. Whether one finds all of this metalevel argument stimulating or exasperating is beside the point: it is a standard part of the academic repertoire, and utterly, completely ordinary. So in my imaginary scenario, were Hasker to shift the disagreement to the metalevel, so that it becomes an argument about what counts as legitimate sources of evidence, he would not be doing anything illicit or unusual.

On Persistent Disagreement

Of course, in my imaginary scenario, Hasker is unlikely to convince his interlocutors—perhaps that goes without saying. Instead, they will continue to insist that he should withdraw from his commitments to (a), (b), and (c), because he is not entitled to use scripture and tradition as evidence. For his part, he will continue to say that he can. Stalemate: neither party will convince the other, and so the

---

[30] Lewis, *Why Philosophy Matters for the Study of Religion*, 46.

disagreement will persist. But so what? In many academic disciplines, especially in the humanities, persistent disagreement is the norm.[31] Scholars in the humanities rarely settle first-order arguments (about how to interpret a specific text, for example); nor do they settle higher-order arguments (about what constitutes, in general, a good interpretation of a text.) As a rough-and-ready approximation, the further we get from the experimental sciences, the more likely it is that an academic discipline allows for persistent disagreement, even about fundamental issues. Needless to say, persistent disagreement is especially common in philosophy, theology, and the academic study of religion. In these other areas of inquiry, scholars typically treat persistent disagreement as a reason to engage in further inquiry, not a reason to block further inquiry. We should do the same in theology.

Critics of the humanities sometimes treat persistent disagreement as a sign that humanistic inquiry as such is illegitimate. We should oppose this residual positivism wherever it occurs. In the humanities, conversations and arguments continue through the centuries; that is their glory. A research program, line of inquiry, or argument may be perfectly legitimate even when it depends on highly contestable assumptions and yields only highly contestable results. We should not conclude from persistent disagreement that all interpretations in the humanities are equally good (or bad), nor that the humanities lack any robust notion of truth. I hardly need to belabor these points. They are among the foundational axioms of the post-positivist humanities. In other academic contexts, they would be accepted without question. I simply want to expand their scope to include academic theology.

Expanding the Norms of Inquiry

The discussion of Hasker suggests two corollaries to the general norms of academic reason:

4.1   When someone challenges our academic commitments, it could be appropriate to shift the disagreement to a higher-level argument.

4.2   Sometimes the right way to respond appropriately to challenges is to hold fast to our own view even in the face of persistent disagreement.

I am skeptical that we can say much in advance about exactly when it is appropriate to shift to a higher-level argument, when we must abandon our views in the face of disagreement, and when we are allowed to hold fast. Sometimes, but not

---

[31] There is a large and growing philosophical literature on the epistemology of disagreement. For a way into the debates, see Richard Feldman and Ted Warfield, eds., *Disagreement* (New York: Oxford University Press, 2010), and David Christensen and Jennifer Lackey, eds., *The Epistemology of Disagreement: New Essays* (New York: Oxford University Press, 2013).

always, these moves would rightly be considered forms of evasion or stubbornness. If we had an algorithm that could tell us when they are allowed in advance, before considering actual cases, then higher-level arguments and persistent disagreement would be rare. They are not rare.

These two corollaries render the general norms of inquiry significantly more permissive than they initially seemed, but I see no realistic alternative. Were we to deny either corollary, we would have to restrict the scope of humanistic inquiry beyond recognition—a clear case of a cure that is worse than the disease. As to (4.1), humanistic inquiry requires that we be able to argue not just about whether our commitments are supported by appropriate evidence, but about what counts as appropriate evidence in the first place. Any scholar of religion, theologian, or philosopher can easily imagine examples from their own subspecialties that are analogous to my Hasker case above, cases where the best way to respond appropriately to a first-order challenge is by shifting the argument to a metalevel dispute about the nature of evidence and rational justification.[32]

As to (4.2), persistent disagreement is an enduring feature of humanistic inquiry, so the only real question is how we should respond to it. Once again, any scholar of religion, theologian, or philosopher can easily recall examples of persistent disagreement in their own subspecialties. Every humanist should agree that some important disagreements are unlikely to be resolved once and for all, and that both parties to a disagreement can sometimes be rational in holding fast to their own considered views. In the humanities, epistemic permissiveness is a virtue, not a vice. Humanistic inquiry works best with a bias toward openness and acceptance, and with a low threshold for what counts as a legitimate scholarly view. If we all faced a general obligation to withdraw from our controversial commitments until we convince (all of? most of?) our epistemic peers to accept those commitments, then humanistic inquiry would grind to a halt.[33]

---

[32] The shift I mean is from "Hasker is not entitled to commitments (a)–(c)" to "Sometimes it is acceptable to treat scripture and tradition as evidence in academic disputes."

[33] With these additions, my overall account of rational inquiry is very similar to Nicholas Wolterstorff's understanding of "dialogic rationality" in philosophy. He writes (Nicholas Wolterstorff, "Then, Now, and Al," in Kelly James Clark and Michael Rea, eds., *Reason, Metaphysics, and Mind: New Essays on the Philosophy of Alvin Plantinga* [New York: Oxford University Press, 2012], 215):

> One enters philosophy as who one is, committed as one is committed, believing what one does believe on matters religious and otherwise; and one participates in the philosophical dialogue taking place. The secular humanist participates as a secular humanist, the Jewish person as Jewish, the secular naturalist as a secular naturalist, the Christian as a Christian. One listens carefully to one's fellow philosophers who contend that one's commitments are misguided, one's beliefs defective, one's philosophical conclusions mistaken. On some matters, large or small, one finds their arguments cogent; on other matters, large or small, one does not. One then retains the commitments, beliefs, and conclusions one already had, perhaps refined by the fuller's fire through which they have gone. What else is one to do? One can't just choose no longer to believe what one did believe. And to those fellow philosophers whose commitments one finds misguided, whose beliefs one finds defective, whose philosophical conclusions one finds mistaken, one offers them arguments to that effect. One hopes they will find those arguments compelling. But one fully expects that often they will not. And so it goes, back and forth.

Does Anything Go?

Still, it is reasonable to ask: Does just anything go? Once we allow that higher-level arguments and persistent disagreement are both normal and healthy, we might worry that there are no longer any constraints left on what counts as an acceptable academic argument. But it is not the case that anything goes. Even with more permissive standards, it is still true (per general norm 6, above) that we should withdraw from commitments to which we are not rationally entitled. This requirement is not just empty rhetoric. No one can be rationally entitled to commitments that are demonstrably incoherent, empirically disproven, or otherwise known to be false. To be sure, interested parties will sometimes disagree about whether a given claim really is generally known to be false or incoherent, but this is unavoidable. We are all epistemically fallible, and if we knew in advance how to determine the difference between true claims and plausible-seeming falsehoods, we would not need to engage in inquiry at all.

Many claims cannot meet even the newly permissive standards. The maxim "innocent until proven guilty" does not mean "innocent until no disagreement remains." Above I gave as representative examples: astrology, young Earth creationism, and parody gods. Even with more permissive standards, all three are still ruled out. Opponents of theology sometimes seem to think that every theological claim is epistemologically equivalent, such that they stand or fall together: either they are all allowed or they all must be barred. But as with every other area of inquiry, there can be better and worse theological claims, which are supported to a greater or lesser degree by reasons and evidence.

Conclusion

I am convinced that some forms of Christian theology can find a place even in secular universities, because I am convinced that the most important Christian doctrines are coherent and rationally defensible. If I am wrong about that, then Christian theology does not belong in the modern research university. But that does not seem to be the position that we are actually in. Instead, the most important Christian doctrines seem at least as plausible as some controversial "secular" philosophical positions that are not regarded as academically beyond the pale. A research program in Christian theology, therefore, seems more analogous to various controversial but still viable research programs in philosophy than to completely discredited research programs like alchemy or astrology. The contemporary academy has room for Platonic realists, Humean empiricists, and computer scientists who believe that we are all just characters in a giant video game. It is hard to see why Christian theologians should be excluded, provided that they are willing to abide by the same norms of argument and inquiry as everyone else.

12

Naturalism as Metaphysics, Reduction without Fears

Here is a very reasonable thing to think. Suppose we grant that analytic theology is a legitimate form of academic inquiry. It still would not follow that it is a legitimate form of inquiry *in the academic study of religion*. Nor would it follow that analytic theologians should be fully integrated into departments of religion. Perhaps they should remain in philosophy departments, or in confessional faculties of theology, or in some other department altogether. The point generalizes. The religious studies critique of theology is often hyperbolic, but we really do need a principled way to distinguish theology from the study of religion. Prima facie, it is reasonable to hold that scholars of religion, properly so called, cannot also be theologians; it is similarly reasonable for any given department to decide to employ only scholars of religion, and not theologians.[1] Speaking as a theologian, I agree that scholars of religion and theologians are usually engaged in very different forms of intellectual work. Qua theologian, I am not especially interested in constructing or assessing general theories about religion, for example. Yet even here we should not be too hasty: if anything counts as a religion, surely Christianity does, and presumably one way to study a religion is to try to understand its doctrinal claims, and so... *voilà*: maybe I am a scholar of religion after all, even qua theologian.

One principled way to distinguish the two would be to say that scholars of religion practice "methodological naturalism" whereas (typically) theologians do not. With a few caveats, I endorse this suggestion. First, the caveats. Some theologians—pantheists, panentheists, and "secular" theologians, for example—do practice methodological naturalism of a sort.[2] Second, it is far from clear what "naturalism"—methodological or otherwise—really means. The label is opaque even in the hard sciences, let alone in the study of religion.[3] In the study of religion,

---

[1] I say "properly so called," because people can wear different disciplinary hats. The same person might be a scholar of religion and also a theologian, but, on a strict separationist view, that would be akin to the same person being both a scholar of religion and (say) an engineer. The same person might well be both, but never in the same respects and at the same time.

[2] See, for example, the discussion on "Secular Theology" in the Council of Societies for the Study of Religion (CSSR) *Bulletin* 37 (2008): 30–52.

[3] The literature here is vast. On naturalism and methodological naturalism in general, I have found the following especially helpful: Hans Halvorsen, "Why Methodological Naturalism?" in Kelly James Clark, ed., *The Blackwell Companion to Naturalism* (Malden, MA: Wiley-Blackwell, 2016), 136–49; Michael Rea, *A World without Design: The Ontological Consequences of Naturalism* (New York: Oxford University Press, 2002); Matthew Bagger, ed., *Pragmatism and Naturalism: Scientific and Social Inquiry*

Analytic Theology and the Academic Study of Religion. William Wood, Oxford University Press (2021). © William Wood. DOI: 10.1093/oso/9780198779872.003.0012

arguments over the place of "naturalism" and the related term "reductionism" are especially heated, because the meanings of the key terms are rarely formulated with sufficient precision. When we define the relevant terms more precisely, we can have a more perspicuous discussion, as I hope to show below.

The outcome of this more perspicuous discussion turns out to be quite surprising. While it makes sense to say that individual scholars of religion should practice methodological naturalism, one cannot justify such a requirement as a global norm that applies to the whole field of religious studies. It follows that any alleged barriers to admitting analytic theology into the field are not global, intellectual barriers. They are, at most, local, prudential barriers that apply at the level of individual departments. The same point holds for other forms of theology, and other forms of normative inquiry. When considering the field as a whole, therefore, I warmly endorse the status quo. That is to say, I endorse the very methodological pluralism that has long been the norm across the academic study of religion. The polarizing discourse around theology and the academic study of religion ignores the fact that both sides have long worked in the same departments, attended the same conferences, and addressed similar topics, albeit from different angles. Theologians and scholars of religion are already in the same room. We just need to talk to each other.

Defining Naturalism

To develop this argument, I first distinguish between "methodological naturalism" (MN) and "ontological naturalism" (ON). Methodological naturalism asserts a rule about how to study things we deem religious.[4] Ontological naturalism asserts a metaphysical claim about what sorts of things exist. More precisely, I formulate MN and ON like this:

Methodological Naturalism (MN):   study religious things by appealing only to natural entities, experiences, and causes.

Ontological Naturalism (ON):   There are no nonnatural entities, experiences, or causes: only natural entities, experiences, and causes exist.

---

after Representationalism (New York: Columbia University Press, 2018). On naturalism in the study of religion, see Jason N. Blum, ed., *The Question of Methodological Naturalism*, Supplements to Method and Theory in the Study of Religion 11 (Leiden: Brill, 2018).

[4] I intend the label "things we deem religious" as maximally encompassing and minimally controversial. The labels "religious matters," "religious objects," and "religious phenomena" would do just as well. For a similar move, see Ann Taves's account of "things deemed religious" and "specialness" in *Religious Experience Reconsidered* (Princeton, NJ: Princeton University Press, 2009), 16–55.

As formulated, most theologians are not methodological naturalists, because they sometimes explain things by appealing to God or to divine action. Nor are they ontological naturalists. I am content to stipulate that analytic theology as a method is not typically a form of naturalistic inquiry, even though it often restricts its appeals to natural sources of evidence. But not always, and so, for the sake of a more interesting argument, I accept the point that analytic theology is not a form of methodological naturalism.

My definitions of MN and ON both depend on an underlying conception of the "natural."[5] Yet defining "the natural" is no less tricky than defining "religion."[6] For my purposes, the philosopher Paul Draper's definition will suffice. According to Draper, the "natural" world is "the spatiotemporal universe of physical entities together with any entities that are ontologically or causally reducible to those entities."[7] On the assumption that "the spatiotemporal universe of physical entities" is also available to our senses, Kevin Schilbrack gets at roughly the same idea when he defines a correlative term, "super-empirical" over against "those realities that are available to our senses...the set of empirical realities"[8] So, in summary, MN asserts that when we study religions, we should appeal to entities, experiences, or causes that are a part of, or reducible to a part of, the empirically available spatiotemporal universe of physical entities. ON asserts that everything that really exists is a part of, or is reducible to a part of, that same spatiotemporal universe.

Both Draper and Schilbrack recognize that on, any reasonable account, there are entities that are not themselves empirically available physical entities but that should still count as natural by virtue of being causally reducible to physical entities—abstractions like "the U.S. economy," for example. Note too that, on the formulation above, MN would include both the causal-empirical explanations associated with scientific and social scientific inquiry, as well as the genealogical and ideological analyses associated with postmodern critique. I take it that this usage captures the self-understanding of most contemporary theorists of religion. A genealogical critic who appeals to categories like power or gender still practices methodological naturalism, on my account, because she (typically) holds that

---

[5] For a similar definition, see Jason N. Blum, "Pragmatism and Naturalism in Religious Studies," *Method and Theory in the Study of Religion* 23 (2011): 84–85:

> As a methodological principle, naturalism holds that phenomena are to be explained solely through natural (mundane, not religious), as opposed to supernatural, categories and causes. By contrast, ontological naturalism is a more thorough-going, metaphysical commitment which claims that all that is, is natural...This is a claim about the nature of reality which explicitly denies the existence of supernatural entities and causes.

[6] Halvorsen makes the point that as science has developed, scientific conceptions of what counts as "natural" have changed. He concludes from this fact that ontological naturalism is "an attitude, stance, or research program" and "not a hypothesis for which we could gather empirical evidence" ("Why Methodological Naturalism?," 139).

[7] Paul W. Draper, "God, Science, and Naturalism," in William J. Wainwright, ed., *The Oxford Handbook of Philosophy of Religion* (New York: Oxford University Press, 2005), 278.

[8] Kevin Schilbrack, *Philosophy and the Study of Religions*, 134.

those categories causally depend on the existence and actions of concrete, physical bodies.

MN is sometimes conflated with a distinct but related norm, "methodological reductionism":

Methodological Reductionism (MR):   study religious things by identifying their physical, economic, social, or political causes.

On my usage, MR is a species of MN: with respect to method, all reductionists are naturalists, but not all naturalists are reductionists. This usage conforms with existing practice. Some scholars study religions naturalistically without also seeking reductive, causal explanations. Consider, for example, an anthropologist who offers a thick description of a religious ritual, or a humanistic scholar who offers an insightful interpretation of a religious text. Such scholars practice MN, insofar as they do not appeal to any nonnatural entities in their analyses, but they are not engaged in reductive, causal-empirical inquiry. Some of the sharpest disputes among theorists of religion have been internecine conflicts between methodological naturalists who are also reductionists and methodological naturalists who are not also reductionists. Reductionists sometimes help themselves to the rhetoric of siege and portray causal-empirical reductionism as the sole bulwark against the ever-present threat of theology.[9] Yet for the most part, their actual opponents are not theologians at all, but fellow methodological naturalists.

Methodological Naturalism: No Conflict with Analytic Theology

I have no objection at all to methodological naturalism. Indeed, on the brief account above, it makes sense to say that scholars of religion should practice methodological naturalism, even if theologians need not. This suggestion seems to reflect the self-understanding of both groups. Most academics who identify as scholars of religion endorse some form of methodological naturalism. They may not regard themselves as social scientists, and they may not seek causal-empirical explanations of religious behavior, but they do not aver to any nonnatural explanations in their academic work either. Conversely, most theologians would not regard themselves as methodological naturalists in the relevant sense. This difference in goals and methods has important implications.

---

[9] One immediately thinks of McCutcheon, *Critics Not Caretakers*; see also Luther H. Martin and Donald Wiebe, "Religious Studies as a Scientific Discipline: The Persistence of a Delusion," *Journal of the American Academy of Religion* 80 (2012): 587–97.

Because they are different forms of inquiry with different aims, there is no essential first-order conflict between the naturalistic study of religion and theology. The possibility of conflict arises only when we move from the level of first-order inquiry to the level of second-order methodological theorizing about how to study religions. And even there, conflict need not arise. It is possible to argue that naturalistic methods of inquiry are legitimate, valuable, and oft-neglected without taking the further step of arguing that naturalistic methods *alone* are legitimate and valuable. Yet it is only this further step that creates any essential conflict with theology.[10]

I would like to develop this point in dialogue with Donovan Schaefer's provocative book *Religious Affects: Animality, Evolution, and Power*.[11] On my interpretation, Schaefer presents an example of what successful, appropriately restrained methodological naturalism looks like in the academic study of religion.[12] Since I spend the rest of this chapter looking at different ways that MN can go awry, I want first to emphasize that it need not go awry. Schaefer is a useful interlocutor because his substantive argument seems very unsympathetic to the arguments, assumptions, and methods of analytic theology. Upon careful consideration, however, it turns out that there is no formal conflict between his project and analytic theology. The wider field of religious studies can easily accommodate both.

Schaefer identifies with the ongoing "materialist shift" in the academic study of religion.[13] He argues that physical, embodied "affects" like fear and pleasure cause religious behavior. His is a materialist story because it is finally an evolutionary story: like other animals, we have evolved to experience specific affects in response to specific stimuli. These affective responses are the building blocks of religious behavior, the atomic structure that supports even our most complex and culturally mediated religious expressions. Ultimately, human beings, like other animals, are religious because religious behavior is a kind of bodily pleasure.

With its sharp focus on animality and embodiment, it is clear that *Religious Affects* is very different from most analytic theology. One might be tempted to go further and think that they are incompatible, such that the field of religious studies could not coherently welcome one without excluding the other. That temptation should be resisted. Analytic theologians do not offer rival theories of religion that

---

[10] In the terms that I develop further in the next section, it is only *restrictive* methodological naturalism that introduces the possibility of conflict. Restrictive methodological naturalism asserts that the *only* legitimate way to study religious things is by appealing to natural entities, experiences, and causes.

[11] Donovan O. Schaefer, *Religious Affects: Animality, Evolution, and Power* (Durham, NC: Duke University Press, 2015).

[12] By singling out Schaefer, I do not mean to imply that he is unique, or that successful, appropriately restrained methodological naturalism is unusual in the academic study of religion.

[13] He draws the term from Manuel A. Vásquez, *More than Belief: A Materialist Theory of Religion* (New York: Oxford University Press, 2011), 3–10.

conflict with Schaefer's affective account, because they do not typically offer theories of religion at all. Similarly, Schaefer is not doing anything like analytic theology. He is not in the business of elucidating key Christian doctrines, or testing and modeling the coherence of Christian truth claims. But for that very reason, he does not show (or try to show) that Christian claims are illegitimate, unwarranted products of false consciousness, or whatnot. To borrow a phrase from the science and religion wars, Schaefer's theory of religion and analytic theology belong to "non-overlapping magisteria," a disjunction that militates against any deep conflict.[14]

Religious Affects begins and ends by asking whether nonhuman animals can have religion. Since, for Schaefer, to be religious is to experience religious affects, he concludes that nonhuman animals can indeed be religious. Many animals exhibit ritual-like behavior, behavior that, were it exhibited by human beings, would probably be deemed religious. According to Schaefer, theorists of religion deny religiosity to animals only because they remain in the grip of what he calls the "linguistic fallacy." To simplify a very complex story, many contemporary theorists of religion identify religion with ideology and power; they then go on to identify ideology and power with language. This latter identification is the linguistic fallacy. The linguistic fallacy assumes that "depth, complex responses, experiences, and decisions cannot take place without the machinery of a linguisticized reason."[15] Rather than being "the window dressing of cognition, behavior, and meaning, affects are their foundation and their substance. Affects are compulsory, directing where bodies go through complex systems of pushes and pulls." Even "religious talk is a way of articulating bodies to systems of power mediated by affect."[16] Unsurprisingly, then, Schaefer denies that religion is "a matter of belief," understood as "the cognitive manipulation and the autonomous affirmation of a set of propositional assertions about the nature of reality." He asks:

> What would happen if we subtracted the framework of human exceptionalism from religion...? What if religion is not only about language, books, or belief? In what ways is religion—for humans and other animals—about the way things feel, the things we want, the way our bodies are guided through thickly textured, magnetized worlds?[17]

These questions set the agenda for the rest of the book, and motivate the "affective" turn in religious studies more generally. In summary, religion, for Schaefer, is

---

[14] The phrase "non-overlapping magisteria" comes from Stephen Jay Gould, "Nonoverlapping Magisteria," *Natural History* 106 (1997): 16–22. Perhaps I should emphasize that by appealing to Gould here I am not making any broader claims about whether science and religion are non-overlapping magisteria in Gould's sense.

[15] Schaefer, *Religious Affects*, 13.   [16] Schaefer, *Religious Affects*, 118.

[17] Schaefer, *Religious Affects*, 2, 3.

primarily about bodies, sensations, and affects, and only secondarily about "language, books, or belief."

Even from this brief summary, it should be easy to see why *Religious Affects* might seem completely antithetical to the project of analytic theology. Yet wherein lies the real conflict? Certainly, as forms of academic inquiry, the two projects are very different. But they are not essentially incompatible. By "not essentially incompatible" I mean something quite specific: it is possible for someone to be wholly convinced by Schaefer's argument and yet still practice analytic theology. And from the other direction, theorists of religion could certainly draw on *Religious Affects* to offer new, affect-based explanations for why some people find analytic theology compelling, but such explanations would not show that its practitioners are *wrong* to find analytic theology compelling.[18]

In fact, when considering *Religious Affects* alongside paradigmatic works of analytic theology, I find very few logically or evidentially incompatible claims, such that affirming some claim of Schaefer entails rejecting some claim of analytic theology. This essential compatibility is instructive, and provides important evidence for my own argument. The wider field of religious studies is capacious enough to accommodate both analytic theology and Schaefer's theory of animal religion. It would be a problem for me if any academic field that regards *Religious Affects* as exemplary work could not also regard analytic theology as acceptable work. Happily, that is not the case.

For that matter, the key claim of affect theory—that affect is more fundamental than ratiocination—has a long history in the Christian tradition and is also compatible with analytic theology. Many Augustinian Christians would say the same thing about affect, albeit in a more Christian idiom.[19] It is true that Schaefer seems to take a dimmer view of human reason and human agency than many analytic theologians would, but they have no need to deny the fundamental role of affect and emotion in the religious life broadly construed. (No one who attends an Anglo-Catholic church in Oxford, England—or, for that matter, an evangelical Baptist church in Oxford, Mississippi—could seriously deny the importance of affect for Christianity.)[20]

---

[18] In the spirit of Schaefer's "materialist shift," we should attend to the tangible, material products of analytic theology: academic books and journal articles about Christian doctrines and practices. It is hard to see why even a materialist affective program must delegitimize the results of these specific, embodied practices of scholarly production and not others.

[19] Indeed, my own first book makes a very similar argument from the perspective of Blaise Pascal and Augustinian accounts of the Fall. William Wood, *Blaise Pascal on Duplicity, Sin, and the Fall: The Secret Instinct* (New York: Oxford University Press, 2013).

[20] Schaefer and the typical analytic theologian are engaged in very different kinds of intellectual work, but their views might be much more compatible than we would initially expect, and many analytic theologians would even agree with some of Schaefer's fundamental assumptions. Several prominent analytic philosophers of religion are "Christian materialists," for example, who deny all forms of mind-body dualism, and hold that human beings are identical to their bodies: the great Christian hope is *the resurrection of the body*, after all. For example, see: Lynne Rudder Baker, "Need a Christian

According to Schaefer, affect theory gives us a new way to think about power, domination, and the darker aspects of religious adherence. He occasionally implies that contemporary (Protestant?) Christianity especially deserves affect-based critique by virtue of its cultural dominance. Even here, I suspect that several prominent analytic theologians would agree with him, especially those discussed in Part 3 of Chapter 5. But in any case, as long as Schaefer does not make the much stronger claim that religion is *reducible without remainder* to power and dominance hierarchies, there is no deep conflict with analytic theology—and I do not find him making that claim. Furthermore, Schaefer recognizes that religion is not always bad, and that "sometimes power may not be out to get you, that the things bodies do with religion may be about healing, joy, or nurturing."[21] Along these lines, the resources of affect theory can even be helpful to analytic theology. Many critics are skeptical of analytic theology precisely because it can seem so detached, disembodied, and "Cartesian." Yet, in my view, analytic theology actually involves a kind of attachment and pleasure, a point I develop in Chapter 14. Those who are sympathetic to Schaefer's affective theory of religion should find this argument thoroughly unsurprising.

No analytic theologian thinks that solving conceptual puzzles equates to religious adherence *tout court*, still less with being a faithful Christian, or being saved, or loving God properly. From the other side, Schaefer does not make the (absurd) claim that there are no cognitive-linguistic dimensions whatsoever to human religious practices. If pressed to theorize about analytic theology, Schaefer would probably explain its recent growth using the vocabulary of affect, embodiment, and power—no doubt including Christian political, cultural, and economic power. He would likely treat the things that analytic theologians value most about their own work—*those sweet, sweet arguments*—as epiphenomenal, downstream effects of power or affect. Without question, this is not the story that analytic theologians would tell about themselves. But my point in this section is that *even if this story is true*, it does not undermine the viability of analytic theology as a scholarly project. Analytic theologians can be wrong about their own motivations while still doing legitimate academic work. In order to construct a deep and

---

be a Mind/Body Dualist?," *Faith and Philosophy* 12 (1995): 489–504; Trenton Merricks, "The Resurrection of the Body and the Life Everlasting," in Rea, ed., *Oxford Handbook of Philosophical Theology* (New York: Oxford University Press, 2009), 364–85; Dean Zimmerman, "The Compatibility of Materialism and Survival," *Faith and Philosophy* 16 (1999): 194–212. The notion that non-human animals are religious has not been the dominant view in the Christian tradition, but it is not utterly without precedent either. Psalm 148 commands *all* of creation to praise God, including "sea monsters," "wild animals and all cattle," and "creeping things and flying birds." The book of Revelation (5:8–9) explicitly uses the ordinary Greek word for animal, ζῷον, to suggest that non-human animals will one day praise God. St Francis of Assisi famously preached to the birds, who apparently, listened raptly—at least according to his hagiographer: Thomas of Celeano, *The First Life of St Francis*, trans. Christopher Stace (London: SPCK, 2000), Chap. 21.

[21] Schaefer, *Religious Affects*, 176.

irreconcilable conflict with analytic theology, one would have to supplement *Religious Affects* with various substantive metaphysical and ontological theses: that there is no God, or no truth; or that human cognitive faculties cannot in principle track the truth. Claims like these would indeed undermine the project of analytic theology. But Schaefer carefully avoids such ontologically extravagant claims.

Religious Affects is a good example of what successful methodological naturalism looks like in the academic study of religion. But as a result of his (laudable) metaphysical restraint, even Schaefer's avowedly materialist, avowedly anti-cognitivist project turns out to be completely compatible with analytic theology. This conclusion is quite revealing. In the broader field of religious studies, we should be very clear about the distinction between the criticism "This is academic work that I, personally, find uninteresting" and the criticism "This is not academic work at all." In any healthy academic field, there is robust disagreement about whether various methods and lines of inquiry are promising or misguided. Schaefer's work might well furnish exclusivist theorists of religion with more reasons for regarding analytic theology as uninteresting, perhaps even misguided, but that kind of reaction still falls under the heading of normal, routine disagreement. It is not a reason to deny that analytic theology belongs in the field at all.

Must We All Be Methodological Naturalists?

Schaefer's book shows us what successful methodological naturalism looks like in the academic study of religion. Yet methodological naturalism, even when successful, does not define the limits of legitimate scholarly work. We should not conflate methodological naturalism with the general norms of academic argument discussed in Chapter 11. On my understanding, a scholar engages in legitimate academic work so long as she offers reasons and evidence for her claims, and is responsive to counterarguments when appropriately challenged. The distinction between naturalism and non-naturalism does not mark the boundary between legitimate and illegitimate academic work.

It is fair to ask why not. Why not make methodological naturalism a necessary condition for doing legitimate academic work? With respect to the study of religion in particular, I address this question below. With respect to the wider university, I would point to other disciplines that do not seem to require methodological naturalism. Some mathematicians are Platonists about mathematical objects, for example, and argue that perfect circles, sets, and numbers really exist in some Platonic realm of forms. On an appropriately equivalent definition of MN in Mathematics, they would not count as methodological naturalists. I could make the same point with respect to mind-body dualists in philosophy, or non-naturalists in ethics. So it seems that methodological naturalism could only be a necessary

condition for doing legitimate academic work of any kind if we are prepared to exclude presumptively legitimate work in other fields. I see no reason to take that step.

Note also that as I have formulated it, MN is a norm of inquiry that defines what counts as legitimate inquiry for individual *scholars* of religion. It thereby defines who counts as a legitimate scholar of religion in the strict sense (namely, those scholars who practice MN). Because it binds at the level of the individual scholar, absent further argument it does not bind at the level of the department or field. MN does not assert the further claim that departments of religion, or the wider field of religious studies, must also be restricted to scholars of religion in the strictest sense. That is, MN on its own does not suffice to exclude theologians from departments of religion or from the wider field of religious studies. So even someone who agrees with the restrictive view that all "proper" scholars of religion should practice MN might still endorse pluralism at the level of the department or field. One would simply allow that individual departments of religion, and consequently the field as a whole, might include non-naturalists, so long as they don't try to pass themselves off as (proper) scholars of religion. This is in fact my own view. I develop it below.

Restrictive Methodological Naturalism

Before I do, however, it is useful to present another set of distinctions. I happily endorse MN and MR, and I agree that inquiry based on naturalistic or reductive methods is valuable—even crucial—to the academic study of religion. But one can hold this view without taking the further step of insisting that *all* inquiry in the study of religion *must* be governed by MN or MR. I have formulated MN and MR in a way that takes no position on whether we should treat them as restrictive or nonrestrictive norms. In other words, MN takes no position on whether we should study religious things *only* by seeking naturalistic explanations (restrictive), or whether the pursuit of naturalistic explanations is one way but not the only way to study religious things (nonrestrictive). The same goes for MR. We need a pair of terms that presents the relevant contrasts explicitly.

restrictive methodological naturalism (RMN):   The only legitimate way to study religious things is by appealing to natural entities, experiences, and causes.

restrictive methodological reductionism (RMR):   The only legitimate way to study religious things is by trying to identify their physical, economic, social, or political causes.

RMN and RMR are more sweeping: by implication, they apply not only to individual scholars, but also to departments, and to the field as a whole. In debates about naturalism and reductionism in the study of religion, it is not always clear whether a given theorist means to argue that scholars of religion should always practice MN or MR, or whether MN and MR are simply among the viable options for the study of religion. In other words, it is not clear whether they are arguing about MN and MR or about RMN and RMR.

Against Restrictive Methodological Naturalism

I now return to the central argument. Some scholars of religion might be prepared to grant that analytic theology is a legitimate form of academic inquiry in some sense. Yet they might still try to claim, on methodological grounds, that it has no place in the academic study of religion. (Again, I will stipulate that analytic theology is not a form of naturalistic or reductive inquiry.) Some opponents of analytic theology might say that the only legitimate way to study religious things is by identifying their physical, economic, social, or political causes (RMR). Others might not go that far, but might still say that the only legitimate way to study religious things is by means of naturalistic methods (RMN). The latter claim is more challenging for my own position, so that is the claim that I will address. There are already several cogent critiques of restrictive methodological reductionism in the study of religion, but comparatively few explicit critiques of restrictive methodological naturalism.[22]

To assess RMN, we need to explore some of the logical consequences of methodological naturalism in the study of religion. Though it may seem as though RMN asserts a metaphysically innocent methodological rule, in fact RMN presupposes a variety of substantive—and controversial—metaphysical assumptions. This fact is awkward for advocates of RMN, who typically affirm it precisely because they want to purge all metaphysics from the study of religion.

Suppose you are an advocate of MN. Moreover, you not only affirm MN; you also affirm RMN, the even stronger claim that all departments of religion and the field as a whole should require MN. On your view, there is no place for theologians, analytic or otherwise, in the academic study of religion. Suppose I ask you to defend that view. What sorts of considerations might you bring to bear? One way, of course, would be to deny that any nonnatural things exist—that is, to assert ON. But that is a metaphysical thesis par excellence, and so it is not available to those who wish to avoid substantive metaphysical arguments. Although I rarely see the claim expressed explicitly, I suspect that exclusivist scholars of religion endorse RMN because they believe that only appropriately "scientific" methods

---

[22] The best response to RMR, which is also the best existing defense of religious studies as a humanistic discipline, is Tyler Roberts, *Encountering Religion*. Roberts criticizes "locativist" scholarship, which corresponds well to the position that I call RMR.

can yield knowledge about religious things.[23] So they likely also affirm what I will call "epistemological naturalism," as expressed by the following claim:

Epistemological Naturalism (EN): Only methods that are relevantly similar to the current methods of the natural and social sciences can yield knowledge, or justified beliefs, about religious things.

EN offers a reason, a justification, for affirming RMN. Note that EN is a *philosophical* claim, one that can be defended only by further philosophical arguments about what counts as knowledge and how we acquire it. It cannot be defended by gathering additional empirical evidence. Leave aside the fact that "relevantly similar" and "current methods" are both quite vague. We all have some grasp of what EN asserts. What should we make of it? EN is not obviously self-defeating. Nor is it obviously true. So EN stands in need of additional argument. But then the cycle simply repeats. We introduced EN to offer rational support for RMN. And just like RMN, EN initially seems like a metaphysically innocent methodological rule. But it turns out to require further supporting argument. And here the real problem arises: we cannot offer that supporting argument without also making a variety of highly contentious substantive theological and metaphysical assumptions.

For example, suppose it is true, as most Christians affirm, that God reveals himself to people through scripture, religious experiences, and the internal testimony of the Holy Spirit. On the plausible assumption that God tells the truth, it would then be the case that divine testimony can yield knowledge, or justified beliefs, about religious things. Believing divine testimony, I take it, is not relevantly similar to the accepted methods of the natural and social sciences.[24] So some common Christian assumptions about sources of knowledge directly contradict EN. But that means that if EN turns out to be true, then those same Christian assumptions turn out to be false. If EN is true, it would be false that divine testimony ever yields knowledge, or justified beliefs, about religious things, and therefore it would be false that God reveals himself. In short, EN entails the falsity of a widely held Christian view about the sources of religious knowledge, and the widely held Christian view in turn entails the falsity of EN. EN is hardly an innocent methodological rule after all.

Before continuing, I want to reiterate that my own argument is an attack on *restrictive* methodological naturalism, not MN or MR as such. Indeed, it is quite easy to repair EN with a small but important change: removing the word "only."

---

[23] Some scholars who are steeped in genealogical and critical forms inquiry might endorse RMN for a different reason. They might think that non-naturalistic forms of inquiry are more likely to be oppressive or especially vulnerable to ideological distortion. I consider this possibility in Chapter 13.

[24] Treating non-divine testimony as a source of evidence (in the absence of contrary defeaters) is, of course, fundamental to any form of inquiry, including the harder sciences.

(EN*):   methods that are relevantly similar to the current methods of the natural and social sciences can yield knowledge, or justified beliefs, about religious things.

EN* seems true to me. I have no quarrel with it, and I happily commend it to everyone. But EN* supports MN and MR. It does not support RMN or RMR, *restrictive* methodological naturalism or reductionism. Let us, therefore, return to the stronger version, EN. I have argued that EN purports to be a methodological rule, but turns out to have substantive theological implications. We can formulate this argument more perspicuously:

(1) If a method of inquiry yields knowledge about religious things, then that method is relevantly similar to the current methods of the natural and social sciences.

(2) Consulting divine testimony is not relevantly similar to the current methods of the natural and social sciences.

(3) So consulting divine testimony does not yield knowledge about religious things.

But if consulting divine testimony does not yield knowledge about religious things, then it is false that God reveals himself to people through scripture, religious experiences, and the internal testimony of the Holy Spirit:

(4) If God reveals himself through scripture, etc., then divine testimony yields knowledge about religious things.

(5) Divine testimony does not yield knowledge about religious things.

(6) So God does not reveal himself through scripture, etc.

Conclusions (3) and (6) are not merely formal-methodological rules, but substantive theological and metaphysical claims about the way God acts. Yet they are entailed by the most plausible interpretation of EN. Since (in my view) EN expresses the main line of support in favor of RMN, it follows that RMN also presupposes the same disguised metaphysical claim. The two principles stand or fall together. At the very least, someone who affirms RMN on a basis other than EN owes us some additional positive arguments on its behalf. I suspect that they will fall into the same trap.

In the study of religion, it is all too easy to treat one's conclusions as the innocent application of a methodological rule, and to ignore the fact that the methodological rule is itself functionally equivalent to a substantive—and contentious—metaphysical position.[25] To consolidate the argument: it is possible

---

[25] This sentence echoes a point made (in a different context) by Gary Gutting in his review of Jeffrey Stout's *Democracy and Tradition* in *Ethics* 115 (2004): 170. "It is suspiciously convenient when

and legitimate for any individual scholar of religion to practice methodological naturalism or reductionism. We can take as a given that these are valuable methods of inquiry. But when we require methodological naturalism of the field as a whole, we find that we cannot justify this restrictive requirement without assuming a variety of substantive metaphysical positions that themselves stand in need of justification. That justification will in turn require arguing about funda- mental matters of ontology and epistemology. Those arguments are not signifi- cantly different from the kinds of metaphysical (indeed, theological) arguments that restrictive methodological naturalism is intended to prevent. So in the study of religion, restrictive methodological naturalism effectively collapses into onto- logical naturalism.

Ontological Naturalism on the Cheap

The proper response to this argument is not to redouble our efforts to purge the study of religion of all metaphysical commitments. The proper response is for scholars of religion to openly avow their metaphysical commitments and then argue about them. As a defender of open-ended metaphysical inquiry, I would not want to forbid theorists of religion from endorsing metaphysical claims, including ontological naturalism. At the moment, however, the prevailing norms of inquiry require scholars of religion to disavow and disguise their commitment to ontological naturalism. As a result, they are never called upon to support their metaphysical views with explicit argument. Instead, they get their ontological naturalism "on the cheap" by virtue of the supposedly innocent demand for restrictive methodological naturalism.

Consider, for example, Russell McCutcheon, a restrictive methodological nat- uralist who has built his career around sharply distinguishing properly academic "critics" of religion from non-scholarly "caretakers," who practice religion. He understands this as a methodological distinction. McCutcheon explicitly con- trasts his own "sociopolitical" reasoning with appeals to "the realm of disembod- ied ideas and beliefs (i.e., metaphysics)" and writes: "It strikes me that transferring [arguments about religion] to the level of metaphysics is obfuscating and regres- sive; it is another instance of the politically conservative, regnant idealist dis- course that I have tried to identify and critique."[26] McCutcheon does not really spell out why he holds that metaphysics is "obfuscating and regressive," still less

what presents itself as a merely methodological rule for rational discussion turns out to be function- ally equivalent to the liberal agnostic's substantive antireligious position."

[26] McCutcheon, *Critics Not Caretakers*, 146.

why metaphysical discourse must be "politically conservative" and "idealist," but in any case, it is clear that he does not regard metaphysics as a legitimate form of truth-directed inquiry.[27] In a later work, McCutcheon advocates "methodological reductionism" and asserts that ontological naturalism "makes no sense."[28]

Let us see what McCutcheon's "methodological" reductionism actually looks like in practice. To take a specific example, many Christian theologians hold that God can act in the world through natural causes, in a way that seems indistinguishable from the normal causal order. On this understanding, the same event can be correctly explained with respect to its natural causes, and yet still admit of further explanation with respect to its divine cause. Among theists, this is not an unusual or esoteric view. It belongs to the standard intellectual toolkit of any Thomist, for example, and has also been a backbone of Kathryn Tanner's influential work.[29] Someone who holds this view has a theological warrant for affirming both of these claims: "Event e has a natural cause" and "Event e has a divine cause."

Suppose you are a scholar of religion who endorses methodological naturalism. You might insist that your own work remains resolutely agnostic about whether there are any divine causes: all you do is look for the natural causes of religious phenomena. Fair enough. But if you assume that the same event cannot have both natural and divine causes, you have ceased practicing methodological naturalism and have instead staked out a substantive metaphysical position. This slip is quite common. For example, McCutcheon writes:

> Not only does the naturalistic approach to the study of religion presume that religious systems are but one aspect of historical, psychological, sociological, political, and cultural systems, it also presumes that the behavior and beliefs of human beings can be studied in much the same way as the behavior of other aspects of the natural world... This tradition models itself after the natural sciences in attempting to generate universal theories of human behavior from the analysis of specific cases, asking not what religion means but why it is that human beings sometimes invoke such things as gods in their analysis of the worlds in which they live.[30]

---

[27] Similarly, Manuel Vasquez writes:

the study of religion can and should proceed without making any appeal to some supernatural or supra-historical force or entity such as God, the Holy, or the Sacred. Whether these forces or entities exist is not a question that religious studies can answer or should spend time contemplating. For getting entangled in these intractable metaphysical questions is both a symptom and a source of Cartesian anxiety, somatophobia, and all kinds of disabling dualisms. (*More Than Belief*, 323–4)

[28] McCutcheon, *Discipline of Religion*, 151. By "metaphysical reductionism" he means what I mean by "ontological naturalism." So his claim is that he himself is not an ontological naturalist.

[29] See Kathryn Tanner, *God and Creation in Christian Theology*.

[30] Russell T. McCutcheon in Russell T. McCutcheon, ed., *The Insider/Outsider Problem in the Study of Religion* (New York: Continuum, 2005), 127–28.

So far, so good. The claim that "the behavior and beliefs of human beings can be studied in much the same way as the behavior of other aspects of the natural world" is an unimpeachable expression of methodological naturalism. I have no issue with it, nor with anything else in the quoted passage. But the following claim, on the same page of the same volume, goes beyond method to metaphysics:

> [T]he naturalistic study of religion...presumes from the outset that religion is not sui generis, not a special case. Instead, *it presumes that when religious people claim to have had supernatural experiences that defy rational explanation, they are mistaken in some way.*[31]

Here McCutcheon claims that religious people are "mistaken in some way" when they say they have had supernatural experiences that defy rational explanation. Yet his claim only makes sense—religious people can only be "mistaken"—if the scholar's naturalistic explanations logically *contradict* the religious explanations offered by religious adherents. But they cannot logically contradict unless the naturalistic explanations are true, while the adherents' own internal religious explanations are false. (McCutcheon may not like the language of "true" and "false" here, but I don't see what else he could mean by "mistaken.") Moreover, he presents his own claims as unrestricted in scope, such that religious people *always* misinterpret their experiences of the supernatural. Yet it is easy to see that this conclusion quickly resolves into the claim that there are no experiences that are genuinely of the supernatural, which implies that there are no nonnatural causes. This is a substantive ontological claim, and a very strong one too.

Once again, let me be clear about my own intentions in making this point. I do not wish to prevent theorists of religion from arguing that religious adherents are mistaken, nor am I engaged in any kind of protective strategy designed to insulate religious adherents from scholarly criticism. (Quite the opposite, in fact, as I discuss below.) But McCutcheon simply cannot assert that the self-interpretations of religious people are always mistaken while also claiming to remain entirely innocent of metaphysics. McCutcheon's own presumption of naturalism must depend on at least one of the following unarticulated warrants: either (i) there are no experiences with nonnatural causes; or (ii) if an experience has a natural cause, then it cannot also have a nonnatural cause. If either (i) or (ii) is true, then every religious person would indeed be mistaken when he believes that his experience has a divine cause. But both (i) and (ii) are metaphysical claims about what kinds of causal agents there are, and so, by his own lights, McCutcheon is not entitled to them.

To be maximally charitable to McCutcheon, perhaps I have ignored the force of his qualifier phrases. After all, the religious person is only mistaken "in some

---

[31] McCutcheon, *The Insider/Outsider Problem*, 127. My emphasis.

way" when he believes that his supernatural experience "defies rational explanation." So, more charitably, perhaps McCutcheon doesn't mean to imply either (i) or (ii) but only either (iii) anyone who believes that an experience has a supernatural cause cannot also believe that the same experience has a natural cause; or (iv) anyone who believes that an experience "defies rational explanation" cannot also believe that the same experience has a natural cause that permits rational explanation. If (iii) or (iv) were true, then our poor deluded religious adherent would indeed be mistaken "in some way," since he would not believe that his experience has a natural cause or a rational explanation when it fact it does, regardless of whether it also has a supernatural cause. True, (iii) and (iv) are not metaphysical claims, but they are universal epistemological generalizations for which we are given no evidence. As a descriptive claim about what all religious adherents actually believe, (iii) is certainly false: I cheerfully present myself as a counterexample. As to (iv), I suppose it depends on what any given religious adherent means by "defies rational explanation."[32] In any case, (iii) and (iv) are substantive philosophical claims, and hardly the product of the restrained reductionism that McCutcheon elsewhere explicitly avows. I suspect the point McCutcheon really wants to make is simply this: we should not *privilege* insider explanations or allow them to block the search for reductive or causal-empirical explanations. This point is perfectly legitimate. McCutcheon is entitled to oppose insider privilege, but he is not entitled to dodge the intellectual consequences of his own supposedly neutral methodological naturalism.

Academic Inquiry and Metaphysical Argument

Thus, in the study of religion, both naturalistic and theistic forms of inquiry rest on controversial metaphysical commitments: even the most avowed reductionists are often covert metaphysicians. From a philosophical point of view, this is thoroughly unsurprising, and no cause for worry. Virtually all interesting claims imply metaphysical commitments of one kind or another. One way to assess a theory, even an empirical theory, is by making its metaphysical commitments explicit. Philosophers see no need to pretend otherwise; nor should scholars of religion. Yet in the study of religion, instead of a proud and open ontological naturalism, we often get something else: an ontological naturalism that is pervasive but implicit, never brought to light, and so never examined, because it is "officially" disavowed—ontological naturalism on the cheap. I want scholars of

---

[32] "Defies rational explanation" should not be understood to be equivalent to "violates a law of nature." Some events might defy rational explanation—and even be deemed miraculous—without violating any natural law. See T. J. Mawson, "Miracles and Laws of Nature," *Religious Studies* 37 (2001): 33–58; William P. Alston, "God's Action in the World," in his *Divine Nature and Human Language* (Ithaca, NY: Cornell University Press, 1989), 197–222.

religion to be able bring their metaphysical commitments into the light, so that we can examine them openly.[33] The only "cost" to this move is really a benefit, in my view: the academic study of religion will allow explicit arguments about metaphysics, including arguments for and against ontological naturalism, as well as arguments for and against the existence of gods, demons, and other "special things."[34]

As long as scholars of religion obey the general norms of academic inquiry, then they are on impeccable methodological ground. When we engage in academic inquiry, we are obligated to support our claims with reasons and evidence, and to respond with reasons and evidence when our rational commitments are appropriately challenged. Insofar as we are able, we ought to offer reasons and evidence that can be accepted even by those who do not share our own commitments. This positive formulation of the norms of academic inquiry is merely another way of expressing the negative point made by Thomas A. Lewis: "The moves that exclude one from the discipline are appeals to an authority that is claimed not to require justification, appeals to an authority conceived as unquestionable, and appeals to private forms of justification for which, in principle, no argument can be given."[35] The general norms of academic inquiry and argument are all we need. More restrictive norms, like RMN, are unnecessary.

I have no wish to render theology immune from rational scrutiny. My argument is the very opposite of a protective strategy. Analytic theology emerges out of a confident disciplinary background in which persistent disagreements about metaphysics and ontology are the norm. From the perspective of my own disciplinary interests, I would love to see historically and empirically informed scholars of religion regularly push analytic theologians to defend their own metaphysical commitments. Everyone in the academy benefits from wide-ranging intellectual critique. In fact, I offer exclusivist scholars a new line of attack against theology: they can try to argue that theology should be excluded from the academy because its fundamental claims are false or irrational. Of course, such a line of attack requires *argument*. It will not work simply to assume from the outset that all theological claims are false or irrational. I am convinced that the most important Christian theological claims can survive such scrutiny. Yet I recognize that many other scholars regard the contrary view as almost self-evident. Fair enough—so let's have the argument. More importantly, let's agree that having that argument is one of the proper tasks of the academic study of religion.

One of the proper tasks, but not the only such task—we certainly do not need to put everything on hold until we settle every important metaphysical question.

---

[33] This does not mean that we should turn the academic study of religion into philosophy. Arguments about metaphysics do not need to take over the discipline. But since we seem to have them anyway, it is better to have them explicitly rather than implicitly.

[34] See note 4 of this chapter.   [35] Lewis, *Why Philosophy Matters for the Study of Religion*, 46.

But as long as metaphysical debates are strictly *verboten* in the academic study of religion, we will continue to have those debates by proxy. Instead of first-order debates about whether there actually are any gods, demons, and experiences of "the sacred," we will continue to see endless second-order disputes about whether scholars who seem a bit too comfortable with such things are really just "theologians" in disguise. Ironically, these methodological disputes have proven just as intractable as the metaphysical arguments they are meant to displace.

Irreducible Methodological Pluralism

When we look at the field as a whole, in all its diversity, the academic study of religion does not look much like one of the natural sciences. It looks a bit more like a social science, but only a bit more. The study of religion also looks quite a lot like one of the humanities—like philosophy, certainly, or the study of literature, or history. Our field is inherently diverse and pluralistic in a way that the harder sciences are not—thus the persistence of our fundamental methodological debates. At the moment, there is no widespread agreement about what a religion is, whether there even are any religions, or how to study them, if it should turn out that there are some. By contrast, scientists broadly agree about the purpose and methods of their scientific work. There are contentious methodological disputes in the natural sciences too, of course, but they are far more constrained. (No one seriously questions whether it is useful to study the physical world by testing predictive hypotheses against intersubjectively available empirical evidence.) The comparable claims and norms in the study of religion cannot be taken for granted in the same way.

This state of affairs is itself an argument for methodological pluralism in the academic study of religion. It holds even if we completely factor out theology. Working scientists are typically engaged only in first-order inquiry. Chemists study the intrinsic properties and behavior of matter. They do not spend time debating the purpose of chemistry or trying to establish the philosophical grounds of the scientific method itself. They leave that sort of thing to philosophers. Other scientific departments and fields have a similarly tight focus. Physics departments house physicists, not philosophers of physics.

By contrast, scholars of religion do more than just study religion. They also debate what it is to study religion. This state of affairs is not only unavoidable; it is a positive good. Unlike chemistry, biology, and physics, the academic study of religion includes more than just first-order inquiry. It also includes wide-ranging, higher-order reflection on the fundamental axioms, methods, and goals of the field itself. This higher-order reflection is a form of humanistic inquiry. Like all forms of humanistic inquiry, this kind of reflection is more likely to flourish in an open, unrestrictive environment that features a diverse array of fundamental assumptions and methodological options. When we reflect on how best to study religious things, we quickly find ourselves thinking more broadly about what it is to study religions in the first place, and why such inquiry is valuable. From there we naturally find ourselves wondering how our inquiry into religions exemplifies the goals of academic inquiry as such, or even about how academic inquiry relates to the still broader project of fostering human flourishing. Reflection on method quickly becomes a form of self-reflection—a broader and deeper reflection about how academic inquiry changes us as inquiring subjects.[36] Scholars of religion should welcome this expansive trajectory.

Analytic Theology and the "Scientific" Study of Religions: Reduction without Fears

Reductionist theorists of religion like to portray themselves as constantly under threat from those who reject the scientific study of religions.[37] Ironically, reductionists might find that they have some surprising allies among analytic theologians. Analytic theology depends on analytic philosophy and, as a field, analytic philosophy features a healthy respect for the natural sciences and for reductive forms of scientific inquiry.[38] (In fact, other humanists sometimes accuse analytic philosophy of excessive reductionism.) For their part, even though analytic theology is not a form of scientific reductionism in the relevant sense, analytic theologians need not be suspicious of reductive forms of inquiry in the study of religion. There is a useful analogy to be drawn with the relationship between theology and the natural sciences. Even though "science" and "religion" are portrayed as bitter enemies in popular culture, more intellectually sophisticated scientists and theologians recognize that there is no fundamental incompatibility between the two, and certainly not at the level of method.[39] Scientific inquiry is compatible

---

[36] See Tyler Roberts, *Encountering Religion*, esp. 85–118.

[37] For example, Martin and Wiebe write:

> Our first assumption is that the modern western research university is a purpose-designed institution for obtaining knowledge about the world. The pursuit of this knowledge is successful only when it is not in service of ideological, theological, and religious agendas. Rather, its primary objective is scientific, that is, to gain public (intersubjectively available) knowledge of public (intersubjectively available) facts.
>
> ("Religious Studies as a Scientific Discipline," 588)

[38] Neil Levy, "Analytic and Continental Philosophy," 284–304; Glock, *What is Analytic Philosophy?*, 134–45, 160–63.

[39] In brief, the crucial point is to distinguish between those theological claims that are subject to empirical disconfirmation and revision from those claims that are not so subject, even in principle. The claim that God continuously creates the universe out of nothing, for example, is not a testable, empirical hypothesis. The claim that Jesus of Nazareth was a real human man is. There are also borderline cases about which reasonable people can disagree: it is not entirely clear whether "Jesus really did work miracles" is a historical claim that is subject to empirical disconfirmation or something else. Furthermore, as discussed above, many theologians hold that God usually acts in the world through

with—though different from—Christian theology. There are a range of intellectually respectable options available to theologians who think that the results of the natural sciences are compatible with major Christian doctrines.[40] The same broad options are available with respect to theology and reductive explanations in the study of religion.

On theological grounds, then, analytic theologians can affirm that the scientific study of the natural world is valuable, and they can agree that the scope of "the natural world" includes human behavior, and even "religious" behavior. They can agree that natural and social sciences have a good track record in uncovering important truths about human behavior using naturalistic and reductive forms of inquiry. Analytic theologians should not be threatened by such forms of inquiry, because—again, on theological grounds—they should also hold that scientific and social scientific truths cannot really conflict with the genuine truths of the Christian faith. How could they, when everything that exists is created and sustained by God? To be sure, analytic theologians should be open to the possibility that scientific findings could cause them to revise or abandon some of their theological views, but, at the same time, the mere possibility of conflict does not entail already existing conflict. In any case, the point of these remarks is not to defend any specific view about the relationship between science and religion, but to establish that, at least prima facie, analytic theologians and reductionist scholars of religion need not regard each other with mutual hostility.

Analytic Theology and the Academic Study of Religion Revisited

As I noted at the start of this chapter, I very much agree that scholars of religion and theologians are usually engaged in different forms of inquiry. Some scholars of religion might worry that my subsequent argument nevertheless erases any distinction between the two. It is important not to overstate this worry. In their academic work, most scholars of religion do not do anything that looks even remotely like Christian theology. Likewise, many theologians are not especially interested in the kinds of inquiry practiced by scholars of religion. Furthermore, for all that I have said, it is even still possible to insist that scholars of religion, properly so called, must practice methodological naturalism. We would then simply have to accept that the wider field also includes some academics who are not scholars of religion, properly so called. At the level of the individual department,

---

secondary causes, in a way that seems indistinguishable from the normal causal order. This view functions as a theological warrant that licenses scientific and social scientific inquiry into religious behavior.

[40] For an accessible overview, see J. B. Stump and Alan Padgett, eds., *The Blackwell Companion to Science and Christianity* (Malden, MA: Wiley-Blackwell, 2012).

this kind of heterogeneity is often already the norm. Many institutions—including my own—have a "Faculty of Theology and Religion," or a pluralistic department of "Religious Studies."

In a way, then, the argument of this chapter is a modest brief in favor of the status quo. Scholars who wish to sharply distinguish theology from the study of religion in their own work can still embrace methodological pluralism as a legitimate way to organize a department. They can also embrace methodological pluralism at the level of the field as a whole. Considered as a field, the academic study of religion can include theologians without fear of contagion, and without violating any important intellectual standards. The worry that allowing theologians through the gates somehow undermines the field as a whole is thoroughly unfounded. Theology is not an infectious disease, such that other scholars are in danger of catching it by dint of contact.

Of course, by itself, this is not a positive case that theology, analytic or otherwise, should be incorporated into the field. (Just because methodological pluralism in general is good, it does not follow that all instances of pluralism are equally good.) Still less is it an argument that all departments of religion must include analytic theologians. Whether it makes sense for a given department to welcome analytic theology will depend on a variety of highly specific local factors. My point is simply that any barriers are practical and prudential, not intellectual. This book as a whole makes the positive case for analytic theology. Much of the case applies equally well to other forms of theology, including non-Christian theology. When otherwise secular departments of religion include Christian theologians, the disciplinary friction can foster unpredictable and fruitful scholarly exchanges. That is a real benefit. But there is no a priori reason to believe that such cross-disciplinary exchanges are more likely to occur with Christian theologians than with other practitioners of normative religious inquiry.

I have never been impressed with "neutral" arguments that purport to show that without *Christian* theology the study of religion is somehow impoverished.[41] Whatever instrumental case there is for analytic Christian theology would also support other kinds of constructive and normative thought—Islamic theology, Buddhist ethics, and so forth. This is a result to welcome, not to fear. What really matters is showing that the field of religious studies can include constructive and normative thought. If I were to offer an additional positive argument to scholars of religion on behalf of analytic Christian theology, I would offer only the following. Whatever the future may hold, it is the case that right now—in the concrete, actually existing world in which we live and work—it would be a genuine public

---

[41] By "neutral" I mean non-faith-based and nonsectarian. There are plenty of good internal Christian reasons for thinking that the study of religions is impoverished without Christian theology. But if we bracket out those internal Christian considerations, I see no reason why the study of religions would benefit from dialogue with Christian theology more than with other traditions.

good to foster a deeper understanding of Christian doctrine among university students, and to model for them what it looks like to engage in open-minded scholarly inquiry into whether those doctrines are coherent and true. This is a task for which analytic theology is especially well suited.[42]

I conclude with an old joke: An evangelical pastor turns to his friend and asks "Do you believe in infant baptism?" The friend exclaims "Believe in it? Why, I've seen it done!" (Sorry.)[43] To use a silly joke to make an important point, I would offer a similar response to hyperbolic worries about whether theology and the academic study of religion can coexist in the secular academy. What is already actual is possible, by definition. In the United Kingdom, Christian theologians work side by side with secular theorists of religion in publicly funded universities, and no one seems unduly concerned that this state of affairs makes genuine academic inquiry impossible for either side. Even in North America, many of the most important, admired, and trenchant theorists of religion have spent their whole careers working alongside theologians, often in explicitly Christian divinity schools. In other words, my argument merely endorses the very pluralism that—happily—already exists in the broader field of religious studies. Our major professional groups, the American Academy of Religion and the Society of Biblical Literature, are hybrid bodies that welcome various forms of theological inquiry along with various forms of naturalistic inquiry. We need not regard this state of affairs as an unhappy and precarious compromise. Instead we should embrace it. That is my proposal.

---

[42] Note that this is not the same project as that of "problematizing one's faith" or "holding one's beliefs in suspension."

[43] I have seen this joke attributed to G. K. Chesterton, Mark Twain, and even (believe it or not) Alvin Plantinga.

13

The Hegemony of Critique

This chapter focuses on the role of "critique" as a specialized kind of academic discourse that has become dominant in the humanities. The term "critique" does not mean negative "criticism," in the sense of disapproval. But it also does not simply mean "careful interpretation," as if the limits of critique were the limits of informed judgment. Rita Felski gives us a sense of the way that many academics practice critique. According to Felski, critique is a "thought style" by which we "expose hidden truths and draw out unflattering and counterintuitive meanings that others fail to see." Rather than being "synonymous with disagreement," critique "is a specific *kind* of disagreement—one that is driven by the protocols of late twentieth and twenty-first-century academic argument." Critique, in this sense, is "the hardening of disagreement into a given repertoire of argumentative moves and interpretative methods." Those moves and methods "include the following: a spirit of skeptical questioning or outright condemnation, an emphasis on its precarious position vis-à-vis overbearing and oppressive social forces, the claim to be engaged in some kind of radical intellectual and/or political work, and the assumption that whatever is *not* critical must therefore be *un*critical."[1]

Felski writes about art and literature, but her description of critique applies very well to the academic study of religion. Consider, for example, Bruce Lincoln's famous "Theses on Method."[2] They read as though they were written specifically to illustrate Felski's own argument. According to Lincoln, scholars of religion must engage in "rigorous critical practice" (Thesis 2); as a part of this practice, they ask "destabilizing and irreverent questions" aimed at "understanding the system of ideology" that operates in the cultures they study (Theses 4, 10); scholars of religion ask such questions because they want to uncover "internal tensions and conflicts, turbulence and incoherence, permeability and malleability" (Thesis 7). By contrast, religious discourse can only ever be the *object* of scholarly critique and can never count as scholarship itself (Theses 12, 13). Religious discourse—theology—thus

---

[1] The quotations in this paragraph are taken, in order, from Rita Felski, *The Limits of Critique* (Chicago: University of Chicago Press, 2015), 2, 1, 187, 2. See also Bruno Latour, "Why Has Critique Run out of Steam? From Matters of Fact to Matters of Concern," *Critical Inquiry* 30 (2004): 225–48. For a counter-view, see Didier Fassin, "The Endurance of Critique," *Anthropological Theory* 17 (2017): 4–29.

[2] Although widely reproduced, they originally appeared in Bruce Lincoln, *Method & Theory in the Study of Religion* 8 (1996): 225–27. In-text citations by thesis number.

Analytic Theology and the Academic Study of Religion. William Wood, Oxford University Press (2021). © William Wood.
DOI: 10.1093/oso/9780198779872.003.0013

gets constructed as *uncritical*, in the pejorative sense because (by assumption) it is not a form of *critique*, in the more technical sense.

The title of this chapter refers to "the hegemony of critique" because the "repertoire of argumentative moves and interpretative methods" associated with critique have thoroughly permeated the academic study of religion. This does not mean that all of its critics are hostile toward religion. In fact, it does not even mean that all of its critics critique *religion*. The converse move is also common: some scholars look at religious practices as a way of critiquing something else—usually some version of the autonomous rational subject supposedly prized by liberal modernity.

To choose one quick example among many, Saba Mahmood's now classic *Politics of Piety* is not a critique of the women's mosque movement in Egypt. Instead, as its back cover tells us, it is "an unflinching critique of the secular-liberal assumptions by which some people hold such a movement to account."[3] Indeed, the argumentative moves and methods identified by Felski are found throughout *Politics of Piety*, notwithstanding Mahmood's obvious sympathy for the religious women she studies. In the preface to the 2012 edition, Mahmood writes that what is "at stake" in her study is "to lay bare a parochial and narrow conception of autonomized agency that refuses to grant legitimacy to any other form of subjectivity or criticality." She further identifies this parochial understanding of agency with common liberal "conceptions of the subject, autonomous reason, and objectivity."[4] Hers is a project of uncovering pervasive hidden assumptions: she wants to "draw attention to the ways in which these liberal presuppositions have become naturalized in the scholarship on gender."[5] Her project is "based on a double-disavowal of the humanist subject":

> The first disavowal is evident in my exploration of certain notions of agency that cannot be reconciled with the project of recuperating the lost voices of those who are written out of "hegemonic feminist narratives"...My project's second disavowal of the humanist subject is manifest in my refusal to recuperate the members of the mosque movement either as "subaltern feminists" or the "fundamentalist Others" of feminism's progressive agenda. To do so, in my opinion, would be to reinscribe a familiar way of being human that a particular narrative of personhood and politics has made available to us, forcing the aporetic multiplicity of commitments and projects to fit into this exhausted narrative mold. Instead, my ruminations on the practices of the women's mosque movement are aimed at unsettling key assumptions at the center of liberal thought through which movements of this kind are often judged.[6]

---

[3] Saba Mahmood, *The Politics of Piety: The Islamic Revival and the Feminist Subject* (Princeton, NJ: Princeton University Press, 2012).

[4] Mahmood, *Politics of Piety*, xii.   [5] Mahmood, *Politics of Piety*, 13.

[6] Mahmood, *Politics of Piety*, 155.

This passage is rife with the rhetoric of critique in Felski's sense: Mahmood wants to "disavow" certain widely held conceptions of agency; she refuses to reify or "reinscribe" them as already all too familiar; she valorizes multiplicity over simplicity—all in the service of "unsettling key assumptions at the center of liberal thought." To her credit, Mahmood also explicitly reflects on her own scholarship and concludes that:

> critique is most powerful when it leaves open the possibility that we might be remade in the process of engaging another worldview... This requires that we occasionally turn the critical gaze upon ourselves, to leave open the possibility that we may be remade through an encounter with the other.[7]

Mahmood thus shows an admirable open-mindedness toward the Muslim women she studies—but then, on my reading, they are not really the objects of her critique at all.

According to Felski, critical scholars are like detectives: "like the detective, the critical reader is intent on tracking down a guilty party. Suspicion sets in motion a search for agents who can be held to account for acts of wrongdoing." The "scholar-turned-sleuth broods over matters of fault and complicity; she pieces together a causal sequence that allows her to identify a crime, impute a motive, interpret clues, and track down a guilty party." The guilty party need not be a person or an author, but the critic assumes that "something, somewhere—a text, an author, a reader, a genre, a discourse, a discipline—is always already guilty of some crime."[8] In short, critique needs villains. As a result, this mode of inquiry can encourage a certain lack of nuance. After all, we need not treat the objects of our critique carefully and precisely when we know that they are "always already guilty."

Even as careful and irenic a critic as Schaefer can fall into this trap. As with Mahmood, Schaefer's critique is not aimed at concrete religious adherents but an abstract scholarly discourse, one that does not give enough agency to bodies because it gives too much agency to language. But the real villain in *Religious Affects* is—once again—"the liberal model of the autonomous self," otherwise known as "the domain of self-determination through sovereign reason."[9] Because the liberal model of the autonomous self is, as Felski puts it, "always already guilty," Schaefer does not ever specify exactly what he means by "autonomous self" or "sovereign reason," and, as a result, he can remain artfully silent about exactly what his proposal really entails. Does he mean to claim that affect wholly determines human behavior, such that human beings do not have rational agency at all, and perhaps no truth-directed faculty of reason? There are passages that

---

[7] Mahmood, *Politics of Piety*, 36–37.
[8] The quotations in this paragraph are taken, in order, Felski, *The Limits of Critique*, 86, 3, 39.
[9] Schaefer, *Religious Affects*, 94, 12; see also 23.

suggest this view.[10] Or, alternatively, is his target merely the bogeyman Cartesian subject who is totally and completely autonomous, utterly free from any external influences, literally disembodied, and perfectly rational? Some passages support this reading.[11] On this latter reading, Schaefer makes the much more modest claim that affect... well, *affects* our free choices and rational decisions in ways that are sometime profound, and in ways that we sometimes cannot recognize ourselves. That is a far more defensible view, but it is also one that is consistent with a robust conception of rational human agency. It is not easy for the reader to determine which of these views Schaefer holds. The often hyperbolic rhetoric of critique enables him to remain vague about exactly how radical his own proposal is.

Critique is a valuable form of inquiry, but when it becomes hegemonic—when it becomes more like an ideology than a method—it can suppress vital questions and avenues of thought. Such is the case in the contemporary religious studies academy. Analytic theologians are well positioned to grasp the limitations of critique precisely because critique's moves and methods are so different from those of analytic theology. To say that critique has "limitations" is not to deny its value. The problem is not with critique as such, but with critique as an all-encompassing ideology of inquiry.[12]

I oppose hegemonic critique on three fronts. First, I argue that in the study of religion, critique has assumed the policing function once played by modern empiricism: caught in the grip of hegemonic critique, exclusivist scholars of religion wrongly insist that theology can only be the object of critique, and that theologians cannot practice critical inquiry themselves. Critique, therefore, functions as a new, "postmodern" way to exclude theology from the religious studies academy at the level of method.[13] Second, I turn an analytic eye toward the study of religion's pervasive critique of "belief." Hegemonic critique has little room for properly epistemological notions like belief and truth, even though we need these notions to understand religious adherents as rational agents. I rehabilitate belief

---

[10] He speaks of "the myth that where bodies go is fundamentally determined by language, either as a sedimentation of verbal instructions teaching us what to want or as a Kantian subject intoning, 'This I desire.'" (*Religious Affects*, 117), and writes "Rather than the window dressing of cognition, behavior, and meaning, affects are their foundation and their substance. Affects are compulsory, directing where bodies go through complex systems of pushes and pulls" (*Religious Affects*, 118).

[11] For example, his frequent rhetorical move of assimilating the modern liberal subject to an angel implies that his target is more like the Cartesian caricature than any complex account of human agency: *Religious Affects*, 2, 4, 10–12, 14, 17, 21, 93, 102, 107, etc. Herein lies the worry: we can all agree that we do not have *angelic* (or, for that matter, straw man-Cartesian) rational agency. But it does not follow that we have no rational agency at all.

[12] I am, therefore, not vulnerable to the charge that I contradict myself by practicing critique even as I point out its problems. My claim is not that critique has no value but that other forms of inquiry also have value.

[13] The term "postmodern" eventually became a placeholder that stands in for "whatever is bad" or "whatever is good," depending on who uses it, and as a result, most contemporary scholars of religion probably would not self-ascribe it anymore. In the main text, I use the hyphen in "post-modern" to indicate that I am using the term in its literal sense, to describe an intellectual move that only becomes available after the demise of modern positivist and empiricist epistemologies.

by showing that some of the most prominent critiques of belief are more limited than they initially appear. Third, I argue that the academic study of religion needs to supplement critical inquiry's "epistemology of power" with a more analytic "epistemology of truth," one that allows us to assess religious adherence as a form of rational behavior.

My engagement with critical inquiry is by no means one-sided. Having presented my brief against hegemonic critique, I turn the tables. Analytic theologians who aspire to any influence beyond the narrow analytic guild must engage sympathetically with critique. Although its limitations are real, critique remains an essential form of inquiry in the humanities, and especially in the study of religion, and analytic theologians in particular have much to learn from critical inquiry. Analytic thought can sometimes be willfully naive, blind to historicist challenges, and inattentive to the deleterious effects of power and dominance relations. Closer contact with critical inquiry can help mitigate these tendencies. Above all, critical theory can help analytic theologians resist the temptation simply to equate their own philosophical intuitions with the voice of timeless universal reason.

Critique as the New Border Patrol

Exclusivist scholars of religion try to deploy critique as the latest weapon in their ongoing efforts to exclude theology from the field. To understand the appeal of this move, it is important first to understand a bit of background about the state of the academic study of religion as a whole. Scholars of religion have long defined themselves over against theology, their ancient but suspect forebear. For more than a century, the two were distinguished on positivist and empiricist grounds, with appeals to the "scientific" status of the study of religion. On this line, the study of religion is a descriptive and explanatory discipline that employs intellectually respectable methods of modern empirical inquiry. Theology is . . . something else, something strange, something not quite *wissenschaftlich* enough for polite academic company. So the story goes, at any rate.[14]

---

[14] This story was easy to tell in the nineteenth and early twentieth centuries. Its scholarly advocates could simply assert that the study of religion is an objective, empirical science. In his 1873 *Introduction to the Science of Religion*, for example, Friedrich Max Müller writes that the science of religion was to be "based on an impartial and truly scientific comparison of . . . the most important religions of mankind" (Friedrich Max Müller, *Introduction to the Science of Religion* [London: Longman, Greens, and Co, 1873], 34). Even in the mid- to late-twentieth century, prominent phenomenologists took a similar line. Mircea Eliade contrasts the study of religion with theology by pointing out that the former, but not the latter, is a kind of empirical inquiry. See Mircea Eliade, "Methodological Remarks on the Study of Religion's Symbolism," in Mircea Eliade and Joseph M. Kitagawa, eds., *The History of Religions: Essays in Methodology* (Chicago: University of Chicago, 1959), 88–89. Ninian Smart insists that religious studies, unlike theology, is "descriptive and explanatory," "impartial," and "tied to the public at large" (Ninan Smart, "Religious Studies and Theology," *CSSR Bulletin* 26 (1997): 67, 68).

In the waning years of the twentieth century, as modernist epistemologies began to lose their grip on the study of religion, its leading figures divided into rival camps and began to fight a series of bitter methodological wars. The battleground explicitly concerned the disciplinary axiom that religion is an irreducible, *sui generis* phenomenon that differs from other forms of culture. Yet the conflict quickly became a wider argument about the intellectual legacy bequeathed by the field's founders, the proper way to study religion, and even whether there is any such thing as "religion" at all.[15] This methodological conflict was not about theology in any immediate sense, but it weaponized the label "theology" as a term of opprobrium to such a degree that it soon came to function as free-floating signifier standing in for whatever one wants to attack at any given moment.[16] Exclusivist theorists of religion regularly liken theology to a contagion: "Although the scientific comparison of religion has made remarkable progress since its nineteenth-century origins, metaphysical (i.e., theological) concerns...continue to infect generalizations about religion," writes Luther Martin.[17] He is not alone. Other leading theorists of religion also display a redoubled distaste for "theology," now understood as a general term for any kind of intellectual and ideological mystification.[18]

At the same time, however, along with the rest of the humanities, the academic study of religion took the "postmodern turn."[19] In the wake of postmodernism, it became much more difficult to regard the study of religion as an impartial, objective, empirical science. Indeed, it became more difficult to see why scientific objectivity is a goal to which the field should aspire in the first place. A central claim of postmodernity is that our language, concepts, and experiences inevitably shape the way we interpret phenomena in the world. We are all culturally and linguistically situated, and we all see the world through ideological filters. This is

---

[15] Key texts include Jonathan Z. Smith, *Map Is Not Territory* (Chicago: University of Chicago Press, 1978) and *Imagining Religion* (Chicago: University of Chicago Press, 1982); Donald Wiebe, *The Irony of Theology and the Nature of Religious Thought* (Montreal: McGill-Queens University Press,1991) and *The Politics of Religious Studies: The Continuing Conflict with Theology in the Academy* (New York: Palgrave,1999); Thomas A. Idinopulos and Edward A. Yonan, eds., *Religion and Reductionism: Essays on Eliade, Segal, and the Challenge of the Social Sciences for the Study of Religion* (Leiden: Brill, 1994); J. Samuel Preus, *Explaining Religion: Criticism and Theory from Bodin to Freud* (New York: Oxford University Press, 1996); Russell T. McCutcheon, *Manufacturing Religion* (New York: Oxford University Press, 1997); Timothy Fitzgerald, *The Ideology of Religious Studies* (New York: Oxford University Press) 2003; Tomoko Masuzawa, *The Invention of World Religions* (Chicago: University of Chicago Press, 2005).

[16] As Catherine Bell writes, "some explanation is needed for the nearly paranoid degree of antitheology polemic of the last decade" (Catherine Bell, "Modernism and Postmodernism in the Study of Religion," *Religious Studies Review* 22 [1996]: 187). She adds: "The underlying logic of the situation also gives one pause: those most interested in studying religion in a no-nonsense fashion appear to be the ones who most fear its proximity and influence."

[17] Luther Martin, "Comparison," in Willi Braun and Russell T. McCutcheon, eds., *Guide to the Study of Religion* (New York: Cassell, 2000), 53–54.

[18] Tyler Roberts has a good discussion in *Encountering Religion*, 49–84.

[19] A representative guide is Mark C. Taylor, *Critical Terms for Religious Studies* (Chicago: University of Chicago Press, 1998).

no less true for the theorist of religion than for the theologian. With a stroke of the postmodern sword, then, the study of religion was cut off from its founding myth: that unlike theologians, scholars of religion are at home in the modern university because they trade only in scientifically valid theories adequately supported by empirical evidence. This state of affairs presents a real dilemma for exclusivist scholars of religion. They must take their own situatedness into account, lest they misrepresent their own field and fall into characteristically modernist errors. But when they do take their situatedness into account, they no longer seem so different from the theologians they wish to expel. Exclusivists need a way to resolve this dilemma.

Enter critique. Some of the study of religion's leading gatekeepers—the usual suspects—now stake the very integrity of the field on critique. Russell McCutcheon's well-known binary opposition between scholarly "critic" and theological "caretaker" is perhaps the apogee of this line of argument.[20] In his essay "My Theory of the Brontosaurus," McCutcheon argues that any properly academic study of religion must take the form of either theory or critique. This is how he defines theory: "(i) a set of related propositions (ii) that possess predictive capability and can therefore be tested empirically (iii) that function to explain the causes of (iv) empirically observable events or processes." Note that this definition hits all the modernist, empiricist high notes. It builds in the demand for falsifiability, it calls for prediction-generating, causal explanations, and it confines its domain to the empirically observable. So much for theory. What about critique? McCutcheon defines critique as metalevel criticism of first-order theories. Crucially, however, it is clear that he has in mind the technical sense of "critique" discussed above. He means critique aimed at relations of power, politics, class, race, and gender. Theological discourse cannot count as critique by definition, since it trades on, as he puts it "grand narratives, teleology, essences, foundationalism, privilege and monolithic identities… [Theology] is the very discourse that is most in need of the radically historicist, postmodern critique."[21]

It is easy to see what is going on here. Recall that Felski associates the rhetoric of critique with "an emphasis on its precarious position vis-à-vis overbearing and oppressive social forces," and "the claim to be engaged in some kind of radical intellectual and/or political work."[22] When we take the emancipatory impulse that often drives critique and apply it to theology, it can start to seem obvious that "theology" is inherently mystifying: precisely what we must be emancipated *from*.

---

[20] See Russell T. McCutcheon, *Critics Not Caretakers*, 103, 111–13; *The Discipline of Religion*, 146–47; "A Direct Question Deserves a Direct Answer: A Response to Atalia Omer's 'Can a Critic Be a Caretaker too?'" *Journal of the American Academy of Religion* 80 (2012): 1079.

[21] All quotations in this paragraph are taken from McCutcheon, *Critics Not Caretakers*, 111–13. For an argument that theology *can* count as critique in the relevant sense, see Tyler Roberts, *Encountering Religion*.

[22] See note 1 of this chapter.

Critique seemingly offers both an explicit methodological warrant and an implicit moral warrant for excluding theology from the academic study of religion. The explicit methodological warrant is that theology is not critical. The implicit moral warrant is that theology is regressive and oppressive, something to be liberated from, and never something to be commended. Taken together, these two warrants solve the otherwise unsolvable conundrum that continues to vex the academic study of religion. Having taken the postmodern turn and bid adieu to the modernist epistemology that sustained the field for its first century, critique appears to offer a principled way to exclude theology again. Critique has assumed the disciplinary policing function once played by scientific empiricism.

Beyond Hegemonic Critique

Yet critique cannot serve as the field's new border cop, because it cannot do the work required: it cannot exclude theology at the level of method. As several prominent scholars have pointed out, there is no essential incompatibility between theology and the method of critique. In fact, many theologians are skilled practitioners of critical inquiry. I do not just mean that they are often "critical" of their own tradition in a more general sense. Rather, I mean that many theologians practice critique even in the technical sense discussed above. That is, they first argue that some of the bedrock assumptions of contemporary discourse are unstable or historically contingent. They then seek to destabilize those assumptions in the service of various emancipatory projects. In fact, in recent years, some of the best, most interesting theology has taken the form of critique.[23]

When critique is understood as one method among others in the study of religion, it can be an alternative to theology, or a supplement to theology, without necessarily being an opponent or rival. It is only when critique becomes all-pervasive and hegemonic that the two start to seem mutually exclusive. That exclusionary move depends on an ideological impetus that is itself ripe for critique. If the field must exclude theology, and if legitimate inquiry must take the form of critique, then of course theology can only be the object of critique, and theologians can never practice critique themselves. But to make this move, one must avoid looking at actual theology, and focus on "theology" instead, where "theology" is an ideological construct called into being precisely to be the object of critique.

---

[23] I think immediately of J. Kameron Carter, *Race: A Theological Account* (Oxford University Press, 2008) and Linn Marie Tonstad, *God and Difference: The Trinity, Sexuality, and the Transformation of Finitude* (New York: Routledge, 2016), and (in my view, at least) Lauren F. Winner, *The Dangers of Christian Practice* (New Haven, CT: Yale University Press, 2018). Also Kwok Pui-lan, *Postcolonial Imagination and Feminist Theology* (Minneapolis, MN: Westminster John Knox, 2005), and Joerg Rieger, *Christ and Empire: From Paul to Postcolonial Times* (Minneapolis, MN: Fortress Press, 2007).

Many forms of theology are completely compatible with critique. This is an absolutely crucial point, but for my own constructive purposes, it still does not go far enough. We should indeed point out that many theologians practice critique, but if we stop there, we implicitly endorse the hegemony of critique instead of challenging it. True, some theology takes the form of critique, but much of the best theology does not. (Analytic theology usually does not.) I also want to defend forms of theology, including analytic theology, that do not look at all like critique. To make this case, I can draw on humanistic scholars who have already begun to question hegemonic critique in other fields. After all, as Felski notes, there is something "perplexing about the ease with which a certain style of reading has settled into the default option" in the contemporary humanities. "Why is it that critics are so quick to the mark to interrogate, unmask, expose, subvert, unravel, demystify, destabilize, take issue, and take umbrage?" she asks. A text "is not exhausted by what it reveals or conceals about the social conditions that surround it." Rather, the text is also important because of "what it sets alight in the reader— what kind of emotions it elicits, what changes of perception it prompts, what bonds and attachments it calls into being." What would it mean, she asks, to "treat experiences of engagement, wonder, or absorption not as signs of naïveté or user error but as clues to why we are drawn to [a text] in the first place? To forge a language of attachment as robust and refined as our rhetoric of detachment?"[24] In Chapter 14, I make the case that theology—including analytic theology—offers a "language of attachment" in Felski's sense.

Felski puts these questions to students of art and literature, but they are just as pertinent for scholars of religion. There is more to the academic study of religion than asking "destabilizing and irreverent questions" of religions in order to uncover their "internal tensions and conflicts, turbulence and incoherence, permeability and malleability."[25] As all sides would agree, religious adherence can also be a source of "engagement, wonder, [and] absorption." Critique is not the only way, or even the best way, of understanding these attractive features of religious adherence. While critique remains hegemonic, then, important dimensions of human religiosity simply go unstudied. I develop this point below.

Hegemonic Critique and Skepticism about Belief

Critique is valuable, and compatible with theological inquiry, but *hegemonic* critique has fostered an intellectual climate that is inimical to many forms of theology, including analytic theology. One especially clear example of this climate concerns the widespread skepticism that many scholars of religion feel about the very concept of *belief*. Because belief is one of the central categories for analytic theology,

---

[24] Felski, *Limits of Critique*, 179–80.   [25] Bruce Lincoln, "Theses on Method," Thesis 4.

any successful defense of analytic thought must rehabilitate it for scholars of religion.[26] Of course, one should often be skeptical about specific acts of believing. But skepticism about the very idea of belief is a function of hegemonic critique. Critique encourages scholars to treat believing as a secondary effect of ideological socialization and power relations. It is a short step from that move to the view that believing itself is epiphenomenal and of no intrinsic theoretical interest.

The analytically inclined would be very surprised to learn how controversial even the most mundane account of believing is for scholars in the contemporary religious studies academy. Consider the 2012 "Yale University Roundtable on Belief," published in the prestigious journal *Method and Theory in the Study of Religions*. The Roundtable's editor, Kathryn Lofton, speaks for the field when she writes: "Like many scholars of my generation, I left graduate school with a knee-jerk nervousness about many categories...Few terms were more ostracized than *belief*."[27] Among analytic philosophers of religion and theologians, by contrast, few terms are *less* problematic than belief. The gap between critical inquiry and analytic inquiry is, therefore, at its widest with respect to the matter of religious belief, and especially propositional belief. With few exceptions, analytic thinkers of all stripes regard it as completely obvious that all human beings have beliefs in some sense. More specifically, analytic philosophers of religion and theologians tend to focus their scholarly work on difficult matters of doctrine, and they tend to express those doctrines in the form of propositions. To an analytic theologian, when we want to understand what a doctrine says or means, or whether it is true, we must first lay out the propositions expressing that doctrine. This process often culminates in, or is constituted by, an argument for why a given proposition should be accepted or rejected, believed as true or abandoned as false. Not so for their non-analytic brethren, who are likely to be less concerned about doctrine, narrow logical coherence, and propositional belief.

In the academic study of religion, widespread skepticism about belief has created an inimical environment for analytic theology. But this same skepticism has also warped the field on its own terms. To develop this point, I first tie skepticism about belief to the rise of hegemonic critique in the study of religion, and argue that the reasons for rejecting belief were never very compelling. Here it is important to distinguish "creedal believing," that is, explicitly assenting to distinctively religious propositions, and "ordinary believing," believing in the more basic sense of "taking as true." Many forms of religious adherence do not require creedal believing, but they do require ordinary believing. In any case, in the academic

---

[26] Kevin Schilbrack has already begun the project of rehabilitating belief. Schilbrack rightly distinguishes between what I would call "creedal believing," that is, explicitly assenting to distinctively religious propositions, and "ordinary believing," believing in the more basic sense of "taking as true." (I discuss this distinction further below.) See Schilbrack, *Philosophy and the Study of Religions*, 53–82. See also Jason Blum, "Belief: Problems and Pseudo-Problems," *Journal of the American Academy of Religion* 86 (2018): 642–64.

[27] Kathryn Lofton, "Introduction to the Yale Roundtable on Belief," *Method and Theory in the Study of Religion* 24 (2012): 52.

study of religion, most of the *legitimate* scholarly animus toward belief has been directed at creedal believing, and especially at the assumption that creedal believing is an essential feature of all religious adherence. That assumption is indeed false. But we can grant this point without also rejecting the explanatory value of belief as such, whether in the creedal or the ordinary sense. One legitimate task for the academic study of religion is to understand how religious adherents view themselves and their own behavior. That task requires some notion of belief, or its functional equivalent.[28]

The Critique of Belief: Donald Lopez

From the outset, skepticism about belief among scholars of religion has developed alongside the rise of critique as the field's dominant method. Genealogical and critical inquiry first became prominent among scholars of religion in the late 1980s, led by Talal Asad's aptly named *Genealogies of Religion*. Asad's influential book associates genealogy and critique with two specific targets: the notion that there is a universal "essence" of religion, and the suggestion that we should identify the essence of religion with propositional belief. According to Asad, this account of religion is far from universal, and is instead specifically Western and Christian: "It is preeminently the Christian church that has occupied itself with identifying, cultivating, and testing belief as a verbalizable inner condition of true religion," he writes.[29] He targets Clifford Geertz and others who unwittingly assumed that all forms of religion necessarily resemble modern Western Protestant forms of religion. Protestant religion gives a central role to religious belief, but other forms of religion, including other forms of Christianity, do not. Asad's essay is foundational for the contemporary study of religion, and it has been widely discussed already. I can, therefore, simply note (with Schilbrack) that, despite appearances, the essay does not repudiate belief as such.[30] Asad does not even repudiate the concept of creedal belief. He simply denies that the essence of religion is private, interior propositional belief.

Another, more febrile wellspring of skepticism about belief is Donald Lopez's essay "Belief," in the 1998 collection *Critical Terms for Religious Studies*, edited by Mark C. Taylor.[31] This essay is worth discussing at length, not only because it is

---

[28] I include the phrase "or its functional equivalent" to signal that I am not committed to any specific ontology of believing (i.e., that beliefs are mental representations) or the object of believing (i.e., abstractly existing propositions), but we do need a way of talking about what occurs when a person takes something as true. I discuss this further below.

[29] Talal Asad, *Genealogies of Religion: Discipline and Reasons of Power in Christianity and Islam* (Baltimore, MD: Johns Hopkins University Press, 1993), 48.

[30] Schilbrack, *Philosophy and the Study of Religions*, 76.

[31] Donald Lopez, "Belief" in Taylor, *Critical Terms*, 21–34. In the 2012 Yale Roundtable on Belief, Lofton mentions three sources of belief skepticism: Asad's *Genealogies of Religion*, Lopez's essay "Belief," and Robert Orsi's *Between Heaven and Earth: The Religious Worlds People Make and the*

influential in its own right, but because other scholars of religion critique belief using the same basic pattern of argument. By showing where Lopez goes wrong, I can also show where the critique of belief in general goes wrong.

At the beginning of his essay, Lopez identifies the target of his critique as the "generally unquestioned assumption that adherents of a given religion, any religion, understand their adherence in terms of belief."[32] At the essay's close, he reiterates this target and concludes: "the problem, then, is not whether belief exists—this is difficult to determine—but whether religion must be represented as something that derives from belief."[33] Leave aside for now that Lopez thinks it is "difficult to determine" whether belief "exists," whatever that might mean. Note instead the logical force of the word "must." If we take it seriously, then, on his own terms, Lopez's stated conclusion is relatively modest. He wants to know whether religion "must" derive from belief. In other words, he commits himself only to these two (logically equivalent) claims: (1) it is not the case that *all* aspects of religious adherence *must* derive from belief, and (2) it is *possible* that *some* aspects of religious adherence do not derive from belief. Neither of these claims entails rejecting belief as such.

Elsewhere in the essay, Lopez criticizes an "ideology of belief...an assumption deriving from the history of Christianity that religion is above all an interior state of assent to certain truths."[34] The ideology of belief is simply the ideology of Christianity run rampant:

> Belief appears as a universal category because of the universalist claims of the tradition in which it has become most central, Christianity. Other religions have made universalist claims, but Christianity was allied with political power, which made it possible to transport its belief to all corners of the globe...making belief the measure of what religion is understood to be.[35]

This is Lopez's conclusion in a nutshell: thanks to Christendom, we tend to "make belief the measure of what religion is understood to be." I agree that we should not regard explicit belief in distinctively religious propositions—that is to say, creedal belief—as the central act of religious adherence as such. The fact that we sometimes make this mistake is, indeed, a product of the cultural influence of Christianity. Note, however, that none of these claims about whether belief is the essence of religion is equivalent to or entails Lofton's later conclusion in the 2012

Scholars Who Study Them (Princeton, NJ: Princeton University Press, 2004). According to Lofton, "for most scholars of religion" this triumvirate "offered compelling evidence that belief ought to be avoided altogether" ("Introduction to the Yale Roundtable on Belief," 53).

[32] Lopez, "Belief," 21.   [33] Lopez, "Belief," 34.   [34] Lopez, "Belief," 29, 31.
[35] Lopez, "Belief," 33.

Yale Roundtable, made on behalf of "most scholars of religion," that "belief ought to be avoided altogether."[36]

Lopez brings us closer to this conclusion by helping himself to a bit of bad philosophy. He challenges the notion that a belief is an "inner assent to a cognitive proposition...a state of mind that produces practice."[37] He writes: "the statement 'I believe in...' is sensible only when there are others who 'do not'; it is an agonistic affirmation of something that cannot be submitted to ordinary rules of verification."[38] This statement conflates a modest, pragmatic claim with an expansive, epistemological claim. The modest claim is that people tend to assert "I believe that p" only when p is questioned. The expansive claim is that beliefs "cannot be submitted to ordinary rules of verification." This conflation allows Lopez to present belief in a tendentious way, as *essentially* private inner assent.[39] There are two elements to the conflation: the notion that believing is an essentially private act, and the notion that believing is unverifiable. Neither element survives scrutiny. The result is that Lopez's critique of belief misfires; it hits only a straw man.

Suppose John believes some proposition, p. What is it, exactly, that is supposed to be essentially private and unverifiable? It is easy to verify the sheer fact of John's belief. We can simply ask him whether he believes p. To be sure, he might not answer the question, or might not answer it honestly. So in some circumstances, it might be difficult to determine whether John really does believe p, given that his behavior strongly suggests that he believes q and not p, or whatnot, but there is nothing especially mysterious about this outcome either: determining whether someone is sincere is a perfectly ordinary human practice. Likewise, it may be difficult to decide how we should factor John's avowed belief that p into our explanations of his behavior, alongside other candidate explanations that do not advert to p. But this difficultly has nothing to do with whether his belief that p is inherently verifiable. In short, if Lopez were correct that belief is an *essentially* private mental state, then perhaps it would be unverifiable. But in most circumstances, there seem to be ordinary, publicly accessible ways of verifying whether

---

[36] Lofton, "Introduction to the Yale Roundtable on Belief," 52. I do not mean to single out Lofton. As far as I can tell, her view accurately represents the views of the field as a whole.

[37] Lopez, "Belief," 34; He strongly suggests—though does not quite assert outright—that this notion of belief is, in fact, specifically Western and Christian, dates only to the early modern period, and indeed arises out of the Inquisition. According to Lopez, when the Inquisition could not find a way to punish heretics for their words and deeds, it punished them for their private, unexpressed beliefs.

[38] Lopez, "Belief," 33; Lopez is, therefore, a source for the view, strange to analytic philosophers, but common among contemporary theorists of religion, that the term "belief" describes a state that is not only private and unexpressed but indeed inexpressible and unverifiable.

[39] One prominent example among many: in a reply to Kevin Schilbrack, Bruce Lincoln emphasizes that "beliefs remain inaccessible" because we have no direct access to them and so cannot know them with certainty: Bruce Lincoln, "Responsa Miniscula," *Method and Theory in the Study of Religion* 17 (2005): 65–66, n. 5.

someone believes *p*. We must conclude, therefore, contra Lopez, that believing is not essentially private.

But perhaps I miss the point. After all, it is supposed to be modern Western Christians and other religionists, not critics like Lopez, who rely on the notion of belief as essentially private inner assent. Lopez wants to attack that notion, and I seem to be upbraiding him for holding the naive view he explicitly repudiates. On the contrary: it matters that Lopez and his fellow critics pick out a single, especially problematic account of belief (the essentially private inner assent account) and then act as if it were the only account on offer. Consider by analogy another complex concept with a modern Western provenance, for example, "the secular." We would not move directly from (1) many people have an untenable account of the secular to (2) therefore, scholars ought to stop talking about the secular and abandon the concept of the secular as an analytical tool. We would instead try to ensure that scholars do not affirm the untenable account of the secular and theorize with a more sophisticated account instead. So too for belief: many people may indeed hold untenable accounts of believing, but that is not itself an argument for abandoning belief as an analytical tool.[40] Indeed, as I argue below, the academic study of religion must appeal to some notion of believing in order to be able to pursue some of its most important scholarly aims.

It need not be especially controversial to say that religious adherents have religious beliefs. Recall the distinction between "creedal beliefs" and ordinary beliefs. To say that all religious adherents have "religious beliefs" in the ordinary sense is just to say that religious adherents have views about what is the case, and take themselves to have reasons for their own actions. Suppose we ask Deborah, an observant Jew, why she does not work on the Sabbath. She might say anything from "because God commands it" to "because it is a nice way to separate my work life from my family life." Either response expresses her own reasons for acting as she does. It should be unproblematic to say that religious adherents have reasons for acting in this sense. Those reasons will include statements, direct or indirect, about what they take to be the case—which is to say, about what they take to be true. It is in this minimal sense that all religious adherents have religious beliefs. There is no reason to suppose that religious beliefs in this minimal sense are essentially inaccessible. Nor need we assimilate the ordinary sense of believing— "taking as true"—to creedal believing. Creedal believing is not a ubiquitous feature of religiosity, but ordinary believing is.

This picture of ordinary believing does not require any particular ontology of belief. In other words, we can accept the picture without committing ourselves to the view that beliefs are interior representations, or dispositions to act, or whatnot. Nor do we require any specific account of "what is believed," i.e., the propositional

---

[40] See Schilbrack, *Philosophy and the Study of Religions*, 73–74.

object of believing. The object of belief could be Platonic abstract propositions, or statements in ordinary language, or sentence types, or many other things besides. We can disagree about the ontology of beliefs and propositions without thereby rejecting the rudimentary account of believing and acting. This account of belief requires only that when religious people engage in religious behavior, they thereby commit themselves to a view about what is the case. (This is what I mean by "taking as true.") We can choose a word other than "belief" to stand in for "a view about what is the case," but we need the basic concept of belief or its functional equivalent to understand human behavior as rational. There are "eliminative materialist" philosophers who think that neuroscience will eventually enable us to replace the "folk category" of belief with a physicalist account of brain states.[41] And there are Heideggerians who associate the concept of belief with unacceptably Cartesian accounts of the mental.[42] On my usage, even though these philosophers reject various specific accounts of the ontology of beliefs, they still affirm some functionally equivalent notion of ordinary believing in the "taking as true" sense. They must, if they allow that human beings ever have reasons for their actions.

The hegemony of critique and widespread skepticism about belief go hand in hand. It is worth asking why. Critique collapses epistemic and semantic categories like knowledge, belief, and truth into political and social categories like power and discipline. The method of critique treats believing as epiphenomenal, as the secondary effects of primary social and political causes that may not be accessible to the believer. There is nothing intrinsically wrong with this emphasis; it can be quite helpful. Indeed, on any sufficiently rich account of human behavior, people often act as a result of motivations that are not immediately transparent. The tradition of critical inquiry tries to uncover these motivations and link them to pervasive social and ideological structures. This is valuable work. But when critique becomes hegemonic, we can lose our grip on other equally valuable forms of inquiry. Critique is not enough.

Epistemologies of Truth and Power

The academic study of religion needs to supplement the idiom of critique with another scholarly idiom that does not treat the beliefs, hopes, and desires of religious adherents as epiphenomenal. We need an epistemology of truth to supplement critique's epistemology of power. Without the vocabulary of belief and

---

[41] For example, Patricia S. Churchland, *Neurophilosophy: Toward a Unified Science of the Mind-Brain* (Cambridge, MA: MIT Press, 1989).

[42] See Hubert Dreyfus, *Being-in-the-World: A Commentary on Heidegger's Being and Time* (Cambridge, MA: MIT Press, 1991), 49, 55, 59, 93.

truth, we cannot even describe the phenomena of religious adherence accurately, since successful explanation presupposes adequate description. Likewise, without the vocabulary of desire and goodness, we cannot talk about how religious adherents understand their own behavior. More importantly for my own project, without this scholarly vocabulary, we cannot evaluate whether religious beliefs are ever true, and whether religious practices are ever good.[43]

The study of religion needs an epistemology of truth because critique presupposes a normative notion of truth. This is not a new point. In different ways, it has already been well made by Nancy Fraser, Charles Taylor, and Amy Allen, among others.[44] Consider again Mahmood's critique of Western liberal subjectivity in *Politics of Piety*. Her critique uses the women's mosque movement in Egypt to show the limitations of the liberal subject. This project can only succeed to the degree that Mahmood sees a truth about liberal subjectivity that previous theorists missed: that it cannot account for the agency of the women she studies. Or consider Schaefer's project in *Religious Affects*, as discussed in Chapter 12. Schaefer only succeeds to the degree that he is right that human behavior is primarily caused by affect and only secondarily caused by language, which is to say that his project only succeeds to the degree that he sees a truth about human behavior missed by theorists before him.[45]

This is a fairly elementary insight, but it is easy to push it further. Following on from the argument in Chapter 12, suppose a given theorist thinks that theology, or perhaps even religion *tout court*, is a form of ideological mystification. This suggestion necessarily assumes that religious adherents have a false understanding of their own religiosity. Put otherwise, it assumes that the scholarly critic is in an epistemically privileged position: he knows important truths about how things really are that are inaccessible to religious adherents themselves. After all, no religious person thinks that their own religious adherence results from ideological mystification. Critique aims at unmasking, destabilizing, and disrupting—but these moves only make sense when the masks in question actually are deceptive, the stability precarious, and the order stifling. In short, critique is always an epistemological project, and like any epistemological project, it presupposes the distinction between true and false.

---

[43] I develop this point in Chapter 14.

[44] They all write specifically in response to Foucault, but the underlying claim applies to critique more generally: Foucault cannot avoid assuming a normative framework that treats some claims as true or false, some situations as oppressive or emancipatory, and some actions as free or constrained. See Nancy Fraser, "Foucault on Modern Power: Empirical Insights and Normative Confusions," *PRAXIS International* 3 (1981): 272–87; Charles Taylor, "Foucault on Freedom and Truth" in his *Philosophical Papers*, Volume 1 (New York: Cambridge University Press, 1985), 152–84; Amy Allen, "Discourse, Power, and Subjectivation: The Foucault/Habermas Debate Reconsidered," *Philosophical Forum* 40 (2009): 1–28.

[45] In making these points, I do not mean to imply that Mahmood or Schaefer would disagree that their critiques presuppose a notion of truth. The examples are purely illustrative.

Scholars of religion should think more about the truth claims that are implicit in their own critiques. This is what I mean when I say that the academic study of religion should supplement its epistemology of power with an epistemology of truth. As a consequence of the demise of the category of belief, scholars of religion now find it very easy to sidestep inconvenient questions about truth. (The notion of belief and the notion of truth are conceptually connected: to believe that p is to believe that p is true.) Their aversion to the discourse of truth comes from multiple directions. Contrary to what many theologians think, few scholars of religion really see themselves as Dawkins-style debunkers. Whether they are anthropologists in the field or theorists in the library, they do not want to find themselves arguing that religious people are mostly wrong about what matters to them most. By downplaying the concept of belief, they can avoid this awkward possibility. The converse also holds, of course. Scholars of religion certainly do not want to find themselves *affirming* religious truth claims in the course of their scholarly work. The threat here is both mundane-methodological and personal-existential. It is mundane and methodological because affirming religious truth claims violates the modernist norms of inquiry that still prevail in many quarters of the academy. It is personal and existential because affirming religious truth claims looks uncomfortably like preaching, or personal conversion, or both. Once again, better to sidestep the whole issue altogether. Yet scholars of religion cannot really sidestep questions of belief and truth, because those questions are presupposed by critique itself.

Moreover, without the theoretical vocabulary of belief and truth, we must abandon some other important avenues of scholarly inquiry. I here mention two. (I discuss a third, normative evaluation, in Chapter 14.) First, even on its own terms, one scholarly task for the academic study of religion is to try to understand what it is like to be religious—that is, to understand religious adherence from the point of view of religious agents themselves. Yet without some notion of believing, at least in the "taking as true" sense, we cannot explain how a religious action can express the first-person perspective of a human agent. In other words, we cannot not explain how religious behavior seems rational from the point of view of the religious agent herself. Return to the case of Deborah, who will not work on the Sabbath. It is natural to say that Deborah keeps the Sabbath because she *believes* that God commands it, or, alternatively because she *believes* that it is a nice way to separate her work life from her family life. We have to advert to her beliefs in order to understand her behavior as rational from her own point of view. Some scholars of religion may have no interest in understanding her behavior as rational from her own point of view. Fair enough. But this does seem like a legitimate task for the academic study of religion, and we need the theoretical vocabulary of belief in order to pursue it.

In short, without some notion of belief, religious behavior becomes (at best) entirely arational. Sadly, I suspect that many scholars of religion would agree that religious behavior is arational, perhaps because they would deny that there is any such thing as rational human agency at all, religious or otherwise. But a note of caution is in order: we should not equate "rational human agent" with the straw man Cartesian subject.[46] We can all distinguish intentional actions, like dancing the tango, from mere bodily happenings, like accidentally tripping on the stairs. The former, but not the latter, is an example of rational human agency, because it is done on purpose—that is, for a reason, even if the reason is as simple as "dancing is fun." Sometimes we also deliberate and choose among available alternatives: *In this dance contest, should I dance the tango or the foxtrot?* Deliberation is another expression of rational agency. There is no need to posit absolute autonomy, utter self-transparency, or any of the other hyperbolic ideas that get packed into the modern liberal subject in order to accept this ordinary picture of rational agency. More to the point, it is one thing to argue toward the (controversial) conclusion that religious behavior is arational, another thing to assume it without argument, and another thing again to uncritically embrace a theoretical vocabulary that guarantees we assume it. Yet without the concepts of belief and truth, the theoretical vocabulary of critique guarantees that we treat religious adherence as arational.

My second point should be even less controversial. The nature of religious believing raises a variety of really interesting conceptual and empirical questions. For example, is believing in God (or gods, or other nonnatural things) the same kind of phenomenon as ordinary empirical believing, e.g., believing that *the book is on the table*? Does the phenomenon of religious believing differ across religious traditions, and if so how? What is the difference, if any, between religious believing and other religiously inflected cognitive notions like acceptance and trust? One does not have to be a Christian to think that these are interesting questions. At the moment, as far as I can tell, these kinds of questions are being asked by cognitive scientists and anthropologists, and sometimes by philosophers of mind, but not by scholars of religion or, for that matter, philosophers of religion.[47] Yet it seems as though ethnographically informed scholars of religion would be especially well positioned to contribute to such discussions. But, of course, that

---

[46] As Charles Taylor reminds us:

> undersigned systematicity has to be related to the purposeful actions of agents in a way that we can understand...It is a mistake to think that the only intelligible relation between a pattern [of behavior] and our conscious purposes is the direct one where the pattern is consciously willed. This is a hang-up which did come down to us from Cartesian-empiricist views of the mind...It is certainly not the case that all patterns *issue* from conscious action, but all patterns have to be made *intelligible* in relation to conscious action.
>
> (Taylor, "Foucault on Freedom and Truth," 171)

[47] For some interesting essays on the nature of religious beliefs, see "Special Issue: What Are Religious Beliefs?" in Thomas J. Coleman III, Jonathan Jong, and Valerie van Mulukom, eds., *Contemporary Pragmatism* 15 (2018): 279–406. Of course, some scholars of religion are interested in the questions above; for example, David Harvey, *Images at Work: The Material Culture of Enchantment* (New York: Oxford University Press, 2018).

requires taking seriously the idea that religious adherents have religious beliefs in the first place.

What Can Analytic Theologians Learn from Critical Inquiry?

The argument of this chapter is not directed against critique as such, but against hegemonic critique as an all-encompassing ideology of inquiry. In a different context, I might even offer a similar argument against hegemonic analytic inquiry. Like critique, analytic philosophy is valuable, but it is certainly not the paradigm for all legitimate inquiry in the humanities. In fact, I am convinced that analytic theologians in particular have much to learn from the tradition of critical inquiry. I especially want to speak up for a sustained dialogue between analytic theologians and critical scholars of religion. The scholarly encounter between analytic theology and critique is valuable largely because their respective assumptions and methods are so different. Scholars of religion are, therefore, especially well positioned to challenge default analytic assumptions in a productive way.

Learning from critical inquiry does not require abandoning the analytic method wholesale or rejecting all existing work in analytic theology. It does require that analytic theologians take critique seriously, actively engage with the challenges that arise from critical inquiry, and even incorporate some critical habits of mind and patterns of argument into their own work. More contact with critical theory—and more conversations with critical theorists—can only help analytic theologians as they pursue their distinctive academic vocation. Just as a deeper engagement with analytic thought can reveal the limitations of critique, a deeper engagement with critique can reveal some of the limitations of analytic theology. I present four promising lines of engagement below.

First, genealogical critique can launch important and often overlooked epistemological challenges to the assumptions of traditional Christian orthodoxy. Analytic theologians tend to divorce the history of doctrine from the history of power. By "the history of power," I mean the myriad ways in which patterns of physical and social force shape our most fundamental concepts, rational norms, and taken-for-granted assumptions. Because they wish to be Christian theologians, good analytic theologians try to be at least somewhat conversant with the history of doctrine. Yet by virtue of their Christian vocation, they often view the history of doctrine in teleological terms, as a divinely guided march toward orthodoxy. They rarely interrogate the messy process of development itself, and so they often sidestep uncomfortable questions about how power and contingency might have shaped what counts as doctrinal truth. I have found that it is difficult to persuade nervous theorists of religion that they ought to investigate whether religious claims are true. But it is just as difficult to persuade complacent analytic theologians that they ought to interrogate whether their own theological concepts developed as a result of contingent historical processes that have no intrinsic orientation toward truth.[48] Of course, no orthodox Christian can agree that their most important theological concepts are socially constructed *rather than* revealed, or that Christian doctrine as a whole has no intrinsic orientation toward truth. But analytic theologians who understand themselves to be responsible to the general norms of academic inquiry are obliged to consider genealogical challenges, even those that threaten the foundations of orthodoxy. Otherwise, those challenges have the epistemological status of unanswered objections.

Second, critical theory, and critical scholars of religion, can invite analytic theologians to consider how their own contingent socialization has affected their philosophical work. Critics from outside the analytic guild are fond of pointing out that analytic Christian theism seems intellectually homogeneous, perhaps because analytic theists seem sociologically homogeneous. Though this intellectual homogeneity is sometimes exaggerated, most prominent analytic theologians do hew quite close to traditional, creedal forms of Christian orthodoxy. It is not unreasonable to ask whether their attachment to orthodoxy is rooted more in sociological factors like race, class, and gender than in the timeless splendor of orthodox truth. Again, analytic theologians themselves rarely consider such challenges, because, as scholars, they remain largely isolated from the tradition of critical inquiry and its distinctive forms of self-reflection.

A more focused example: analytic thinkers often appeal to philosophical intuitions about what "seems true" or "seems plausible." Yet critical scholars of religion will likely have radically different assumptions and intuitions about truth and plausibility. Mutual dialogue can bring these differences to light in a fruitful way. We might then have a valuable meta-philosophical conversation about how we form intuitions and how we can know whether they are reliable. This conversation can also inform the way we understand the basic patterns of reasoning that we all use, like inference to the best explanation. For example, it seems to me (really!) that when we consider the reported postmortem appearances of Christ in conjunction with other relevant data, the claim "Christ rose from the dead" is a legitimate inference to the best explanation of the totality of the evidence. At the same time, I must also admit that my own intuitions about what counts as the "best" explanation are far from universal. They are the product of my own upbringing and disciplinary training, as well as an ambient intellectual culture that remains broadly Christian. To endorse this moment of self-critique does not by itself entail that my inference is mistaken. But surely something would be amiss if I continually refuse to ask such self-critical questions at all. I am more

---

[48] In my experience, many analytic philosophers of religion are too quick to assimilate genealogical criticism to the genetic fallacy. It is true that showing the causal origins of my belief that *p* cannot, by itself, show that *p* is false. But if it can be established that my belief that *p* was caused by some process that is not likely to aim at truth, that fact should count as evidence that my belief is epistemically unjustified or unwarranted.

likely to ask them, and to take them seriously as genuine questions, when I am in conversation with others who press me about them, because they do not share my assumptions and intuitions. This is another reason why analytic theology would benefit from deeper engagement with critical scholars of religion.

As another example, consider analytic "perfect being theology." When theologians practice perfect being theology, they try to identify the attributes possessed by a perfect being. This method usually involves appealing to broadly shared philosophical intuitions about, for example, what power is, why it is good to have more power, and what counts as having maximum power. Ideally, these intuitions are meant to be universal, but they are also highly contestable. Should it turn out that our supposedly "universal" intuitions about power are actually distinctively Western, white, and masculine, then the whole project of perfect being theology starts to seem unstable.[49] Of course, to raise this challenge is not to assume that it is unanswerable. If I assert "I believe p because of reasons a, b, and c," and you counter with "No, you really believe p because of sociological factors x, y, and z," then you at least owe me some arguments showing that a, b, and c are not good reasons for believing p. But at the moment we are nowhere close to having this kind of discussion in analytic theology. Analytic theologians rarely consider whether race, class, and gender affect their theorizing, largely because analytic theology has been so isolated from the critical tradition where such questions are fundamental.

Third, as an alternative to analytic inquiry, critical inquiry invites analytic theologians to think more carefully about the way we understand the nature of reason. As I argued in Chapter 6, all broadly orthodox Christian theology is committed to some notion of universal reason. Whether or not analytic philosophy is also so committed in theory, it certainly seems to be in practice. Analytic theology, therefore, seems doubly committed to a viable account of universal reason. Yet, in the contemporary academy, few notions are regarded with more suspicion. From the Foucauldian power/knowledge epistemology to contemporary feminist standpoint theory, diverse but reinforcing trajectories of critical inquiry argue that so-called "universal" reason is a malign fiction. From these critical perspectives, universal reason is merely a tool of the dominant, another strategy to ensure that oppressed "irrational" groups deserve their domination.

Needless to say, this hypercritical perspective on universal reason is not common among analytic theologians. But they cannot simply ignore it if they want to speak to anyone outside the narrow analytic guild. Perhaps I am wrong that Christian theology as such requires some notion of universal reason. Even if I am

---

[49] I take this point from Sameer Yadav's "Toward an Analytic Theology of Liberation," in Michelle Panchuk and Michael Rea, eds., *Voices from the Edge*. See also William Jones, *Is God a White Racist?* (Boston, MA: Beacon Press, 1998); Anna Mercedes, *Power For: Feminism and Christ's Self-Giving* (New York: Bloomsbury, 2011).

wrong, however, it is certainly fair to press *analytic* theologians about the account of reason implied by their own theological work. After all, analytic theologians seem especially confident in the power of reason; that is part of what makes analytic theology different from other forms of Christian theology. If they ignore contemporary critical theory, analytic theologians will be vulnerable to charges that their confidence in the power of reason is misplaced.

Furthermore, Christian theologians who are sensitive to the noetic effects of sin have an even greater obligation to take critique seriously. Woven into the very fabric of Christian orthodoxy, we find the claim that, as a result of the Fall, the inner voice of reason is often self-serving and self-deceptive.[50] Many analytic theologians seem to accept this claim as an abstract proposition but grant it no apparent role in their own intellectual work. In other words, they accept the truth of the claim, but proceed as though it does not apply to them. In our current intellectual climate, I do not think it is possible to take seriously the noetic effects of sin and also simply dismiss or ignore the vibrant tradition of critique. At its best, critique speaks in the name of marginalized and oppressed groups who have been victimized, sometimes by individual Christians, and sometimes by the wider social and political structures of Christendom. The grammar of Christian orthodoxy requires theologians to listen to their voices precisely because that grammar includes the story of sin and the Fall.

Finally, critique can help analytic theologians become more self-aware about how their own disciplinary socialization affects their intellectual work. In Chapter 4, I noted that analytic philosophers often overlook the tradition-bound nature of analytic inquiry, and find analytic writing "clear" only because they have been socialized into the analytic tradition's distinctive rhetorical and intellectual virtues.[51] Critique as a method aims at revealing the contingent effects of disciplinary socialization. By turning a critical eye toward their own training, analytic thinkers can resist the tendency to treat distinctive analytic virtues as universal, as well as the tendency to regard other kinds of humanistic inquiry as deficient forms of analytic philosophy. This self-critical stance should help analytic theologians to be better colleagues and more sophisticated thinkers. One could make a similar point about the hyper-aggressive "argument culture" of much analytic philosophy. Analytic philosophers and theologians often claim that they argue so aggressively because they are only interested in truth. But wielding the rhetoric of truth like a sword is not the same thing as genuinely seeking the truth. A strong academic culture of argument and counterargument can be healthy, but taken too far it can also be inimical to genuine inquiry. A greater openness to the tradition of genealogy and critique could help analytic theology flourish by

---

[50] See Wood, *Blaise Pascal on Duplicity, Sin, and the Fall.*
[51] See also William Wood, "Traditions, Trajectories, and Tools in Analytic Theology," *Journal of Analytic Theology* 4 (2016): 254–66.

encouraging analytic theologians to be more attentive to the ways in which their own disciplinary socialization can impede clear thinking.

Conclusion: Against Hegemonic Critique

Critical inquiry is certainly valuable, but the hegemony of critique has warped the academic study of religion, even on its own terms. Exclusivist scholars of religion valorize critique in part because they think it offers a principled way to distinguish the study of religion from theology. But under the pressures of hegemonic critique, the field has abandoned other equally valuable lines of inquiry. The field's skepticism about theology has, therefore, come at a cost.

We see this cost very clearly when we look at the way contemporary scholars of religion have treated the concept of belief. The important but relatively modest point that belief is not the universal essence of religious adherence has somehow exploded into the much larger claim that scholars of religion ought to abandon the concept of belief altogether, or the even more radical suggestion that religious adherents have no relevant religious beliefs. The lesson seems clear: we should not abandon the theoretical vocabulary of critique, but we do need to supplement it. In order to understand religious adherents as rational agents, we need a way to talk about their beliefs, desires, and hopes. The point becomes stronger if we also wish to evaluate whether their religious beliefs are true, or whether their desires and hopes are good.

Critical theory lacks the theoretical vocabulary required for this form of assessment, a vocabulary that is central to analytic philosophy. Accordingly, analytic theologians can model what it looks like to move beyond the limits of critique. I emphasize that to say "analytic theology can help" is not identical to saying "only analytic theology can help." But analytic theologians are already comfortable with asking whether religious beliefs and practices are justifiably affirmed, or laudable, or true. They are accustomed to evaluating religious adherence using the epistemological vocabulary of reasons, arguments, and evidence instead of the genealogical vocabulary of social and structural causes. Both idioms are properly academic, and both are useful. They allow us to ask and answer different kinds of questions.

Yet analytic theology has no monopoly on truth, and the analytic method no monopoly on rigor. Analytic philosophers of religion and theologians would benefit immensely from a serious scholarly engagement with critical inquiry. Critique's tools and methods can supplement those of analytic philosophy, because critique allows us to ask some interesting questions that are rarely considered by members of the analytic guild. Are Christian doctrines socially constructed in a way that matters? Should we care about the social location and background of analytic theologians? These questions are hardly at the forefront of analytic inquiry, but analogous questions are central to the rest of the humanities. A *via media* between analytic thought and critical theory seems desirable, one in which the strengths of each side can mitigate the weaknesses of the other.

The academic study of religion understands itself as inherently interdisciplinary. Scholars of religion draw as needed from anthropology, psychology, sociology, and more. The fact that the avowedly interdisciplinary study of religion mostly ignores analytic philosophy is a strange artifact of a bygone era. To a field that rightly celebrates its own porous disciplinary boundaries, nothing useful should be alien. I commend the analytic discourse on rationality—what I have called the "epistemology of truth"—not because it is analytic but because it is useful. I would make a similar point to analytic theologians. Analytic theology also understands itself as inherently interdisciplinary. It is intellectually unhealthy for analytic theologians to avoid all contact with critique, and to sidestep the "epistemology of power" that is so central to the rest of the humanities. Scholars of religion and analytic theologians alike should ask: What can we learn from intellectual traditions other than our own? We cannot begin to address our limitations while we do not even realize what they are.

14

Analytic Theology as Rigorous Appreciation

On Normative Inquiry in the Academic Study of Religion

Once we move beyond hegemonic critique, what comes next? Exclusivist scholars of religion want to enlist critique as the field's new border guard, and use it to keep theology at bay. Yet, ironically, instead of excluding theology, hegemonic critique inadvertently reopens the gates to theology. Critique is inherently normative, and once we agree that the field not only welcomes but depends on normative inquiry in the form of critique, it becomes much more difficult to make a principled case against other forms of normative inquiry, including theology. Thus, relative to what came before, the critical turn in the study of religion has actually fostered a better intellectual climate for theology. When we reject positivist strictures on truth, meaning, and inquiry, previously unacceptable forms of argument again become viable. While the field as a whole remained in thrall to modernist assumptions about method, it was easier to make a principled case against theology simply by drawing a sharp line between empirical and normative approaches. After the field's decisive turn toward critique, however, it is no longer clear what exactly is wrong with normative inquiry.

"Normative inquiry" is broader than theology, of course. In the study of religions, normative inquiry can also include socially engaged scholarship as political advocacy, normative ethics, and various forms of spiritual development. But by now it should be unsurprising that debates about normativity in the study of religion frequently become proxy debates about the proper place of theology in the academy. Advocates of normative inquiry do not always defend theology as such, but because of the field's continuing anxiety about theology, any defense of normative inquiry also becomes, *ipso facto*, a defense of theology. Opponents worry that by opening the door to normative approaches they thereby open the door to theology.

In this chapter, I position analytic theology amid recent debates about the place of normativity in the academic study of religion. I first introduce those debates. I then argue that critique is a form of normative inquiry, yet one that is negatively

Analytic Theology and the Academic Study of Religion. William Wood, Oxford University Press (2021). © William Wood.
DOI: 10.1093/oso/9780198779872.003.0014

charged.[1] It follows that the field already allows normative evaluation of religious claims—so long as "evaluate" means "subvert," "destabilize," or "historicize," and never "endorse" or "commend." By itself, this point does not constitute a principled case for positive forms of normative evaluation like theology, however. I therefore make the positive case for analytic theology. (Much of that case applies to other forms of theology too.) I argue that analytic theology is a form of "rigorous appreciation" that can contribute to the study of religions while also maintaining its own distinctive focus on evaluating Christian truth claims and practices. I conclude with a modest proposal on behalf of comparative analytic theology.

The New Normativity in the Study of Religion

In recent years, normative approaches to the study of religion have enjoyed a newfound respect. The field's leading defenders of normative approaches include Thomas A. Lewis, Tyler Roberts, and Kevin Schilbrack.[2] Lewis argues that normative claims are inevitable in the study of religion, and that "the drive to define religious studies largely through the contrast with theology" has obscured this fact, in part because the contrast assumes that "normative claims related to religion are fundamentally a matter of faith," where faith is typically opposed to reason. He concludes: "What is important is not to try somehow to exclude normative claims but rather to be willing to offer justification for the norms we invoke."[3] Kevin Schilbrack's wide-ranging manifesto *Philosophy and the Study of Religions* proposes that "evaluating religious phenomena" is one of the proper tasks for the academic study of religion. He specifies: "Evaluative approaches to the study of religion pursue the questions whether religious beliefs are true, religious practices moral, religious experiences real, and religious institutions just."[4] As Schilbrack notes, explicitly evaluative approaches are rare among self-identified scholars of religion, but they are not rare among philosophers of religion. Schilbrack and Lewis discuss theology only in passing, but Tyler Roberts defends theology at length in his *Encountering Religion*. His robust defense of broadly postmodern forms of theology is also a defense of normative inquiry in the humanities more generally.

These proposals run in tandem with a general resurgence in post-critical, humanistic, and evaluative inquiry that spans several academic disciplines. "Post-critical" here means "no longer in the grips of hegemonic critique." For example, as I discussed in Chapter 13, some literary theorists have begun to push back against the hegemony of critique by developing a complementary hermeneutics

---

[1] Felski, *The Limits of Critique*, 127–34.
[2] Lewis, *Why Philosophy Matters for the Study of Religion*; Roberts, *Encountering Religion*; Schilbrack, *Philosophy and the Study of Religions*.
[3] Lewis, *Why Philosophy Matters for the Study of Religion*, 44–45.
[4] Schilbrack, *Philosophy and the Study of Religions*, 185.

of appreciation and pleasure. Felski asks, "What would it mean to treat experiences of engagement, wonder, or absorption not as signs of naïveté or user error but as clues to why we are drawn to [a text] in the first place? To forge a language of attachment as robust and refined as our rhetoric of detachment?"[5] Suppose we ask this question as scholars of religion. What *would* it look like to treat experiences of engagement, wonder, and absorption "not as signs of naïveté or user error" but as "clues" to why one might wish to be religious? What would it look like, in the study of religion, "to forge a language of attachment as robust and refined as our rhetoric of detachment"? The questions answer themselves. It would look like theology.[6]

In the academic study of religion, "theology" names the discourse that prizes attachment, wonder, and absorption instead of detachment, suspicion, and distance. When we grasp this point, two paths open. The first insists theology cannot be a form of critique, and so cannot be properly academic at all. So far, exclusivist theorists of religion have taken the first path. But there is a second path. Suppose the academic study of religion, along with Felski, comes to recognize the limits of critique? Then theology becomes a useful discussion partner that can offer many examples of the ways that affective attachment and rigorous scholarship can work together.

I recognize that this is not a straightforward move. In the academic study of religion, advocates of post-critical appreciation and normative inquiry have a much more difficult task than colleagues in other branches of the humanities. It is one thing for humanistic scholars in other fields to foster a deeper, more informed sense of wonder and beauty in response to art and literature. It is another thing altogether to foster a similar response toward religious adherence. The worry, I take it, is that scholarly appreciation can easily become preaching or apologetic endorsement. The worry is by no means groundless, but as I discuss below, the way beyond it is clear: as long as everyone abides by the general norms of academic inquiry, there is no reason to treat theology differently from other forms of normative evaluation—including, for that matter, critique.

Critique as Normative and Negative

It is utterly obvious that critique is a form of normative inquiry, and just as obvious that critical theorists pursue their academic work in the service of various value-laden agendas. So it is, and so they do—and we are all the better for it. Unsurprisingly, I have no objection to normative inquiry or to value-laden

---

[5] Felski, *Limits of Critique*, 179–80.
[6] Here I mean theology in general, though I also think this description applies to analytic theology, as I discuss below.

scholarship, as long as everyone recognizes it as such. Nor do I have any objection to the fact that in the study of religion, normative evaluation—in the form of critique—is usually negatively charged. But even though the normative dimensions of critique are obvious, its practitioners rarely avow them, and it is this disguised normativity that I find troubling. Here is a quick example of what I mean when I say that critique is normative and negative: Consider Craig Martin's *Critical Introduction to the Study of Religion*. According to Martin, his textbook is a "critical" introduction because it focuses "narrowly on how the cultural elements of religious traditions have been used to legitimate social domination."[7] He analogizes scholars of religion to "homicide detectives approaching possible murder suspects—with a very critical eye."[8] He wants students to adopt a "hermeneutic of suspicion" toward religious claims; that is, when faced with religious claims or religious practices, we should "approach those claims with skepticism...become culture detectives, taking nothing at face value and looking for hidden motivations, unstated assumptions, or unseen effects in how elements of culture are formed and used."[9] Martin's textbook therefore instantiates Bruce Lincoln's injunction that real scholars of religion must ask "destabilizing and irreverent questions" about religious traditions in order to uncover their "internal tensions and conflicts, turbulence and incoherence, permeability and malleability."[10] Martin is more explicit than Lincoln about his own political agenda: because he "sympathize[s] with those who are victims of oppression," he wants "first, to demonstrate to students that societies are never set up in ways that serve everyone's interests equally and, second, to give students the skills to identify who benefits and who does not, and how disproportionate social structures are legitimated and maintained."[11] Presumably, on this line, religion serves to legitimate the interests of those who benefit from disproportionate social structures.

This is a perfectly sound way to conduct academic inquiry into religion, but it is normative through and through. Martin's critical introduction presents a negative evaluation of religion as a social phenomenon: for Martin, religion functions "to legitimate social domination." If we also "sympathize with victims of oppression," then, presumably, when we encounter religious claims, we too should approach them with skepticism, like "homicide detectives approaching possible murder suspects." Martin's critique is normative, and negatively charged. To be fair, Martin does not explicitly say that religions do *nothing other* than legitimate social domination, nor does he say, for example, that most religious beliefs are false. These further claims

---

[7] Craig Martin, *A Critical Introduction to the Study of Religion*, 2nd ed. (New York: Routledge, 2017), xv. Martin is a critical theorist of religion and the word "Critical" in his textbook's title is chosen advisedly.

[8] Martin, *Critical Introduction*, 22. See Felski on the figure of the critic as detective: *The Limits of Critique*, 85–116.

[9] Martin, *Critical Introduction*, 22. [10] Lincoln, "Theses on Method."

[11] Martin, *Critical Introduction*, xv.

are not strictly entailed by his approach, as he also recognizes. But we also speak through our omissions. The conjunction of what Martin does say about religion and what he does not say conveys a clear message. When all we learn about religion is that it legitimates oppression, it is hard to conclude that religious adherence could ever be genuinely attractive or commendable.

And that's fine too. My point is about inquiry in the field as a whole, not about Martin as an individual scholar. No individual scholar is obliged to engage in meticulous tit-for-tat balancing of positive and negative assessment. But on what principled grounds could the field as a whole welcome Martin's negative evaluation but stigmatize more positive commendations of religious adherence? The question is not whether negative evaluations of religion count as genuine scholarly work—they do—but whether negative evaluations *alone* count as genuine scholarly work. Critical theorists of religion do not eschew normative evaluation. What they actually eschew is affirmative evaluation: the positive appreciation of religious claims and practices. Theorists like Martin or Lincoln, who are content to pass negative judgments on religious adherence owe us a good explanation for why negative evaluation is acceptable when positive evaluation is not. I very much doubt that there is such an explanation.

"Normativity" Is Not Enough

Still, to say just this is not enough. Theologians should certainly point out that the academic study of religion is already thoroughly normative. At the same time, however, they should not make the mistake of thinking that a defense of "normativity" suffices as a defense of theology. "Normativity" alone is not enough. Everyone makes normative claims: theorists of religion and theologians alike. True as this point is, it does not go very far. The really pressing question is: *What kinds* of normative claims are permitted and why? The defense of bare "normativity" can obscure this issue. Consider Thomas A. Tweed's 2015 presidential address to the American Academy of Religion, "Valuing the Study of Religion."[12] Tweed argues, sensibly enough, that value judgments are inevitable in the study of religion. But the examples that he adduces are trivial and uncontroversial. For the most part, they concern only basic norms of academic inquiry that no one

---

[12] Thomas A. Tweed, "Valuing the Study of Religion: Improving Difficult Dialogues within and beyond the AAR's 'Big Tent,'" *Journal of the American Academy of Religion* 84 (2016): 287–322. Tweed explicitly sets his own remarks in a context that by now seems depressingly familiar:

> disagreements about the scope of the academic study of religion: our divisive internal AAR debates between humanistic and scientific approaches, between scholarship alone or advocacy too, *and, most of all, between theology and religious studies. The complaints about theologians on the 2015 AAR election ballot confirmed my original sense that we need more and better talk about what we share and what we don't.*   (288–89; my italics)

seriously disputes. For example, Tweed notes that scientists sometimes describe theories in terms of beauty and elegance, and that they value "precision, coherence, and explanatory power" in their work.[13] He points out that humanists "sometimes turn to language that implies there is an 'ethics of reading' when [they] assert that a criticism is 'uncharitable' or 'unfair.'"[14] With somewhat more bite, he points out that critical theorists typically begin by announcing "a value priority—that attending to power as we analyze practices is more admirable than attending to meaning as we read symbols—and declare that the most praiseworthy scholarly aim is to 'problematize' standard accounts."[15]

Tweed's point—that scholarly inquiry as such is a normative enterprise—is true as far as it goes, and well worth reiterating to anyone who actually denies it. But his focus on the rudimentary values of sound scholarship leaves him with surprisingly little to say about the real methodological debates that vex the field. Even a straw man positivist can accept "normativity" in Tweed's sense. We cannot purge inquiry in the study of religion of all norms whatsoever. (After all, "Don't invent data!" is a normative claim.) But conceding this point does not require one to concede any actually contested ground. One could consistently accept the normative dimensions of inquiry in general without also accepting the value of specific forms of normative inquiry like theology, scholarship as political advocacy, or prescriptive ethics.

Lewis does a better job. According to Lewis, *controversial* normative claims are inevitable in the study of religion. Any time we assert that "human behavior can be explained in a particular way," we invoke claims about "the nature of human existence" with "important consequences for how we should live." Moreover, even our supposedly descriptive claims are often metaphysical and evaluative: "to describe an experience as delusional or transcendent, for instance, is to make a claim about the nature of reality."[16] Controversial normative claims are inevitable in the study of religion because we must use evaluative language to formulate our theoretical explanations and descriptions. As Lewis notes, the proper response to this state of affairs is not to try harder to purify our scholarly vocabulary of all controversial evaluative terms. Rather, the proper response is to accept the scholarly obligation to justify one's evaluative vocabulary when it is appropriately challenged. Lewis advances the dialectic beyond the bare defense of "normativity," but his argument still remains mostly formal and methodological. He makes a very important point: since all scholars make controversial normative claims, the study of religion should allow normative claims that are well supported by argument. But he does not really assert that any specific normative claims are well supported;

---

[13] Tweed, "Valuing the Study of Religion," 292.
[14] Tweed, "Valuing the Study of Religion," 294.
[15] Tweed, "Valuing the Study of Religion," 294–95.
[16] The previous three quotations are from Lewis, *Why Philosophy Matters for the Study of Religion*, 49–50.

nor does he tell us much about the specific evaluative vocabularies that are appropriate for scholars of religion. This need not be Lewis's task, of course, but it must be *someone's* task.

The task falls to anyone who endorses not just "normativity" in general, but some specific form of normative inquiry. From the general fact that all scholars of religion make normative claims, we cannot validly infer that any specific kind of normative claim is allowed or disallowed. After all, no one holds that every kind of normative claim without exception is welcome in the academic study of religion. So the question remains: Which forms of normativity are welcome and which remain beyond the pale? Advocates of specific forms of normative inquiry—like, say, analytic theology—therefore need to make a positive, substantive case for the kinds of normativity that they endorse.

The Rigor of Appreciation

This book as a whole is my attempt to make that case for analytic theology. In my view, theology in general is a normative academic discourse that prizes attachment and appreciation in addition to critique. I would even make the same claim about analytic theology. This move will no doubt earn some rolled eyes and raised eyebrows. In my experience, scholars outside the analytic guild sometimes find it difficult to imagine why anyone would find analytic philosophy, or analytic theology, appealing at all. To many, they seem like closed-off, narrow-minded discourses, fit only for people who are interested in reductively "solving" the tiniest, most technical problems—a world away from the humanistic appreciation commended by Felski and others.

Yet, as a sometime analytic theologian myself, I read "post-critical" theorists like Felski with a warm sense of recognition. I find in analytic theology many of the same attractions and appeals that they associate with post-critical reading. That is, I find analytic-style inquiry into the meaning, coherence, and truth of Christian doctrines to be an adventure, a rich wellspring of attachment, enchantment, wonder, and absorption. So for those scholars who find analytic thought detached, alien, and off-putting, I can at least offer my own experience as a representative counterexample. Behold: there are people in the world who find in analytic theology the very same sense of aesthetic pleasure praised by avant-garde humanists in the rest of the academy.

I use the label "rigorous appreciation" as a general term to describe post-critical attitudes and practices in theology and the study of religion. I say "rigorous" appreciation because I want to signal that these attitudes and practices feature reasoned arguments and interpretations. They are not just emotive expressions of taste. This section presents the general idea of rigorous appreciation. The next section narrows the focus to analytic theology in particular. As always, just because I commend analytic theology as a form of rigorous appreciation does not mean that I think other forms of theology are non-rigorous.

There is a rigor, a properly academic rigor, to skillful appreciation. Perhaps we can recognize this point more easily with art and literature. Sometimes an adroit interpretation of a poem deconstructs the poem so thoroughly that it unravels before our very eyes. But not always. Adroit interpretation can also show why the poem is more beautiful, more pleasurable, and more insightful than we had previously grasped. It can identify "moments of recognition, enchantment, shock, and knowledge."[17] The scholar qua scholar need not distance herself from these moments; she can use her academic work to foster them.[18] Such work may require advanced historical or philological training. Certainly, it will require specific skills and forms of attention. As Toril Moi puts it, "to read well is to bring to the text a certain quality of attention...a willingness to participate in the 'adventure' offered by the text."[19] She continues: "To be open to adventure is to be ready to be illuminated by the text, to assume that it can work the 'miracle of literature' and show us things we had never suspected, show us 'another world.'"[20] In my own terminology, reading with "rigorous appreciation" is a way to participate in the "adventure" offered by the text.

In another piece, Felski identifies four modes of post-critical inquiry: curating, conveying, criticizing, and composing.[21] Though it is not her intention, I am struck by how easily all of them can be transposed into the theological register. "Curating" involves "a process of caring for—the word has its origins in *caritas*—of guarding, protecting, conserving, caretaking, and looking after," and "conveying" means passing on the things we curate, making them present for people today; conveying is also a kind of interpretation, ensuring that what we curate can become salient to diverse audiences with very different concerns.[22] "Criticizing" gets at the idea that we can be critical without practicing critique. Criticizing can also be a way of curating and conveying. After all, curating and conveying are not the same as simply repeating. Finally, "composing" is a synthetic word, about

---

[17] Felski, *The Limits of Critique*, 191.

[18] In addition to Felski, see also Toril Moi, *Revolution of the Ordinary: Literary Studies after Wittgenstein, Austin, and Cavell* (Chicago: University of Chicago Press, 2017); Eve Kosofsky Sedgwick, "Paranoid Reading and Reparative Reading, or, You're So Paranoid, You Probably Think is Essay Is about You," in *Touching Feeling: Affect, Pedagogy, Performativity* (Durham, NC: Duke University Press, 2003), 123–52. In very different ways, Wendy Steiner and Hans-Georg Gadamer show what it looks like for critics to try to find hidden beauty and pleasure in uncomfortable artistic objects in (respectively): *The Scandal of Pleasure: Art in an Age of Fundamentalism* (Chicago: University of Chicago Press, 1995); and the title essay of his *The Relevance of the Beautiful and Other Essays*, trans. Nicholas Walker, ed. Robert Bernasconi (Cambridge: Cambridge University Press, 1986).

[19] Toril Moi, "The Adventure of Reading," *Literature & Theology* 25 (2011): 136. In the quotation Moi is discussing the work of Cora Diamond, who introduces the idea of reading as an adventure.

[20] Moi, "Adventure of Reading," 137.

[21] Rita Felski, "Introduction: Recomposing the Humanities—with Bruno Latour," *New Literary History* 47 (2016): 215–29.

[22] Felski, "Introduction," 217, 218.

"making rather than unmaking, adding rather than subtracting, translating rather than separating."[23]

Like critique, "rigorous appreciation" is normative; unlike critique, it is positively charged. Both critique and rigorous appreciation can be self-reflexive and personally transformative. Tyler Roberts's *Encountering Religion* is especially instructive on this point. The key analytical category in *Encountering Religion* is—unsurprisingly, given its title—"the encounter." According to Roberts, scholars should allow themselves to "encounter" religion, rather than merely trying to explain it reductively. Encountering religion requires open-minded, hermeneutical inquiry: when we encounter religious texts and actors, we let them speak to us on their own terms. We do not insist on reducing religions or redescribing them with our own scholarly vocabulary. Instead we think *with* religion, critically yet sympathetically. In so doing, we put ourselves at risk: we might even find ourselves changed by the encounter. Roberts's notion of the scholarly "encounter" with religion is very similar to my own category of "rigorous appreciation." To consolidate, then, leading post-critical literary theorists embrace the personally transformative "adventure" of art and literature. And some broad-minded scholars of religion accept that good academic work can foster a transformative "encounter" with the religious other.

The Risks of Rigor

Now that we have gone this far, the next step should not seem so large, even though it leads us toward a similarly generous attitude toward theology. A thought experiment: imagine a classroom of undergraduates who are assigned an especially difficult novel. Upon first reading, they find it by turns impenetrable and off-putting. Yet after the students have studied it carefully with a skillful teacher, they understand the novel more deeply and can now regard it as profound and insightful. I doubt that there is a single person who would claim that such an outcome is unscholarly. Indeed, precisely this sort of pedagogical encounter is the lifeblood of the humanities classroom.

Now recall my example of Hypothetical Hasker, in Chapter 11. Hypothetical Hasker is a committed Platonist, and when he teaches the theory of the Forms, he does his best to present that theory as coherent and plausible, and he argues that it has great explanatory power. As it happens, his students regularly agree with him and start to take Platonism seriously themselves. This sort of outcome is very common in philosophy. Students enter the classroom as mind-body dualists and

---

[23] Felski, "Introduction," 219.

leave as materialists, or vice versa. Or they enter as relativists and leave as realists, or vice versa. One could multiply such examples at will.

Finally, imagine a similar scene, where the topic of discussion is some matter of Christian theology. Once again, the students find the assigned texts opaque, and cannot sympathize with the thought-world from which they emerged. Once again, the skillful teacher leads them to a place of deeper understanding and sympathy. She presents the Christian worldview as attractive, and the doctrinal claims under discussion as reasonable and credible, the sorts of claims that a sophisticated, intelligent person might find persuasive. Part of her presentation includes raising and answering objections about whether the claims are coherent or perhaps even true. The students leave the classroom with a newfound appreciation for the Christian tradition and its core doctrines. Whereas the first two scenario just seem like ordinary cases of good teaching, I suspect that to many scholars, the third scenario will seem like something else—perhaps even vaguely sinister evangelism. This is unfortunate. All three scenarios present examples of good teaching. Someone who endorses the first two and rejects the third owes us a principled explanation of the difference. Again, I very much doubt that there is a real difference.

Still, there are some legitimate worries about power and exclusion even in this toy scenario. One does not have to be a Dawkins-level secularist to worry about Christian philosophers or theologians who turn their lecterns into pulpits. Perhaps they present all religious views other than their own in an unsophisticated, one-sided way, and then compel their students to agree with their dogmatic assessments, on penalty of receiving poor grades. (Religious adherents will, of course, imagine the same scenario in reverse.) The worry extends still further. Any classroom features obvious power imbalances, and even the most well-meaning teachers find themselves shaping their students into their own intellectual image. The shaping is subtle, and results from deep social and systemic factors of which neither side is fully aware. The danger is that when teachers try to evaluate or commend religious truth claims in the classroom, they might find that they are shaping students religiously rather than just academically. Teaching could become indoctrination.

Nor are worries about the effects of power confined to classroom settings. The same worries also apply to research and other professional activities. No one wants to see the academic study of religion devolve (further?) into a spiral of religiously motivated polemic and counter-polemic. Advocates of scientific and social scientific approaches already worry that their work has been marginalized by "religionists." And scholars of religion—who disagree about almost everything else—agree that the field remains "too Christian." This broad consensus is also finally about power. It expresses the worry that, all too often, properly academic norms are subordinated to Christian theological norms, because of the social and political power of contemporary Christians.

These are genuine concerns, but the remedy, as always, is ready to hand. First, we should lower the temperature. We do not need to dream up speculative scenarios about the dangers that might arise if universities suddenly started allowing theology. They already allow theology. We can look at the actually existing theology courses in (mostly) private universities in the U.S. and in (mostly) public universities in the U.K. to see that academic theology is really just another one of the humanities, something perfectly ordinary, and not an object of fearful, fetishized suspicion. Second, whether in the classroom or in the research seminar, all scholars must support their evaluations with reasoned arguments and maximally accessible evidence. This commitment to the norms of academic inquiry is what guarantees that rigorous appreciation remains a respectful academic dialogue rather than an exercise in dogmatic proclamation. As long as they remain committed to the norms of academic inquiry, scholars who commend religious truth claims treat their interlocutors as fellow truth-seekers, engaged in a common endeavor of trying to understand the world better.

With these caveats in mind, let us extend the previous thought experiment. There surely is a difference between presenting the Christian tradition sympathetically, as broadly credible or "belief-worthy" in some general sense, and presenting it as true, as something "to be believed." Perhaps the former is allowed but the latter is not. But even this difference is not as sharp as one might think. The difference seems especially salient in the academic study of religion, because studying religion inevitably raises so many difficult moral and existential questions. Yet purely as a matter of the logic of inquiry, there is no sharp difference between "Here are some good reasons why *someone* might believe *p*" and "Here are some good reasons why *you* might believe *p*." You are someone, after all.[24]

Suppose we want to ask whether some religious claim is supported by reasons. We ask: "Why would someone believe *p*?" We could treat this line of inquiry as purely descriptive: we could say no more than "Someone—that is, any arbitrary person—might believe *p* because of reasons *a*, *b*, and *c*." But we could also go a step further: we could assess whether *a*, *b*, and *c* are good reasons for believing *p*. When we ask that question, we might ask whether *a*, *b*, and *c* are good reasons for *some specific person* to believe *p*. Or we might ask whether they are good reasons for *anyone* to believe *p*. Once we get to the final question, we are in effect considering whether *p* is true, full-stop. And we certainly cannot rule out in advance that the answer to this question might be yes. A similar chain of steps would involve considering whether some practice is good. This kind of normative evaluation is a mainstay of philosophical inquiry. It should also be welcome in the

---

[24] As Thomas Nagel points out: "Reasons are by definition general, and we aim always to extend their generality" and "Unless we think that anyone should draw the same conclusion from the same premises, we cannot regard the conclusion as justified by reason" (Nagel, *The Last Word*, 79).

academic study of religion.[25] "Welcome" does not mean "universally required." Of course, many individual scholars of religion will have no interest in exploring evaluative questions about truth and goodness. Fair enough—anthropologists doing fieldwork probably should not get into philosophical arguments with their local informants, for example. But even though some scholars of religion have no interest in such questions, others do. There is no methodological canon that requires scholars in general to suppress their interest in questions of truth and goodness, and so there is no reason to insist on such a canon in the study of religion.

Like the study of religion, philosophy raises difficult moral and existential questions, but the pedagogical norms that govern philosophy classrooms very much allow teachers to commend views they regard as true; that is, to try to convince students that they themselves should adopt some specific, often controversial metaphysical or normative view. Again, this needn't look like preaching. A good teacher in the humanities should never *require* that her students agree with any particular viewpoint, including her own. Good teachers encourage students to develop their own views, and allow students to challenge the views of their teachers. But the norms of philosophy certainly do permit teachers to advocate, rather than just neutrally present, their own views, even when those views are highly controversial. What matters is that all parties aim at rational persuasion by means of evidence and argument instead of by coercion. This can be tricky, of course, but it is not impossible. The best way to make the case why it is not only possible but valuable is by returning to the discussion of analytic theology.

Analytic Theology as Rigorous Appreciation

Scholars of religion are not required to subvert religious experiences, beliefs, and practices. They need not unmask them, reduce them to something else, or show that they really express some form of ideological mystification. They can forgo critique without thereby becoming uncritical. Instead, precisely as scholars, they can use their highly developed powers of attention and interpretation to appreciate religious beliefs, practices, and experiences, to understand why they are attractive, and assess whether they are valuable. But there is no principled way to draw a sharp line between these kinds of intellectual activities and commendation or endorsement. This conclusion furnishes another reason to agree that the wider field of religious studies has no principled, intellectual grounds for excluding many forms of normative inquiry, including analytic theology.

---

[25] Kevin Schilbrack makes a similar point about philosophy of religion. He writes: "The distinctive contribution of philosophy of religion has to do with the evaluation of truth claims, which means the assessment of reason-giving and arguments." See *Philosophy and the Study of Religions*, 25. I agree, and I would extend the point to analytic theology, as long we bear in mind that evaluation and assessment are not confined to *negative* evaluation and assessment.

It remains to argue that analytic theology exhibits the virtues of rigorous appreciation. Analytic theology shows clearly what it looks like to engage in reasoned, evidence-based evaluation of theological, metaphysical, and otherwise non-empirical claims. But, crucially, evaluation can include positive evaluation, even affirmation. Analytic theology inherits the tools and methods of analytic philosophy, but it also inherits from theology the fundamentally positive, appreciative stance discussed above. Because it is a form of theology, analytic theology is an engaged, "insider" discourse, and not a detached, "outsider" discourse. It is true that the analytic method is often reductive. In this sense, it can even seem superficially similar to the technical sense of critique. But whatever we might say about analytic philosophy, analytic *theology* is a fundamentally positive, constructive enterprise. Analytic theologians typically aim to develop their own accounts of various theological topoi and to present them as attractive and worthy of endorsement. Non-analytic thinkers might assume that such accounts are motivated (at best) by a desiccated love of coherence for its own sake, or (at worst) by the desire to find fault with others. This assumption is uncharitable. I would say that far more often, analytic theologians are actually motivated by a kind of pleasure: the intellectual pleasure that results from sincere attempts to understand the complex intellectual inheritance of Christianity. One does not have to feel this specific form of pleasure oneself, or endorse the technical philosophical means by which analytic theologians pursue it, to accept my central point. Analytic theologians theorize from the kind of positive, engaged stance that humanistic scholars in other contexts happily commend.

Consider again Felski's four modes of post-critical inquiry. It is easy to see how analytic theology involves criticizing and composing: I doubt anyone needs to be persuaded that analytic theology involves criticizing, even though it may not involve critique. With respect to composing, I argued in Chapter 5 that analytic theology is paradigmatically a form of constructive theology that aims at creating new theological models and syntheses. Despite the connotations of the word "analytic," the contemporary analytic task, in both philosophy and theology, very much includes positive synthesis. This is especially the case with analytic theology, which often aims at constructing models that display the coherence, truth, and value of key Christian doctrines and practices.

Historically minded critics may doubt that analytic theology really involves "curating" and "conveying" the authentic Christian tradition, but it does. Analytic theologians often try to show that some Christian doctrine is actually coherent and credible. Using Felski's own terminology, this seems like a way of "guarding" and "protecting" Christian claims from contemporary challenges, which is a way of "conserving," and "looking after" the broader Christian tradition in which those claims are embedded.[26] Likewise, if by "conveying" we mean making

---

[26] Felski, "Introduction," 217.

important Christian claims present for people today, then the method of logical paraphrase—laying out those claims in propositional fashion—can be understood as a way to convey them in a contemporary idiom. When we bring Felski's four modes of post-critical inquiry into dialogue with analytic theology, we see again that post-critical inquiry is more than traditionalism—more than simply repeating the same formulae over and over. Because post-critical inquiry also requires argument, it also requires genuine intellectual risk.

As a form of rigorous appreciation, analytic theology has a distinctive academic mission. That mission revolves around the normative evaluation of Christian truth claims and practices. Normative evaluation may include negative assessment—as when Hasker denies the coherence of divine simplicity, for example—but it may also include positive endorsement.[27] As a field, the academic study of religion is growing more comfortable with normative inquiry. It is only a small further step to agree that affirmative, constructive theology (analytic or otherwise) has a place in the religious studies academy. As always, analytic theologians remain bound by the general norms of academic inquiry, and so they cannot legitimately commend claims that are demonstrably false or irrational. Like all responsible academics, they should endorse only those theological claims that arc sufficiently well supported by evidence and argument. And, of course, there will be second-level questions about what counts as "demonstrably false or irrational" and "sufficiently well-supported." This kind of open-ended, ramifying interrogation is a feature, not a flaw, of humanistic inquiry.

Because analytic theology is *theology*, it will draw in part on the standards of evidence and argument that govern any form of historical and textual study. At the same time, because it is *analytic*, it will also draw on the standards of evidence and argument that prevail in contemporary philosophy. These standards include considerations like logical coherence, modal status (e.g. necessity, possibility, impossibility), and even appeals to expert philosophical intuitions. The norms of inquiry that prevail in philosophy departments are significantly different from those in the study of religion. The dual nature of analytic theology is what enables its distinctive contributions to the religious studies guild. By drawing on all aspects of its intellectual inheritance, analytic theology can model forms of reasoned argument that are now comparatively rare in the religious studies academy. Analytic theology can show that it is possible to evaluate and even commend theological claims without departing from the general standards of academic reason. Analytic theology is not the only form of inquiry that can show this; but it is a form of inquiry that is especially well suited to showing it.

Consider the question: "Is Christ both fully human and fully divine?" or the closely related question "Is it rational to believe that Christ is fully human and

---

[27] Hasker denies divine simplicity in Hasker, *Metaphysics and the Tri-Personal God*, 36–39.

fully divine?" (I use Christian examples because they are the examples I know. But it would be easy for an expert in non-Christian religions to substitute equivalent questions.) These are not the kinds of questions that are typically asked in religious studies classrooms or addressed in specialist religion journals.[28] They are—obviously—fundamentally different from the causal and empirical questions that natural scientists and social theorists usually ask. Nor do they lend themselves to the kind of critical inquiry favored by postmodern theorists. They are, nevertheless, interesting and important questions. Not to everyone, perhaps, but to many people—there can be no serious doubt about that.

Furthermore, we can imagine at least two ways in which we might engage the arguments used to answer such questions. We could take a purely descriptive interest in the proffered arguments—this group of Christians argues like this, that group argues like that, and so on. Alternatively, we could take a more philosophical interest. Someone who takes a more philosophical interest will also want to assess them as *arguments*. Yet assessing them as arguments means assessing whether the proffered reasons are good reasons, which means assessing whether the arguments themselves are sound and their conclusions true. Here "assessing" is not simply identical to *negatively* assessing. One might fairly and honestly assess the evidence and arguments for some theological claim and conclude that it is actually on a sound footing.

This kind of positive conclusion could itself happen in two ways. The conclusion could be conditional: *if* we accept assumptions X, Y, and Z, then this account of (for example) the incarnation presents a plausible way to understand the claim that Christ is both human and divine. On this line, because it remains conditional, positive commendation still looks quite close to pure description. Given the nature of theological argument, conditional justifications of this sort are likely to be very common.[29] It is at least possible, however, that one might reach an unconditional conclusion: this account is justified, full-stop. Such an outcome cannot be ruled out in principle. One cannot fix in advance the outcome of any genuinely academic argument.

Analytic Appreciation in the Academic Study of Religion

I have said that analytic theology is centrally concerned with the normative evaluation of Christian truth claims and practices. This is a distinctively theological task, but it can also contribute to the academic study of religion more generally.

---

[28] Much depends on "typically," I suppose, and if we take "religion" here to include theology, the point becomes less salient. The point is that these kinds of questions are rarely regarded as questions for the academic study of religion properly so called.

[29] This is Timothy Pawl's method in *In Defense of Conciliar Christology*, 20.

First, analytic theologians can help scholars of religion understand the normative core of Christian doctrine. Second, they can also help scholars of religion understand the way theological elites reason, either directly, as a part of their own work, or indirectly, by providing contemporary examples of theological disputation.

The study of religion is broader than the study of Christianity, and not even all scholars of Christianity need to be well versed in Christian doctrine. But surely many of them do. Analytic theology can be a useful resource. Analytic theologians aspire to the all-important virtue of clarity, and they typically strive to present key Christian doctrines in explicit, propositional form. This mode of writing is not without its faults, but because its claims are so explicit and its steps of reasoning so transparent, it can be comparatively easy for non-specialists to understand. So the best analytic theology features a wealth of useful material for scholars who simply want to understand the normative core of the Christian tradition better.

Consider, for example, the way Hasker handles the rather technical issue of the "divine processions." The orthodox Christian creeds do not just specify that the Father, Son, and Spirit are numerically distinct beings that share a single divine nature. The creeds also specify the sense in which each divine person possesses or receives that nature. The Father alone possesses the divine nature without receiving it. The Father in turn communicates the divine nature to the Son and the Spirit: in the traditional language, this is what it means to say that the Son is *begotten* of the Father, and that the Spirit *proceeds* from the Father (and the Son).[30] The patristic tradition embraced the most natural interpretation of this view: in some sense the Father causes the Son and the Spirit to exist—to be sure, the Father necessarily and eternally causes the Son and Spirit to exist, and so it is impossible for the Father to exist without them, but nevertheless, there is a sense in which it is true that the Father is causally prior to the Son and Spirit. Hasker does a very good job of explaining these ideas, and scholars of religion who do not know much about the doctrine of the divine processions can find in Hasker a perspicuous statement of its outlines.[31]

Analytic theology can also be useful to theorists of religion as an example of elite theological reasoning. Elite theological reasoning is one form of religious behavior. If the academic study of religion aims to study all aspects of religious behavior, it should also study elite theological reasoning. By "elite theological reasoning," I mean things like how theological elites construct arguments, how they understand argumentation, evidence, and persuasion, and why they appeal to *these* kinds of considerations in *those* kinds of disputes. Martin Kavka makes the welcome point that "one of the things that the study of religion should be able

---

[30] Eastern Orthodox Christians typically deny that the Spirit proceeds from both the Father and the Son—hence the parentheses.

[31] Hasker, *Metaphysics and the Tri-Personal God*, 214–29.

to do is to give an account of theological disputation."[32] Yet being able to give an account of theological disputation requires being able to think like a theologian, at least to a degree: it requires a substantial grasp of the theological claims under dispute, why they are regarded as normative, what their implications are taken to be, and so forth. Theorists of religion need not accept internal Christian accounts of these matters, but they at least need to understand what those internal Christian accounts are before constructing explanatory theories about them. (This is another instance of the general point that successful explanation first requires an adequate description of the *explanandum*.) Kavka calls this kind of work "profane theology." It is "profane" because one can study the structure of theological disputation, and to some extent even learn to think like a theologian, without being a believer oneself.[33] Scholars of religion could view constructive analytic theologians through this lens, as skilled practitioners of theological disputation. This suggestion comes close to the "theologians as native informants" model that strikes some theologians as quite offensive. I prefer the idiom of "artists in residence," but in any case, nothing about the model strikes me as inherently offensive, provided that all sides agree that theologians are also engaged in academic inquiry. There is nothing offensive about insisting that theologians and scholars of religion are engaged in fundamentally different forms of academic inquiry. What is offensive is insisting that *only* scholars of religion are engaged in academic inquiry.

I have presented several ways in which analytic theology can contribute—either directly or indirectly—to the academic study of religion. In terms of the structure of my own argument, however, I want to be clear that I do not stake the academic legitimacy of analytic theology on the degree to which it can contribute to the academic study of religion. As long as analytic theology follows the general norms of academic inquiry, it is a legitimate academic discourse in its own right, with its own legitimate task: evaluating Christian beliefs and practices. Yet even as analytic theologians pursue this distinctively Christian mission, they may also contribute to the wider enterprise of the study of religions. In a suitably confident and open religious studies academy, this contribution should be welcome to all sides.

Toward Comparative Analytic Theology

This contribution should be welcome, but will it be? It certainly wouldn't hurt if Christian analytic theologians took more interest in non-Christian religions.

---

[32] Kavka, "Profane Theology," 109.
[33] As I have noted at various points, a fair amount of analytic theology is already "profane" in Kavka's sense, in that it can be understood as arguing the mode of the conditional: *if* we accept assumptions X, Y, and Z, then conclusion C follows.

The academic study of religion prizes comparative work in a way that analytic philosophy of religion does not. As discussed in Chapter 1, scholars of religion often regard analytic philosophy of religion as excessively "narrow," which is to say, as excessively Christian. In my view, there is nothing intrinsically wrong with narrowness—everyone should study what most interests them, even if those interests are narrow. Still, when we face the charge squarely, we can see real opportunities for mutual growth. It would be good for the religious studies academy to welcome more analytic theologians, and it would be good if more analytic theologians also did comparative work. I therefore present a modest proposal. Imagine a thriving new subfield called "comparative analytic theology." Comparative analytic theology would be an especially welcome form of rigorous appreciation.

By embracing comparative inquiry, analytic theologians could contribute directly to the academic study of religion while moving into new and potentially fruitful areas of research. Many scholars of religion are explicitly engaged in comparative work, and even those who are not so engaged still regard comparison as the backbone of the field. At the same time, however, there is one kind of comparison that scholars of religion carefully avoid—comparative evaluation of religious truth claims and ethical norms. Scholars of religion, including philosophers based primarily in departments of religion, rarely seem willing to make comparative judgments about the truth claims and ethical norms of different religious traditions. Yet these kinds of judgments come naturally to scholars trained in the analytic method. Analytic theology can, therefore, contribute to the academic study of religion by advancing this neglected dimension of comparative study.

Comparative theology is not new. It already exists as an academic discipline, though it is not unproblematic in the religious studies guild, precisely because it is a form of theology. Comparative theology joins the comparative impulse found in the study of religions with the religiously engaged perspective found in theology. Like all good theology, comparative theology is a form of faith seeking understanding, but the understanding sought only emerges from a serious study of other religious traditions. As Francis X. Clooney, one of the leading exponents of comparative theology, puts it:

> Comparative theology—comparative and theological beginning to end—marks acts of faith seeking understanding which are rooted in a particular faith tradition but which, from that foundation, venture into learning from one or more other faith traditions. This learning is sought for the sake of fresh theological insights that are indebted to the newly encountered tradition/s as well as the home tradition. Comparative theology thus combines tradition-rooted theological concerns with actual study of another tradition.[34]

---

[34] Francis X. Clooney, *Comparative Theology: Deep Learning across Religious Borders* (Malden, MA: Wiley-Blackwell, 2010), 10.

More succinctly, comparative theology is a "mode of interreligious learning."[35] We should take this focus on interreligious *learning* seriously. Comparative analytic theology should always be practiced in the mode of interreligious learning, rather than in the mode of interreligious apologetics.

Comparative analytic theologians could maintain their distinctively analytic focus on truth claims, reason-giving, and explicit argumentation. But they could also assess the truth claims, reasons, and arguments of religious traditions other than their own in a way that aims at learning from them rather than merely refuting them. (This can be tricky. Depending on the circumstances, showing that an interlocutor's arguments do not succeed could contribute to mutual learning or inhibit it.) Interreligious learning does not have to be adversarial, and it does not have to be one-sided. Analytic theologians might also find that non-Christian traditions offer interesting criticisms or interesting new solutions to perennial philosophical and theological problems.[36] Analytic theology is a form of theology that prizes rigorous argumentation aimed at assessing truth claims. Even on their own terms, analytic theologians would benefit from considering the arguments of non-Christian traditions. For example, analytic "perfect being theology" would certainly benefit from a deeper engagement with non-Christian and non-Western notions of the nature of divine perfection. It seems likely that the converse holds as well.

I foresee several lines of resistance to comparative analytic theology. First, given the cultural prominence of Christianity and the argumentative proclivities of many analytic philosophers, one might worry that any dialogue between analytic theologians and their non-Christian counterparts will be superficial and one-sided. No one would welcome an army of analytically trained "comparativists" with little to offer beyond uninformed arguments about the truth and falsity of religious doctrines they do not really understand. Parimal Patil's comments on Francis X. Clooney's *Hindu God, Christian God* are especially apt:

> Without the presence of professional Hindu theologians in the academy, for example, the interreligious project of *Hindu God, Christian God* will remain an entirely Christian enterprise. It will represent just another subdiscipline of Christian theology and will radically alter the comparative and dialogical dimensions of the project. It is also likely that in such an environment Hindu theology will only be used in service of Christian theology and will not be given an opportunity to respond. Without institutional space for Hindu theologians

---

[35] Clooney, *Comparative Theology*, 3.
[36] As examples of responses to the problem of evil that have not been considered by (largely Christian) philosophers of religion, see Tyron Goldschmidt and Beth Seacord, "Judaism, Reincarnation, and Theodicy," *Faith and Philosophy* 30 (2013): 393–417; Samuel Lebens and Tyron Goldschmidt, "The Promise of a New Past," *Philosopher's Imprint* 17 (2017): 1–25.

and the study of Hindu theology, moreover, it is difficult to imagine that Hindu traditions would not be more easily misused.[37]

In order for comparative analytic theology really to flourish, analytic theologians must treat non-Christian philosophers and theologians as their intellectual peers. So the very idea of comparative analytic theology also implies that the academy should be more open to non-Christian theology, which, of course, could include non-Christian analytic theology.[38] Second, critics might also worry that comparative evaluation is a waste of time, and will only lead to irresolvable disagreements. But the likelihood of disagreement is not a reason to disallow comparative evaluation. Agreeing to disagree is often a perfectly legitimate—and perfectly scholarly—outcome in its own right. To suggest that we should engage in rational inquiry only when that inquiry is likely to yield a single definitive result strikes me as deeply anti-humanistic. When we argue about competing religious truth claims, we are engaged in open-ended humanistic inquiry, with all its attendant risks and rewards. So I am unimpressed with objections to comparative theology that do no more than repeat general objections to humanistic inquiry.

I have much more sympathy with those objections that (once again) express legitimate worries about power and domination. After all, scholars are never completely isolated from broader patterns of culture and politics. In a society with a culturally dominant religious tradition, evaluating the reasons, arguments, and evidence of non-dominant religions could end up unjustifiably reinforcing the supremacy of the dominant. This is a real concern. But comparative evaluation need not be a form of dominance. It can also be a form of respect. Evaluating religious truth claims is a way of taking them seriously. When we sincerely evaluate the claims of others, we show that we are open to the possibility that they might be true. Insofar as everyone ought to believe claims that are true, we thereby show that we are open to the possibility that we ourselves should believe them too. That openness is very much a mark of respect. In fact, the wholesale refusal to evaluate religious truth claims often expresses its own kind of cultural dominance and disrespect. It is a way of implicitly denying that religious truth claims are even worthy of evaluation, or perhaps even denying that they are truth claims at all. The idea that comparative evaluation is always disrespectful or dangerous rests on the assumption that there can be no good reasons for religious believing, from which it "follows" that religious adherents must be protected, like small children, from rational criticism.

---

[37] Parimal Patel, as quoted in Francis X. Clooney, *Hindu God, Christian God: How Reason Helps Break Down the Boundaries between Religions* (New York: Oxford University Press, 2001), 186–87.

[38] See, for example, Samuel Lebens, *The Principles of Judaism* (New York: Oxford University Press, 2020).

One virtue of analytic philosophy as a method is that it is quite conducive to identifying exactly where religious traditions agree and disagree about deep axiological, ontological, and epistemological matters. Analytic evaluation can, therefore, sharpen our grasp of both the similarities and the differences that obtain among different religious traditions. Both are equally important. It is easy to exaggerate doctrinal differences across religious traditions, especially in a scholarly climate that (rightly) celebrates difference, diversity, and distinctiveness. In such a climate, it can be a useful corrective to discover that sharply different religious traditions sometimes make similar claims. At the same time, however, evaluating truth claims is a way to sharpen our grasp of the real differences that do obtain across traditions. We can do this in a divisive way; but we can also do it respectfully, as a way of letting the religious other remain other.

Who are the natural interlocutors for comparative analytic theologians? They might find historical conversation partners in the various forms of Western but non-Christian medieval thought, or in the non-Western forms of scholasticism associated with Indian traditions—and, of course, they might find contemporary conversation partners among the scholars of those traditions.[39] But I hope that eventually comparative analytic theologians also look to traditions and forms of thought that are radically *dissimilar* to contemporary analytic theology. And even though I have focused on Christian analytic theology, there is nothing inherently Christian about the analytic method itself. So we can also look forward to a time in which Christian analytic theologians have non-Christian analytic theological counterparts, and to the interreligious dialogues that will ensue.[40]

Comparative analytic theology would be a welcome member of the guild of analytic theology and religious studies. But I do not want to overstate my case. I do not claim that all good analytic theology must be comparative, or that only comparative analytic theology deserves a place in the religious studies academy. (I am not a comparativist myself, so that would be a very strange claim for me to make.) As ever, my real argument is modest: it would be good if more analytic theologians did comparative work, and good if more scholars of religion welcomed their efforts.

---

[39] See, for example, José Cabezón, ed. *Scholasticism: Cross-Cultural and Comparative Perspectives* (Albany, NY: SUNY Press, 1998).

[40] See Samuel Lebens, "It Is Time for the Analytic Philosophy of Judaism," *Marginalia Review of Books*, December 8, 2015, https://marginalia.lareviewofbooks.org/it-is-time-for-the-analytic-philosophy-of-judaism-by-samuel-lebens/, accessed July 11, 2020:

> Analytic philosophy of Judaism is the new chapter of Jewish philosophy waiting to be written . . . The analytic philosophy of Judaism promises to give rise to clearheaded accounts of what it is, in our various streams of Jewish thought, that we actually stand for; and why it matters to us so much. The tools of analytic philosophy equip a thinker to articulate their position and better stake their ground.

See also Samuel Lebens, Dani Rabinowitz, and Aaron Segal, eds., *Jewish Philosophy in an Analytic Age* (New York: Oxford University Press, 2019). See also Lebens, *The Principles of Judaism*.

Conclusion

According to Kevin Schilbrack, the subdiscipline of philosophy of religion investigates legitimate academic questions about "whether religious beliefs are true, religious practices moral, religious experiences real, and religious institutions just."[41] Theology is not a species of philosophy of religion, but like philosophy of religion, theology is a normative and evaluative form of inquiry. The academic study of religion has resisted normative and evaluative inquiry—or, at least, it has resisted *positive* forms of normative and evaluative inquiry. But as long as all parties follow general academic norms, there is no principled case for allowing negative evaluation and barring positive evaluation. Analytic theology is a form of rigorous appreciation focused on evaluating and commending Christian truth claims and practices. So understood, analytic theology can contribute in various ways to the academic study of religion, while also remaining faithful to its distinctive academic vocation.

Whether we call it "rigorous appreciation" or something else, we should all welcome forms of inquiry that are post-critical, engaged, and *attached*. At its best, humanistic inquiry is transformative, but not all transformations destabilize and subvert. Some transformations renew and solidify what is already strong. We need a scholarly language that allows us to cultivate—in our students and in ourselves—intellectually responsible ways of inhabiting our own deepest convictions. We need to understand the complexity and fragility of those convictions, and their particularity, and to grasp that they are not always obvious to other people, because those other people also have their own convictions that are not always obvious to us. Sometimes humanistic inquiry can transform us into better versions of who we already are. We can learn from each other without abandoning or bracketing what matters to us most.

---

[41] Schilbrack, *Philosophy and the Study of Religions*, 185.

Conclusion

Analytic Theology after the Postsecular

The religious studies academy is like a house that is perpetually under construction, constantly demolished and rebuilt anew, the better to comport with current fashion. The structure we now inhabit was raised in the early 1990s, after the previous one, designed by Mircea Eliade, no longer seemed inhabitable.[1] Our present structure has many architects, but two are especially important: John Milbank and Talal Asad.[2] One a theologian, the other an anthropologist—unwitting and unlikely collaborators, perhaps, but so far the structure they helped build has endured. I call that structure the "postsecular consensus."[3]

In a way, the theologian Milbank laid the initial foundations for the postsecular consensus.[4] In 1990, nearly a decade before *Radical Orthodoxy*, the edited volume, and well before "Radical Orthodoxy," the self-styled theological brand, Milbank published *Theology and Social Theory*, a trenchant critique of modern, social scientific approaches to the study of religion. It still remains unsurpassed in force and scope, and its oracular opening paragraphs turned out to be a charter for the next thirty years of theorizing on the postsecular:

> Once, there was no "secular." And the secular was not latent, waiting to fill more space with the steam of the "purely human," when the pressure of the sacred was

---

[1] For some current histories of the field, see Chapter 13, note 17. See also Stephen S. Bush, *Visions of Religion: Experience, Meaning, and Power* (New York: Oxford University Press, 2014).

[2] Like all genealogies, this one is simplified for the sake of a better story. Although I do think that Milbank and Asad are uniquely important architects of the postsecular consensus in theology and the study of religion, they are joined by many others, and if we were to broaden the scope of the claim to include sociologists involved in rethinking the "secularization thesis," the list would be very long indeed. To single out a few additional sources in the United States, among scholars of religion, see the whole corpus of J. Z. Smith; among theologians one should consider "post-liberal" theologians and the so-called Yale-Chicago debates. See William Placher, *Unapologetic Theology* (Louisville, KY: Westminster John Knox, 1989).

[3] I first encountered the phrase "after the postsecular" in Anthony Paul Smith and Daniel Whistler, eds., *After the Postsecular and the Postmodern: New Essays in Continental Philosophy of Religion* (Newcastle upon Tyne: Cambridge Scholars, 2010).

[4] I say "in a way," because Milbank's landmark *Theology and Social Theory* appeared before Asad's *Genealogies of Religion*. But in *Theology and Social Theory*, Milbank cites the 1983 essay ("Anthropological Conceptions of Religion: Reflections on Geertz," *Man* 18 [1983]: 237–59) that would become the key first chapter of Asad's *Genealogies of Religion*.

Analytic Theology and the Academic Study of Religion. William Wood, Oxford University Press (2021). © William Wood.
DOI: 10.1093/oso/9780198779872.003.0015

relaxed... The secular as a domain had to be instituted or *imagined*, both in theory and in practice.[5]

In the modern age, we have been conditioned to think that the secular is simply the empty unmarked space that remains when religion withdraws from public life. Yet, according to Milbank, "the secular" is not neutral, natural, or given, but actively constructed: ironically birthed, in the first instance, by a decadent, late medieval Christian church that could no longer fully understand its own historic teachings. Three years after *Theology and Social Theory*, the anthropologist Asad's truly field-changing book *Genealogies of Religion* arrived. While many theorists of religion would resist the suggestion that Milbank is a major architect of the post-secular consensus, nearly everyone would give that honor to Asad. *Genealogies of Religion* presents itself as a work of anthropology, but for the most part it is an anthropology without ethnography—a work of metalevel philosophical critique. It is still widely read and widely cited, because it pointedly criticizes an idea that had long been a mainstay of the academic study of religion, the idea that there is a transcultural and transhistorical "essence" of religion as such. That idea is now almost universally rejected by scholars of religion, due in no small part to Asad. *Genealogies of Religion* is more concerned with critiquing modernist notions of religion than with unmasking the pretenses of the secular, but the seeds of Asad's equally influential 2003 work *Formations of the Secular* are all present in the earlier work, since Asad, like Milbank, holds that "the secular" and "the religious" develop together.[6]

Milbank and Asad are mutually reinforcing. Both deny that the essence of religion lies with private, individual acts of believing; both regard this false view as a modern, Western ideological construct that was unknown before the Reformation, even in Christendom.[7] Both tie this modern notion of religion to specific historical developments in Christian theology, and insist that the supposedly secular disciplines of anthropology and history are constituted by disguised theological assumptions. Both Milbank and Asad argue that the modern liberal state has constructed the distinction between "religious" and "secular" in order to delegitimize theological challenges to state authority.[8] Both go on to identify this distinction with colonialist and orientalist projects.

This, then, is the postsecular consensus in contemporary theology and the academic study of religion. It begins with a genealogy that portrays "religion" as a category invented in the early modern period to serve the interests of Western

---

[5] Milbank, *Theology and Social Theory*, 9.

[6] Talal Asad, *Formations of the Secular: Christianity, Islam, Modernity* (Stanford, CA: Stanford University Press, 2003).

[7] See Milbank, *Theology and Social Theory*, 10, 18, 42, 43, 76; Asad, *Genealogies*, 28–29, 39, 42, 45–46, 47.

[8] Asad, *Genealogies*, 28–29; Milbank, *Theology and Social Theory*, 7–48.

state power. Yet the genealogy of religion is also a genealogy of "the secular," because the idea of the secular as a neutral, unmarked public space can only emerge in tandem with the modern notion of religion. Both "the religious" and "the secular" are specifically Christian-theological constructions. But they shore up a Christianity that had already become modern, because it had already departed considerably from its original home in patristic and medieval forms of thought. Theologians and theorists of religion alike accept this consensus. They differ only in whether they treat it as the story of a fall from a divinely appointed harmony or as just another accident of history, further grist for the genealogical mill.

On the whole, the postsecular consensus has been comparatively friendly to theology, because it makes possible a common intellectual framework to which all sides can appeal. Theologians and theorists of religion can agree that the secular is a historically contingent, constructed category that yields an equally contingent, constructed account of rationality. They then go on to argue that alternative forms of rationality are equally legitimate. For their part, at least some postsecular scholars of religion now want to engage directly with religious forms of reasoning.[9] Yet such scholars are typically interested primarily in those forms of religious reasoning that anticipate their own critique of secular reason. That is, they are interested in distinctively religious reasoning as a *counterweight* to the constricting, modernist epistemologies they wish to resist. They value forms of religious reasoning that embrace play, freedom, chaos, disorder, incongruity, uncertainty, and excess. They denigrate modernist reasoning because it prizes grasping, certainty, fixity, and closure.

Analytic theology stands in a complicated relationship to the postsecular consensus. Analytic thinkers like Alvin Plantinga, Nicholas Wolterstorff, and other key forerunners of analytic theology developed their own critique of secular reason in the 1980s.[10] Yet postsecular theologians and scholars of religion ignore this legacy and typically assimilate analytic theology to the deleterious, modernist patterns of reasoning they themselves resist. After all, analytic theology, like analytic philosophy of religion, foregrounds propositional argumentation and rational assent. From the perspective of the postsecular consensus, then, analytic theology probably seems like a form of disembodied, rationalist deism, perhaps even modernist fundamentalism.

Analytic theologians tell a different story. In their version, analytic theology simply carries on the same form of theology practiced by the great patristic and

---

[9] For example, I would name Amy Hollywood, most recently in *Acute Melancholia and Other Essays: Mysticism, History, and the Study of Religion* (New York: Columbia University Press, 2016); Roberts, *Encountering Religion*; Orsi, *Between Heaven and Earth*; Mahmood, *Politics of Piety*.

[10] See Alvin Plantinga, "Advice for Christian Philosophers," *Faith and Philosophy* 1 (1984): 253–71; Alvin Plantinga and Nicholas Wolterstorff, eds., *Faith and Rationality: Reason and Belief in God* (Notre Dame, IN: University of Notre Dame Press, 1984).

scholastic thinkers.[11] By contrast, contemporary academic theology has become sloppy, anti-rational, and perversely heterodox. Analytic theologians deny that modern thinkers like Kant, Nietzsche, or Freud have successfully challenged orthodox Christianity, and so they see no need to construct new forms of post-secular or postmodern Christianity in order to escape those challenges. Instead, they respond to the modern intellectual challenge with additional intellectual arguments. Yet they explicitly construe that response as a return to patristic and scholastic theology.

In fact, both sides miss the mark. Analytic theology is not easy to categorize, because it blurs the boundaries that divide premodern, modern, and postmodern theology. For example, analytic theologians join postmodern thinkers in rejecting modern epistemological foundationalism and verificationism. And as I have argued throughout this book, analytic theology is not a "disengaged," rationalist project, but a traditional form of faith seeking understanding, one that prizes attachment, wonder, and intellectual pleasure (see especially Chapters 10 and 14). Analytic theology also foregrounds traditional theological questions about God, and addresses them using a traditional premodern metaphysical vocabulary. Yet analytic theology does not simply reproduce patristic or scholastic thought, as if the Enlightenment and the scientific revolution had no lasting effects. So analytic theology is also a modern form of inquiry: it draws on analytic philosophy, which is itself distinctively modern, and it shares certain modern presuppositions and patterns of argument, as I discuss below.

Analytic theology is a modern form of inquiry, and that is why it can flourish in the secular university, which continues to enforce modern intellectual norms. Yet analytic theology is not exclusively or deleteriously modern, and that is why it can also count as fully theological. These two claims pull together several strands of argument found across the book as a whole, and so they serve as its fitting conclusion. Other theologians should welcome analytic theology as a legitimate form of theology, and other scholars of religion should agree that analytic theology is a legitimate form of academic inquiry that follows the same norms of argument found in other academic disciplines.

Analytic Theology in the Secular Age

To develop this conclusion, it is helpful to put another concrete view on the table. Consider Charles Taylor's well-known genealogy of the secular in *A Secular Age*.[12] Notwithstanding the title of his magnum opus, Taylor is very much a theorist of

---

[11] I have heard this view expressed in personal communication many times. In print, the closest I have found is Oliver Crisp's statement in Crisp and Rea, *Analytic Theology*, 39.

[12] Charles Taylor, *A Secular Age* (Cambridge, MA: Belknap Press, 2008).

the *post*secular. Like Milbank and Asad, Taylor argues that the secular is not natural, but constructed, and furthermore constructed out of theological materials furnished by late medieval Christianity. Taylor's story is dense, and far from uncontroversial. For my own purposes, it does not matter whether his genealogy gets all the details right. *A Secular Age* can still help us understand the place of analytic theology in the contemporary university. In Taylor's terminology, analytic theology shows us one way to affirm transcendence from within the immanent frame, under the conditions of modern secularity.

After all, even after we have recognized that "the secular" is a constructed and contingent category, we cannot simply leave it behind. According to Taylor, we continue to live in a secular age, because the conditions of modern secularity shape everyone's beliefs about transcendence, whether we understand ourselves as religious believers or skeptics. What defines our age as secular is the fundamentally modern character of religious belief itself. Everyone, no matter how personally devout, recognizes that believing otherwise, including outright disbelief, remain genuine options, if not for oneself, then certainly for others. In short, "belief in God is no longer axiomatic. There are alternatives."[13]

As Taylor recognizes, the sheer fact of religious diversity is not a uniquely modern phenomenon. Some scholars also push back on Taylor's suggestion that atheism is a uniquely modern phenomenon, or inherently parasitic upon Christianity.[14] In anticipation of such challenges, Taylor tends to emphasize how much easier unbelief is under the conditions of modernity. In modernity, "the other becomes more and more like me, in everything else but faith: same activities, professions, opinions, tastes, etc. Then the issue posed by difference becomes more insistent: why my way, and not hers? There is no other difference left to make the shift preposterous or unimaginable." When it is even so much as possible for religious adherence to become one more item on a list of personal preferences, an option to choose or reject at will, the phenomenon itself must have changed significantly; a premodern person could never have understood religious adherence this way. Taylor concludes: it was "virtually impossible not to believe in God in, say, 1500 in our Western society, while in 2000 many of us find this not only easy, but even inescapable."[15] Western Christendom has always been marked by a degree of pluralism, but pluralism becomes a properly existential challenge only in modernity, according to Taylor. Only within the conditions of modern

---

[13] Taylor, *A Secular Age*, 3.
[14] Peter E. Gordon, "The Place of the Sacred in the Absence of God: Charles Taylor's *A Secular Age*," *Journal of the History of Ideas* 69 (2008): 647–73; Tim Whitmarsh, *Battling the Gods: Atheism in the Ancient World* (New York: Knopf, 2015); Joseph Blankholm, "The Ghost of Immanentism," *The Immanent Frame*, November 14, 2017, https://tif.ssrc.org/2017/11/14/the-ghost-of-immanentism/, accessed July 11, 2020.
[15] Taylor, *Secular Age*, 304, 25.

secularity can we really *feel* that it is a live option to adopt someone else's religion, or no religion at all.

Notwithstanding his own best efforts, the best way to see the force of Taylor's argument is by focusing on a slightly different phenomenon. Instead of religious diversity, atheism or unbelief, consider instead religious *indifference*. Only under the conditions of modern secularity is it possible to be utterly indifferent to religion, to have no interest at all in determining which gods to follow or whether there even are any gods. Even if there were atheists, agnostics, or materialists in the ancient and medieval world, they did not slouch toward nonbelief out of inertia and sheer lack of interest, as so many modern people do. Something has changed. Even the most committed religious adherent cannot fail to recognize this situation intellectually and feel it viscerally.

The Immanent Frame

In Taylor's terminology, we all live within "the immanent frame." The immanent frame derives from modern natural science: even though there is no intrinsic incompatibility between science and religion, we cannot help but see ourselves and the world differently after the scientific revolution. The immanent frame "constitutes a 'natural' order, to be contrasted to a 'supernatural' one, an 'immanent' world, over against a possible 'transcendent' one."[16] Although the very idea of a "frame" implies a limited perspective, the immanent frame has in fact become all-pervasive, "common to all of us in the modern West," because it runs hand in hand with "the major theoretical transformation of Western modernity, vis., the rise of post-Galilean natural science."[17] Religious or not, we all live in a secular, scientific age and so we all live within the immanent frame.

Nevertheless, it is a mistake to regard the immanent frame as implacably hostile to religious belief. The steady progress of secularization does not demonstrate the triumphal march of newly liberated reason, but neither does it represent a funeral procession for traditional forms of religiosity. Again, Taylor is instructive. He distinguishes multiple senses of "secular." In the sense of "secular" outlined above, the key point is that theological assumptions no longer compose the background framework of everyone's shared experience. But this sense of "secular" is very different from *normative secularism*, an ideology that insists on the nonreligious character of all public institutions and rational debates.[18] We should

---

[16] Taylor, *Secular Age*, 543.   [17] Taylor, *Secular Age*, 542.

[18] Talyor distinguishes three concepts of "the secular." The first is the term's original usage, to mark the distinction between people who are not in religious orders, in distinction from priests, monks, and nuns. The second is the typical Enlightenment understanding discussed above where we understand the realm of the secular as coextensive with the realm of the public, the rational, etc., over against private non-rational religion. The third sense is the sense in which everyone is now "secular," according

not conflate the two. Even though theological assumptions no longer figure in the background framework of our shared experience, the conditions of secularity do not entail normative secularism. On the contrary, they can even create valuable new possibilities for religious belief and practice. Analytic theology is one such possibility.

Affirming Transcendence in the Immanent Frame

I now make two claims. The first is descriptive: analytic theology is a product of modernity, and arises in response to the conditions of secularity discussed by Taylor and others. The second is normative: analytic theology is a *valuable* response to modernity, valuable precisely because it is well suited for our secular age. Advocates of the postsecular consensus, including theological opponents of analytic theology, are likely to agree with the descriptive claim. They are unlikely to agree with the normative claim. I endorse both.

First, the descriptive claim. Even if it is not wholly modern—for reasons discussed above—analytic theology does exhibit preoccupations and patterns of reasoning that arise only in modernity and that typify the modern age. This claim should be unsurprising: analytic theology is modern because analytic philosophy is modern. It is important to be clear about what I mean. Obviously, there is nothing especially modern about formulating clear and precise arguments, nor appealing to *modus ponens, modus tollens,* and other basic forms of logical inference.[19] But analytic philosophy as a method is much more than a system for drawing basic logical inferences. The method itself depends on a rich intellectual culture that socializes its practitioners into treating certain figures as authoritative, certain problems as especially salient, others as unimportant, and so on.[20]

Analytic philosophy also shares one of the defining features of modernity, a preoccupation with scientific modes of inquiry. From its origins in the early twentieth century, and especially during the heyday of logical positivism, analytic philosophy has always presented itself as the philosophical face of modern, scientific empiricism and naturalism.[21] As Jaegwon Kim, a leading philosopher of mind, writes:

to Taylor, because the character of religious belief itself has changed, and become optional, contestable, and contested. See *A Secular Age,* 1–4.

[19] For that matter, even in the domain of logic, the backbone of analytic philosophy is first-order predicate logic. First-order predicate logic is a modern achievement, unknown before the nineteenth century, and furthermore one that makes certain traditional ideas—that existence is a genuine property, for example—more difficult to express. So, on its own, modern logic helps shape us into modern thinkers.
[20] See Wood, "Traditions, Trajectories, and Tools."
[21] A variety of historians of analytic philosophy make this point. See Hans-Johann Glock, *What Is Analytic Philosophy?,* 134–55. Neil Levy argues that analytic philosophy models itself on the methods

If contemporary analytic philosophy can be said to have a philosophical ideology, it undoubtedly is naturalism. Naturalism is often invoked as a motivating ground for many philosophical projects, and "naturalization" programs abound everywhere, in theory of knowledge, philosophy of mind, theory of meaning, metaphysics, and ethics.[22]

Even now, in the middle of the ongoing revival of analytic metaphysics, most metaphysicians are naturalists, or at least understand themselves to be elucidating the metaphysics implicit in the natural sciences.[23] If a metaphysical theory conflicts with some well-established scientific claim, that generally counts as a reason to discard the theory. All of this is true even though most analytic theologians and philosophers of religion are not naturalists. Even though they are not naturalists themselves, they still inherit this default attitude of respect for the methods and results of modern science.[24] That is why they are so acutely aware of the threats that naturalism and physicalism pose to traditional Christian belief.

The chief opponents of analytic philosophy of religion are metaphysical naturalism and physicalism, together with verificationist epistemologies that threaten religious claims with empirical vacuity or logical incoherence. Unlike more continental forms of religious reflection, analytic philosophy of religion has rarely addressed challenges like spiritual malaise, the meaninglessness of lived experience, or existential anxiety and finitude. Perhaps more surprisingly, (largely Christian) analytic philosophy of religion has not worried much about the philosophical challenges posed by non-Christian religions.[25] Naturalism and physicalism

of the physical sciences, and implicitly follows Thomas Kuhn's "normal science" paradigm (Neil Levy, "Continental and Analytic Philosophy," 301). As a result, analytic philosophers tend to see their task as one of theory-building and problem solving, and they work on a fairly narrow range of well-defined problems (Levy, "Continental and Analytic Philosophy," 293).

[22] Jaegwon Kim, "The American Origins of Philosophical Naturalism," *Journal of Philosophical Research* 28, Supplement (2003): 83–98. Thanks to Daniel De Haan for pointing me toward this reference.

[23] See Daniel Nolan, "Method in Analytic Metaphysics," in Herman Cappelen, Tamar Szabó Gendler, and John Hawthorne, eds., *The Oxford Handbook of Philosophical Methodology* (New York: Oxford University Press, 2016), 164.

Analytic metaphysicians are often accused of neglecting science…But I think this is just an error about the majority of contemporary analytic metaphysicians, who do keep at least one eye on the sciences. Metaphysicians are often wary of having their theories conflict with the best current science, and many want to go further, and use scientific findings to be a positive guide about which metaphysical theories are most likely to be correct.

[24] By the standards of the rest of the academy, some analytic philosophers of religion do seem a bit too comfortable with so-called intelligent design creationism. (See, for example, Alvin Plantinga, *Where the Conflict Really Lies: Science, Religion, and Naturalism* (New York: Oxford University Press, 2008), esp. chap. 8). Yet this sympathy for intelligent design actually evinces excessive *deference* to natural science, so it would not count against my argument. Intelligent design creationism is so worried that natural science has a monopoly on truth that it tries to show that the doctrine of creation is not only consistent with natural science but established by natural science.

[25] There is a body of analytic literature on the comparatively abstract issue of whether religious pluralism is a defeater for Christian belief, but very little in the way of detailed engagement with the

are the real opponents, not rival forms of theism, still less rival forms of non-theistic religion. In all these ways, analytic philosophy of religion shows itself to be characteristically modern.

Because analytic theology descends from analytic philosophy of religion, analytic theologians tend to have a similar focus. For example, analytic theologians are especially concerned to show the logical coherence and epistemic possibility of Christian doctrines. This single-minded focus on logical coherence is itself quite modern, as is the typical analytic suspicion of mystery and paradox.[26] Both reflect the background assumptions of the immanent frame. Only a modern person would expect to be able to give a rational account of Christian doctrine without appealing to mystery and paradox. Even though analytic theologians are orthodox Christian theists, and even though (as I have argued) analytic theology is an authentic form of Christian theology, the ferocity of analytic opposition to the naturalistic worldview shows that analytic theologians clearly feel its force.

In short, analytic theologians find their conceptual home in the post-Galilean immanent frame. How could it be otherwise? This is the question that Taylor presses on us all. We all live and think within the immanent frame: not just the analytic theologian, who wants to out-argue the Enlightenment, but also the post-secular theologian, who wants to out-preach or out-narrate the Enlightenment, and even the postsecular scholar of religion, who wants to critique it. Taylor shows us that these activities are not so different, because they are all constituted by the very modernity they want to resist.

Analytic Theology's Open Space

Taylor writes—not without a certain melancholy—of "that open space where you can feel the winds pulling you, now to belief, now to unbelief," a space where one can "actually feel some of the force of each opposing position."[27] Is it valuable to be able to stand in this open space? Taylor seems to think so. But the space itself is uniquely modern, as is the vantage point it offers. Its inhabitants are not disengaged or neutral, and Taylor does not say that they are *suspended* between belief and unbelief. Yet the fact that they can actually feel the force of both sides means that they are not entirely comfortable on either side. It is not uniquely modern

specific theological claims of non-Christian religions. (Thus, the narrowness that other thinkers attribute to analytic philosophy of religion.)

[26] Contrary to the line pushed by some critics of analytic theology, premodern Christians were not *unconcerned* with logical coherence, but it is true that worries about logical coherence were not the principle focus of patristic or medieval doctrinal disputes. Patristic and medieval debates focused much more on the proper interpretation of scripture, and the fundamental axioms that governed exegetical disputes were soteriological, not narrowly logical.

[27] Taylor, *A Secular Age*, 549.

to be able to recognize opposing positions. To feel their force existentially is uniquely modern.

Analytic theologians are well equipped to stand in Taylor's "open space," because they find themselves both pulled toward and pushed away from scientific naturalism. That is my second, normative claim. Analytic theology is a valuable theological response to the conditions of modern secularity, because analytic theologians can affirm transcendence from within the immanent frame. Moreover, in order to feel the force of opposing positions, one must cultivate certain epistemic virtues: one must have a keen grasp of one's own fallibility, and one must be open to argument and evidence, and responsive to countervailing reasons. These may not be uniquely modern virtues, but because they are presupposed by the scientific method, they are highly prized in modernity. They are also highly prized in analytic philosophy, and in analytic theology.

Analytic theologians can feel the force of belief and unbelief because they live out their Christian convictions alongside their distinctive professional commitments. By virtue of their training in analytic philosophy, analytic theologians find themselves steeped in a secularist academic culture. I would venture to say that this description holds even for analytic theologians who work in Christian universities or divinity schools. By "secularist academic culture" I do not just mean the day-to-day interlocutors in one's own department. I mean the wider culture of analytic philosophy and the academy at large. Even someone who works in a day-to-day environment that is friendly to theology still must wrestle with opposing, very unsympathetic positions when they read journals, attend conferences, and interact with the wider field. Yet analytic theology can flourish in such an environment because it draws on the same norms of argument deployed by theology's secularist despisers.

Analytic Theology and Modern Inquiry

It is striking just how well analytic theology fares when measured against the methodological norms of modern "secular" inquiry. I say this even though I continue to hold that analytic theology is best treated as a form of faith seeking understanding. Consider: the direct scholarly aim of analytic theology is the production of knowledge, not preaching, praxis, or moral improvement.[28] Here we should recall Michael Rea's point that analytic philosophy—and therefore analytic theology—tries "to discover such true explanatory theories as we can in areas of

---

[28] In Chapter 10, I argued that analytic theology can be understood as a spiritual practice. Even if I am right about this, this feature of analytic theology is indirect, and has as much to do with the attitude of the inquirer as with the nature of the inquiry. It does not change the fact that the direct scholarly aim of analytic theology is knowledge, not spiritual insight.

inquiry (metaphysics, morals, and the like) that fall outside the scope of the natural sciences."[29] Analytic theology also evaluates Christian doctrines and practices with generally accessible evidence and arguments. Even when analytic theologians rely on explicitly Christian premises, they do not shield those premises from counterarguments and counter-evidence. Nor do they defend them solely with appeals to authority or to private revelatory experiences. Analytic theologians frequently revise the conclusions of their academic work as a result of rational criticism. By virtue of their philosophical training, most are fallibilists about knowledge, and are open to criticism from any quarter. No type of criticism (historical, scientific, or social scientific) is ruled out of bounds a priori. In summary, analytic theology can flourish in the modern university precisely because it conforms to modern norms of academic inquiry.

In an academic context—in colleges, universities, and academic seminaries and divinity schools—it is good that there are theologians who foreground these modern norms. They are widely regarded as essential to the task of academic inquiry as such, and especially so regarded by opponents of theology. It is good that there are academic theologians who can argue in a way that largely conforms to the academic practices of other disciplines. It is good that there is a branch of academic theology that explicitly appeals to common standards of rationality and commonsense notions about truth. One can understand this point in a variety of ways, but it is perhaps most helpful to regard it in purely pragmatic terms, as a point about what it takes for an academic discipline to thrive in the contemporary academy. No matter how valuable they are in other contexts, forms of theology that explicitly reject the prevailing norms of the secular academy are less likely to survive *in the academy*. By contrast, forms of theology that are well adapted to those norms are more likely to survive. I can make this pragmatic point without denigrating other forms of theology, including those forms that privilege narrative or embodied practice over intellectual argument. But it is good that there are theologians who are at home in the contemporary university, and who can argue using its prevailing norms.

Conclusion

This book has sought three very different groups of interlocutors: analytic theologians and philosophers of religion, other academic theologians, and scholars of religion. All three groups have something to learn from this tour of analytic theology's place in the postsecular consensus. The lessons they can learn are also, I hope, the lessons of this book as a whole.

---

[29] Michael Rea, "Introduction," in Crisp and Rea, *Analytic Theology*, 4.

Analytic theologians can learn that because analytic philosophy is distinctively modern, they too are modern. This is a useful lesson, because analytic theologians must first understand their own style of inquiry as modern in order to appreciate the real value of premodern ways of reading and thinking, on the one hand, and broadly postmodern forms of argument like critique, on the other. We can only learn from different forms of inquiry when we accept that they *are* genuinely different, which presupposes that we properly recognize the character of our own preferred modes of inquiry. So the postsecular consensus can reinforce the lesson that analytic philosophy and analytic theology have much to learn from other forms of inquiry. That is all to the good.

Other theologians can learn that analytic theology is a valuable form of *theological* reasoning, even though it is modern. Historically minded theologians are fond of pointing out that contemporary analytic theologians focus on a very narrow—very modern—range of intellectual problems, problems that did not preoccupy our patristic and early medieval forebears. So they do and so they should. Much of the value of analytic theology, in my view, lies in the fact that it uses the modern tools and methods of analytic philosophy to show that historic Christian orthodoxy is on solid rational ground, even within the unfriendly terms established by our secular age. Too often, that kind of intellectual work gets tarred with the label of "deism" or even "fundamentalism." That response reflects a profound lack of charity. Just as analytic theologians should not denigrate other kinds of theology as silly, unserious, uninterested in truth, or whatnot, neither should other theologians dismiss analytic theology as intellectually shallow deism, or crudely rationalistic fundamentalism. Like all forms of inquiry, analytic argumentation is limited and vulnerable to characteristic deformations, but it remains important and valuable. Many people really do want to know whether core Christian doctrines make sense, how they could be even possibly true, and how they could be consistent with the natural sciences and other things we take ourselves to know. Analytic theology can help answer these kinds of questions. Answering them well requires the kind of technical apparatus that flourished in the scholastic period and flourishes again in the modern dress of analytic theology.

Scholars of religion can learn to take analytic theology seriously as a form of theological *reasoning*. It then becomes impossible to make a principled case that analytic theology is not a legitimate form of academic inquiry, with a legitimate place in the contemporary, secular university. The exclusivist attack on theology never made a great deal of sense, even at its strongest point, when modern empiricist methods and secularist assumptions reigned supreme. The attack makes even less sense now, amid the postsecular consensus. And it makes less sense still when directed specifically at analytic theology. Analytic theology cannot be excluded from the academy at the level of method.

But to learn this lesson about analytic theology, scholars of religion need to relearn how to take reasoning as such more seriously. Genealogy and critique are now the main modes of inquiry practiced by contemporary theorists of religion. These methods are not "irrational," of course. As I have emphasized many times— as recently as three paragraphs ago—genealogy and critique are valuable, but in the contemporary religious studies academy they have become hegemonic. When critique becomes a hegemonic ideology instead of merely one method among others, it cannot help but obscure important dimensions of the multifaceted phenomenon of religious adherence. Among those now obscured dimensions are rational belief and rational agency.

One of the key lessons of the postsecular consensus has been that religious adherence is more than religious belief. That lesson is important and true, but postsecular scholars of religion have learned it too well. In reacting against earlier modernist paradigms of religion, they have overcorrected. Religious adherence does not belong exclusively to the domain of the irrational or the arational, and so the vocabulary of reasoning, believing, and acting on the basis of one's reasons should remain an important part of the scholarly vocabulary. Even on its own terms, one legitimate task for the academic study of religion is to try to understand religious adherence as a form of rational agency, as something rational from the first-personal point of view of religious agents themselves. Yet too many scholars of religion seem to have lost all interest in understanding religious adherence as an expression of rational agency.

Critics of analytic theology threaten to put it in an impossible double bind: either analytic theology is not really theology because it is too modern or it is not a legitimate form of academic inquiry because it is too theological. The goal of this book has been to show that neither prong of this attack succeeds. Analytic theology really is theology, fully Christian theology, and no more vulnerable to worries about idolatry, ontotheology, and univocity than any other form of theology. Even so, analytic theologians rightly hold themselves responsible to the same norms of inquiry and argument followed by scholars in other academic fields, especially philosophy. At several points, I have emphasized that I see this book as an exercise in bridge-building. Even though the methods of analytic theology are very different from the methods currently employed by postsecular theologians and theorists of religion, the difference need not be regarded as an unbridgeable gap rooted in mutual hostility. Analytic theology represents one way that theology can find a place in the secular research university. That is all I have argued, but that is enough.

Bibliography

Abraham, William, "Systematic Theology as Analytic Theology," in Oliver D. Crisp and Michael C. Rea, eds., *Analytic Theology: New Essays in the Philosophy of Theology* (New York: Oxford University Press, 2009), 54–69.

Adams, Marilyn McCord, "Anselm on Faith and Reason," in Brian Davies and Brian Leftow, eds., *The Cambridge Companion to Anselm* (New York: Cambridge University Press, 2004), 32–60.

Adams, Marilyn McCord, "What's Wrong with the Ontotheological Error?" *Journal of Analytic Theology* 2 (2014): 3–8.

Adler, Jonathan E., *Belief's Own Ethics* (Cambridge, MA: MIT Press, 2002).

Adorno, Theodor, *Minima Moralia*, trans. E. F. N. Jephcott (New York: Verso, 2005 [1951]).

Aldama, S. J. J. A. and Iesu Solano, S. J., *Sacrae Theologiae Summa IIIA: On the Incarnate Word on the Blessed Virgin Mary*, trans. S. J. Kenneth Baker (Saddle River, NJ: Keep The Faith, 2014).

Allen, Amy, "Discourse, Power, and Subjectivation: The Foucault/Habermas Debate Reconsidered," *Philosophical Forum* 40 (2009): 1–28.

Alles, Gregory D., ed., *Religious Studies: A Global View* (New York: Routledge, 2008).

Alston, William P., "Referring to God," *International Journal for Philosophy of Religion* 24 (1988): 113–28.

Alston, William P., *Divine Nature and Human Language* (Ithaca, NY: Cornell University Press, 1989).

Alston, William P., *Perceiving God* (Ithaca, NY: Cornell University Press, 1991).

Alston, William P., "Two Cheers for Mystery!" in Andrew Dole and Andrew Chignell, eds., *God and the Ethics of Belief: New Essays in Philosophy of Religion* (Cambridge: Cambridge University Press, 2005), 99–116.

Anatolios, Khaled, ed., *The Holy Trinity in the Life of the Church* (Grand Rapids, MI: Baker, 2014).

Anatolios, Khaled, "Personhood, Trinity, and Communion in Some Patristic Texts," in Khaled Anatolios, ed., *The Holy Trinity in the Life of the Church* (Grand Rapids, MI: Baker, 2014), 147–64.

Anselm, *Basic Writings*, ed. and trans. Thomas Williams (Indianapolis, IN: Hackett, 2007).

Aquinas, Thomas, *On Evil*, ed. Brian Davies (New York: Oxford University Press, 2003).

Aquinas, Thomas, *Summa Theologiae: The Treatise on the Divine Nature*, trans. Brian J. Shanley, O.P. (Indianapolis, IN: Hackett, 2006).

Arcadi, James M., *An Incarnational Model of the Eucharist* (Cambridge: Cambridge University Press, 2018).

Armstrong, A. H., ed., *The Cambridge History of Later Greek and Early Medieval Philosophy* (New York: Cambridge University Press, 1967).

Asad, Talal, "Anthropological Conceptions of Religion: Reflections on Geertz," *Man* 18 (1983): 237–59.

Asad, Talal, *Genealogies of Religion: Discipline and Reasons of Power in Christianity and Islam* (Baltimore, MD: Johns Hopkins University Press, 1993).

Asad, Talal, *Formations of the Secular: Christianity, Islam, Modernity* (Stanford, CA: Stanford University Press, 2003).

Asad, Talal, *Secular Translations: Nation-State, Modern Self, and Calculative Reason* (New York: Columbia University Press, 2018).

Augustine, *City of God*, trans. Henry Bettenson (New York: Penguin,1972).

Augustine, *Tractates on the Gospel of John in the Fathers of the Church*, vol. 88, trans. John W. Rettig (Washington, DC: Catholic University of America Press, 1993).

Augustine, *On Christian Teaching*, trans. R. P. H. Green. Oxford World's Classics (New York: Oxford University Press, 1997).

Ayres, Lewis, *Nicaea and Its Legacy* (New York: Oxford University Press, 2004).

Bagger, Matthew, ed., *Pragmatism and Naturalism: Scientific and Social Inquiry after Representationalism* (New York: Columbia University Press, 2018).

Baker-Hytch, Max, "Analytic Theology and Analytic Philosophy of Religion: What's the Difference?" *Journal of Analytic Theology* 1 (2016): 1–16.

Barron, Robert, *Priority of Christ: Towards a Postmodern Catholicism* (Grand Rapids, MI: Brazos, 2007).

Barth, Karl, *Fides Quaerens Intellectum: Anselm's Proof of the Existence of God in the Context of His Theological Scheme* (London: SCM, 1960).

Barth, Karl, "The First Commandment as an Axiom of Theology," in H. Martin Rumscheidt, ed., *The Way of Theology in Karl Barth: Essays and Comments* (Eugene, OR: Pickwick, 1986), 63–78.

Bayne, Tim and Nagasawa, Yujin, "The Grounds of Worship," *Religious Studies* 42 (2006): 299–313.

Bell, Catherine, "Modernism and Postmodernism in the Study of Religion," *Religious Studies Review* 22 (1996): 179–90.

Bennett, M. R. and Hacker, P. M. S. *Philosophical Foundations of Neuroscience* (Malden, MA: Blackwell, 2003).

Blankholm, Joseph, "The Ghost of Immanentism," *The Immanent Frame*, November 14, 2017, https://tif.ssrc.org/2017/11/14/the-ghost-of-immanentism/, accessed July 11, 2020.

Blum, Jason N., "Pragmatism and Naturalism in Religious Studies," *Method and Theory in the Study of Religion* 23 (2011): 83–102.

Blum, Jason N., "Belief: Problems and Pseudo-Problems," *Journal of the American Academy of Religion* 86 (2018): 642–64.

Blum, Jason N., ed., *The Question of Methodological Naturalism*, Supplements to Method and Theory in the Study of Religion 11 (Leiden: Brill, 2018).

Bockmuehl, Markus, "Creatio ex Nihilo in Palestinian Judaism and Early Christianity," *Scottish Journal of Theology* 65 (2012): 254–70.

Bonevac, Daniel, "Two Theories of Analogical Predication," *Oxford Studies in the Philosophy of Religion* 4 (2012): 20–42.

Booth, Wayne C., Colomb, Gregory G., and Williams, Joseph M., *The Craft of Research* (Chicago: University of Chicago Press, 2003).

Brandom, Robert B., *Making It Explicit: Reasoning, Representing, and Discursive Commitment* (Cambridge, MA: Harvard University Press, 1994).

Brandom, Robert B., *Articulating Reasons* (Cambridge, MA: Harvard University Press, 2000).

Braun, Willi and McCutcheon, Russell T., eds., *Guide to the Study of Religion* (New York: T&T Clark, 2000).

Buckley, Michael J., *At the Origins of Modern Atheism* (New Haven, CT: Yale University Press, 1990).

Bultmann, Rudolph, *Kerygma and Myth* (New York: Harper and Row, 1961).

Burrell, David, *Faith and Freedom: An Interfaith Perspective* (Malden, MA: Blackwell, 2004).

Burrell, David, "Creator/Creatures Relation: 'The Distinction' vs. 'Ontotheology,'" *Faith and Philosophy* 25 (2008): 177–89.

Bush, Stephen S., *Visions of Religion: Experience, Meaning, and Power* (New York: Oxford University Press, 2014).

Butler, Judith, "A 'Bad' Writer Bites Back," *New York Times*, March 20, 1999.

Butler, Judith, "Values of Difficulty," in Jonathan Culler and Kevin Lamb, eds., *Just Being Difficult? Academic Writing in the Public Arena* (Stanford, CA: Stanford University Press, 2003), 199–216.

Cabezón, José, ed., *Scholasticism: Cross-Cultural and Comparative Perspectives* (Albany, NY: SUNY Press, 1998).

Cady, Linell and Brown, Delwin, eds., *Religious Studies, Theology, and the University: Conflicting Maps, Changing Terrain* (New York: SUNY Press, 2002).

Calvin, John, *Institutes of the Christian Religion* (1559 ed.), ed. J. T. MacNeill, trans. F. L. Battles (London: S. C. M. Press, 1961).

Candler Jr., Peter M., "Reading Immemorially: The Quaestio and the Paragraph in the Summa Theologiae," *American Catholic Philosophical Quarterly* 78 (2004): 531–57.

Caputo, "How to Avoid Speaking of God: The Violence of Natural Theology," in Eugene Long, ed., *The Prospects for Natural Theology* (Washington, DC: Catholic University of America Press, 1992), 128–50.

Carter, J. Kameron, *Race: A Theological Account* (Oxford University Press, 2008).

Catholic Church, *Catechism of the Catholic Church*, 2nd ed. (Vatican: Libreria Editrice Vaticana, 2012).

Chignell, Andrew, "As Kant Has Shown: Analytic Theology and the Critical Philosophy," in Oliver D. Crisp and Michael C. Rea, *Analytic Theology: New Essays in the Philosophy of Theology* (New York: Oxford University Press, 2009), 117–35.

Christensen, David and Lackey, Jennifer, eds., *The Epistemology of Disagreement: New Essays* (New York: Oxford University Press, 2013).

Churchland, Patricia S., *Neurophilosophy: Toward a Unified Science of the Mind-Brain* (Cambridge: MIT Press, 1989).

Clooney, Francis X., *Hindu God, Christian God: How Reason Helps Break Down the Boundaries between Religions* (New York: Oxford University Press, 2001).

Clooney, Francis X., *Comparative Theology: Deep Learning across Religious Borders* (Malden, MA: Wiley-Blackwell, 2010).

Coady, C. A. J., *Testimony: A Philosophical Study* (New York: Clarendon, 1992).

Coakley, Sarah, *God, Sexuality, and the Self* (New York: Cambridge University Press, 2013).

Coleman, Thomas J. III, Jong, Jonathan, and van Mulukom, Valerie, eds., *Contemporary Pragmatism* 15 (2018): 279–406.

Collini, Stefan, *What Are Universities for?* (London: Penguin, 2012).

Conee, Earl, "Review of Jonathan Adler, *Belief's Own Ethics*," *Notre Dame Philosophical Reviews* (October 15, 2002), https://ndpr.nd.edu/news/belief-s-own-ethics/, accessed July 10, 2020.

Cottingham, John, *Cartesian Reflections* (New York: Oxford University Press, 2008).

Council of Societies for the Study of Religion (CSSR), "Secular Theology," *Bulletin* 37 (2008): 30–52.

Crisp, Oliver, ed., *A Reader in Contemporary Philosophical Theology* (New York: Continuum, 2009).

Crisp, Oliver, *Analyzing Doctrine* (Waco, TX: Baylor University Press, 2019).

Crisp, Oliver D. and Rea, Michael C., eds., *Analytic Theology: New Essays in the Philosophy of Theology* (New York: Oxford University Press, 2009).

Cross, Richard, "Where Angels Fear to Tread: Duns Scotus and Radical Orthodoxy," *Antonianum* 76 (2001): 7–41.

Cross, Richard, *Duns Scotus on God* (Burlington, VT: Ashgate, 2005).

Cross, Richard, "Idolatry and Religious Language," *Faith and Philosophy* 25 (2008): 190–96.

Cross, Richard, "The Incarnation," in Thomas P. Flint and Michael Rea, eds., *The Oxford Handbook of Philosophical Theology* (New York: Oxford University Press, 2009), 452–75.

Cross, Richard, "Disability, Impairment, and Some Medieval Accounts of the Incarnation: Suggestions for a Theology of Personhood," *Modern Theology* 27 (2011): 639–58.

Cuneo, Terrence, *Ritualized Faith: Essays on the Philosophy of Liturgy* (New York: Oxford University Press, 2016).

Davies, Brian, "A Timeless God?" *New Blackfriars* 64 (1983): 215–24.

Davies, Brian, *An Introduction to the Philosophy of Religion* (New York: Oxford University Press, 2000).

Davies, Brian, *The Reality of God and the Problem of Evil* (New York: Continuum, 2006).

Davies, Brian, "Divine Simplicity," in Charles Taliaferro and Chad Meister, eds., *The Cambridge Companion to Christian Philosophical Theology* (Cambridge: Cambridge University Press, 2010), 31–45.

Davies, Brian, "Are Names Said of God and Creatures Univocally?" *American Catholic Philosophical Quarterly* 92 (2018): 324–25.

de Ridder, Jeroen and van Woudenberg, Rene, "Referring to, Believing in, and Worshipping the Same God: A Reformed View," *Faith and Philosophy* 31 (2014): 46–67.

Donnellan, Keith, "Reference and Definite Descriptions," *Philosophical Review* 75 (1966): 281–304.

Draper, Paul W., "God, Science, and Naturalism," in William J. Wainwright, ed., *The Oxford Handbook of Philosophy of Religion* (New York: Oxford University Press, 2005): 272–303.

Dreyfus, Hubert, *Being-in-the-World: A Commentary on Heidegger's Being and Time* (Cambridge: MIT Press, 1991).

Dummett, Michael, *Origins of Analytical Philosophy* (London: Duckworth, 1993).

Dumont, Stephen, "The Univocity of the Concept of Being in the Fourteenth Century: John Duns Scotus and William of Alnwick," *Medieval Studies* 49 (1987): 1–75.

Dunn, James D. G., *Christology in the Making: An Inquiry into the Origins of the Doctrine of the Incarnation*, 2nd ed. (London: SCM, 1989).

Eliade, Mircea, "Methodological Remarks on the Study of Religion's Symbolism," in Mircea Eliade and Joseph M. Kitagawa, eds., *The History of Religions: Essays in Methodology* (Chicago: University of Chicago, 1959), 86–107.

Emery, Giles and Levering, Matthew, eds., *The Oxford Handbook of the Trinity* (New York: Oxford University Press, 2011).

Evans, C. Stephen, "On Taking God Seriously," in William J. Wainwright, ed., *God, Philosophy and Academic Culture* (New York: Oxford University Press, 1996), 59–70.

Fassin, Didier, "The Endurance of Critique," *Anthropological Theory* 17 (2017): 4–29.

Feenstra, Ronald J. and Plantinga, Jr., Cornelius, *Trinity, Incarnation, and Atonement: Philosophical and Theological Essays* (Notre Dame, IN: University of Notre Dame Press, 1989).

Feldman, Richard and Warfield, Ted, eds., *Disagreement* (New York: Oxford University Press, 2010).

Felski, Rita, *The Limits of Critique* (Chicago: University of Chicago Press, 2015).

Felski, Rita, "Introduction: Recomposing the Humanities—with Bruno Latour," *New Literary History* 47 (2016): 215–29.

Feser, Edward, "Why Is There Anything at all? It's Simple," http://edwardfeser.blogspot.com/2013/10/why-is-there-anything-at-all-its-simple.html, accessed May 15, 2019.

Fitzgerald, Timothy, *The Ideology of Religious Studies* (New York: Oxford University Press, 2003).

Fleischacker, Samuel, *Divine Teaching and the Way of the World: A Defense of Revealed Religion* (New York: Oxford University Press, 2011).

Flew, Antony, "The Presumption of Atheism," *Canadian Journal of Philosophy* 2 (1972), 29–46.

Forrest, Peter, "The Incarnation: A Philosophical Case for Kenosis," *Religious Studies* 26 (2000): 127–40.

Foucault, Michel, "Truth and Power," in Paul Rabinow, ed., *The Foucault Reader* (New York: Pantheon, 1984), 51–75.

Foucault, Michel, *Discipline and Punish: The Birth of the Prison* (New York: Vintage, 1991).

Fraser, Nancy, "Foucault on Modern Power: Empirical Insights and Normative Confusions," *PRAXIS International* 3 (1981): 272–87.

Fricker, Miranda, *Epistemic Injustice: Power and the Ethics of Knowing* (New York: Oxford University Press, 2007).

Gadamer, Hans-Georg, *The Relevance of the Beautiful and Other Essays*, ed. Robert Bernasconi, trans. Nicholas Walker (Cambridge: Cambridge University Press, 1986).

Gaon, Saadya, *The Book of Doctrines and Beliefs*, trans. Alexander Altmann (Indianapolis, IN: Hackett, 2002).

Gavrilyuk, Paul, "Creation in Early Christian Literature: Irenaeus against the Gnostics and Athanasius against the Arians," in Janet Soskice, ed., *Creation "Ex Nihilo" and Modern Theology* (Malden, MA: Wiley-Blackwell, 2013), 22–32.

Gillett, Carl and Rives, Bradley, "The Non-Existence of Determinables: Or, a World of Absolute Determinates as Default Hypothesis," *Noûs* 39 (2005): 483–504.

Gilson, Étienne, *The Spirit of Mediaeval Philosophy* (Notre Dame, IN: University of Notre Dame Press, 1991 [1936]).

Glasgow, Joshua, Haslanger Sally, Jeffers, Chike, and Spencer, Quayshawn, *What Is Race? Four Philosophical Views* (New York: Oxford University Press, 2019).

Gleeson, Andrew, "The Power of God," *Sophia* 49 (2010): 603–16.

Glock, Hans-Johann, *What Is Analytic Philosophy?* (New York: Cambridge University Press, 2008).

Godfrey-Smith, Peter, "Metaphysics and the Philosophical Imagination," *Philosophical Studies* 160 (2012): 97–113.

Goldschmidt, Tyron and Seacord, Beth, "Judaism, Reincarnation, and Theodicy," *Faith and Philosophy* 30 (2013): 393–417.

Goodman, Nelson, *Fact, Fiction, and Forecast*, 4th ed. (Cambridge, MA: Harvard University Press, 1983).

Gordon, Peter E., "The Place of the Sacred in the Absence of God: Charles Taylor's *A Secular Age*," *Journal of the History of Ideas* 69 (2008): 647–73.

Gould, Paul, ed., *Beyond the Control of God? Six Views on the Problem of God and Abstract Objects* (New York: Bloomsbury Academic, 2014).

Gould, Stephen Jay, "Nonoverlapping Magisteria," *Natural History* 106 (1997): 16–22.

Grant, W. Matthews, *Free Will and God's Universal Causality: The Dual Sources Account* (London: Bloomsbury, 2019).

Gregory, Brad, *The Unintended Reformation* (Cambridge, MA: Harvard University Press, 2012).

Gregory of Nyssa, *The Life of Moses,* trans. Abraham Malherbe and Everett Ferguson. Classics of Western Spirituality (New York: Paulist Press, 1978).

Gutiérrez, Gustavo, *A Theology of Liberation* (New York: Orbis, 1973).

Gutting, Gary, "Review of Jeffrey Stout's *Democracy and Tradition,*" *Ethics* 115 (2004): 169–75.

Hadot, Pierre, *Philosophy as a Way of Life: Spiritual Exercises from Socrates to Foucault* (Malden, MA: Blackwell, 1995).

Halbertal, Moshe and Margalit, Avishai, *Idolatry* (Cambridge, MA: Harvard University Press, 1998).

Halvorsen, Hans, "Why Methodological Naturalism?" in Kelly James Clark, ed., *The Blackwell Companion to Naturalism* (Malden, MA: Wiley-Blackwell, 2016), 136–49.

Hankey, Wayne J., "Why Philosophy Abides for Aquinas," *Heythrop Journal* 43 (2001): 329–48.

Hankey, Wayne J., "Philosophy as Way of Life for Christians? Iamblichan and Porphyrian Reflections on Religion, Virtue, and Philosophy in Thomas Aquinas," *Laval théologique et philosophique* 59 (2003): 193–224.

Harris, Harriet and Insole, Christopher, eds., *Faith and Philosophical Analysis: The Impact of Analytical Philosophy on the Philosophy of Religion* (Burlington, VT: Ashgate, 2005).

Harrison, Peter, *The Bible, Protestantism, and the Rise of Natural Science* (New York: Cambridge University Press, 1998).

Harrison, Peter, *The Fall of Man and the Foundations of Science* (New York: Cambridge University Press, 2007).

Hart, David Bentley, *The Beauty of the Infinite* (Grand Rapids, MI: Eerdmans, 2004).

Hart, David Bentley, *The Experience of God: Being, Consciousness, Bliss* (New Haven, CT: Yale University Press, 2014).

Harvey, David, *Images at Work: The Material Culture of Enchantment* (New York: Oxford University Press, 2018).

Hasker, William, *Metaphysics and the Tri-Personal God* (New York: Oxford University Press, 2013).

Hasker, William, "Can Social Trinitarianism Be Monotheist?: A Reply to Dale Tuggy," *Faith and Philosophy* 30 (2013): 439–43.

Hasker, William, "God's Only Begotten Son: A Reply to R. T. Mullins," *European Journal for Philosophy of Religion* 9 (2017): 217–38.

Haslanger, Sally, *Resisting Reality: Social Construction and Social Critique* (New York: Oxford University Press, 2012).

Hector, Kevin, *Theology without Metaphysics* (Cambridge: Cambridge University Press, 2011).

Heidegger, Martin, *Identity and Difference*, trans. Joan Stambaugh (New York: Harper and Row, 1969).

Heil, John, "Levels of Reality," *Ratio* 16 (2003): 205–21.

Hereth, Blake and Timpe, Kevin, eds., *The Lost Sheep in Philosophy of Religion: New Perspectives on Disability, Gender, Race, and Animals* (New York: Routledge, 2020).

Hick, John, "Jesus and the World Religions," in John Hick (ed.), *The Myth of God Incarnate* (London: SCM Press, 1977), 167–85.

Hollywood, Amy, *Acute Melancholia and Other Essays: Mysticism, History, and the Study of Religion* (New York: Columbia University Press, 2016).

Horan, Daniel P., *Postmodernity and Univocity* (Minneapolis, MN: Fortress Press, 2014).

Hughes, Gerard, *Nature of God* (New York: Routledge, 1995).

Hyman, Gavin, *A Short History of Atheism* (New York: Tauris, 2010).

Idinopulos, Thomas A. and Yonan, Edward A., eds., *Religion and Reductionism: Essays on Eliade, Segal, and the Challenge of the Social Sciences for the Study of Religion* (Leiden: Brill, 1994).

Irenaeus, "*Adversus Haereses*," in trans. Alexander Roberts and William Rambaut, eds. Alexander Roberts, James Donaldson, and A. Cleveland Coxe, *Ante-Nicene Fathers,* Vol. 1 (Buffalo, NY: Christian Literature Publishing Co., 1885). Revised and edited for New Advent by Kevin Knight, http://www.newadvent.org/fathers/0103.htm, accessed July 6, 2020.

Jacobs, Jonathan D., "The Ineffable, Inconceivable, and Incomprehensible God: Fundamentality and Apophatic Theology," in Jonathan L. Kvanvig, ed., *Oxford Studies in Philosophy of Religion 6* (New York: Oxford University Press, 2015), 158–76.

Jones, William, *Is God a White Racist?* (Boston, MA: Beacon Press, 1998).

Jordan, Mark, "Theology and Philosophy," in Norman Kretzmann and Eleonore Stump, eds., *The Cambridge Companion to Aquinas* (New York: Cambridge University Press, 1993), 232–51.

Jordan, Mark, *Rewritten Theology: Aquinas after His Readers* (Malden, MA: Blackwell, 2006).

Justin Martyr, "*First Apology* and *Second Apology*," in trans. Marcus Dods and George Reith, eds. Alexander Roberts, James Donaldson, and A. Cleveland Coxe, *Ante-Nicene Fathers*, Vol. 1 (Buffalo, NY: Christian Literature Publishing Co., 1885). Revised and edited for New Advent by Kevin Knight, http://www.newadvent.org/fathers/0126.htm, accessed July 6, 2020, http://www.newadvent.org/fathers/0127.htm, accessed July 6, 2020.

Kant, Immanuel, *Religion within the Limits of Mere Reason and Other Writings*, trans. and ed. Allen Wood and George di Giovanni (New York: Cambridge University Press, 2018).

Kavka, Martin, "Profane Theology," *Method and Theory in the Study of Religion* 27 (2015): 104–15.

Keller, Lorraine Juliano, "Defending Divine Ineffability" (forthcoming).

Keller, Lorraine Juliano, "Semantics for Divine Intrinsic Predications" (forthcoming).

Kelly, J. N. D., *Early Christian Doctrines* (London: A&C Black, 1985).

Kim, Jaegwon, "The American Origins of Philosophical Naturalism," *Journal of Philosophical Research* 28, Supplement (2003): 83–98.

Knight, John Allen, "Descriptivist Reference and the Return of Classical Theism," in Jeanine Diller and Asa Kasher, eds., *Models of God and Alternative Ultimate Realities* (Dordrecht: Springer, 2013), 207–23.

Kripke, Saul, *Naming and Necessity* (Cambridge, MA: Harvard University Press, 1980).

Kvanvig, Jonathan, "Divine Transcendence," *Religious Studies* 20 (1984): 377–87.

LaCugna, Catherine Mowry, *God for Us: The Trinity and Christian Life* (New York: Harper Collins, 1991).

Latour, Bruno, "Why Has Critique Run out of Steam? From Matters of Fact to Matters of Concern," *Critical Inquiry* 30 (2004): 225–48.

Lebens, Samuel, "It Is Time for the Analytic Philosophy of Judaism," *Marginalia Review of Books*, December 8, 2015. https://marginalia.lareviewofbooks.org/it-is-time-for-the-analytic-philosophy-of-judaism-by-samuel-lebens/, accessed July 11, 2020.

Lebens, Samuel, *The Principles of Judaism* (New York: Oxford University Press, 2020).

Lebens, Samuel and Goldschmidt, Tyron, "The Promise of a New Past," *Philosopher's Imprint* 17 (2017): 1–25.

Lebens, Samuel, Rabinowitz, Dani, and Sega, Aaron, eds. *Jewish Philosophy in an Analytic Age* (New York: Oxford University Press, 2019).

Leftow, Brian, "Anselm on the Cost of Salvation," *Medieval Philosophy and Theology* 6 (1997): 73–92.

Leftow, Brian, "Anti Social Trinitarianism," in Stephen T. Davis, S. J. Daniel Kendall, and S. J. Gerald O'Collins, eds. *The Trinity: An Interdisciplinary Symposium* (New York: Oxford University Press, 1999), 203–50.

Leftow, Brian, "A Latin Trinity," *Faith and Philosophy* 21 (2004), 304–33.

Leftow, Brian, "Omnipotence," in Thomas P. Flint and Michael C. Rea, eds., *The Oxford Handbook of Philosophical Theology* (New York: Oxford University Press, 2009), 167–98.

Leftow, Brian, "Why Perfect Being Theology?," *International Journal for Philosophy of Religion* 69 (2011): 103–18.

Leftow, Brian, *God and Necessity* (New York: Oxford University Press, 2012), 11–12.

Lepojärvi, Jason, "Worship, Veneration, and Idolatry: Observations from C. S. Lewis," *Religious Studies* 51 (2015): 543–62.

Levy, Neil, "Analytic and Continental Philosophy: Explaining the Differences," *Metaphilosophy* 34 (2003): 284–304.

Lewis, Thomas A., *Why Philosophy Matters to the Study of Religion and Vice Versa* (New York: Oxford University Press, 2015).

Lincoln, Bruce, "Theses on Method," *Method and Theory in the Study of Religion* 8 (1996): 225–27.

Lincoln, Bruce, "Responsa Miniscula," *Method and Theory in the Study of Religion* 17 (2005): 59–67.

Lofton, Kathryn, "Introduction to the Yale Roundtable on Belief," *Method and Theory in the Study of Religion* 24 (2012): 51–54.

Lopez, Donald, "Belief" in Mark C. Taylor, ed., *Critical Terms for Religious Studies* (Chicago: University of Chicago Press, 1998), 21–34.

MacIntyre, Alasdair, *Whose Justice? Which Rationality?* (Notre Dame, IN: University of Notre Dame Press, 1989).

Mahmood, Saba, "Secularism and the Hermeneutics of Empire," *Public Culture* 18, no. 2 (2006): 323–47.

Marcuse, Herbert, *The One-Dimensional Man: Studies in the Ideology of Advanced Industrial Society* (New York: Routledge, 1991 [1964]).

Marion, Jean-Luc, *God without Being*, trans. Thomas A. Carlson (Chicago: University of Chicago Press, 1995).

Marion, Jean-Luc, "In the Name: How to Avoid Speaking of 'Negative Theology'," in John D. Caputo and Michael J. Scanlon, eds., *God, the Gift, and Postmodernism* (Bloomington, IN: Indiana University Press, 1999), 20–53.

Marion, Jean-Luc, *The Idol and Distance*, trans. Thomas A. Carlson (New York: Fordham University Press, 2011).

Marmodoro, Anna and Hill, Jonathan, eds., *The Metaphysics of the Incarnation* (New York: Oxford University Press, 2011).

Marshall, Bruce, "*Quod scit unda uetula*: Aquinas on the Nature of Theology," in Rik Van Nieuwenhove and Joseph Peter Wawrykow, eds., *The Theology of Thomas Aquinas* (Notre Dame, IN: University of Notre Dame Press, 2005), 1–35.

Martin, Craig, *A Critical Introduction to the Study of Religion*, 2nd ed. (New York: Routledge, 2017).

Martin, Luther, "Comparison," in Willi Braun and Russell T. McCutcheon, eds., *Guide to the Study of Religion* (New York: Cassell, 2000), 45–56.

Martin, Luther H. and Wiebe, Donald, "Religious Studies as a Scientific Discipline: The Persistence of a Delusion," *Journal of the American Academy of Religion* 80 (2012): 587–97.

Masuzawa, Tomoko, *The Invention of World Religions* (Chicago: University of Chicago Press, 2005).

Mawson, T. J., "Miracles and Laws of Nature," *Religious Studies* 37 (2001): 33–58.

Mawson, T. J., *Belief in God* (New York: Oxford University Press, 2005).

Mawson, T. J., *The Divine Attributes* (Cambridge: Cambridge University Press, 2019).

May, Gerhard, *Creatio Ex Nihilo: The Doctrine of "Creation out of Nothing" in Early Christian Thought* (Edinburgh: Edinburgh University Press, 1994).

McCabe, Herbert, *God Matters* (New York: Continuum, 1987).

McCutcheon, Russell T., *Manufacturing Religion* (New York: Oxford University Press, 1997).

McCutcheon, Russell T., *Critics Not Caretakers: Redescribing the Public Study of Religion* (New York: SUNY Press, 2001).

McCutcheon, Russell T., *The Discipline of Religion: Structure, Meaning, Rhetoric* (New York: Routledge, 2003).

McCutcheon, Russell T., ed., *The Insider/Outsider Problem in the Study of Religion: A Reader* (New York: Continuum, 2005).

McCutcheon, Russell T., "A Direct Question Deserves a Direct Answer: A Response to Atalia Omer's 'Can a Critic Be a Caretaker too?'" *Journal of the American Academy of Religion* 80 (2012): 1077–82.

McDaniel, Kris, *The Fragmentation of Being* (New York: Oxford University Press, 2017).

McInerny Ralph, *Aquinas and Analogy* (Washington, DC: Catholic University of America Press, 1996).

Mercedes, Anna, *Power for Feminism and Christ's Self-Giving* (New York: Bloomsbury, 2011).

Merricks, Trenton, "The Resurrection of the Body and the Life Everlasting," in Thomas P. Flint and Michael C. Rea, eds., *The Oxford Handbook of Philosophical Theology* (New York: Oxford University Press, 2009), 364–85.

Migliore, Daniel L., *Faith Seeking Understanding: An Introduction to Christian Theology*, 2nd ed. (Grand Rapids, MI: Eerdmans, 2004).

Milbank, John, "Intensities," *Modern Theology* 15 (1999): 454–55.

Milbank, John, *The Suspended Middle: Henri de Lubac and the Debate Concerning the Supernatural* (London: SCM, 2005).

Milbank, John, *Theology and Social Theory*, 2nd ed. (Malden, MA: Wiley-Blackwell, 2006).

Milbank, John, *The Word Made Strange* (Malden, MA: Blackwell, 2007).

Milbank, John, *The Future of Love* (Eugene, OR: Cascade, 2009).

Milbank, John, *Beyond Secular Order* (Oxford: Wiley-Blackwell, 2013).

Milbank, John, Pickstock, Catherine, and Ward, Graham, eds., *Radical Orthodoxy: A New Theology* (New York: Routledge, 1999).

Miller, Barry, *From Existence to God* (New York: Routledge, 1991).

Miller, Barry, *A Most Unlikely God* (Notre Dame, IN: University of Notre Dame Press, 1996).

Min-ha, Trinh T., *Woman, Native, Other* (Bloomington, IN: Indiana University Press, 1989).

Minns, Denis, *Irenaeus* (London: Geoffrey Chapman, 1994).

Moi, Toril, "The Adventure of Reading," *Literature & Theology* 25 (2011): 125–40.

Moi, Toril, *Revolution of the Ordinary: Literary Studies after Wittgenstein, Austin, and Cavell* (Chicago: University of Chicago Press, 2017).

Moore, Andrew, "Reason," in Kathryn Tanner, John Webster, and Iain Torrance, eds., *The Oxford Handbook of Systematic Theology* (New York: Oxford University Press, 2007), 394–412.

Morris, Thomas V., *Our Idea of God* (Downers Grove, IL: InterVarsity Press, 1991).

Müller, Friedrich Max, *Introduction to the Science of Religion* (London: Longman, Greens, and Co, 1873).

Murphy, Mark, *God's Own Ethics* (New York: Oxford University Press, 2017).

Nagasawa, Yujin, "A New Defense of Anselmian Theism," *Philosophical Quarterly* 58 (2008): 577–96.

Nagasawa, Yujin, *Maximal God* (New York: Oxford University Press, 2017).

Nagel, Thomas, *The Last Word* (New York: Oxford University Press, 2001).

Nolan, Daniel, "Method in Analytic Metaphysics," in Herman Cappelen, Tamar Szabó Gendler, and John Hawthorne, eds., *The Oxford Handbook of Philosophical Methodology* (New York: Oxford University Press, 2016), 159–78.

Nongbri, Brent, *Before Religion: A History of a Modern Concept* (New Haven, CT: Yale University Press, 2015).

Norman, A. P., "The Normative Structure of Adjudicative Dialogue," *Argumentation* 15 (2001): 489–98.

Norris, Rebecca Sachs, "Examining the Structure and Role of Emotion: Contributions of Neurobiology to the Study of Embodied Religious Experience," *Zygon* 40 (2005): 181–99.

Oliver, Simon, "Analytic Theology," *International Journal for Systematic Theology* 12, no. 4 (2010): 464–75.

Oliver, Simon, "Henri de Lubac and Radical Orthodoxy," in Jordan Hillebert, ed., *T&T Clark Companion to Henri de Lubac* (London: T&T Clark, 2017), 393–418.

Origen, *Homilies on Jeremiah and 1 Kings 28*, trans. John Clark Smith. Fathers of the Church (Washington, DC: Catholic University of America Press, 1998), 43.

Orilia, Francesco and Swoyer, Chris, "Properties," in Edward N. Zalta, ed., *The Stanford Encyclopedia of Philosophy* (Summer 2020 edition), https://plato.stanford.edu/archives/sum2020/entries/properties/, accessed July 8, 2020.

Orsi, Robert, *Between Heaven and Earth: The Religious Worlds People Make and the Scholars Who Study Them* (Princeton, NJ: Princeton University Press, 2004).

Orwell, George, *Politics and the English Language* (Peterborough: Broadview Press, 2006 [1946]).

Orzel, Chad, *Eureka: Discovering Your Inner Scientist* (New York: Basic Books, 2014).

Page, Ben, "Wherein Lies the Debate? Concerning Whether God Is a Person," *International Journal for Philosophy of Religion* 85 (2019): 297–317.

Panchuk, Michelle, "Created and Uncreated Things: A Neo-Augustinian Solution to the Bootstrapping Problem," *International Philosophical Quarterly* 56 (2016): 99–112.

Panchuk, Michelle and Rea, Michael, eds., *Voices from the Edge: Centering Marginalized Voices in Analytic Theology* (New York: Oxford University Press, 2020).

Pawl, Timothy, "Traditional Christian Theism and Truthmaker Maximalism," *European Journal for Philosophy* of Religion 4 (2012): 197–218.

Pawl, Timothy, "A Solution to the Fundamental Philosophical Problem of Christology," *Journal of Analytic Theology* 2 (2014): 62–85.

Pawl, Timothy, *In Defense of Conciliar Christology* (New York: Oxford University Press, 2016).

Pawl, Timothy, *In Defense of Extended Conciliar Christology* (New York: Oxford University Press, 2019).

Pickstock, Catherine, "Duns Scotus: His Historical and Contemporary Significance," *Modern Theology* 21 (2005): 543–74.

Placher, William, *Unapologetic Theology* (Louisville, KY: Westminster John Knox, 1989).

Plantinga, Alvin, *Does God Have a Nature?* (Milwaukee, WI: Marquette University Press, 1980).

Plantinga, Alvin, "Advice for Christian Philosophers," *Faith and Philosophy* 1 (1984): 253–71.

Plantinga, Alvin, "Christian Philosophy at the End of the Twentieth Century," in James F. Sennett, ed., *The Analytic Theist: An Alvin Plantinga Reader* (Grand Rapids, MI: Eerdmans, 1998), 328–52.

Plantinga, Alvin, *Warranted Christian Belief* (New York: Oxford University Press, 2000).

Plantinga, Alvin, *Where the Conflct Really Lies: Science, Religion, and Naturalism* (New York: Oxford University Press, 2008).

Plantinga, Alvin and Wolterstorff, Nicholas, eds., *Faith and Rationality: Reason and Belief in God* (Notre Dame, IN: University of Notre Dame Press, 1984).

Pouivet, Roger, "Against Theistic Personalism," *European Journal for Philosophy of Religion* 10 (2018): 1–19.

Powell, Jeffrey, ed., *Heidegger and Language* (Bloomington, IN: Indiana University Press, 2013).

Preus, J. Samuel, *Explaining Religion: Criticism and Theory from Bodin to Freud* (New York: Oxford University Press, 1996).

Prinz, Jesse, "Emotions Embodied," in Robert C. Solomon, ed., *Thinking about Feeling: Contemporary Philosophers on Emotions* (New York: Oxford University Press, 2004), 44–60.

Pseudo-Dionysius, *Pseudo-Dionysius: The Complete Works*, trans. Colm Luibheid (New York: Paulist Press, 1987).

Pui-lan, Kwok, *Postcolonial Imagination and Feminist Theology* (Minneapolis, MN: Westminster John Knox, 2005).

Quine, W. V. O., *From a Logical Point of View* (New York: Harper, 1953).

Rea, Michael C., *A World without Design: The Ontological Consequences of Naturalism* (New York: Oxford University Press, 2002).

Rea, Michael C., ed., *Oxford Readings in Philosophical Theology*. Volume 1: *Trinity, Incarnation, Atonement*; Volume 2: *Providence, Scripture, and Resurrection* (New York: Oxford University Press, 2009).

Reynolds, Jack, "Common Sense and Philosophical Methodology: Some Metaphilosophical Reflections on Analytic Philosophy and Deluze," *Philosophical Forum* 41 (2010): 231–58.

Rieger, Joerg, *Christ and Empire: From Paul to Postcolonial Times* (Minneapolis, MN: Fortress Press, 2007).

Roberts, Tyler, *Encountering Religion: Responsibility and Criticism after Secularism* (New York: Columbia University Press, 2013).

Rockmore, Tom, *Kant and Phenomenology* (Chicago: University of Chicago Press, 2011).

Rogers, Katherin, *Perfect Being Theology* (Edinburgh: Edinburgh University Press, 2000).

Rogers, Katherin, "Anselm on God's Perfect Freedom," *The Saint Anselm Journal* 1 (2003): 1–8.

Rudder Baker, Lynne, "Need a Christian Be a Mind/Body Dualist?," *Faith and Philosophy* 12 (1995): 489–504.

Rutledge, Jonathan C., "Analyzing the Muddles of Analysis: (Some Of) What Analytic Theologians Can Learn from the History of Analytic Feminism," *Modern Theology* (6 May 2019), doi:10.1111/moth.12525.

Schaefer, Donovan O., *Religious Affects: Animality, Evolution, and Power* (Durham, NC: Duke University Press, 2015).

Schellenberg, J. L., "Is Plantinga-Style Christian Philosophy Really Philosophy?" in J. Aaron Simmons, ed., *Christian Philosophy: Conceptions, Continuations, and Challenges* (New York: Oxford University Press, 2018), 229–43.

Schilbrack, Kevin, *Philosophy and the Study of Religions: A Manifesto* (Malden, MA: Wiley-Blackwell, 2014).

Schwartz, Stephen P., *A Brief History of Analytic Philosophy: From Russell to Rawls* (Chichester: Wiley-Blackwell, 2012).

Sedgwick, Eve Kosofsky, "Paranoid Reading and Reparative Reading, or, You're So Paranoid, You Probably Think Is Essay Is about You," in *Touching Feeling: Affect, Pedagogy, Performativity* (Durham, NC: Duke University Press, 2003), 123–52.

Sedgwick, Eve Kosofsky, *Touching Feeling: Affect, Pedagogy, Performativity* (Durham, NC: Duke University Press, 2003).

Shanley, Brian J., "Divine Causation and Human Freedom in Aquinas" *American Catholic Philosophical Quarterly* 72 (1988): 99–122.

Simmons, J. Aaron, "Living in the Existential Margins: Reflections on the Relationship between Philosophy and Theology," *Open Theology* 5 (2019): 147–57.

Slater, Michael R., *Pragmatism and the Philosophy of Religion* (New York: Cambridge University Press, 2014).

Smart, Ninian, "Religious Studies and Theology," *CSSR Bulletin* 26 (1997): 66–68.

Smith, Anthony Paul and Whistler, Daniel, eds., *After the Postsecular and the Postmodern: New Essays in Continental Philosophy of Religion* (Newcastle upon Tyne: Cambridge Scholars, 2010).

Smith, James K. A., *How (Not) to Be Secular: Reading Charles Taylor* (Grand Rapids, MI: Eerdmans, 2015).

Smith, Jonathan Z., *Map Is Not Territory* (Chicago: University of Chicago Press, 1978).

Smith, Jonathan Z., *Imagining Religion* (Chicago: University of Chicago Press, 1982).

Smith, Quentin, "The Metaphilosophy of Naturalism," *Philo* 4 (2001): 195–215.

Sokolowski, Robert, *The God of Faith and Reason: Foundations of Christian Theology* (Washington, DC: Catholic University of America Press, 1982).

Sonderegger, Katherine, *That Jesus Christ Was Born a Jew: Karl Barth's Doctrine of Israel* (University Park, PA: Pennsylvania State University Press, 1992).

Soskice, Janet Martin, "Names of God: Or Why Names Are Not Attributes," *New Blackfriars* 101 (2020): 182–95.

Speaks, Jeff, "The Method of Perfect Being Theology," *Faith and Philosophy* 31 (2014): 256–66.

Speaks, Jeff, "Perfect Being Theology and Modal Truth," *Faith and Philosophy* 33 (2016): 465–73.

Steiner, Wendy, *The Scandal of Pleasure: Art in an Age of Fundamentalism* (Chicago: University of Chicago Press, 1995).

Stoller, Paul, "Rationality," in Mark C. Taylor, ed., *Critical Terms for Religious Studies* (Chicago: University of Chicago Press, 1998), 239–55.

Stout, Jeffrey, *Democracy & Tradition* (Princeton, NJ: Princeton University Press, 2004).

Stout, Jeffrey, "Radical Interpretation and Pragmatism: Davidson, Rorty, and Brandom on Truth," in Nancy Frankenberry, ed., *Radical Interpretation in Religion* (New York: Cambridge University Press, 2004), 25–52.

Studer, Basil, *Trinity and Incarnation: The Faith of the Early Church*, trans. Matthias Westerhoff (Edinburgh: T&T Clark, 1993).

Stump, J. B. and Padgett, Alan, eds., *The Blackwell Companion to Science and Christianity* (Malden, MA: Wiley-Blackwell, 2012).

Swinburne, Richard, *The Coherence of Theism* (New York: Oxford University Press, 1977).

Swinburne, Richard, *The Christian God* (New York: Oxford University Press, 1994).

Tanner, Kathryn, *God and Creation in Christian Theology: Tyranny or Empowerment?* (Minneapolis, MN: Fortress Press, 2005).

Tanner, Kathryn, *Christ the Key* (New York: Cambridge University Press, 2010).

Taves, Ann, *Religious Experience Reconsidered* (Princeton, NJ: Princeton University Press, 2009).

Taylor, Charles, "Foucault on Freedom and Truth," in Charles Taylor, ed., *Philosophical Papers*, Vol. 1 (New York: Cambridge University Press, 1985), 152–84.

Taylor, Charles, *A Secular Age* (Cambridge, MA: Belknap Press, 2008).

Taylor, Mark C., *Critical Terms for Religious Studies* (Chicago: University of Chicago Press, 1998).

Tertullian *De idololatria* [On Idolatry], trans. J. H. Waszink and J. C. M. van Winden (Leiden: Brill, 1987).

Thomas of Celeano, *The First Life of St Francis*, trans. Christopher Stace (London: SPCK, 2000).

Thomson, Iain, *Heidegger on Ontotheology* (Cambridge: Cambridge University Press, 2005).

Timpe, Kevin and Cobb, Aaron, "Disability and the Theodicy of Defeat," *Journal of Analytic Theology* 5 (2017): 100–20.

Tonstad, Linn Marie, *God and Difference: The Trinity, Sexuality, and the Transformation of Finitude* (New York: Routledge, 2016).

Tracy, David, *The Achievement of Bernard Longergan* (New York: Herder and Herder, 1970).

Trakakis, N. N., "Does Univocity Entail Idolatry?" *Sophia* 49 (2010): 535–55.

Tweed, Thomas A., "Valuing the Study of Religion: Improving Difficult Dialogues within and beyond the AAR's 'Big Tent,'" *Journal of the American Academy of Religion* 84 (2016): 287–322.

Vanhoozer, Kevin J., ed., *The Cambridge Companion to Postmodern Theology* (New York: Cambridge University Press, 2003).

van Inwagen, Peter, "It Is Wrong, Everywhere, Always, for Anyone, to Believe Anything upon Insufficient Evidence," in Jeffrey Jordan and Daniel Howard-Snyder, eds., *Faith, Freedom and Rationality* (Savage, MD: Rowman and Littlefield, 1996), 137–54.

van Inwagen, Peter, "God and Other Uncreated Things," in Kevin Timpe, ed., *Metaphysics and God: Essays in Honor of Elenore Stump* (New York: Routledge, 2009), 3–20.

van Inwagen, Peter, *Existence: Essays in Ontology* (Cambridge: Cambridge University Press, 2014), 60–71.

Vásquez, Manuel A., *More than Belief: A Materialist Theory of Religion* (New York: Oxford University Press, 2011).

Ward, Graham, *Barth, Derrida and the Language of Theology* (New York: Cambridge University Press, 1995).

Weil, Simone, *Waiting for God* (New York: Harper and Row, 1951).

Weinandy, Thomas, *Does God Suffer?* (Notre Dame, IN: University of Notre Dame Press, 2000).

Westphal, Merold, "The Emergence of Modern Philosophy of Religion," in Philip L. Quinn and Charles Taliaferro, eds., *Blackwell Companion to Philosophy of Religion* (Malden, MA: Blackwell, 1997), 111–20.

Westphal, Merold, *Overcoming Ontotheology* (New York: Fordham University Press, 2001).

Westphal, Merold, "Theological Anti-Realism," in Andrew Moore and Michael Scott, eds., *Realism and Religion: Philosophical and Theological Perspectives* (Burlington, VT: Ashgate, 2007), 131–46.

Whitmarsh, Tim, *Battling the Gods: Atheism in the Ancient World* (New York: Knopf, 2015).

Wiebe, Donald, *The Irony of Theology and the Nature of Religious Thought* (Montreal: McGill-Queens University Press, 1991).

Wiebe, Donald, *Politics of Religious Studies* (New York: Palgrave, 1999).

Wierenga, Edward, *The Nature of God* (Ithaca, NY: Cornell University Press, 1989).

Wierenga, Edward, "Augustinian Perfect Being Theology and the God of Abraham, Isaac, and Jacob," *International Journal for Philosophy of Religion* 69 (2011): 139–51.

Williams, Scott M., "John Duns Scotus," in William J. Abraham and Frederick D. Aquino, eds., *The Oxford Handbook of the Epistemology of Theology* (New York: Oxford, 2017), 423–25.

Williams, Scott M., ed., *Disability in Medieval Philosophy and Theology* (New York: Routledge, 2020).

Williams, Thomas, "The Doctrine of Univocity Is True and Salutary," *Modern Theology* 21 (2005): 575–85.

Williamson, Timothy, "How Did We Get Here from There? The Transformation of Analytic Philosophy," *Belgrade Philosophical Annual* 27 (2014): 7–37.

Williamson, Timothy, *Doing Philosophy: From Common Curiosity to Logical Reasoning* (New York: Oxford University Press, 2018).

Winner, Lauren, *The Dangers of Christian Practice* (New Haven, CT: Yale University Press, 2018).

Wippel, John F., *The Metaphysical Thought of Thomas Aquinas* (Washington, DC: Catholic University of America Press, 2000).

Wolterstorff, Nicholas, *On Universals* (Chicago: University of Chicago Press, 1970).

Wolterstorff, Nicholas, "Between the Pincers of Increased Diversity and Supposed Irrationality," in William J. Wainwright, ed., *God, Philosophy and Academic Culture: A Discussion between Scholars in the AAR and the APA* (Atlanta, GA: Scholars Press, 1996), 13–20.

Wolterstorff, Nicholas, "How Philosophical Theology Became Possible within the Analytical Tradition of Philosophy," in Oliver D. Crisp and Michael C. Rea, eds., *Analytic Theology: New Essays in the Philosophy of Theology* (New York: Oxford University Press, 2009), 155–70.

Wolterstorff, Nicholas, "Then, Now, and Al," in Kelly James Clark and Michael Rea, eds., *Reason, Metaphysics, and Mind: New Essays on the Philosophy of Alvin Plantinga* (New York: Oxford University Press, 2012), 215.

Wood, Allen W., *Kant's Rational Theology* (Ithaca, NY: Cornell University Press, 2009).

Wood, William, "On the New Analytic Theology, or: The Road Less Travelled," *Journal of the American Academy of Religion* 77 (2009): 941–60.

Wood, William, *Blaise Pascal on Duplicity, Sin, and the Fall: The Secret Instinct* (New York: Oxford University Press, 2013).

Wood, William, "Thomas Aquinas on the Claim That God Is Truth," *Journal of the History of Philosophy* 51 (2013): 21–47.

Wood, William, "Analytic Theology as a Way of Life," *Journal of Analytic Theology* 2 (2014): 43–60.

Wood, William, "On Behalf of Traditional Philosophy of Religion" [Roundtable on Kevin Schilbrack, *Philosophy and the Study of Religions*], *Journal of the American Academy of Religion* 83 (2015): 236–60.

Wood, William, "Modeling Mystery," *Scientia et Fides* 4 (2016): 1–21.

Wood, William, "Review of William Hasker, *Metaphysics and the Tri-Personal God*," *Scottish Journal of Theology* 69 (2016): 234–36.

Wood, William, "Traditions, Trajectories, and Tools in Analytic Theology," *Journal of Analytic Theology* 4 (2016): 254–66.

Yadav, Sameer, "Mystical Experience and the Apophatic Attitude," *Journal of Analytic Theology* 4 (2016): 18–43.

Yadav, Sameer, "Toward an Analytic Theology of Liberation," in Michelle Panchuk and Michael Rea, eds., *Voices from the Edge: Centering Marginalized Voices in Analytic Theology* (New York: Oxford University Press, 2020), 47–74.

Zagzebski, Linda, *Epistemic Authority: A Theory of Trust, Authority, and Autonomy in Belief* (New York: Oxford University Press, 2012).

Zimmerman, Dean, "The Compatibility of Materialism and Survival," *Faith and Philosophy* 16 (1999): 194–212.

Zimmerman, Dean, "Three Introductory Questions: Is Analytic Philosophical Theology an Oxymoron, Is Substance Dualism Incoherent, What's in This Book Anyway," in Peter van Inwagen and Dean Zimmerman, eds., *Persons Human and Divine* (New York: Oxford University Press, 2007), 1–13.

Index

For the benefit of digital users, indexed terms that span two pages (e.g., 52–53) may, on occasion, appear on only one of those pages.